Computer Organization and Architecture

Express Learning Series

Computer Organization and Architecture

Express Learning Series

ITL Education Solutions Ltd.
Research and Development Wing

ISBN 978–81–317–7339–0

First Impression, 2012
Fifth Impression, 2022
Sixth Impression, 2024

Published by Pearson India Education Services Pvt. Ltd, CIN: U72200TN2005PTC057128

Head Office: 1st Floor, Berger Tower, Plot No. C-001A/2, Sector 16B, Noida – 201 301,Uttar Pradesh, India.

Registered Office: Featherlite, 'The Address' 5th Floor, Survey No 203/10B, 200 Ft MMRD Road, Zamin Pallavaram, Chennai - 600044
Website: in.pearson.com; Email:companysecretary.india@pearson.com

Digitally printed in India by Trinity Academy for Corporate Training Ltd, New Delhi in the year of 2024.

Contents

Preface

A computer system comprises a set of hardware components including central processing unit, memory, and I/O devices. At lower abstraction level, each of these components can be viewed as consisting of several sub-components such as microprocessor, ALU, control memory, and processor registers. The way these sub-components operate and are connected with each other—computer organization—greatly affects the performance of system. In addition to computer organization, computer architecture affects the performance of system. Computer architecture is concerned with the attributes of system visible to programmer including addressing modes, instruction set, instruction format, and number of bits used to represent a data type. Thus to design a high-performance system, it is necessary to have the knowledge of computer organization and architecture.

Keeping in mind the importance of computer organization and architecture, almost all the universities have included this subject in B.Tech (CSE), B.Tech (IT), and MCA courses. The book in your hands, *Computer Organization and Architecture*, in its unique easy-to-understand question-and-answer format directly addresses the need of students enrolled in these courses. The questions and corresponding answers in this book have been designed and selected to cover all the necessary material in computer organization and architecture as per the syllabi of most universities. The text has been designed to make it particularly easy for students to understand the hardware operations of digital computers. An attempt has been made to make the book self-contained so that the students can learn the subject by them. The organized and accessible format allows students to quickly find the questions on specific topics.

The book *Computer Organization and Architecture* is a part of series named *Express Learning* which has a number of books designed as quick reference guides.

Unique Features

1. Designed as a student friendly self-learning guide. The book is written in a clear, concise, and lucid manner.
2. Easy-to-understand question-and-answer format.
3. Includes previously asked as well as new questions organized in chapters.
4. All types of questions including MCQs, short, and long questions are covered.
5. Solutions to numerical questions asked at examinations are provided.
6. All ideas and concepts are presented with clear examples.
7. Text is well structured and well supported with suitable diagrams.
8. Inter-chapter dependencies are kept to a minimum.
9. A comprehensive index at the end of the book for quick access to desired topics.
10. Chapter Organization

All the question-answers are organized into fifteen chapters. A brief description of these chapters is as follows:

- *Chapter 1* describes digital computers, layered view of computer, the functional units of computer, and the difference between computer organization and architecture. The chapter provides an insight into the factors used to calculate system performance in addition to the Von Neumann architecture and Flynn's classification of computer.
- *Chapter 2* familiarizes the reader with the logic gates that are the building blocks of every digital circuit. It also covers the Boolean algebra that deals with binary variables and logic operations.
- *Chapter 3* explains combinational and sequential digital circuits such as half and full adders, encoders and decoders, multiplexers and demultiplexers, flip-flops, registers, and counters.
- *Chapter 4* presents how the data types found in computer are represented in binary form. It also discusses the methods of representing negative binary numbers including signed-magnitude, 1's complements and 2's complements form.
- *Chapter 5* discusses the algorithms for performing various arithmetic operations on binary data along with their hardware implementation.
- *Chapter 6* introduces the register transfer language that is used to represent the internal operations of computer in symbolic form. It describes all types of microoperations that are register, arithmetic, logic, and shift.
- *Chapter 7* deals with the design and organization of a basic digital computer. It concerns with the instruction set, instruction format, and instruction types, which are the basic elements of any computer. It also discusses how instructions are executed.
- *Chapter 8* focuses on the control unit. It commences with the basic functions performed by the control unit. Then, the discussion moves on to its implementation using hardware and software.
- *Chapter 9* concentrates on the brain of computer system that is CPU. It explains the register and stack organization of CPU and various addressing modes.
- *Chapter 10* begins with a brief description of the I/O devices and then describes the methods used by the computer to interact with the I/O devices.
- *Chapter 11* discusses the various components of memory hierarchy, which include cache memory, main memory and auxiliary memory. It also throws light on operation and organization of associative memory.
- *Chapter 12* introduces the concept of pipelining and illustrates how pipelining speeds up the processing, thus enhancing the performance of computer.
- *Chapter 13* familiarizes the reader with other organizations of parallel systems which include vector and array processors.
- *Chapter 14* describes the architectural models of multiprocessor systems including loosely and tightly coupled multiprocessors. In addition, it discusses various interconnection structures using which components of multiprocessors communicate with each other.
- *Chapter 15* introduces the 8085 microprocessor along with its architecture, pin diagram, instruction set and addressing modes. A brief overview of assembly language programming in 8085 is also provided.

Acknowledgements

- ❑ Our publisher Pearson Education, their editorial team, and panel reviewers for their valuable contributions toward content enrichment.
- ❑ Our technical and editorial consultants for devoting their precious time to improve the quality of the book.
- ❑ Our entire research and development team who have put in their sincere efforts to bring out a high-quality book.

Feedback

For any suggestions and comments about this book, please feel free to send an e-mail to **itlesl@rediffmail.com**.

Hope you enjoy reading this book as much as we have enjoyed writing it.

Rohit Khurana
Founder and CEO
ITL ESL

1

Introduction to Computer

1. What is a digital computer?

Ans. Digital computer is a machine that processes the input given in digital or discrete form and produces the output in the same form. The first digital computer was developed in late 1940s and was used for numerical calculations. Digital computers use binary number system, which consists of only two digits 0 and 1. These are known as binary digits (also known as **bit** in short). A group of 8 bits is called a **byte**. The information in a digital computer is represented in the groups of bits. These groups of bits not only represent the binary numbers but also represent other discrete symbols including letters of the alphabets or decimal digits with the help of various coding techniques. Digital computer cannot process analog quantities directly; therefore, the analog quantities must be first converted into digital form before being processed. Similarly, if one wants output in a form other than digital, then the digital output needs to be converted into the desired form. For such conversion, the digital computer uses the components that can convert information in one form into some other form.

2. Give the layered view of the computer system.

Ans. A computer system is made up of different hardware and software layers as shown in Figure 1.1. The innermost layer comprises the **data path** that interconnects various components of CPU, I/O devices and memory. The next layer is the **controller** hardware, which controls the flow of data between various CPU modules, I/O devices and memory in accordance with the processing required for an instruction. These two layers collectively constitute the **computer hardware**, which is controlled by the next layer called **machine language** instruction set. Depending on the type of microoperations associated with a machine language instruction, the control signals are generated by the controller to transfer data on the data path of the innermost layer. The next layer above is the **system software**, which operates on the three inner layers. System software includes compiler, operating system, linkage editor, etc. The outermost layer is the **application software**, which includes modules like DBMS, sorting package and various other special-purpose packages. A user from the external environment can interact with the system with the help of a high-level language (HLL).

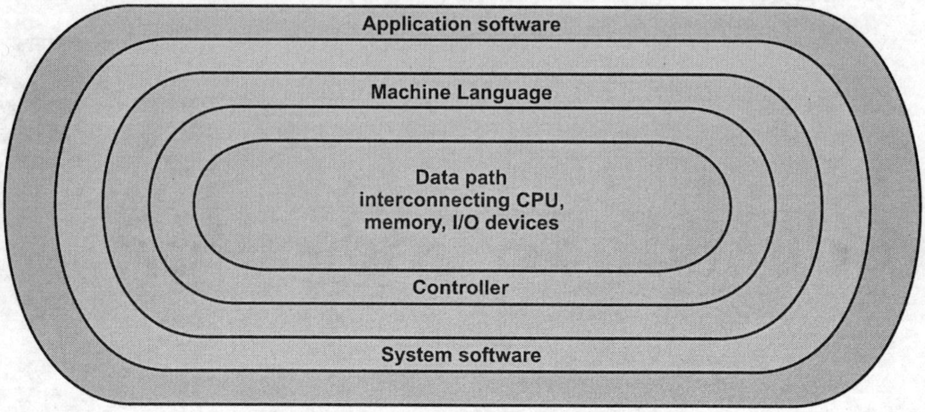

Figure 1.1 Layered View of a Computer System

3. Explain different functional units of a computer.

Ans. Digital computer system consists of four distinct functional units, namely, *input unit*, *central processing unit*, *memory* (or *storage*) *unit* and *output unit* (see Figure 1.2). All these units are interconnected allowing communication among them and thus, helping the computer to function as a system.

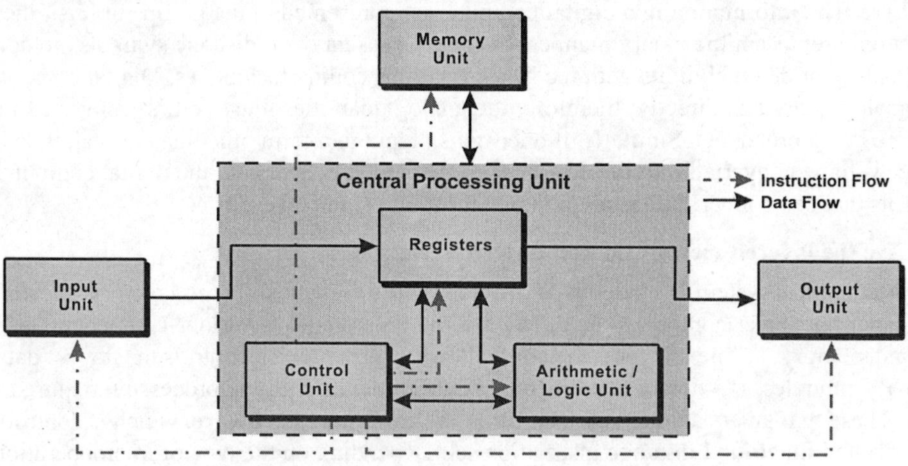

Figure 1.2 Block Diagram of a Digital Computer

The description of these functional units is as follows:

- **Memory unit:** The memory unit is responsible for managing programs and acting as a storage unit for holding the data. There are two types of memory, namely, *primary memory* and *secondary memory*. **Primary memory**, also known as **main memory**, is a high-speed memory that temporarily holds the instructions and data currently being processed by the CPU, the intermediate results produced during the course of calculations, and the recently processed data. While the instructions and data remain in main memory, the CPU can access them directly and quickly. It is classified into two categories: *random access memory* (*RAM*) and *read only memory* (*ROM*). **Secondary memory**, also known as **auxiliary memory**, is used for storing the data and instructions permanently. It supplies the stored information to the other units of computer as and when required. Some commonly used secondary storage devices are optical disks, hard disks and pen drives.

- **Central processing unit (CPU):** CPU, also known as *processor*, is the brain of the computer system that processes data (input) and converts it into meaningful information (output). It is referred to as the *administrative section* of the computer system that interprets the data and instructions, coordinates the operations and supervises the instructions. It consists of three components, namely, *arithmetic logic unit* (*ALU*), *control unit* (*CU*) and *memory unit* (*MU*), which are discussed as follows:
  - **Arithmetic logic unit (ALU):** This unit performs all the arithmetic and logical operations on data such as addition, subtraction, multiplication, XOR and AND. Whenever an arithmetic or logical operation is to be performed, the required data is transferred from the memory unit to ALU, the operation is performed and the result is returned to the memory unit. It has got internal logic capabilities through which the various conditions encountered during processing are tested and the actions are taken accordingly.
  - **Control unit (CU):** The task of CU is to direct the data flow among various units, control computer operations and retrieve the programs instructions stored in memory one-by-one. After fetching the instruction, it interprets the instruction and sends the signal to ALU and storage areas so that the instruction can be executed. It also controls the input/output (I/O) devices and directs the overall functioning of the other units of the computer.
  - **Registers:** These are the special-purpose, high-speed temporary memory units that can hold varied information such as data, instructions, addresses and intermediate results of calculations. Essentially, they hold the information that the CPU is currently working on. Registers can be considered as the CPU's working memory, an additional storage location that provides the advantage of speed.
- **Input and output unit:** The user must enter instructions and data into the computer system before any operation can be performed on the given data. Similarly, after processing the data, the information must go out from the computer system to the user. For this, every computer system incorporates input and output unit that serve as a communication media between the computer system and the user.

  An **input unit** accepts instructions and data from the user with the help of input devices such as keyboard, mouse and light pen. Since the data and instructions entered through different input devices will be in different form, the input unit converts them into the form that the computer can understand. After this, the input unit supplies the converted instructions and data to the computer for further processing.

  The **output unit** performs just opposite to that of input unit. It accepts the outputs (which are in machine-coded form) produced by the computer, converts them into the user understandable form, and supplies the converted results to the user with the help of an output device such as printer, monitor and plotter.

4. State the difference between computer architecture and computer organization.

Ans. There is a thin line difference between computer architecture and computer organization as both are interrelated to each other. Computer architecture is like building a design and architecture of the house, while computer organization is like building the house with the bricks keeping the architecture of house in mind. Some differences between them are listed in Table 1.1.

Table 1.1 Differences between Computer Architecture and Computer Organization

Computer architecture (CA)	Computer organization (CO)
A computer's architecture is an abstract model and is programmer's view in terms of instructions, registers and addressing modes.	A computer organization is a realization of the architectural specifications.
It deals with the structural and behavioural attributes of a system visible to the user.	It deals with the operations of the hardware components and the way these components are arranged to form the computer system.
The architectural attributes of a computer include the number of bits used for representing various data types, instruction set, memory addressing techniques and I/O mechanisms.	The organizational attributes of a computer include hardware details that are transparent to the user, such as the interfaces between the computer, peripherals and control signals.
It describes what the computer does.	It describes how the computer does.
It shows the physical address memory, CPU and the coordination between both.	It shows the linking of the operational attributes and contribution to realize architectural specification.
It depends on the nature of the components.	It depends on the technology being used.
Change in the architecture will bring a drastic change in the computer organization.	Change in the organization of a computer can be done without changing its architecture.
For example, the architecture specifies that the computer will have multiplication and division operations.	For example, the organization specifies whether to implement multiplication and division with the help of a special unit or by making use of add and subtract units.

5. What do you mean by performance of a computer?

Ans. The performance of a computer means different for different persons. For example, an individual user can define the performance in terms of **response time**, also referred to as **execution time** (that is, the time between the start and completion of a task). If the same program is run on two different computers, then the computer that takes less time to execute the program is said to be faster and thus, having a better performance than another. On the other hand, a computer centre manager can define the performance in terms of **throughput**—the amount of work completed in a given time. If the computer centre has two timeshared computers, then the computer that completes more jobs in a given time period is said to have better throughput and thus, having a better performance. While discussing the performance of machines, we are primarily concerned with the execution time.

An individual computer user is generally interested in reducing the execution time of a task to improve the performance. Thus, the performance of a computer (say A) and its execution time can be related by the following equation.

$$\text{Performance}_A = 1/\text{Execution time}_A$$

It is clear from this equation that less is the execution time, better will be the performance of a computer.

The above-mentioned performance equation can also be used to compare the performance of two different computers. For example, consider two computers (A and B) where the performance of A is better than that of B. That is,

$$\text{Performance}_A > \text{Performance}_B$$

$$1/\text{Execution time}_A > 1/\text{Execution time}_B$$

$$\text{Execution time}_B > \text{Execution time}_A$$

It is clear from this equation that if machine A is faster than B, then it means B takes longer time to execute a task than A.

If the machine A performs n times better than B, then the relationship between their performances can be quantitatively expressed as:

$$\text{Performance}_A/\text{Performance}_B = n$$

$$\text{Execution time}_B/\text{Execution time}_A = n$$

Thus, the execution time of machine B will be n times longer than that of A.

6. What are the factors used for calculating the performance of a computer?

Ans. New age computers are more powerful because of their underlying hardware facilities, which are driven by a range of software packages. Therefore, for analyzing the performance of computers, basic hardware and software factors are determined. In general, a computer system can perform ideally when there subsists a perfect match between the machine capability and program behavior. The machine capability can be enhanced by managing the resources efficiently and using better hardware technology. On the other hand, the program behavior is very difficult to predict as it depends heavily on application, run-time conditions, data structures, algorithm design and compiler technology. It is impossible to achieve the perfect match between the hardware and software of a computer by improving only a few factors. Some factors that are taken into account while projecting the performance of a computer are as follows:

- **Processor clock:** The processor of a digital computer is driven by a clock with a constant cycle time. This clock is referred to as the **processor clock**. The important parameter affecting processor performance is the period of one clock cycle (time taken by the clock to complete one clock cycle at a constant rate). This time period is denoted by P and is the inverse of the clock rate (R). That is, the clock rate can be determined by using the following formula:

  $$P = \frac{1}{R}$$

  It is clear from this equation that higher the clock rate, higher is the performance of the computer. Clock rate is generally measured in cycles per second or hertz (Hz). The computers are now coming with the clock rates ranging between megahertz (MHz) and gigahertz (GHz).
- **CPU time:** It is the time that CPU spends in computing a particular task. It excludes the time spent on waiting for I/O or running other programs. The CPU time is divided into two parts: **user CPU time** which is the time spent by the CPU in the program and the **system CPU time** which is the time spent by the CPU for performing operating system task on behalf of the user program. It is difficult to differentiate between times accurately; thus, generally, the term CPU performance refers to user CPU time.
- **Performance metrics:** The performance from users and designers point of view is examined using different metrics. The effect of a design change on the performance as seen by the user can be determined by relating these different metrics. The CPU time can be related with the basic metrics including clock cycles and clock cycle time with the help of a single formula given here:

CPU execution time for a program = CPU clock cycle for a program × Clock cycle time for a program

Now since the clock rate and clock cycle time are inverse of each other, the above formula can be written as follows:

$$\text{CPU excution time for a program} = \frac{\text{CPU clock cycles for a program}}{\text{Clock rate}}$$

From this equation, it is clear that the performance of a computer can be improved by reducing either the length of the clock cycle or the number of clock cycles required for a program.

- **Hardware software interface**: The above given equation does not take into account the number of instructions needed to be executed for the execution of program. However, as the compiler generates machine instructions that are executed to run the program, the execution time of a program must depend on the number of instructions required for the program execution. If `N` denotes the actual number of instructions that are to be executed to run the program, `S` denotes the average number of steps required to run a single machine instructions and `R` denotes the clock rate, then the execution time (`T`) can be given as shown here:

$$T = \frac{N \times S}{R}$$

This equation is called the basic performance equation. In case the execution time of a machine instruction is measured in cycles per instruction (`CPI`), the execution time for the program can be given as:

$$T = \frac{N \times CPI}{R}$$

7. Why benchmark programs are used to measure computer performance?

Ans. A new computer would be best evaluated by the user who executes the same program again and again. The user can evaluate the performance of two computer systems by executing the same workload (set of programs that are run) on them and then compare their execution time. This is the general situation under which the performance can be evaluated; however, sometimes some users are not in the situation to measure the performance. Therefore, they must rely on alternative methods for measuring the system performance. This alternative method involves evaluation of a machine using a set of benchmarks—the programs specifically selected for measuring the performance. The benchmarks from a workload are run on the machine hoping that they will predict the performance of actual workload.

Real applications are the best type of programs used for benchmarking. The applications might be typical ones or the ones that the user uses regularly. For example, in an environment of engineers, typical engineering applications would be the best set of benchmarks and in software developer's environment, the compiler applications would form the best benchmarks. Though, real applications are the best candidates as benchmarks, it becomes very difficult to find ways for speeding up the benchmark execution.

8. Explain the basic operational concepts of a modern computer system.

or

Describe the connections between the processor and memory with a neat structure diagram.

or

Mention the registers used for communication between processor and main memory.

Ans. Executing a sequence of instructions (program) is the basic task of a computer system. All the functional units of the computer contribute to the execution of a program. The input unit accepts data and instructions to be executed from the external environment and loads them into the main memory. The memory unit holds the data and instructions loaded by the input unit. The control unit fetches the data and instructions from the memory, decodes them and makes them to execute. During processing, the ALU performs the required arithmetic and logical operations. After the data has been processed, the output obtained is either stored in memory for future reference or given to the output unit, which transmits the output to the external environment. Along with the arithmetic logic unit and control unit, the CPU also has a number of general-purpose registers as well as special-function registers (see Figure 1.3).

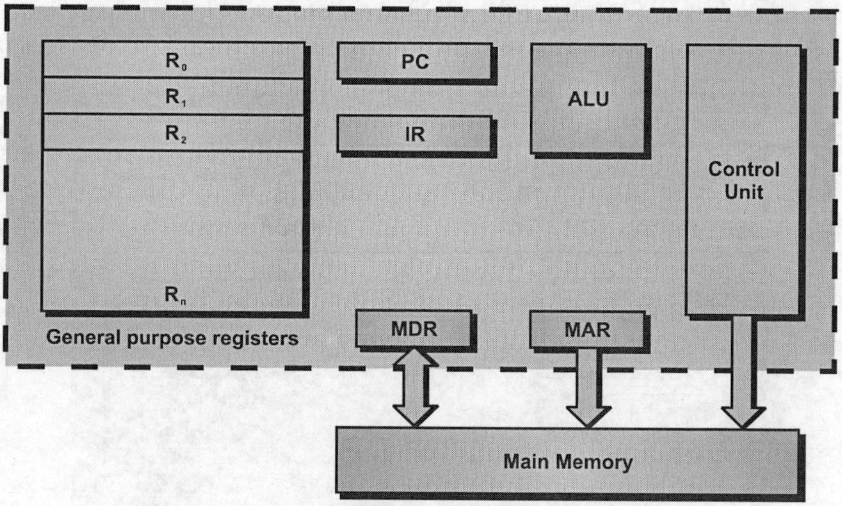

Figure 1.3 Connections between the Main Memory and the Processor

The general purpose registers are used to hold the data temporarily, while the special-function registers perform one or the other important tasks in the processor. The description of each special function register is as follows:

- **Program counter (PC):** A program produces the desired output if its instructions are executed in specific order. The order of instruction execution is monitored by PC register. This register keeps track of the instruction that is to be executed next.
- **Instruction register (IR):** This register holds the instruction that is presently being executed. The control unit can view the contents of IR for generating the timing signals controlled by various processing elements.
- **Memory address register (MAR) and memory data register (MDR):** These two registers are responsible for transferring data between the main memory and the processor. The address of the

main memory to or from which data is to be transferred is kept in the MAR. The data which is being written into or read from the main memory is contained in the MDR. Notice that MAR and MDR can be simply mentioned as AR and DR, respectively.

9. Explain Von Neumann architecture.

Ans. The earliest computers, such as ENIAC and Colossus, were program-controlled machines in which writing a new program or changing some existing program required rewiring, restructuring or redesigning the machines. Thus, programming in these computers was a quite tedious task. To ease the programming process, an idea known as **stored program concept** was proposed by a mathematician and an early computer scientist named John Von Neumann. According to this concept, both data and instructions are kept in the main memory. Thus, a computer could get its instructions from the memory and the programs could be setup or changed from within the memory as well, without having to redesign the computer. All the computers based on stored program concept are known as Von Neumann systems employing the **Von Neumann architecture.**

Most of the conventional and today's modern computers that are based on Von Neumann architecture consists of four hardware components: a CPU with control unit, ALU, main memory and an I/O system (see Figure 1.4). In addition, these computers can process the instructions in a sequential manner.

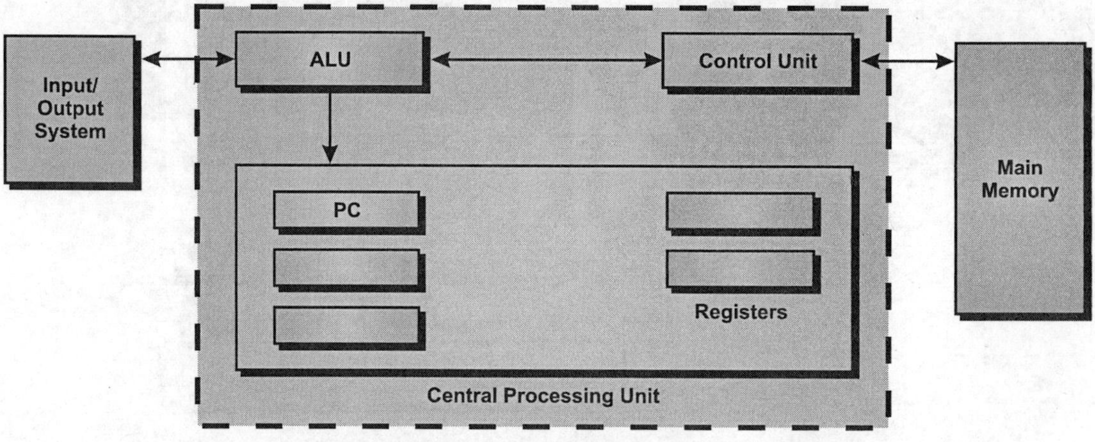

Figure 1.4 Von Neumann Architecture

The architecture shown in Figure 1.4 depicts the working of a Von Neumann computer. Here, the I/O instructions are passed through ALU to the control unit. All the programs are executed by following the **Von Neumann execution cycle** or **fetch–decode–execute cycle**, which describes the working of the machine. One iteration of this cycle involves the following steps:

1. The control unit determines the location of the next program instruction to be executed using the program counter and fetches it from the main memory.
2. The instruction is then decoded into the language understandable by the ALU.
3. The required data operands for executing the instructions are fetched from main memory and stored into the CPU registers.
4. The instructions are executed by ALU and the results are placed in registers or memory.

10. Explain Von Neumann bottleneck.

Ans. Although Von Neumann architecture was accepted as the basis for modern computers, it too had a drawback. As shown in Figure 1.4, there is a single path between the control unit and the memory unit of Von Neumann computer. This leads to limited throughput (rate of data transfer) between the CPU and memory unit. The throughput is much smaller than the actual CPU rate. This is what is known as **Von Neumann bottleneck**. As a result of this bottleneck, the effective processing speed of CPU reduces greatly especially when CPU has to do only a minimal processing on a large amount of data. In such cases, the CPU is forcibly made to wait continuously until the required data gets transferred to or from the memory thus, resulting in poor CPU utilization.

11. Specify possible strategies for handling Von Neumann bottleneck.

Ans. Von Neumann bottleneck can be overcome by bringing changes in the computer and/or processor architecture. The different approaches or strategies applied to overcome this problem are as follows:

- **Caching:** In this approach, the most frequently used data are stored in a special area in RAM. This helps in speedy access of those data and thus, increases overall performance.
- **Pre-fetching:** In this approach, some data are moved into the cache before being requested, so that if a request for these data comes, the data could be accessed faster.
- **Multithreading:** In this approach, multiple requests are managed at the same time by creating a separate thread for each request.
- **New types of RAM:** In this approach, different type of RAMs are used where the output is activated on both the rising and falling edge of the system clock thus, doubling the output. An example of such RAM is DDR SDRAM.
- **Processing in memory (PIM):** This approach tends to overcome the problem by integrating a processor and memory in a single microchip.

12. Describe the Flynn's classification of computer system.

Ans. In 1972, **Michael J. Flynn** introduced the scheme for classifying digital computers on the basis of multiplicity of instruction and data streams. The term **instruction stream** refers to the sequence of instructions read from the memory and the term **data stream** refers to the operations performed on the sequence of data in the processor. Such classification of the computer systems is known as **Flynn's classification**. Flynn classified computers into four organizations, namely, *single instruction stream, single data stream (SISD) organization, single instruction stream, multiple data stream (SIMD) organization, multiple instruction stream, single data stream (MISD) organization* and *multiple instruction stream, multiple data stream (MIMD) organization*. Notice that only three types of system components including memory unit, processor unit and control unit are required to illustrate the classification. The memory units provide instruction and data streams, control unit decodes the instruction stream and sends it to the processor unit which then processes it. In shared memory subsystems, these components exist in multiple numbers. The four organizations are discussed as follows:

- **SISD organization:** This class corresponds to computers with a single processor. An SISD computer consists of a single control unit, a processor unit and a memory unit. The processor executes the instruction in a sequential manner and some internal parallel processing may or may not be there. Figure 1.5 shows an SISD computer organization where a single stream of data and instructions are accessed through processing elements from the main memory and the result is stored back into the main memory.

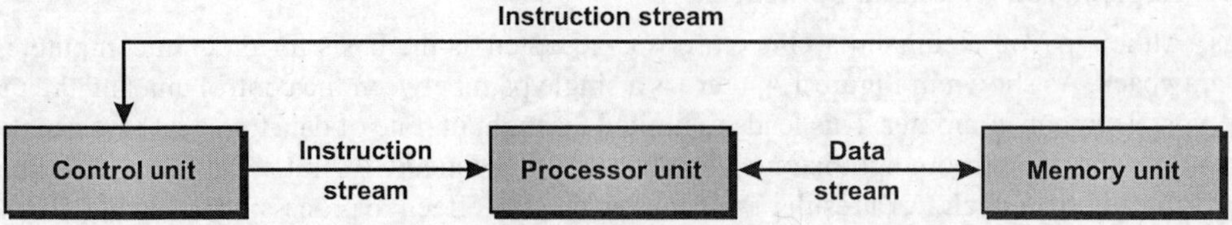

Figure 1.5 SISD Organization

- **SIMD organization:** This class corresponds to computers with multiple processors supervised by a common control unit. All processors operate on different items of data from different data streams but receive the same instructions from the control unit. The shared memory unit has to communicate simultaneously with all the processors, and for this it has multiple modules in it. The SIMD computers are similar to array processors and are capable of solving many scientific problems. SIMD computer organization is shown in Figure 1.6.

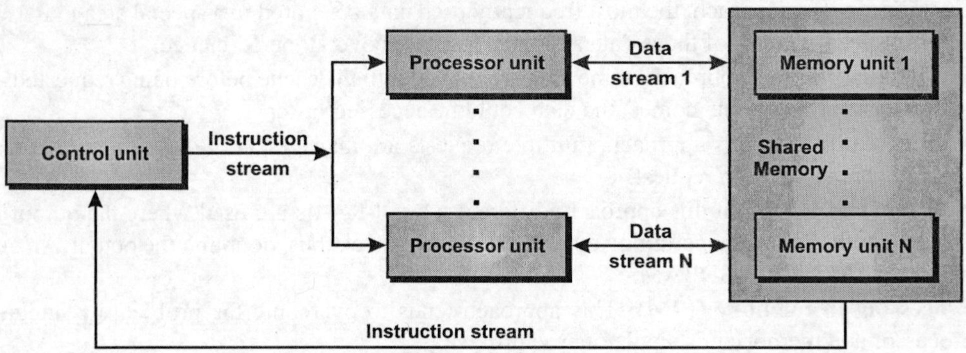

Figure 1.6 SIMD Organization

- **MISD organization:** This class corresponds to computers with multiple processing elements that receive different instruction streams and operate on a single data stream. That is, the same data stream is manipulated by several instructions. An MISD processor may be viewed as a two-dimensional arrangement (matrix) of processing elements known as **systolic processor**. This kind of structure is not practically implemented and therefore, is not in much use. MISD computer organization is shown in Figure 1.7.

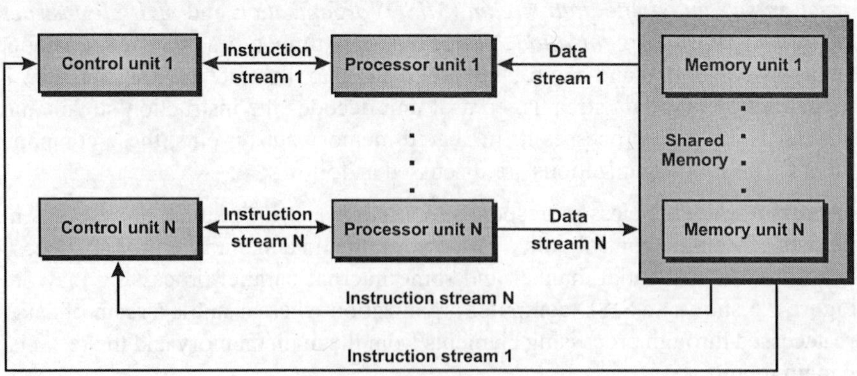

Figure 1.7 MISD Organization

- **MIMD organization:** This class corresponds to computers that can process several programs at the same time and are used for general purpose parallel computing. Most of the multiprocessor systems fall under this category. MIMD computer organization is shown in Figure 1.8.

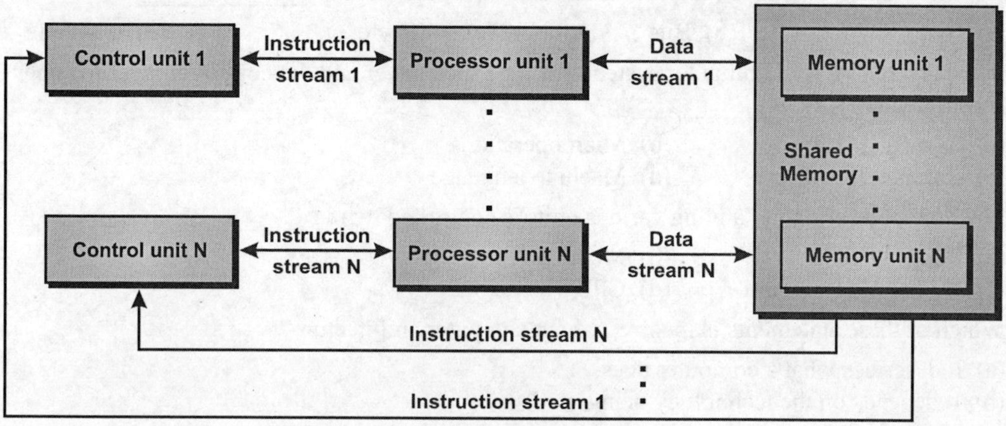

Figure 1.8 MIMD Organization

13. Two computers use same instruction set architecture. Computer X has a clock cycle time of 300 ps and a CPI of 2.5 for some program and computer Y has a clock cycle time of 400 ps and a CPI of 1.5 for the same program. Which computer is faster for this program and by how much?

Ans. Since each computer executes same number of instructions for the program, let the number of instructions be *N*. Now, the processor clock cycles for each computer can be calculated as follows:

$\text{CPU clock cycles}_X = N \times CPI_X = N \times 2.5$

$\text{CPU clock cycles}_Y = N \times CPI_Y = N \times 1.5$

After calculating the CPU clock cycles, we can determine the CPU execution time as follows:

$\text{CPU time}_x = \text{CPU clock cycle}_x \times \text{Clock cycle time}_x$

$= N \times 2.5 \times 300 \text{ ps} = 750 \text{ N ps}$

$\text{CPU time}_y = \text{CPU clock cycle}_y \times \text{Clock cycle time}_y$

$= N \times 1.5 \times 400 \text{ ps} = 600 \text{ N ps}$

Therefore, it can be seen clearly that computer Y is faster for the program as it has less execution time than X. The amount by which Y is faster than X can be calculated by computing the ratio of their execution times, as shown here.

$$\frac{\text{CPU Performance}_X}{\text{CPU Performance}_Y} = \frac{\text{Execution time}_Y}{\text{Execution time}_X} = \frac{600 \text{ N ps}}{750 \text{ N ps}} = 0.8$$

This implies that computer Y is 0.8 times faster than computer X.

MULTIPLE CHOICE QUESTIONS

1. The information in digital computer is represented in the form of ________.
   (a) Bytes (b) Bits (c) Kilobyte (d) Gigabyte
2. In the layered view of computer system, the innermost layer and the controller layer together constitute the ________.
   (a) Computer software (b) Microoperations
   (c) Computer hardware (d) Machine language
3. The flow of information among various units is controlled by the ________.
   (a) Control unit (b) Memory unit
   (c) Arithmetic logic unit (d) CPU
4. Which of these statements is incorrect about computer architecture?
   (a) It describes what a computer does.
   (b) It depends on the technology being used.
   (c) The architectural attributes of a computer include the number of bits used for representing various data types.
   (d) It is an abstract model.
5. The unit of clock rate is ________.
   (a) Meters per second (b) Seconds (c) Hertz (d) Hours
6. The basic principle of Von Neumann computer is to:
   (a) Store program and data in separate memory (b) Use pipeline concept
   (c) Store program and data in the same memory (d) Use a large number of registers
7. In Von Neumann architecture, can each bit be accessed independently?
   (a) No (b) Yes (c) Cannot be determined (d) None of these
8. Which of the following are the components of Von Neumann architecture?
   (a) Buses, memory and input/output controllers (b) Hard disks, floppy disks and CPU
   (c) Memory, CPU and printers (d) Memory, input/output modules and CPU
9. Which of the following strategies are used for handling Von Neumann bottleneck?
   (a) Caching (b) Multithreading
   (c) Pre-fetching (d) All of these
10. In which computer organization, all processors operate on different items of data but receive same instructions from the control unit?
    (a) SIMD (b) MIMD (c) SISD (d) MISD

Ans. 1. b 2. c 3. a 4. b 5. c 6. c 7. a 8. d 9. d 10. a

2

Logic Gates and Boolean Algebra

1. What do you mean by logic gate?

Ans. The term **gate** can be defined as the logic circuit that is used to manipulate the binary information. The logic gates are the elementary building blocks of a computer, which are used to implement most of the functions in a computer. A **logic gate** is defined as an electronic (digital) circuit that takes one or more input signals (binary 0 or 1) and produces an output signal of binary 0 or 1 depending on the input signals and its internal circuitry.

A number of logic gates are used in digital computer systems. Each gate is represented by different graphic symbols and its operation can be identified by the way of an algebraic expression (or function). The relationship between input and output binary variables for each gate can be expressed in a tabular form called the **truth table.**

2. What are the different logic gates used for the design of digital circuits? Give their logic symbols and truth tables.

Ans. There are seven different logic gates including AND, OR, NOT, NAND, NOR, XOR and XNOR, which are used for the design of digital circuits. Out of these, the logic gates AND, NOT and OR are called the **basic gates**, while the logic gates NAND, NOR, XOR and XNOR are called the **derived gates**. Each logic gate takes one or more binary variables as input and produces a binary variable as output. These logic gates are described as follows:

- **AND gate:** This logic gate has two or more binary input variables (say A and B) and one binary output variable (say F). It performs the **logical multiplication** operation and is represented by the '·' symbol. The algebraic expression for the AND gate (for two inputs) is written as $F = A \cdot B$ or simply as $F = AB$. The logic symbol and truth table for the AND gate (for two inputs) are shown in Figure 2.1.

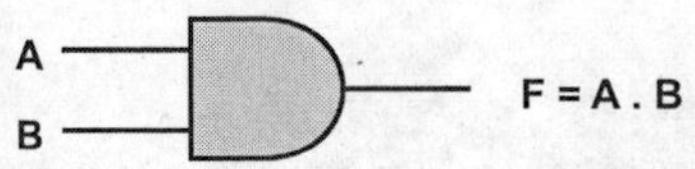

A	B	F = A . B
0	0	0
0	1	0
1	0	0
1	1	1

Figure 2.1 Logic Symbol and Truth Table for AND Gate

It can be observed from the truth table that the output of AND gate is 1 only if all of the inputs are 1; otherwise, the output is 0.

- **OR gate:** This logic gate consists of two or more binary inputs and one binary output. It performs the **logical addition** operation and is represented by the '+' symbol. The algebraic expression for the OR gate (for two inputs) is written as `F = A + B`. The logic symbol and truth table for the OR gate (for two inputs) are shown in Figure 2.2.

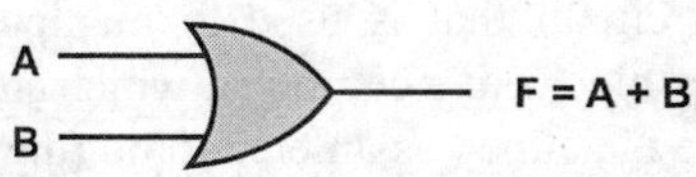

A	B	F = A + B
0	0	0
0	1	1
1	0	1
1	1	1

Figure 2.2 Logic Symbol and Truth Table for OR Gate

It can be observed from the truth table that the output of OR gate is 1 if at least one of the inputs is 1.

- **NOT gate:** This logic gate has only one binary input (say `A`) and one binary output. It performs an operation called **inversion** or **complementation** and that's why also referred to as the **inverter**. It simply changes one logic level to the opposite, that is, 1 to 0 and 0 to 1. The NOT operation is represented by either '′' or '¯' symbol and the algebraic expression for this gate is written as `F = A′` or F = $\overline{A}$. The logic symbol and the truth table for NOT gate are shown in Figure 2.3. Note that the small circle (o) in the logic symbol indicates the inversion.

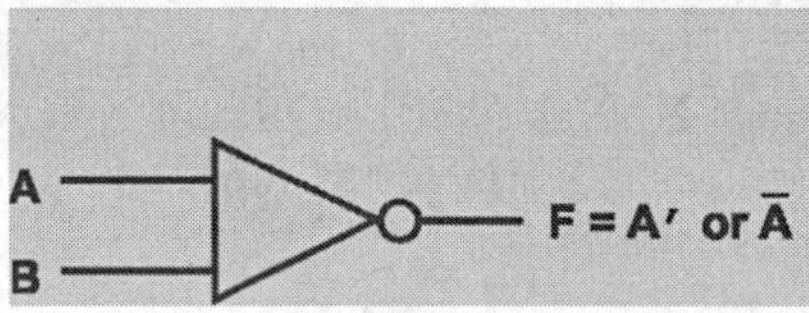

A	F = A′ or $\overline{A}$
0	1
1	0

Figure 2.3 Logic Symbol and Truth Table for NOT Gate

- **NAND gate:** As the name suggests, this logic gate is the combination of NOT and AND gates. It complements the function of AND gate, that is, it gives the output 1 if any of the inputs is 0 and if all the inputs are 1, then the output of NAND gate is 0. The algebraic expression for the NAND gate (for two inputs) is written as `F = (A·B)′` or simply as `(AB)′`. The logic symbol and the truth table for NAND gate are shown in Figure 2.4. Note that the logic symbol of NAND gate consists of logic symbol of AND gate followed by the small circle indicating the inversion.

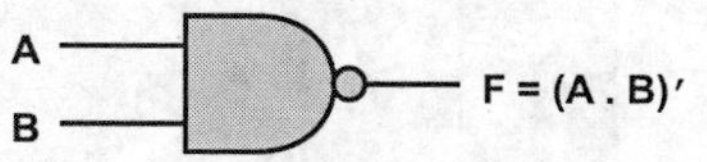

A	B	F = (A . B)′
0	0	1
0	1	1
1	0	1
1	1	0

Figure 2.4 Logic Symbol and Truth Table for NAND Gate

- **NOR gate:** As the name suggests, this logic gate is the combination of NOT and OR gates. It complements the function of OR gate, that is, it gives the output 1 if all the inputs are 0 and if any of the inputs is 1, then the output of NOR gate is 0. The algebraic expression for the NOR gate (for two inputs) is written as `F = (A + B)'`. The logic symbol and the truth table for NOR gate are shown in Figure 2.5. Note that the logic symbol of NOR gate consists of logic symbol of OR gate followed by the small circle indicating the inversion.

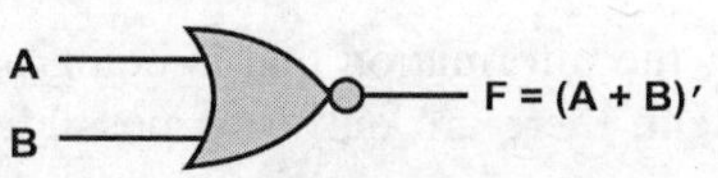

A	B	F = (A + B)′
0	0	1
0	1	0
1	0	0
1	1	0

Figure 2.5 Logic Symbol and Truth Table for NOR Gate

- **XOR (exclusive OR) gate:** This logic gate produces an output 1 if any input is 1 but excludes the combination when both inputs are 1. For more than two inputs, the output is 1 when an odd number of inputs are 1. For example, in case of five inputs, the output of XOR gate is 1 if one, three or five inputs are 1. The XOR operation is represented by the symbol '⊕' and the algebraic expression for XOR gate (for two inputs) is written as `F = A ⊕ B` or simply as `A'B + AB'`. The logic symbol and truth table (for two inputs) for XOR gate are shown in Figure 2.6. Note that the logic symbol of XOR gate is similar to OR gate except the additional curved line on the input side.

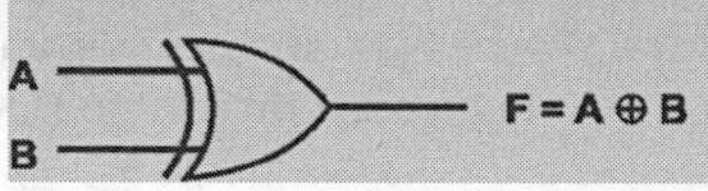

A	B	F = A ⊕ B
0	0	0
0	1	1
1	0	1
1	1	0

Figure 2.6 Logic Symbol and Truth Table for XOR Gate

- **XNOR (exclusive NOR) gate:** This logic gate complements the function of XOR gate, that is, it gives the output 1 if all the inputs are same; otherwise, the output is 0. The algebraic expression for XNOR gate (for two inputs) is written as `F = (A ⊕ B)'` or simply as `A'B' + AB`. The logic symbol and truth table for XNOR gate (for two inputs) are shown in Figure 2.7. Note that the logic symbol of XNOR gate is similar to XOR gate followed by a small circle that indicates the inversion.

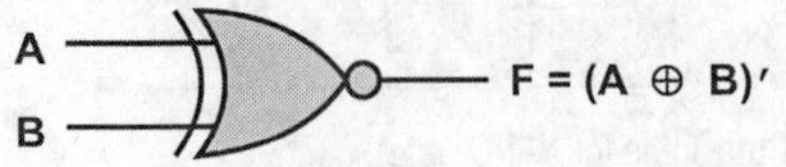

A	B	F = (A ⊕ B)′
0	0	1
0	1	0
1	0	0
1	1	1

Figure 2.7 Logic Symbol and Truth Table for XNOR Gate

3. Why NAND and NOR gates are known as universal gates?

Ans. Any logic function such as AND, OR and NOT can be produced from the NAND and NOR gates. Therefore, they are referred to as the universal gates. Both NAND and NOR gates are sufficient to realize any logic expression.

4. Define the following terms:

(a) Boolean algebra

(b) Boolean function

(c) Logic diagram

Ans. (a) Boolean algebra: In the digital system, the information that is being processed is usually presented in the binary form. In a binary system, there are only two possible values for any digit; on/off, high/low, true/false or 1/0. The various complex computations performed by the digital systems on these binary numbers are done through Boolean algebra. **Boolean algebra** is defined as an algebraic system that deals with binary variables and logic operations. The Boolean variables are represented by letters such as `A`, `B`, `x` and `y`, while three basic logic operations include AND, OR and NOT operations.

(b) Boolean function: An algebraic expression consisting of binary variables, logic operation symbols, parentheses and an equal to (=) sign is referred to as a Boolean function. For example, consider the following algebraic expression:

`F = AB′C + A′BC′`

Here, `F` is the Boolean function, `A` and `B` are the binary variables and '+' denotes the logic OR operation. Note that the value of a Boolean function can be either 0 or 1 depending on the values of input variables. In addition to algebraic form, a Boolean function can be expressed in the form of a truth table.

(c) Logic diagram: The logic diagram is the graphical representation of a Boolean function, which is composed of AND, OR and NOT gates. For example, the logic diagram for the Boolean function `F` is as shown in Figure 2.8.

5. State the duality principle of Boolean algebra. Also give an example.

Ans. The **duality principle** states that any valid Boolean expression of Boolean algebra remains valid even if the logical operators (+ and ·) and the identity elements (1 and 0) in the expression are interchanged, that is, by replacing + with ·, · with +, 1 with 0 and 0 with 1. This is an easy way to derive a new expression from an existing one. The derived expression is known as the **dual of an expression**.

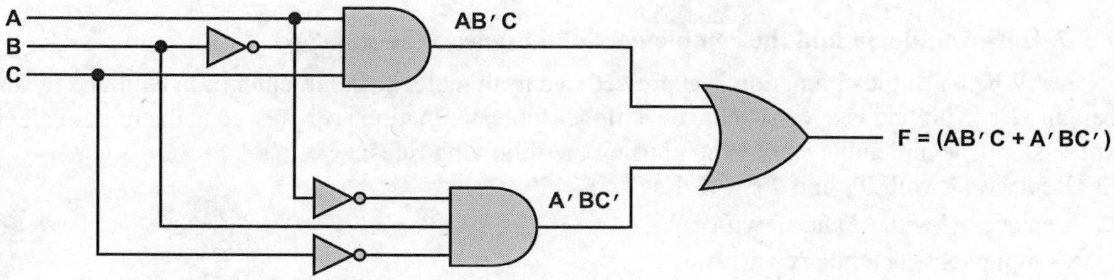

Figure 2.8 Logic Diagram for Boolean Function F

For example, consider a Boolean expression (A + B) · (A + C). Now, the dual of this expression will be (A·B) + (A·C).

6. List various laws of Boolean algebra.

Ans. While operating with Boolean expressions, certain laws are followed. These laws are listed in Table 2.1.

Table 2.1 Laws of Boolean Algebra

Rules	Property
Identity law	A + 0 = A
	A·1 = A
Null law	A·0 = 0
	A + 1 = 1
Idempotent law	A + A = A
	A·A = A
Inverse law	A + A′ = 1
	A·A′ = 0
Commutative law	A + B = B + A
	A·B = B·A
Associative law	A + (B + C) = (A + B) + C
	A· (B·C) = (A·B) ·C
Distributive law	A· (B + C) = A·B + A·C
	A + (B·C) = (A + B) · (A + C)
De Morgan's law	(A + B)′ = A′.B′
	(A·B)′ = A′ + B′
Absorption law	A + A·B = A
	A· (A + B) = A
Involution law	(A′)′ = A

All these laws can be verified either algebraically or by means of truth table.

7. How would you find the complement of a Boolean function?

Ans. When a Boolean function is expressed in a truth table, its complement can be found by simply changing 1's to 0's and vice versa. However, if the Boolean function is expressed in the form of algebraic expression, its complement can be found using the following rules:

- Replace 1's with 0's and 0's with 1's.
- Replace '+' with '·' and '·' with '+'.
- Complement each binary variable.

For example, consider the following Boolean function:

$F = (A' + B + C)(A + B + C')$

The complement of the function F is

$F' = (AB'C') + (A'B'C)$

8. State and prove the De Morgan's theorem using the algebraic method.

Ans. There are two theorems stated by De Morgan. Both these theorems are stated as follows:

Theorem 1: The complement of the sum of binary variables is equal to the product of the complements of the individual variables. That is, the complement of two or more variables ORed together is equal to the AND of the complements of the individual variables. Formally, this theorem can be expressed as:

$(A + B +, \ldots, + Z)' = A'B', \ldots, Z'$ (1)

Theorem 2: The complement of the product of binary variables is equal to the sum of the complements of individual variables. That is, the complement of two or more variables ANDed together is equal to the OR of the complements of the individual variables. Formally, this theorem can be expressed as:

$(AB, \ldots, Z)' = A' + B' +, \ldots, + Z'$ (2)

For simplicity, we are giving the proof of De Morgan's theorems for two input variables.

Proof of Theorem 1: $(A + B)' = A'B'$

R.H.S. $A'B'$

$= (A'B') + 0$	$[X + 0 = X]$
$= (A'B') + [(A + B) \cdot (A + B)']$	$[X \cdot X' = 0]$
$= [A'B' + A + B] \cdot [A'B' + (A + B)']$	$[X + YZ = (X + Y)(X + Z)]$
$= [(A' + A)(A + B') + B] \cdot [A'B' + (A + B)']$	$[X + YZ = (X + Y)(X + Z)]$
$= [1 \cdot (A + B') + B] \cdot [A'B' + (A + B)']$	$[X + X' = 1]$
$= [A + B' + B] \cdot [A'B' + (A + B)']$	
$= (A + 1) \cdot [A'B' + (A + B)']$	
$= A'B' + (A + B)'$	$[X + 1 = 1]$
$= [A'B' + (A + B)'] \cdot 1$	$[X \cdot 1 = X]$
$= [A'B' + (A + B)'] \cdot [(A + B) + (A + B)']$	$[X + X' = 1]$
$= (A + B)' + [(A'B') \cdot (A + B)]$	$[(X + Y)(X + Z) = X + YZ]$
$= (A + B)' + (A'B'A + A'B'B]$	
$= (A + B)' + [0 + 0]$	$[X \cdot X' = 0]$
$= (A + B)' + 0$	$[0 + 0 = 0]$
$= (A + B)'$	$[X + 0 = X]$

= L.H.S. Hence proved.

Proof of Theorem 2: $(AB)' = A' + B'$

R.H.S. $A' + B'$

$= (A' + B') \cdot 1$	$[X \cdot 1 = X]$
$= (A' + B') \cdot [AB + (AB)']$	$[X + X' = 1]$
$= (A' + B')AB + (A' + B')(AB)'$	$[X \cdot (Y + Z) = (X \cdot Y) + (X \cdot Z)]$
$= A'AB + B'AB + A'(AB)' + B'(AB)'$	
$= 0 + 0 + A'(AB)' + B'(AB)'$	$[X \cdot X' = 0]$
$= A'(AB)' + B'(AB)'$	
$= (AB)'(A' + B')$	
$= (AB)'(A' + B') + 0$	$[X + 0 = X]$
$= (AB)'(A' + B') + (AB)'(AB)$	$[X \cdot X' = 0]$
$= (AB)'[(A' + B') + AB]$	$[XY + XZ = X(Y + Z)]$
$= (AB)'[A' + B' + AB + AB]$	$[X + X = X]$
$= (AB)'[A' + AB + B' + AB]$	
$= (AB)'[(A' + A)(A' + B)$	
$+ (B' + B)(B' + A)]$	$[X + YZ = (X + Y)(X + Z)]$
$= (AB)'[A' + B + B' + A]$	$[X' + X = 1]$
$= (AB)'[(A' + A)(B + B')]$	
$= (AB)'[1 \cdot 1]$	
$= (AB)' \cdot 1$	$[1 \cdot 1 = 1]$
$= (AB)'$	

= L.H.S. Hence proved.

9. Explain Sum of Products (SOP) and Products of Sum (POS) forms.

Ans. The number of logic gates needed to implement a Boolean function depends on the number of terms involved in a Boolean expression. Lesser is the number of terms, lesser will be the number of gates required. For implementing a Boolean function with minimum number of logic gates, we need to arrange the terms in Boolean expression in one of the two standard forms: *SOP* and *POS*.

A Boolean expression in **SOP form** consists of two or more AND terms that are ORed together. Each AND term (also referred to as **product term**) in the expression has one or more variables either in normal or complemented form.

Example: $ABC + A'B + BC + D$

A Boolean expression in **POS form** consists of two or more OR terms that are ANDed together. Each OR term (also referred to as **sum term**) in the expression has one or more variables either in normal or complemented form.

Example: $(A + B + C) \cdot (A + B') \cdot (C' + D)$

10. What are minterms and maxterms?

Ans. Minterms: In a Boolean expression, the AND terms (product terms) that contain all the variables (either in normal form or in complemented form) involved in Boolean function are called **minterms** or **standard products**. For example, for a Boolean function of two variables A and B, there are four possible minterms: $A'B'$, $A'B$, AB' and AB. In general, there are 2^n minterms for n input variables. Table 2.2 lists the minterms for a Boolean expression involving three variables. Each minterm is represented by m_i, where i indicates the decimal equivalent of the binary number of the minterm designated (see Table 2.2). Note that in each minterm, a binary variable is in complemented form if its corresponding bit in the binary variable is 0; otherwise, the variable is in normal form.

Table 2.2 Minterms for Three Binary Variables

	Minterms	
A B C	**Term**	**Symbolic notation**
000	A′B′C′	m_0
001	A′B′C	m_1
010	A′BC′	m_2
011	A′BC	m_3
100	AB′C′	m_4
101	AB′C	m_5
110	ABC′	m_6
111	ABC	m_7

Maxterms: In a Boolean expression, the OR terms (sum terms) that contain all the variables (either in normal form or in complemented form) involved in Boolean function are called **maxterms** or **standard sums**. For example, for a Boolean function of two variables A and B, there are four possible maxterms: (A′ + B′), (A′ + B), (A + B′) and (A + B). In general, there are 2^n maxterms for n input variables. Table 2.3 lists the maxterms for a Boolean expression involving three variables. Each maxterm is represented by m_i, where i indicates the decimal equivalent of the binary number of the maxterm designated (see Table 2.3). Unlike minterms, in each maxterm, a binary variable is in complemented form if its corresponding bit in the binary variable is 1; otherwise, the variable is in normal form.

Table 2.3 Maxterms for Three Binary Variables

	Maxterms	
A B C	**Term**	**Symbolic notation**
000	A + B + C	M_0
001	A + B + C′	M_1
010	A + B′ + C	M_2
011	A + B′ + C′	M_3
100	A′ + B + C	M_4
101	A′ + B + C′	M_5
110	A′ + B′ + C	M_6
111	A′ + B′ + C′	M_7

Note that a maxterm M_i is the complement of the minterm m_i and vice versa.

11. When a Boolean function is said to be in canonical form? How would you convert an SOP or POS Boolean expression into canonical form? Explain with the help of an example.

Ans. A Boolean function is said to be in **canonical form** if it is expressed as a **sum of minterms (canonical SOP** form) or **product of maxterms (canonical POS** form). In other words, a Boolean expression is in canonical form if all terms in the expression are minterms or maxterms.

A Boolean function can be expressed as sum of minterms that produce output 1 in the truth table and as product of maxterms that produce output 0 in the truth table.

Converting an SOP expression into canonical SOP form:

A Boolean expression in SOP form can be converted into canonical SOP form by following the steps listed below:

1. Multiply each product term (that is not a minterm) in the given SOP expression by $(X + X')$, where X denotes the variable missing in that term and expand the expression.
2. Repeat step 1 until all the resulting product terms become the minterms, that is, contain all the variables either in normal form or in complemented form.

Example: Consider a Boolean function $F = AB + A'C$ that is in SOP form. This function can be converted into canonical SOP form or sum of minterms as follows:

$F = AB + A'C$

$= AB(C + C') + A'C(B + B')$

$= ABC + ABC' + A'BC + A'B'C$

Rearranging the minterms in ascending order, we get

$F = A'B'C + A'BC + ABC' + ABC$

$= m_1 + m_3 + m_6 + m_7$ [From Table 2.2]

The function F can also be written in the following short notation:

$F(A, B, C) = \Sigma(1, 3, 6, 7)$

Here, the summation (Σ) sign indicates ORing of the terms.

Converting a POS expression into canonical form:

A Boolean expression in POS form can be converted into canonical POS form by following the steps listed below:

1. Add (XX') to each sum term (that is not a maxterm) in the given POS expression, where X denotes the variable missing in that term.
2. Apply the distributive rule $[A + BC = (A + B)(A + C)]$ on that term.
3. Repeat step 1 and step 2 until all the resulting sum terms become the maxterms, that is, contain all the variables either in normal form or in complemented form.

Example: Consider a Boolean function $F = (A + B)(B' + C)$ that is in POS form. This function can be converted into canonical POS form or product of maxterms as follows:

$F = (A + B)(B' + C)$

$= (A + B + CC')(B' + C + AA')$

On applying distributive law, we get

$F = (A + B + C)(A + B + C')(B' + C + A)(B' + C + A')$

$= (A + B + C)(A + B + C')(A + B' + C)(A' + B' + C)$ [Rearranging the terms]

$= M_0\ M_1\ M_2\ M_6$ [From Table 2.3]

The function F can also be written in the following short notation:

$F(A, B, C) = \Pi(0, 1, 2, 6)$

Here, the product (Π) symbol indicates ANDing of the terms.

12. Suppose you are given a truth table. How would you represent the Boolean function expressed by means of truth table as sum of minterms and product of maxterms?

Ans. To represent the Boolean function expressed in the form of truth table as sum of minterms, we will take OR of the terms that are generating output 1 in the truth table and the variables of those terms will be ANDed together. On the other hand, for product of maxterms form, we will take AND of the terms that are generating output 0 in the truth table and the variables of those terms will be ORed together.

To understand this concept, consider the following truth table.

A	B	C	F
0	0	0	0
0	0	1	1
0	1	0	0
0	1	1	1
1	0	0	0
1	0	1	1
1	1	0	0
1	1	1	0

We can represent the function F as sum of minterms as shown here.

$F = A'B'C + A'BC + AB'C$

$= m_1 + m_3 + m_5$

That is,

$F(A, B, C) = \Sigma(1, 3, 5)$

We can represent the function F as product of maxterms as shown here.

$F = (A + B + C)(A + B' + C)(A' + B + C)(A' + B' + C)(A' + B' + C')$

$= M_0\ M_2\ M_4\ M_6\ M_7$

That is,

$F(A, B, C) = \Pi(0, 2, 4, 6, 7)$

13. How would you convert a Boolean function from one canonical form to another? Explain with the help of a suitable example.

Ans. As we know that a Boolean function can be expressed as sum of minterms that produce output 1 in the truth table. If we take complement of such function, then we get those minterms that produce output 0 in the truth table. For example, consider a Boolean function represented as the sum of minterms is:

$F(X, Y, Z) = \Sigma(0, 2, 5, 7)$

The function F has a complement function, which is as follows:

$$F'(X, Y, Z) = \Sigma(1, 3, 4, 6)$$
$$= m_1 + m_3 + m_4 + m_6$$

Now, if we again complement the function F′, we get the function F as shown here.

$$F(X, Y, Z) = (m_1 + m_3 + m_4 + m_6)'$$
$$= m_1' \cdot m_3' \cdot m_4' \cdot m_6' \quad \text{[De Morgan's theorem]}$$
$$= M_1 \cdot M_3 \cdot M_4 \cdot M_6 \quad [m_1' = M_1]$$

Thus, $F(X, Y, Z) = \Pi(1, 3, 4, 6)$

There is also a shortcut method for converting a Boolean function from one canonical form into another. For this, interchange the summation sign and the product symbol and list those terms that are missing from the given form.

14. List various ways to simplify the Boolean function.

Ans. Simplifying a Boolean function means reducing the number of terms in the Boolean function as possible so that it can be implemented using the simple hardware. There are various methods using which a Boolean function can be simplified. Out of these, two most commonly used methods are *algebraic* and *Karnaugh map* (or simply *K-map*). In **algebraic** method, the Boolean function is simplified by applying rules and laws of Boolean algebra. It is a trial- and error-based method and does not guarantee the optimal simplification. Therefore, an alternate graphical method, K-map, is preferred. In **K-map**, the Boolean function is represented pictorially and then simplified by applying certain rules.

15. What is K-map? Describe the steps used to simplify a Boolean expression.

Ans. The **K-map** is a graphical arrangement of a truth table, which is used to simplify and manipulate the Boolean function. It enables easier interpretation for selecting the minimum number of terms required to express the function algebraically. This diagram is composed of squares where each square represents a minterm. As we know that the truth table of a Boolean function involving n variables consists of 2^n minterms, correspondingly, there are 2^n squares in the K-map. For some minterms in the truth table, the Boolean function is equal to 1, while for others, it is equal to 0. In the K-map, the squares that correspond to minterms producing 1 are marked by 1 and the rest are either marked by zero or left blank.

A Boolean expression can be simplified using the K-map in three steps, which are as follows:

1. Design the K-map

Before designing a K-map, a Boolean expression must be in canonical form. The K-map can be designed for any number of variables. However, using the K-map to optimize Boolean functions is practical only for functions of two, three or four variables. Simplifying the expressions having five or six variables using K-map becomes a cumbersome task but is possible. However, beyond six variables K-map is not practically feasible. Figure 2.9 shows the K-maps for two, three and four variables, where each square in the K-map indicates a minterm.

Note that each minterm represented by a square in K-map is identified with the help of binary assignment of the variables along the top and left edges. For example, the minterm m_{11} in the four-variable

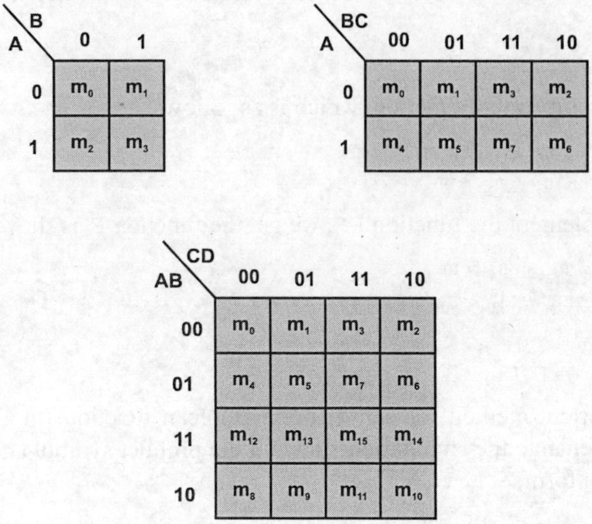

Figure 2.9 K-maps for Two, Three and Four Variables

K-map (that is, 1011 in binary) can be determined from 10 in the fourth row concatenated with 11 of the third column. This minterm represents the term `AB'CD` (variable `B` in complemented form and variables `A`, `C` and `D` in normal form).

In addition to minterms, the K-map can also be designed to represent the maxterms, if the given Boolean expression is in canonical POS form. The difference is that the maxterms are represented by 0's in the K-map instead of 1's.

2. Grouping of Terms

After the Boolean function has been represented in a K-map, we start grouping the squares containing 1's or 0's depending on whether the given Boolean expression is in canonical SOP or POS form, respectively. The squares are grouped based on certain rules that are listed as follows:

- Grouping of squares is always done in the power of 2 such as 21, 22, 23, 24 and so on. A group of two 1's or 0's is called a **pair**, a group of four 1's or 0's is called a **quad** and a group of eight 1's or 0's is known as an **octet**.
- The K-map is considered as cylindrical or folded. Therefore, the squares at the left and right ends of a row or a column are considered adjacent.
- A group can be horizontal or vertical but not diagonal.
- Overlapping of groups is also possible. Overlapping implies that same 1's or 0's can appear in more than one group.
- Each group should be as large as possible so that there are fewer groups. Moreover, each square containing 1 or 0 must be in at least one group.
- Redundant groups are not allowed. That is, a group whose all 1's or 0's are overlapped by other groups should not be present.

3. Cancellation of Variables

Once grouping of the squares is done, the next step is to simplify the Boolean function by cancelling the unwanted variables from the groups. There are different rules for cancelling the variables for a pair, a quad and an octet. A pair cancels one variable, a quad cancels two variables and an octet cancels three variables.

- **Cancellation in a pair:** Cancel the variable (either horizontally or vertically) that exists in both the normal and the complemented state.
- **Cancellation in a quad:** Cancel the two variables (either horizontally or vertically) that exist in both the normal and the complemented state.
- **Cancellation in an octet:** Cancel the three variables (either horizontally or vertically) that exist in both the normal and the complemented states.

After all the unwanted variables have been cancelled out from the groups formed, the simplified Boolean expression is obtained. Here, it is important to note that the simplified Boolean expression obtained from a K-map may not be unique. This is because the squares in K-map can be grouped in different ways thus, resulting in more than one simplified expression. One more thing to note that the resultant expression is expressed as sum of minterms; however, you can also express it as product of maxterms, if desired.

16. What are don't care conditions? Explain.

Ans. The 1's and 0's entries in the K-map indicate the combination of variables for which the Boolean function produces outputs 1 and 0, respectively. However, in some applications, either certain combinations of variables never occur or it does not matter whether the function produces output 1 or 0 for given combination of variables. In both cases, we can say that we don't care about the function output for those combinations of variables.

The don't care conditions are represented in the K-map by the cross (x) symbol and are helpful in further simplification of Boolean expressions. While making groups of adjacent squares, the don't care conditions (that is, x's) can be assumed 0's or 1's. Note that it is not necessary to include an x in the groups if it does not contribute in covering a large area.

17. Implement all basic logic gates function with the help of NAND gate.

Ans. As we know that the output expression for the NAND gate is

$$F = (A \cdot B)'$$

The function of **NOT gate** can be implemented using the NAND gate by making both inputs to the NAND gate equal [see Figure 2.10(a)] as shown here.

$$\begin{aligned} F &= (A \cdot A)' \\ &= A' + A' && \text{[De Morgan's theorem]} \\ &= A' && \text{[Idempotent law]} \end{aligned}$$

The functionality of **OR gate** can be produced by using three NAND gates [see Figure 2.10(b)]. The first NAND gate produces A', the second produces B' and the third produces $(A' \cdot B')'$, which is equivalent to $(A + B)$, that is, the function of OR gate as shown here.

$$\begin{aligned} F &= (A' \cdot B')' \\ &= [(A')' + (B')'] && \text{[De Morgan's theorem]} \\ &= (A + B) && \text{[Involution law]} \end{aligned}$$

The functionality of **AND gate** can be produced by using two NAND gates one after the other [see Figure 2.10(c)]. The first NAND gate produces $(A \cdot B)'$ and the second produces $[(A \cdot B)']'$, which according to involution law is equivalent to $A \cdot B$, that is, the function of AND gate.

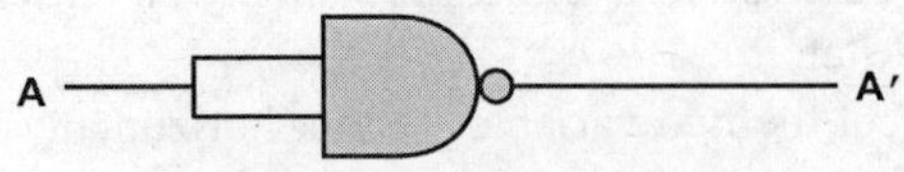

(a) NOT gate using NAND gate

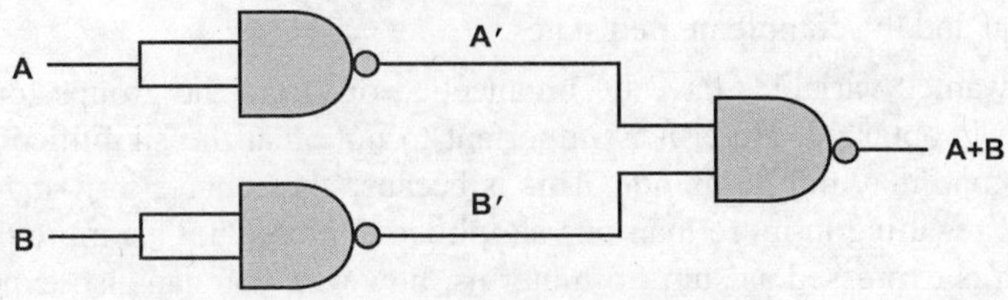

(b) OR gate using NAND gate

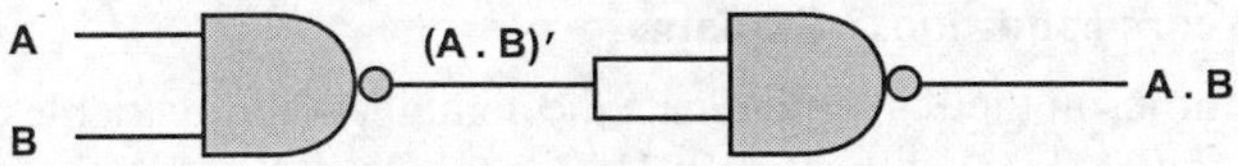

(c) AND gate using NAND gate

Figure 2.10 NOT, OR and AND Gates using NAND Gate

18. Implement all basic logic gates function with the help of NOR gate.

Ans. As we know that the output expression for the NOR gate is

F = (A + B)′

The function of **NOT gate** can be implemented using the NOR gate by making both inputs to the NOR gate equal [see Figure 2.11(a)] as shown here.

F = (A + A)′

= A′ [Idempotent law]

(a) NOT gate using NOR gate

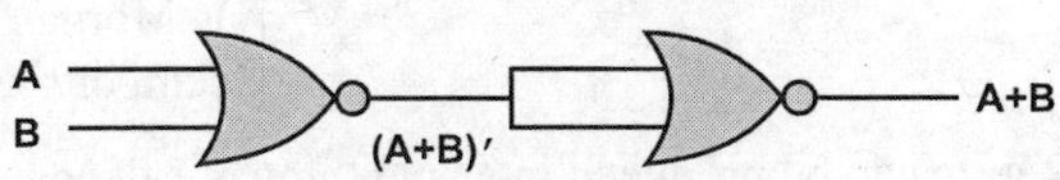

(b) OR gate using NOR gate

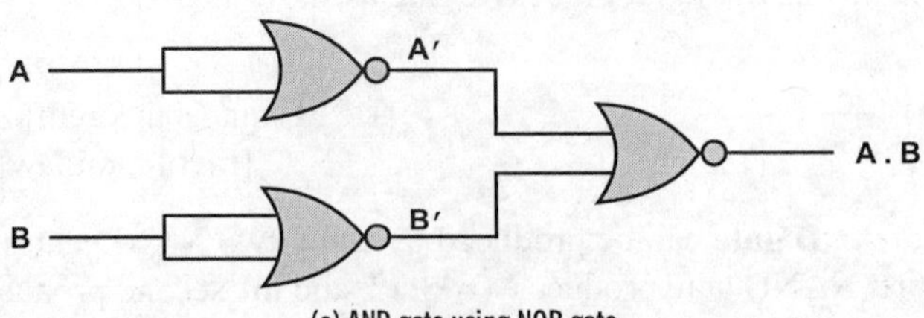

(c) AND gate using NOR gate

Figure 2.11 NOT, OR and AND Gates using NOR Gate

The functionality of **OR gate** can be produced by using two NOR gates one after the other [see Figure 2.11(b)]. The first NOR gate produces $(A + B)'$ and the second produces $[(A + B)']'$, which according to involution law is equivalent to $A + B$, that is, the function of OR gate.

The functionality of **AND gate** can be produced by using three NOR gates [see Figure 2.11(c)]. The first NOR gate produces A', the second produces B' and the third produces $(A' + B')'$, which is equivalent to $(A \cdot B)$, that is, the function of AND gate as shown here.

$$\begin{aligned} F &= (A' + B')' \\ &= [(A')' \cdot (B')'] && \text{[using De Morgan's law]} \\ &= A \cdot B && \text{[using Involution law]} \end{aligned}$$

19. Construct the XOR and XNOR gates using the basic gates.

Ans. As we know that the output expression for XOR gate is

$$F = A'B + AB'$$

The logic circuit for this expression using the basic gates is shown in Figure 2.12.

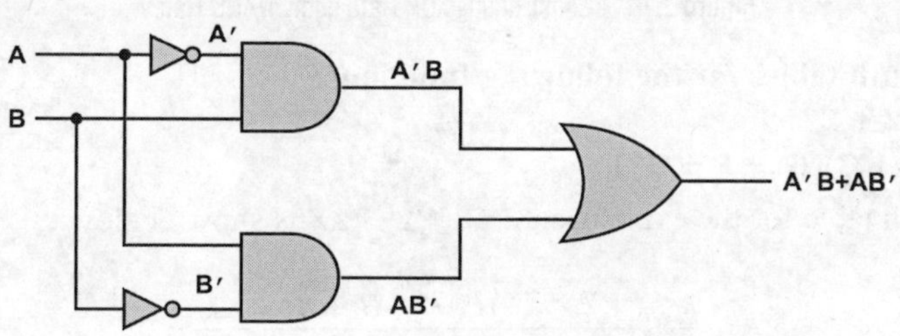

Figure 2.12 Logic Circuit for XOR Gate using Basic Gates

The output expression for XNOR gate is the complement of that of XOR gate. That is,

$$\begin{aligned} F &= (A'B + AB')' \\ &= (A'B)' \cdot (AB')' \\ &= (A + B') \cdot (A' + B) \\ &= AA' + A'B' + AB + B'B && \text{[Distributive law]} \\ &= 0 + A'B' + AB + 0 && \text{[Inverse law]} \\ &= A'B' + AB \end{aligned}$$

The logic circuit for this expression is designed by adding a NOT gate to the logic circuit of the XOR gate as shown in Figure 2.13.

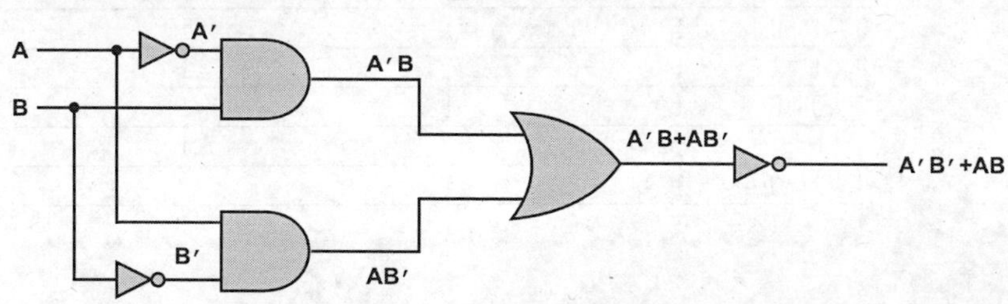

Figure 2.13 Logic Circuit for XNOR Gate using Basic Gates

20. How many minimum NAND gates are required to construct XOR gate?

Ans. The minimum four NAND gates are required to construct an XOR gate. As shown in Figure 2.14, the first NAND gate produces (A·B)′, that is, (A′ + B′). The second NAND gate produces [A·(A′ + B′)]′, that is, A′ + AB. The third NAND gate produces [B·(A′ + B′)]′ that is equal to B′ + AB. Finally, the fourth NAND gate produces [(A′ + AB)·(B′ + AB)]′, which when solved gives A′B + AB′, the output of XOR gate.

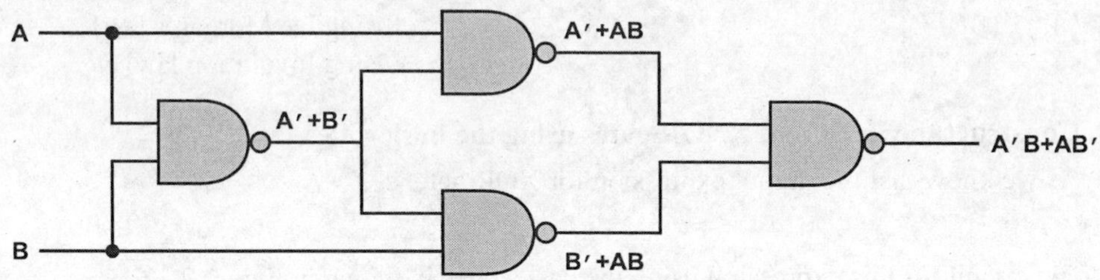

Figure 2.14 Constructing XOR Gate using NAND Gates

21. Find the truth tables for the following functions:

(a) XY + YZ + ZX

(b) (A + B + C) (A + B + C′)

Ans. **(a)** The truth table for the expression XY + YZ + ZX is shown below:

X	Y	Z	XY	YZ	ZX	XY + YZ + ZX
0	0	0	0	0	0	0
0	0	1	0	0	0	0
0	1	0	0	0	0	0
0	1	1	0	1	0	1
1	0	0	0	0	0	0
1	0	1	0	0	1	1
1	1	0	1	0	0	1
1	1	1	1	1	1	1

(b) The truth table for the expression (A + B + C) (A + B + C′) is shown below:

A	B	C	(A + B + C)	C′	(A + B + C′)	(A + B + C) (A + B + C′)
0	0	0	0	1	1	0
0	0	1	1	0	0	0
0	1	0	1	1	1	1
0	1	1	1	0	1	1
1	0	0	1	1	1	1
1	0	1	1	0	1	1
1	1	0	1	1	1	1
1	1	1	1	0	1	1

22. Draw the logic circuit for the following expressions:

(a) `y = (a' + b + c) (a + b + c')`
(b) `y = (a' + b' + c) (a' + b + c')`

Ans. (a) The logic circuit for the expression `y = (a' + b + c) (a + b + c')` is shown in Figure 2.15.

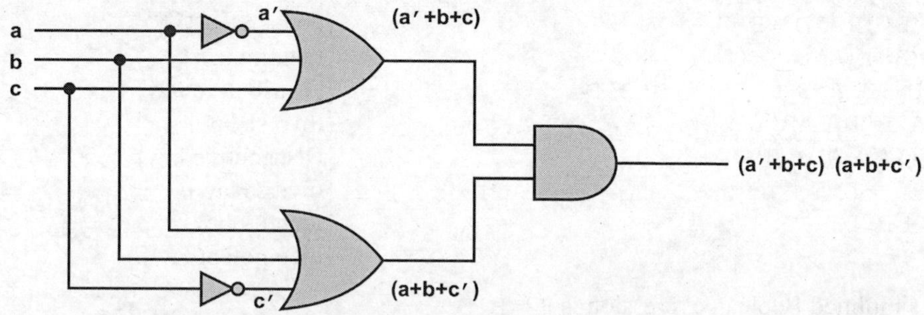

Figure 2.15 Logic Circuit

(b) The logic circuit for the expression `y = (a' + b' + c) (a' + b + c')` is shown in Figure 2.16.

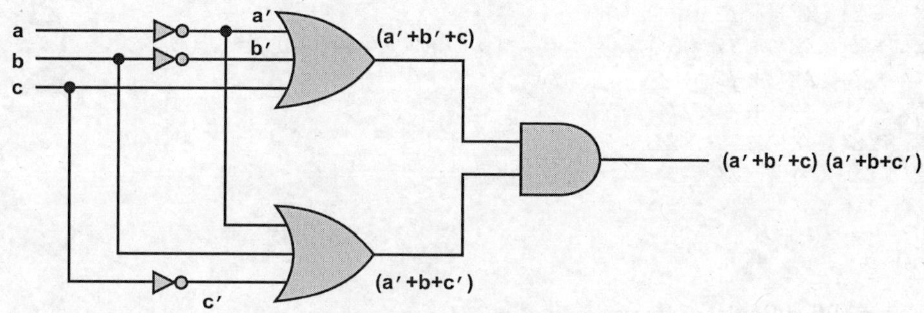

Figure 2.16 Logic Circuit

23. Prove the identity `A(A' + B) = AB` using truth table.

Ans. The truth table for the given expression is as shown below:

A	B	A′	A′ + B	A (A′ + B)	AB
0	0	1	1	0	0
0	1	1	1	0	0
1	0	0	0	0	0
1	1	0	1	1	1

From the above truth table, it is proved that $A(A' + B) = AB$.

24. Simplify the expression $F = (A + B')(A' + B' + D')D$.

Ans. The given expression is

$F = (A + B')(A' + B' + D')D$	
$= (A + B')(A'D + B'D + D'D)$	
$= (A + B')(A'D + B'D + 0)$	[Inverse law]
$= (A + B')(A'D + B'D)$	[Identity law]
$= AA'D + B'A'D + AB'D + B'B'D$	[Distributive law]
$= 0 + A'B'D + AB'D + B'D$	[Inverse law]
$= B'D(A' + A) + B'D$	[Distributive law]
$= B'D\cdot 1 + B'D$	[Inverse law]
$= B'D + B'D$	[Identity law]
$= B'D$	[Idempotent law]

Thus, the simplified Boolean expression is $F = B'D$.

25. Simplify the expression $F = (X' + Y)(X + Y + Z)Z'$.

Ans. The given expression is

$$F = (X' + Y)(X + Y + Z)Z'$$
$$= (X' + Y)(XZ' + YZ' + ZZ')$$
$$= (X' + Y)(XZ' + YZ' + 0)$$
$$= (X' + Y)(XZ' + YZ')$$
$$= X'XZ' + YXZ' + X'YZ' + YYZ'$$
$$= 0 + XYZ' + X'YZ' + YZ'$$
$$= YZ'(X + X') + YZ'$$
$$= YZ'\cdot 1 + YZ'$$
$$= YZ' + YZ'$$
$$= YZ'$$

Thus, the simplified Boolean expression is $F = YZ'$.

26. Prove that

$$(xy + y'x + yz')x'y' + xy' + yz' = xy' + yz'$$

Ans.

$$\text{L.H.S} = (xy + y'x + yz')x'y' + xy' + yz'$$
$$= [x(y + y') + yz']x'y' + xy' + yz'$$
$$= [x\cdot 1 + yz']x'y' + xy' + yz'$$
$$= (xx'y' + yz'x'y') + xy' + yz'$$
$$= (0 + 0) + xy' + yz'$$
$$= xy' + yz' = \text{R.H.S.}$$

Hence proved.

27. Convert the following logic function into minterms:

$$A'B'C'D' + A'B'C'D + ABCD + AB'CD'$$

Ans. The given logic function is

$F = A'B'C'D' + A'B'C'D + ABCD + AB'CD'$

$= m_0 + m_1 + m_{15} + m_{10}$

Arranging the minterms in ascending order, we get

$F = m_0 + m_1 + m_{10} + m_{15}$

The function F can be expressed as:

$F(A, B, C, D) = \Sigma(0, 1, 10, 15)$

28. Express the function F = pq + p′r as sum of minterms.

Ans. The function F contains three variables p, q and r and it consists of two terms: pq and p′r. There is one variable missing in both the terms. Therefore, to express this function as sum of minterms, we first have to include the missing variable in each term as shown here.

$F = pq + p'r$

$= pq(r + r') + p'r(q + q')$

$= pqr + pqr' + p'qr + p'q'r$

$= m_7 + m_6 + m_3 + m_1$

Arranging the minterms in ascending order, we get

$F = m_1 + m_3 + m_6 + m_7$

The function F can be expressed as:

$F(p, q, r) = \Sigma(1, 3, 6, 7)$

29. Express the Boolean function F = pr′ + q′r as product of maxterms.

Ans. To express the given function F as a product of maxterms, we first need to convert each term of the function into an OR term. This can be done by applying distributive law which states that $x + yz = (x + y)(x + z)$.

The given function is

$F = pr' + q'r$

$= (pr' + q')(pr' + r)$

$= (p + q')(r' + q')(p + r)(r' + r)$

$= (p + q')(q' + r')(p + r) \cdot 1 \qquad [x + x' = 1]$

$= (p + q')(q' + r')(p + r)$

Now, there is one variable missing in each OR term of the expression. Thus, we need to include the missing term in each OR term as shown here.

$F = (p + q')(q' + r')(p + r)$

$= (p + q' + rr')(pp' + q' + r')(p + qq' + r)$

$= (p + q' + r)(p + q' + r')(p + q' + r')(p' + q' + r')(p + q + r)(p + q' + r)$

$= (p + q' + r)(p + q' + r')(p' + q' + r')(p + q + r)$

$= M_2 \cdot M_3 \cdot M_7 \cdot M_0$

Arranging the maxterms in ascending order, we get

$F = M_0 \cdot M_2 \cdot M_3 \cdot M_7$

The function F can be expressed as:

$F(p, q, r) = \prod(0, 2, 3, 7)$

30. Implement a Boolean function with the help of Gates for F(w, x, y) = Σ(0, 2, 5, 6).

Ans. The given function is

$F(w, x, y) = \Sigma(0, 2, 5, 6)$

$= m_0 + m_2 + m_5 + m_6$

$= w'x'y' + w'xy' + wx'y + wxy'$

The logic circuit for this function is shown in Figure 2.17.

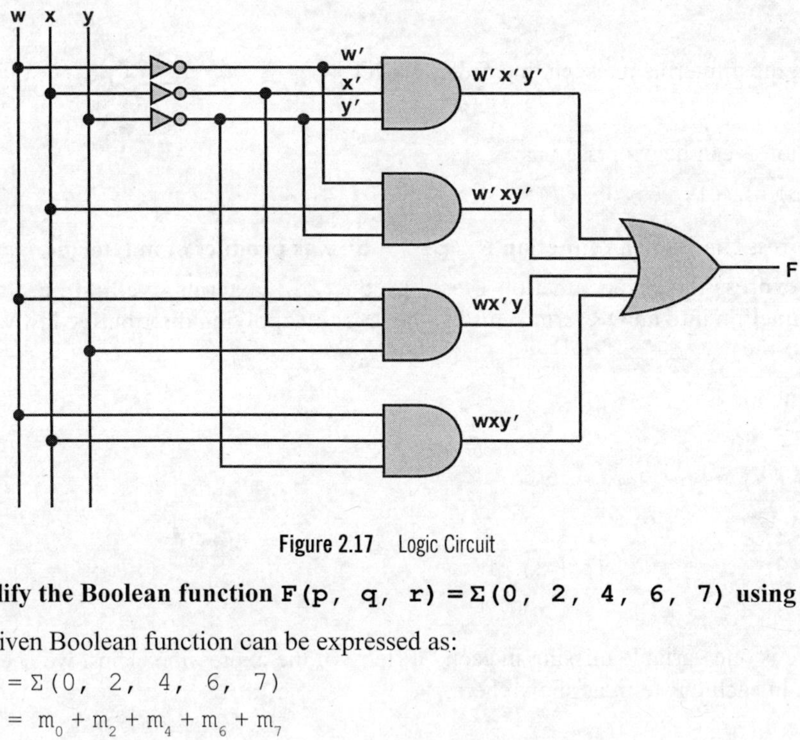

Figure 2.17 Logic Circuit

31. Simplify the Boolean function F(p, q, r) = Σ(0, 2, 4, 6, 7) using K-map.

Ans. The given Boolean function can be expressed as:

$F(p, q, r) = \Sigma(0, 2, 4, 6, 7)$

$= m_0 + m_2 + m_4 + m_6 + m_7$

$= p'q'r' + p'qr' + pq'r' + pqr' + pqr$

The K-map for this function is shown in Figure 2.18.

In the K-map shown in Figure 2.18, the 1's is marked in the squares corresponding to the minterms 0, 2, 4, 6 and 7. Minterms 0, 2, 4 and 6 are combined to form a quad, thus producing r' (the variables p and q are cancelled out as they are appearing in normal as well as in complemented form). Similarly, the minterms 6 and 7 are combined to form a pair that produces pq (the variable r is cancelled out as it is appearing in normal as well as in complemented form).

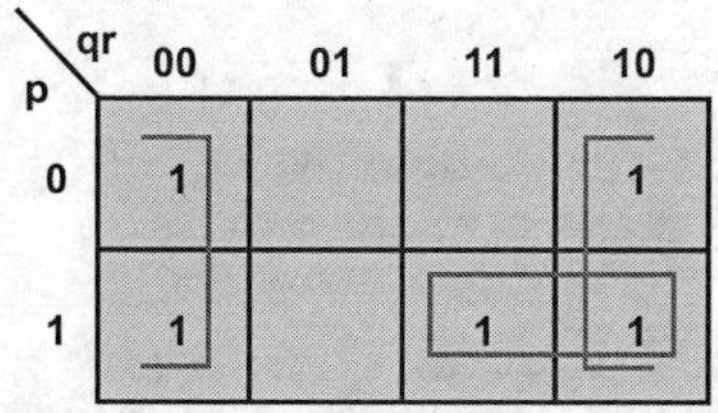

Figure 2.18 K-map for F (p, q, r) = Σ(0, 2, 4, 6, 7)

Thus, the simplified Boolean function is

F = r′ + pq.

32. Simplify the expression Z(A, B, C, D)= Σ(0, 1, 3, 5, 8, 9, 10, 13, 14, 15) using K-map.

Ans. The given Boolean function can be expressed as:

Z(A, B, C, D) = Σ(0, 1, 3, 5, 8, 9, 10, 13, 14, 15)

$= m_0 + m_1 + m_3 + m_5 + m_8 + m_9 + m_{10} + m_{13} + m_{14} + m_{15}$

The K-map for this expression is shown in Figure 2.19.

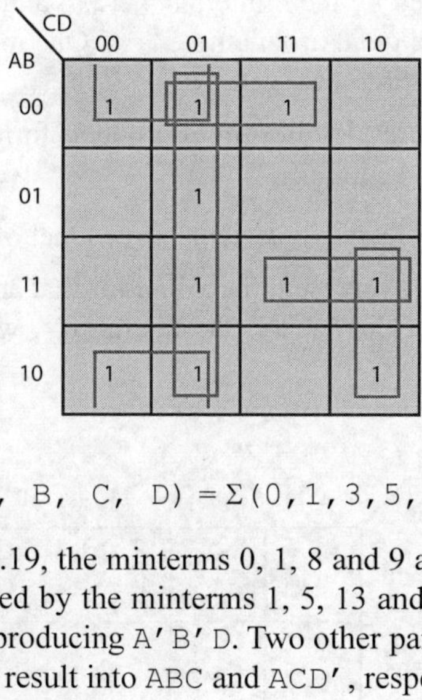

Figure 2.19 K-map for F (A, B, C, D) = Σ(0,1,3,5,8,9,10,13,14,15)

In the K-map shown in Figure 2.19, the minterms 0, 1, 8 and 9 are grouped together, producing the term B′C′. Another group is formed by the minterms 1, 5, 13 and 9 and this group results into C′D. The minterms 1 and 3 make a pair producing A′B′D. Two other pairs are formed by minterms (14 and 15) and (14 and 10) and these pairs result into ABC and ACD′, respectively.

Thus, the simplified Boolean expression is

F = B′C′ + C′D + A′B′D + ABC + ACD′

33. Simplify the Boolean expression Z(a, b, c, d) = Σ(0, 1, 4, 6, 7, 8, 9, 12, 14, 15) using K-map in

(a) Sum of products

(b) Products of sums

Ans. (a) The given Boolean function can be expressed as:

Z(a, b, c, d)= Σ(0, 1, 4, 6, 7, 8, 9, 12, 14, 15)

$$= m_0 + m_1 + m_4 + m_6 + m_7 + m_8 + m_9 + m_{12} + m_{14} + m_{15}$$

The K-map for this expression is shown in Figure 2.20.

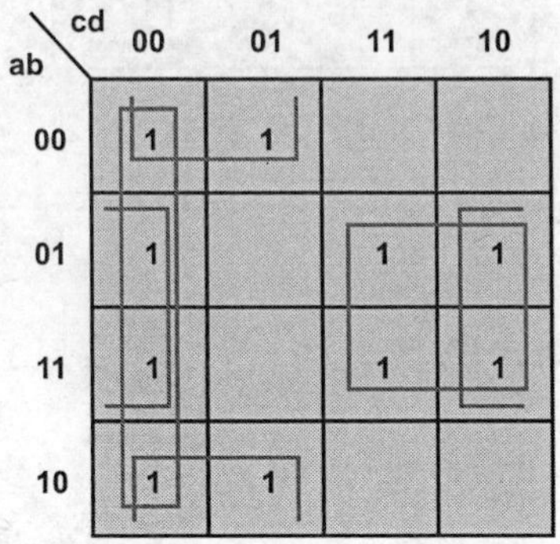

Figure 2.20 K-map for F(a, b, c, d) = Σ(0, 1, 4, 6, 7, 8, 9, 12, 14, 15)

In the K-map shown in Figure 2.20, the minterms 0, 1, 8 and 9 are grouped into a quad, producing the term b'c'. Another group is formed by the minterms 4, 12, 6 and 14 and this group results into bd'. The minterms 0, 4, 12 and 8 make a quad producing c'd'. One more quad is formed by the minterms 6, 7, 14 and 15 and this quad results into the term bc.

Thus, the simplified Boolean expression in sum of products form is

F = b'c' + bd' + c'd' + bc

(b) The K-map for the given Boolean expression F in product of sums is shown in Figure 2.21.

Here, the squares marked with 0's represent the minterms that are not included in F and thus, denote the complement of F. On grouping the squares containing 0's, we get the simplified complemented function F' as shown here.

F' = b'c + bc'd

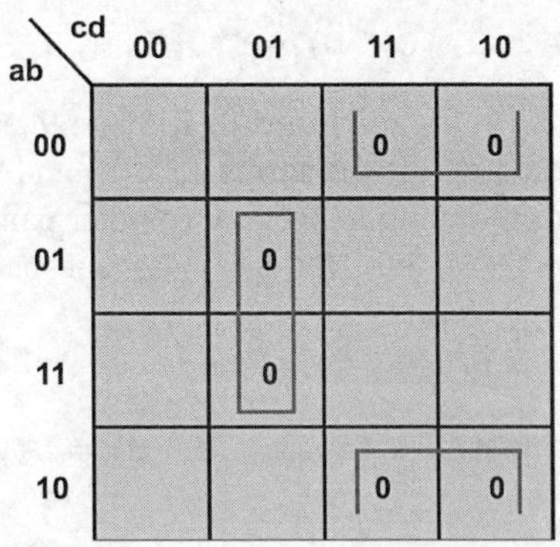

Figure 2.21 K-map for Function F in POS Form

Now, if we take the complement of F′, we get the simplified function F in product of sums form as shown here.

F = (b′c + bc′d)′

On applying De Morgan's theorem, we get

F = (b + c′)(b′ + c + d′)

34. Obtain the simplified expression for function F(a, b, c, d) = ∏(1, 3, 5, 7, 13, 15) in POS form.

Ans. The K-map for the function F(a, b, c, d) = ∏(1, 3, 5, 7, 13, 15) in POS form is shown in Figure 2.22. The 0's are marked in the squares corresponding to the maxterms 1, 3, 5, 7, 13 and 15, which represent the complement of F.

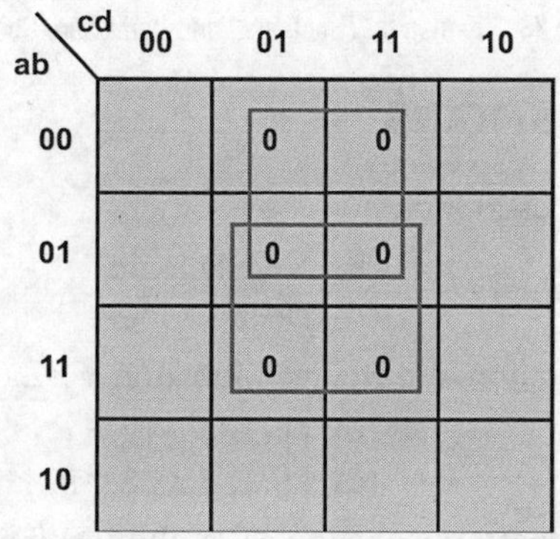

Figure 2.22 K-map for F(a, b, c, d) = Σ(1, 3, 5, 7, 13, 15)

From this K-map, we get the following simplified complemented expression F′ as:

F′ = a′d + bd

Now, if we take the complement of F′, we get the simplified function F in product of sums form as shown here.

F = (a′d + bd)′

On applying De Morgan's theorem, we get

F = (a + d′)(b′ + d′)

35. Simplify the function F using don't care condition d.

F(p, q, r, s) = Σ(0, 3, 7, 8, 9, 11, 12, 13)

d(p, q, r, s) = Σ(1, 4, 14, 15)

Ans. The K-map for the function F including the don't care condition d is shown in Figure in 2.23.

On combining the groups of squares containing 1's and x's, we get the simplified expression F as:

F = r′s′ + rs + pr′

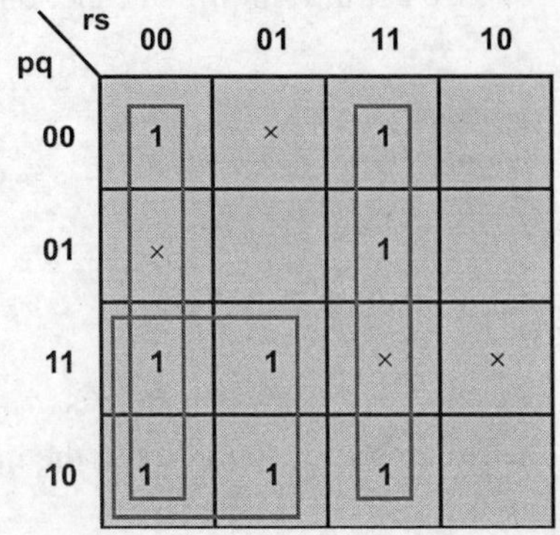

Figure 2.23 K-map for Function F and Don't Care Condition d

MULTIPLE CHOICE QUESTIONS

1. Which logic is known as universal logic?
   (a) PAL logic (b) NAND logic
   (c) MUX logic (d) Decoder logic
2. The equivalent POS representation of a Boolean function Y = Σ (0, 2, 3, 5) + d (7, 9, 12, 15) is
   (a) $\prod$ (0, 2, 3, 5) (b) $\prod$ (1, 4, 6) + d (7, 9, 12, 15)
   (c) $\prod$ (1, 4, 6, 8, 10, 11, 13, 14) (d) $\prod$ (1, 4, 6, 8, 10, 11, 13, 14). d (7, 9, 12, 15)
3. Which of the following gates performs the logical multiplication operation?
   (a) OR (b) AND
   (c) NOT (d) NAND
4. __________ is defined as the system that deals with binary variables and logic operations.
   (a) Boolean function (b) Logic circuit
   (c) Boolean algebra (d) None of these
5. The complement of the function F = (BC′ + A′D) is
   (a) (B′ + C) (A + D′) (b) (B + C′) (A′ + D)
   (c) BC′ · AD (d) None of these
6. In a Boolean expression, the OR terms that contain all the variables (either in normal form or in complemented form) involved in Boolean function are called __________.
   (a) Maxterms (b) Minterms
   (c) Standard products (d) None of these
7. Which of the following are the methods to simplify a Boolean function?
   (a) Algebraic (b) K-map
   (c) Both (a) and (b) (d) Neither (a) nor (b)
8. The table showing the relationship between input and output of binary variables is referred to as __________.
   (a) State table (b) Excitation table
   (c) Reduction table (d) Truth table

9. Which of the following is a valid minterm in a Boolean function of three variables?

   (a) AB
   (b) A′B′C
   (c) B′C
   (d) All of these

10. Which of the following Boolean expressions is true?

    (a) X + X′Y = X + Y
    (b) (X + Y) X′ = X′Y
    (c) X′Y + YZ = X′YZ′ + X′YZ + XYZ
    (d) All of these

Ans. 1. b 2. d 3. b 4. c 5. a 6. a 7. c 8. d 9. b 10. d

3

Digital Circuits

1. Define two types of digital circuits.

Ans. Any digital device can have two types of circuits, namely, *combinational* and *sequential*. A **combinational circuit** is a logic circuit that consists of a set of interconnected logic gates with a set of binary inputs and outputs. The binary values of output at any instant of time are a function of the combination of the binary values of the inputs. The operation of a combinational circuit can be described by means of truth table or Boolean expression. Figure 3.1 shows the block diagram of a combinational circuit with N inputs and M outputs.

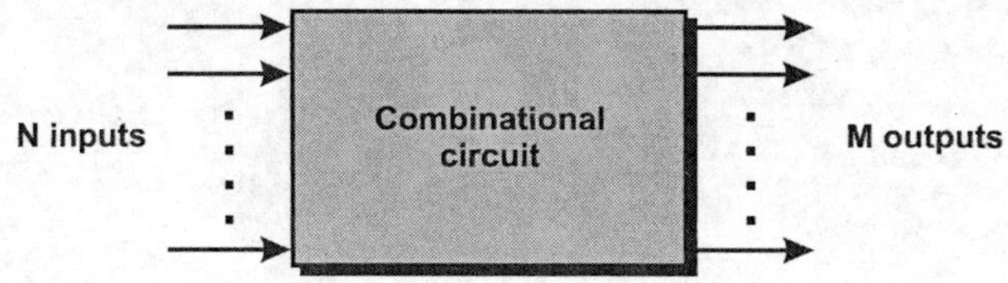

Figure 3.1 Block Diagram of a Combinational Circuit

On the other hand, a **sequential circuit** consists of a set of interconnected logic gates (that is, combinational circuit) and memory elements. The **memory elements** are the devices that can store the binary information (0 or 1). The binary values of the output at any instant depend on the combination of binary values of inputs as well as the current state of memory elements. As shown in Figure 3.2, the combinational part of the sequential circuit receives two types of inputs: **primary input** from the external environment and the **secondary input** from the memory elements.

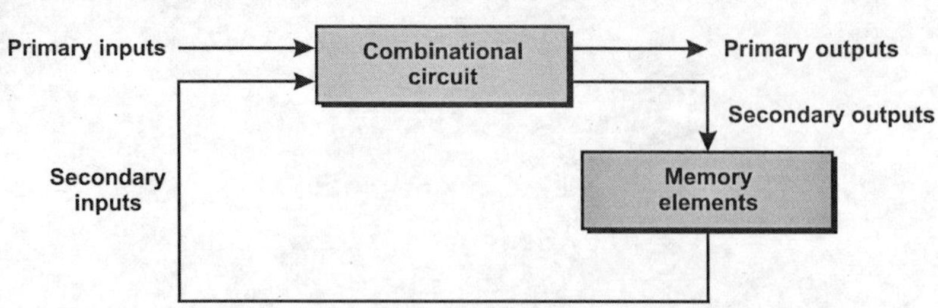

Figure 3.2 Block Diagram of a Sequential Circuit

2. Differentiate between combinational and sequential circuit.

Ans. The differences between combinational and sequential circuits are listed in Table 3.1.

Table 3.1 Differences between Combinational and Sequential Circuit

Combinational circuit	Sequential circuit
A combinational circuit is an interconnection of logic gates with many input and output variables.	A sequential circuit is an interconnection of combinational circuit and memory elements.
The output at any instance of time depends only on the present input. As soon as the input is changed, the information of previous input is lost. This implies that the combinational circuits have no memory.	The output at any instance of time depends not only on the present input but also on the previous input. Memory elements store the previous input and are connected to the combinational circuit forming a feedback path.
Some commonly used combinational circuits include adders (half and full), subtractors (half and full), decoders, encoders, multiplexers and de-multiplexers.	Some of the commonly used sequential circuits include flip-flops, registers and counters.
This circuit is easier to design.	This circuit is difficult to design because of the presence of memory.
This circuit is faster in speed as compared with sequential circuit because all inputs of this circuit are primary and are applied simultaneously.	This circuit is slower in speed because it consists of primary as well as secondary inputs and the secondary inputs are applied after a delay.
The realization of this circuit requires more hardware. Therefore, it is expensive in cost.	This circuit can be realized using less hardware. Therefore, it is cheaper in cost.

3. Write the steps involved in designing a combinational circuit.

Ans. The steps involved in designing a combinational circuit are as follows:

1. State the problem and determine the number of inputs and outputs.
2. Assign the letter symbols to input and output variables.
3. Derive the truth table representing the relationship between the input and output variables.
4. Obtain the simplified Boolean expression for each output using the K-map.
5. Draw the logic diagram for the output expression obtained from the previous step.

4. What is half adder? Give the logic diagram and truth table of half adder.

Ans. A **half adder** is a combinational circuit that performs the arithmetic addition of two binary digits (bits). It accepts two binary inputs of one bit each: *augend* (x) and *addend* (y) and produces two binary outputs: *sum* (S) and *carry* (C) of one bit each. The reason behind specifying two outputs is that the addition of two binary 1's is binary 10, which has two digits. Figure 3.3 shows the block diagram and truth table for the half adder.

It can be observed from the truth table that the output S is 1 if either of the inputs (that is, x or y) but not both are 1 and the output C is 1 if both inputs (x and y) are 1. Thus, the simplified Boolean functions for the two outputs can be written as:

$$S = x'y + xy' \text{ or } x \oplus y$$

$$C = xy$$

(a) Block diagram

x	y	S	C
0	0	0	0
0	1	1	0
1	0	1	0
1	1	0	1

(b) Truth table

Figure 3.3 Block Diagram and Truth Table for Half Adder

The logic diagram for the half adder combinational circuit consists of an XOR gate and an AND gate as shown in Figure 3.4.

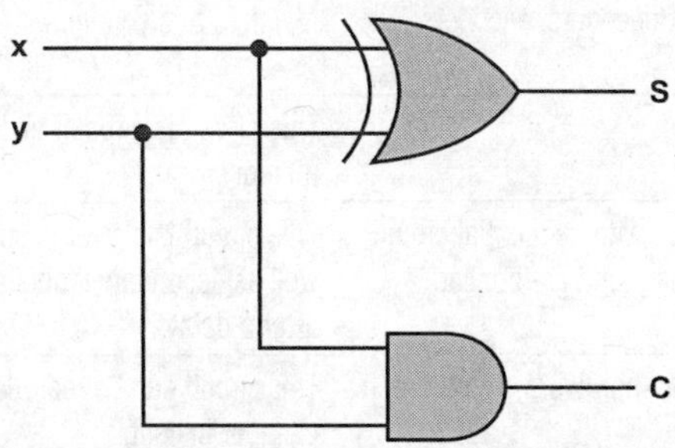

Figure 3.4 Logic Diagram for Half Adder

5. What is full adder? Give the logic diagram and truth table of full adder.

Ans. A **full adder** is a combinational circuit that performs the arithmetic addition of three bits. It accepts three binary inputs (x, y and z) of one bit each and produces two binary outputs (S for sum and C for carry) of one bit each. Here, the first two inputs x and y represent the significant bits that are to be added, while the third input z represents the carry input from the previous lower significant position. The block diagram and the truth table for the full adder are shown in Figure 3.5.

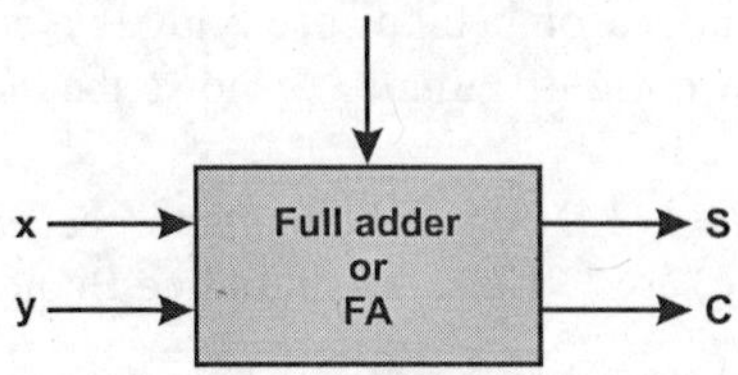

(a) Block diagram

x	y	z	S	C
0	0	0	0	0
0	0	1	1	0
0	1	0	1	0
0	1	1	0	1
1	0	0	1	0
1	0	1	0	1
1	1	0	0	1
1	1	1	1	1

(b) Truth table

Figure 3.5 Block Diagram and Truth Table for Full Adder

Figure 3.6 shows the K-map representation for the outputs S and C of full adder.

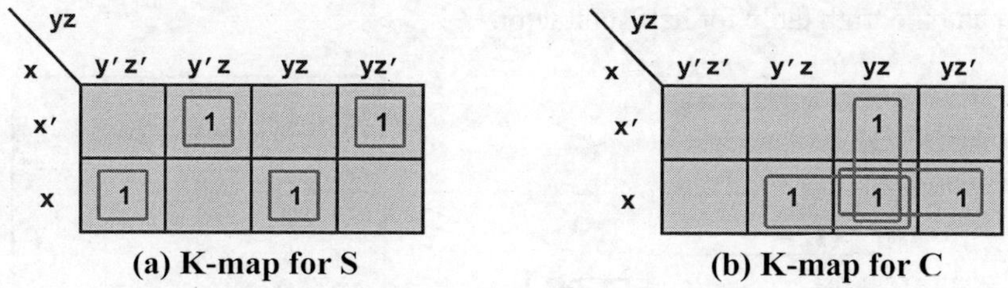

Figure 3.6 K-maps for the Outputs of Full Adder

From the K-maps, the Boolean functions for the outputs S and C can be obtained as:

$$S = x'y'z + x'yz' + xy'z' + xyz$$
$$C = xy + xz + yz$$

The Boolean function for S can be further simplified as shown here.

$$\begin{aligned} S &= x'y'z + x'yz' + xy'z' + xyz \\ &= x'(y'z + yz') + x(y'z' + yz) \\ &= x'(y \oplus z) + x(y \oplus z)' \\ &= x \oplus (y \oplus z) \text{ or } x \oplus y \oplus z \end{aligned}$$

With these simplified Boolean functions, the circuit for full adder can be implemented as shown in Figure 3.7.

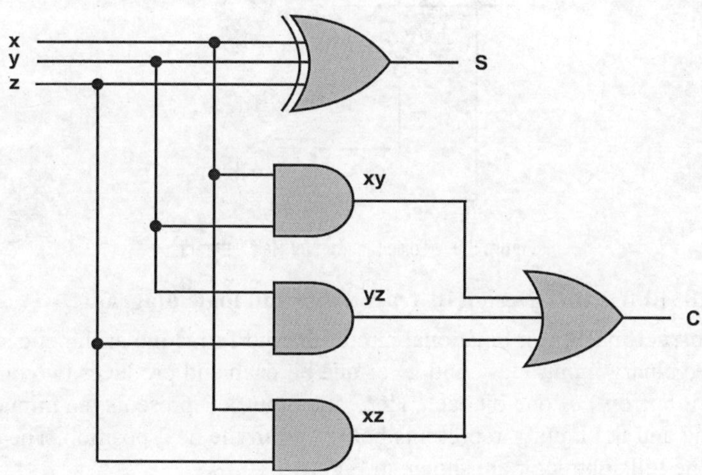

Figure 3.7 Implementation of Full Adder

6. What is half subtractor? Give its truth table and logic diagram.

Ans. A **half subtractor** is a combinational circuit that performs the arithmetic subtraction of two binary digits (bits). It accepts two binary inputs: *minuend* (x) and *subtrahend* (y) each of one bit and produces two binary outputs: *difference* (D) and *borrow* (B) of one bit each. The borrow (B) bit indicates that a binary 1 has been borrowed from the next higher significant bit position. Figure 3.8 shows the block diagram and the truth table for half subtractor.

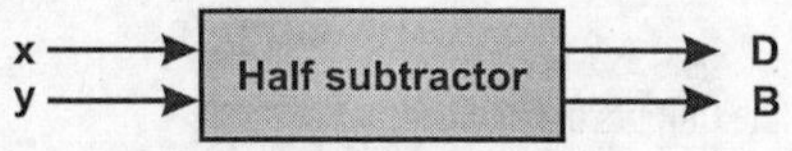

(a) Block diagram

x	y	D	B
0	0	0	0
0	1	1	1
1	0	1	0
1	1	0	0

(b) Truth table

Figure 3.8 Block Diagram and Truth Table for Half Subtractor

From the truth table, the simplified Boolean functions for the two outputs D and B can be directly derived as:

$D = x'y + xy'$ or $x \oplus y$
$B = x'y$

The logic diagram for the half subtractor combinational circuit consists of an XOR gate, an AND gate and a NOT gate as shown in Figure 3.9.

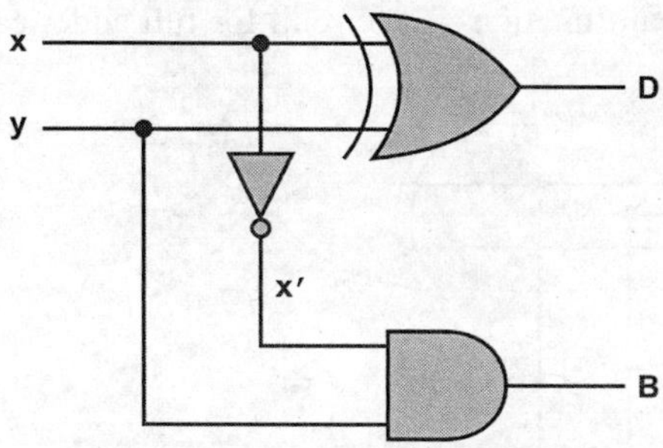

Figure 3.9 Logic Diagram for Half Subtractor

7. What is full subtractor? Design its truth table and logic diagram.

Ans. A **full subtractor** is a combinational circuit that performs the arithmetic subtraction of three bits. It accepts three binary inputs (x, y and z) of one bit each and produces two binary outputs (D for difference and B for borrow) of one bit each. Here, the input x represents the minuend, input y represents the subtrahend and the input z represents borrow from the next position. The block diagram and the truth table for the full subtractor are shown in Figure 3.10.

The Boolean functions for the outputs D and B can be obtained from the truth table as follows:

$D = x'y'z + x'yz' + xy'z' + xyz$
$B = x'y'z + x'yz' + x'yz + xyz$

The Boolean expression for the output D is equivalent to the XOR of x, y and z as explained in Q5. That is,

$D = x \oplus (y \oplus z)$

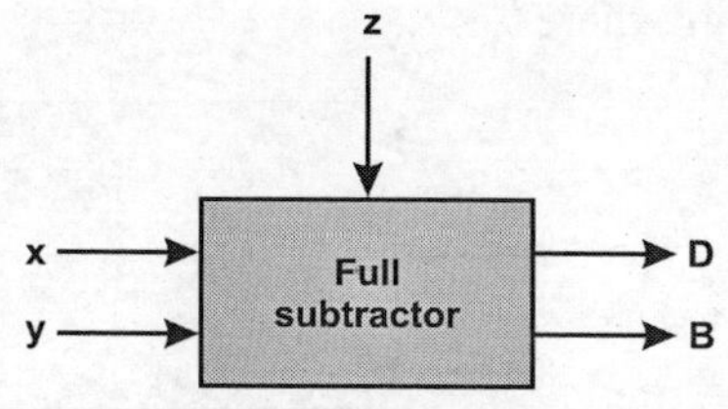

(a) Block diagram

x	y	z	D	B
0	0	0	0	0
0	0	1	1	1
0	1	0	1	1
0	1	1	0	1
1	0	0	1	0
1	0	1	0	0
1	1	0	0	0
1	1	1	1	1

(b) Truth table

Figure 3.10 Block Diagram and Truth Table for Full Subtractor

The Boolean expression for the output B can be simplified using the K-map as shown in Figure 3.11.

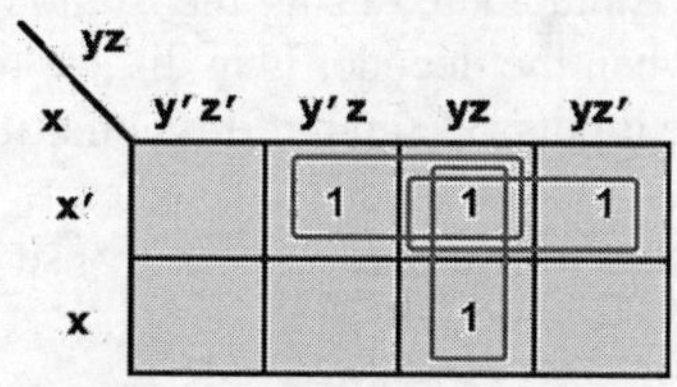

Figure 3.11 K-map for Output *B*

From the K-map shown in Figure 3.11, the simplified Boolean expression for the output B is obtained as

$$B = x'z + x'y + yz$$

The logic diagram for the full subtractor combinational circuit is shown in Figure 3.12.

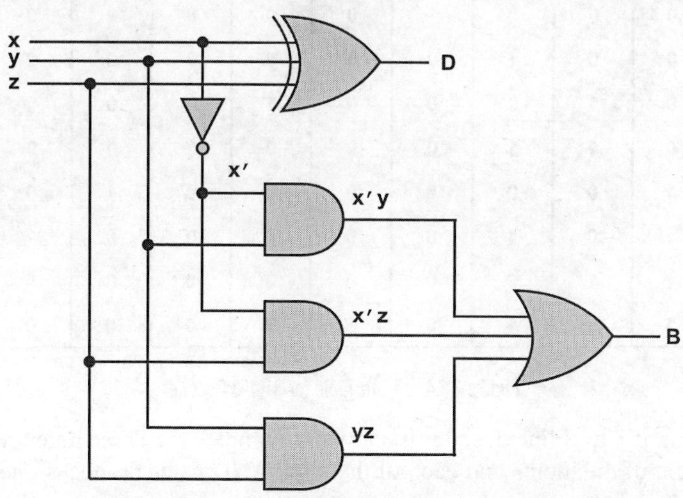

Figure 3.12 Logic Diagram for Full Subtractor

8. What is decoder? Explain 3 × 8 line decoder.

Ans. A **decoder** is a combinational circuit that converts the binary information from N encoded input lines to a maximum of 2^N distinct output lines. The output may be less than 2^N in case some input combinations are unused in N-bit coded input information. A decoder with N inputs and M outputs is referred to as an **N-to-M line decoder** or **N × M decoder** where M ≤ N.

A **3-to-8 decoder** takes three inputs (x, y and z) and decodes them into eight outputs (from Y_0 to Y_7). Generally, decoders include one or more enable inputs for controlling the operation of the circuit. The block diagram of 3-to-8 line decoder shown in Figure 3.13 includes one enable input (labelled as E). When E = 1, the decoder is in enable mode else is in disable mode. The 3-to-8 decoder is useful in conversion of binary into octal numbers.

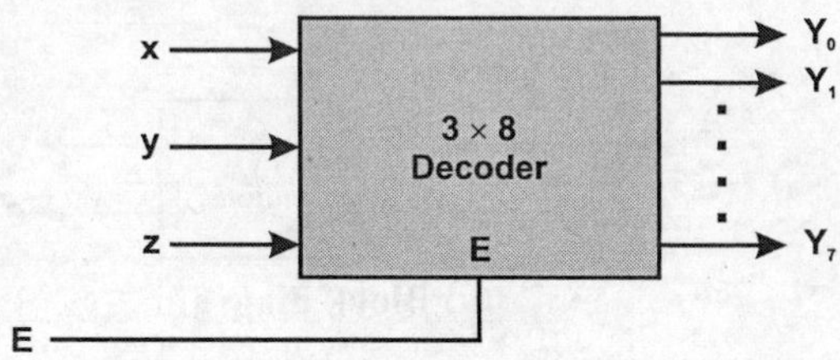

Figure 3.13 Block Diagram of 3-to-8 Line Decoder

The operation of 3-to-8 decoder is elucidated using the truth table shown in Figure 3.14. It can be observed from the truth table that when the decoder is in disable mode (that is, E = 0), all the outputs are 0 irrespective of the values of the inputs x, y and z; this condition is represented by ×'s in the inputs and designate do not care conditions. On the other hand, when E = 1, the decoder operates in regular mode and for each possible combination of inputs x, y and z, seven outputs (Y_0 to Y_7) are produced out of which six are 0's and one is 1.

Inputs				Outputs							
Enable (E)	x	y	z	Y_0	Y_1	Y_2	Y_3	Y_4	Y_5	Y_6	Y_7
0	×	×	×	0	0	0	0	0	0	0	0
1	0	0	0	1	0	0	0	0	0	0	0
1	0	0	1	0	1	0	0	0	0	0	0
1	0	1	0	0	0	1	0	0	0	0	0
1	0	1	1	0	0	0	1	0	0	0	0
1	1	0	0	0	0	0	0	1	0	0	0
1	1	0	1	0	0	0	0	0	1	0	0
1	1	1	0	0	0	0	0	0	0	1	0
1	1	1	1	0	0	0	0	0	0	0	1

Figure 3.14 Truth Table for 3-to-8 Decoder

The logic diagram of 3-to-8 line decoder is shown in Figure 3.15. Three inverters have been used to show the complement of the inputs and each of the eight AND gates produces one of the binary combinations as output.

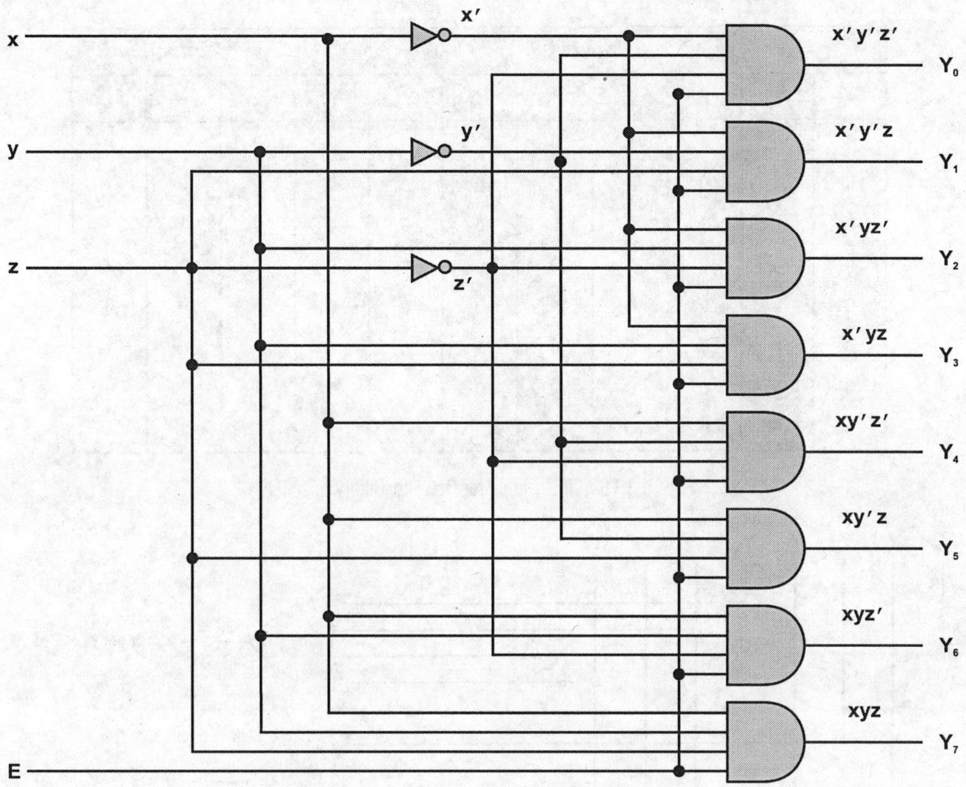

Figure 3.15 Logic Diagram for 3-to-8 Decoder

9. Explain encoder.

Ans. An **encoder** is a combinational logic circuit that performs the reverse function from that of a decoder. It has 2^N or less number of input lines and N output lines that produce the binary code corresponding to the values of inputs. The octal-to-binary encoder is an example of encoder consisting of eight inputs (Y_0 to Y_7) one corresponding to each of the octal digits and three outputs (x, y and z) that produce the corresponding binary number. The truth table for octal-to-binary encoder is shown in Figure 3.16. Notice that at any given time only one input is 1, while all other inputs are 0's.

From the truth table, it can be observed that the output x is 1 if the octal digit 4, 5, 6 or 7 is used as input. Similarly, the output y is 1 if the octal digit 2, 3, 6 or 7 is the input and the output z is 1 if the octal digit 1, 3, 5 or 7 is the input. Thus, the Boolean functions for these outputs can be written as:

$$x = Y_4 + Y_5 + Y_6 + Y_7$$

$$y = Y_2 + Y_3 + Y_6 + Y_7$$

$$z = Y_1 + Y_3 + Y_5 + Y_7$$

The logic diagram for octal-to-binary encoder can be constructed using three OR gates as shown in Figure 3.17.

Inputs								Outputs		
Y_0	Y_1	Y_2	Y_3	Y_4	Y_5	Y_6	Y_7	x	y	z
1	0	0	0	0	0	0	0	0	0	0
0	1	0	0	0	0	0	0	0	0	1
0	0	1	0	0	0	0	0	0	1	0
0	0	0	1	0	0	0	0	0	1	1
0	0	0	0	1	0	0	0	1	0	0
0	0	0	0	0	1	0	0	1	0	1
0	0	0	0	0	0	1	0	1	1	0
0	0	0	0	0	0	0	1	1	1	1

Figure 3.16 Truth Table for Octal-to-Binary Encoder

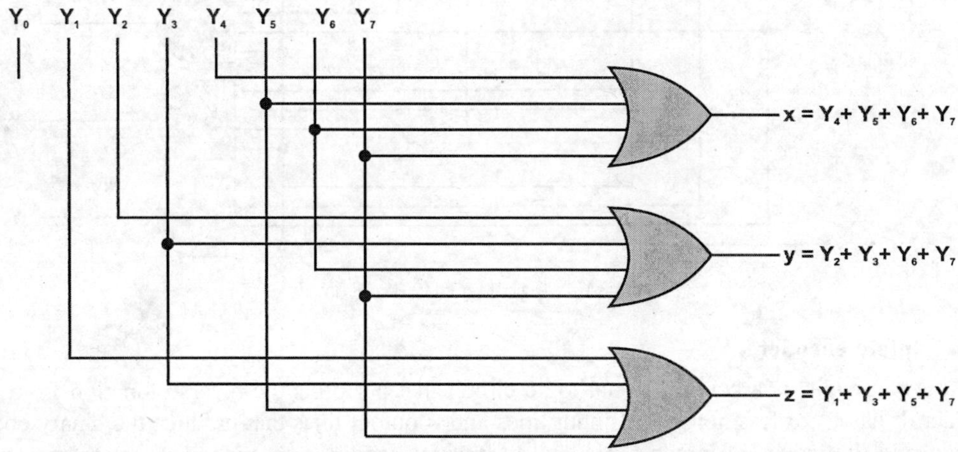

Figure 3.17 Logic Diagram for Octal-to-Binary Encoder

10. What is multiplexer? Construct 4 ¥ 1 multiplexer circuit and explain its working also.

Ans. A **multiplexer (MUX)**, also known as **data selector**, is a combinational circuit that selects one binary input from 2^N input lines and sends it to a single output line. The decision of selecting a specific input from 2^N inputs is made on the basis of a set of input variables called **selection inputs**. For a 2^N-to-1 line (also denoted as $2^N \times 1$) multiplexer, there are N input selection lines (S_0, S_1, ... ,S_{N-1}) and the binary combinations of these selection inputs identify which input is to be selected.

A **4 × 1 multiplexer** has four data inputs (A_0, A_1, A_2 and A_3), two selection inputs (S_0 and S_1) and a single output (Y). Figure 3.18 shows the logic diagram for a 4 × 1 multiplexer. It consists of four AND gates where each AND gate takes three inputs: one input comes from one of the four input lines and two inputs come from the selection lines. The bit combinations of S_0 and S_1 determine which of the four AND gates will be selected. The outputs from the AND gates are ORed together to produce the single output Y.

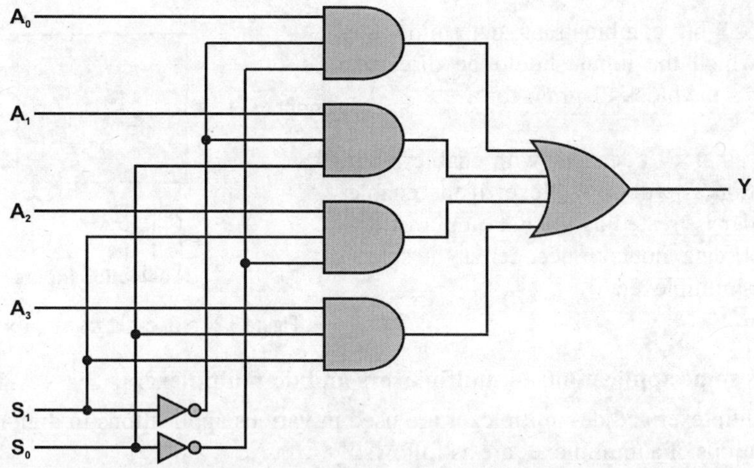

Figure 3.18 Logic Diagram for a 4×1 Multiplexer

To understand the operation of 4 × 1 multiplexer, let us consider the case when $S_1 = 0$ and $S_0 = 1$. In this case, the inputs to the AND gates are $A_0$10, $A_1$11, $A_2$00 and $A_3$01. Since all AND gates except the second one have at least one of their inputs equal to 0, they will produce 0's as outputs, while the output from the second AND gate will be A_1. Thus, the final output from the OR gate (that is the sum of outputs from AND gates) will be equal to A_1. That is, the input A_1 will be selected and directed it to the output line.

The 4 × 1 multiplexer has total six inputs (leading to $2^6 = 64$ binary combinations) and one output; thus, total 64 rows are required in the truth table for describing the operation of this multiplexer. As it seems inconvenient to represent such a long table, we can use a function table to describe the operation of the multiplexer. The function table shows that combinations of the selection inputs (S_0 and S_1) lead to output (Y). Figure 3.19 shows the function table and block diagram for the 4 × 1 multiplexer.

Selection Inputs		Output
S_1	S_0	Y
0	0	A_0
0	1	A_1
1	0	A_2
1	1	A_3

(a) Function table

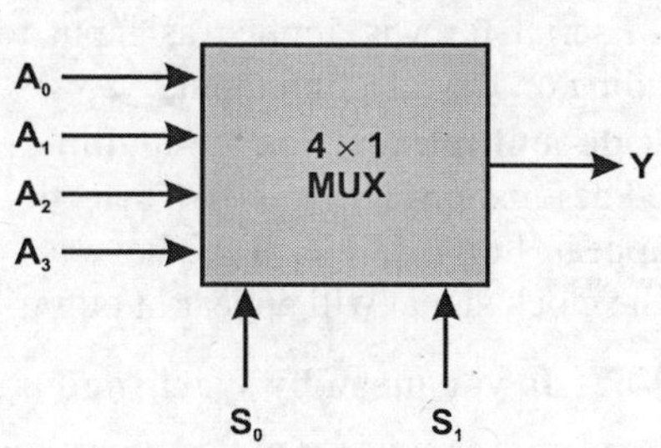

(b) Block diagram

Figure 3.19 Function Table and Block Diagram of 4 × 1 Multiplexer

11. What is de-multiplexer?

Ans. A **de-multiplexer** (or **DEMUX**) is a combinational circuit that performs reverse operation from that of multiplexer. That is, it accepts binary information from a single input line and transmits it to one of the 2^N possible output lines. Like multiplexer, the de-multiplexer also has N selection input lines whose bit combinations determine the output line to which the input should be directed. Figure 3.20 shows the block diagram for a 1 × 2^N de-multiplexer.

Observe that an N × 2^N decoder with enable input E can also function as a de-multiplexer if the enable input E of decoder is treated as the data input of de-multiplexer and N data inputs of decoder as the selection inputs of de-multiplexer.

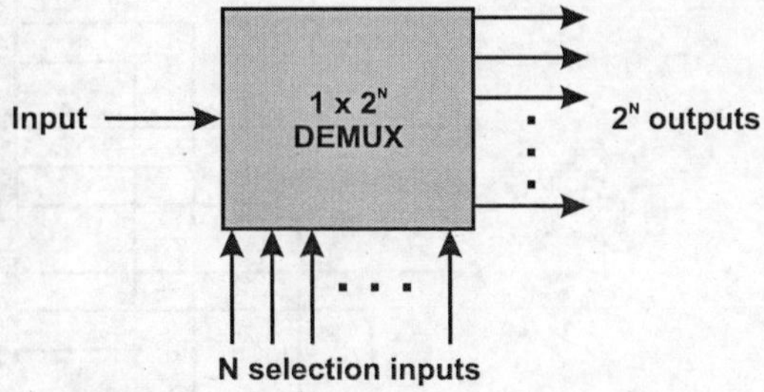

Figure 3.20 Block Diagram for 1 × 2^N De-multiplexer

12. Discuss some applications of multiplexers and de-multiplexers.

Ans. The multiplexer and de-multiplexer are used in various applications in digital systems. Some common applications of a multiplexer are as follows:

- **Data routing:** Multiplexers enable to route data from one of the various sources to one destination. Depending on the values of selection inputs, the data from the sources can be directed to a destination.
- **Parallel-to-serial conversion:** A multiplexer can be used as a parallel-to-serial converter. The data in parallel form is applied to the data inputs of the multiplexer and it comes out of the circuit in serial form.
- **Logic function generator:** A multiplexer with N data inputs can be used to generate an N input truth table and thus, to implement a Boolean equation. The logic function is formed by setting the values of data inputs (A_0, A_1, etc.) to either 0 or 1. The selection inputs of the multiplexer become the input variables of the Boolean equation to be implemented. If the number of input variables used in the logic function is greater than the number of selection inputs, then one or more variables are also applied as data inputs to the multiplexer.

Some common applications of a de-multiplexer are as follows:

- **Serial-to-parallel conversion:** A de-multiplexer can be used as serial-to-parallel converter. The data in serial form is applied as input to the de-multiplexer and is converted to parallel form depending on the selection inputs.
- **Clock de-multiplexer:** The de-multiplexer can be used for distributing the clock signal to the desired destination. The values of selection inputs determine the destination where the clock signal will appear. For example, if we have a 1 × 8 de-multiplexer and the selection inputs $S_2S_1S_0$ are 110, the clock signal will appear at output Y_5.

13. What do you mean by synchronous and asynchronous sequential circuit?

Ans. Sequential circuits are of two types: *synchronous* and *asynchronous*. **Synchronous** (or **clocked**) **sequential circuits** use a clock that provides regular timing pulses and the events occur only during one of these timing pulses. On the other hand, the **asynchronous sequential circuits** do not use any clock and an event can take place after the other event has completed without waiting for any timing pulse. These circuits are also known as **unclocked sequential circuits**.

14. What is flip-flop? Explain with the help of logic diagram.

Ans. The memory (or storage) elements that are used in synchronous or clocked sequential circuits are called flip-flops. A **flip-flop** is binary cell that can store only a single bit of information. It has more than one input and two outputs; one output is for the normal value (Q) and another is for the complemented value (Q′) of the bit stored in it as shown in Figure 3.21(a). Once it enters a binary state (either 0 or 1), it continues to remain in that state until the clock pulse occurs.

As shown in Figure 3.21(b), a flip-flop can be constructed by using two inverters in series where the output of one inverter becomes the input of another one. Thus, the outputs of both the inverters are the complement of each other.

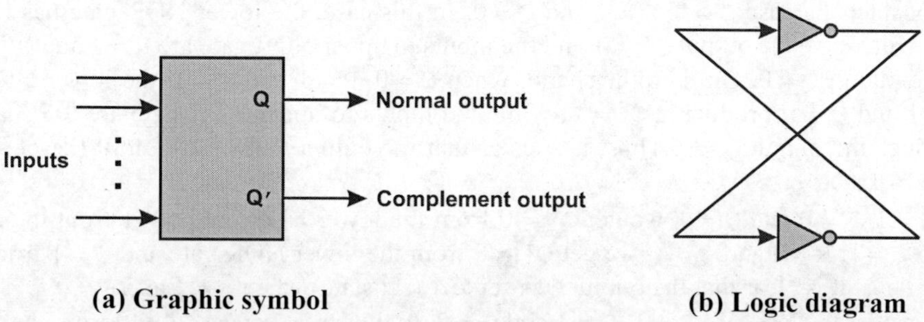

Figure 3.21 Logic Symbol and Logic Diagram for the Filp-flop

There are four common types of flip-flops including SR, D, JK and T flip-flop. These flip-flops differ from one another in terms of number of inputs and the way the binary state is affected by the inputs.

15. Explain the operation of SR flip-flop.

Ans. An **SR** (or **RS**) **flip-flop** has three inputs: S (set), R (reset) and C (clock) and two outputs: one normal (say, Q) and other complemented (Q’). Figure 3.22 (a) shows the graphic symbol of SR flip-flop where a small circle at the output terminal indicates the complemented output. In addition, an arrow-head in front of input C indicates the **dynamic input,** which refers to the fact that the flip-flop responds when the input clock signal C changes from 0 to 1 (that is, positive transition).

The logic diagram for SR flip-flop shown in Figure 3.22 (b) consists of a NOR flip-flop where the output of one NOR gate is the input of the other NOR gate. In addition, the logic diagram comprises two AND gates. The outputs of the AND gates remains 0 as long as there is no signal at clock (that is, C=0) no matter what the values of S and R are. As a result, the output Q remains unaffected. However, when the value of C changes from 0 to 1, only then the inputs S and R reach the NOR flip-flop and thus, the output Q changes according to the values of S and R.

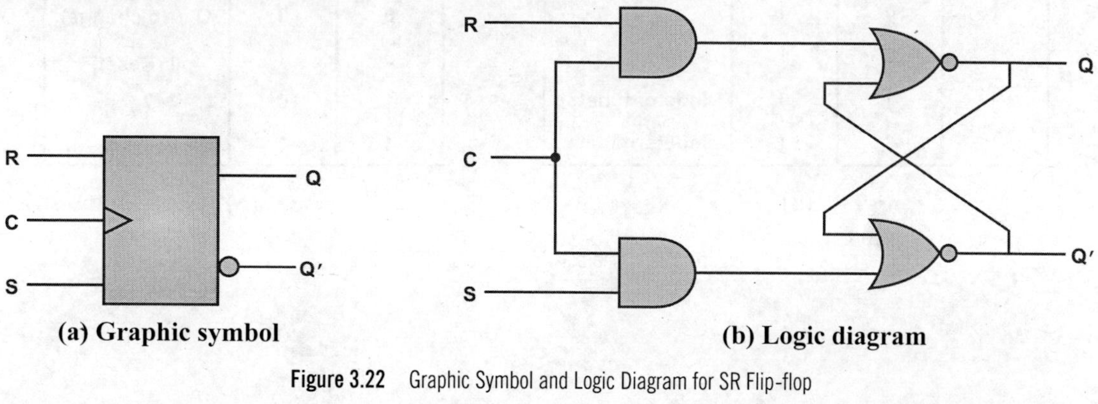

Figure 3.22 Graphic Symbol and Logic Diagram for SR Flip-flop

To understand the operation of SR flip-flop, suppose when C changes from 0 to 1, S = 0, R = 0 and Q = 0. In this case, the lower NOR gate has inputs S = 0 and Q = 0, which produce Q′ = 1. Now, the inputs to upper NOR gate are R = 0 and Q′ = 1, which produce the output Q = 0. On the other hand, if S = 0, R = 0 and Q = 1, the lower NOR gate has inputs S = 0 and Q = 1, producing the output Q′ = 0. And, the inputs to upper NOR gate are R = 0 and Q′ = 0, which produce the output Q = 1. Thus, we can say that the output does not change (that is, remains in the previous state) as long as S = 0 and R = 0.

Now, consider the case S = 0, R = 1 and Q = 0. In this case, the lower NOR gate has inputs S = 0 and Q = 0, which give the output Q′ = 1 and the inputs to upper NOR gate are R = 1 and Q′ = 1, which produce the output Q = 0. On the other hand, when S = 0, R = 1 and Q = 1, the lower NOR gate has inputs S = 1 and Q = 1, producing Q′ = 0, while the inputs to upper NOR gate are R = 1 and Q′ = 0, which produce the output Q = 0. Thus, it is clear that the output Q is cleared to 0 (**reset state**) when S = 0 and R = 1.

When S = 1, R = 0 and Q = 0, we get Q′ = 0 from the lower NOR gate Q = 1 from the upper NOR gate. When S = 1, R = 0 and Q = 1, we get Q′ = 0 from the lower NOR gate and Q = 1 from the upper NOR gate. Thus, it is clear that the output Q is set to 1 (set state) when S = 1 and R = 0.

Now, consider the last case S = 1, R = 1 and Q = 0. In this case, we get Q′ = 0 from the lower NOR gate and Q = 0 from the upper NOR gate. When S = 1, R = 1 and Q = 1, we get Q′ = 0 from the lower NOR gate and Q = 0 from the upper NOR gate. As both Q and Q′ are 0, this indicates the unstable (indeterminate) state.

The operation of a flip-flop can be described in tabular form by means of a **characteristic table** which depicts the next state of the flip-flops as a function of the inputs and the current state. Figure 3.23 (a) shows the characteristic table of SR flip-flop. In the table, Q_n refers to the binary state of the output Q at a given time (that is, **present state**), Q_{n+1} refers to the binary state of Q after the clock pulse occurs (that is, **next state**). This table can be further simplified as shown in Figure 3.23 (b).

S	R	Q_n	Q_{n+1}
0	0	0	0
0	0	1	1
0	1	0	0
0	1	1	0
1	0	0	1
1	0	1	1
1	1	0	Indeterminate
1	1	1	Indeterminate

(a)

S	R	Q_{n+1}
0	0	Q_n (No change)
0	1	0 (Reset)
1	0	1 (Set)
1	1	Indeterminate

(b)

Figure 3.23 Characteristic Table of SR Flip-flop

16. What is data flip-flop? Give its logic diagram a.nd characteristic table.

Ans. The **D (Data) flip-flop** is the modified version of the SR flip-flop, which is constructed by placing a NOT gate (inverter) between the S and R inputs and the single input is assigned the symbol D. The graphic symbol and logic diagram of D flip-flop are shown in Figure 3.24.

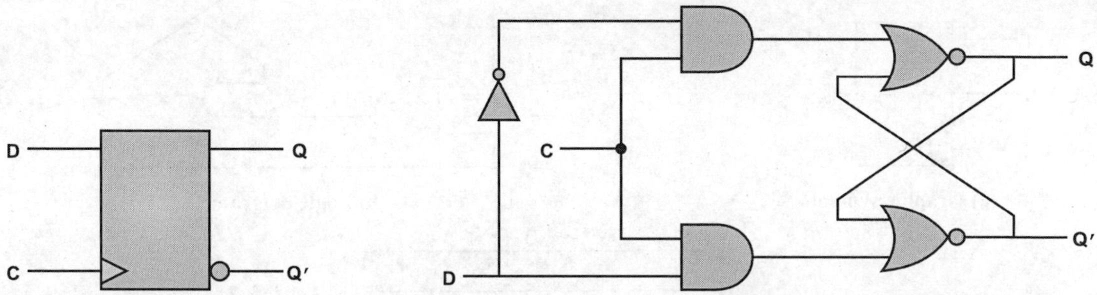

(a) Graphic symbol **(b) Logic diagram**

Figure 3.24 Graphic Symbol and Logic Diagram for D Flip-flop

During the occurrence of a clock transition (clock pulse) from 0 to 1, the input D is sampled. If D = 0, the output of the flip-flop goes to state 0 but if D = 1, the output of the flip-flop goes to the state 1. The characteristic table of D flip-flop is shown in Figure 3.25.

D	Q_{n+1}
0	0 (Reset)
1	1 (Set)

Figure 3.25 Characteristic Table of D Flip-flop

From the characteristic table, it is clear that we can determine the next state Q_{n+1} from the D input. This relationship can be expressed by the following characteristic equation:

$$Q_{n+1} = D$$

The advantage of D flip-flop over SR flip-flop is that it has only one input D excluding the clock input. However, its disadvantage is that no input condition in the *D* flip-flop leads to 'no change' state, that is, $Q_{n+1} = Q_n$. To achieve this state, either the clock signal should be disabled or the output should be fed back into the input.

17. Explain JK flip-flop.

Ans. As we know that the SR flip-flop suffers from the problem of 'indeterminate' condition when both the inputs (S and R) are 1. To overcome this problem, another flip-flop called **JK flip-flop** is designed in which the indeterminate condition of SR type has become defined. The inputs J and K behave similarly to the inputs S and R to set and reset the flip-flop, respectively, and when J = K = 1, a clock transition occurs that changes the outputs of the flip-flop to their complemented state. Figure 3.26 shows the graphic symbol, logic diagram and the characteristic table of the JK flip-flop.

From the characteristic table, it is clear that the inputs J and K are equivalent to S (set) and R (reset) inputs of the SR flip-flop, respectively. In addition, the JK flip-flop has a complement condition $Q_{n+1} = Q_n'$ in place of indeterminate condition when both the inputs J and K are equal to 1.

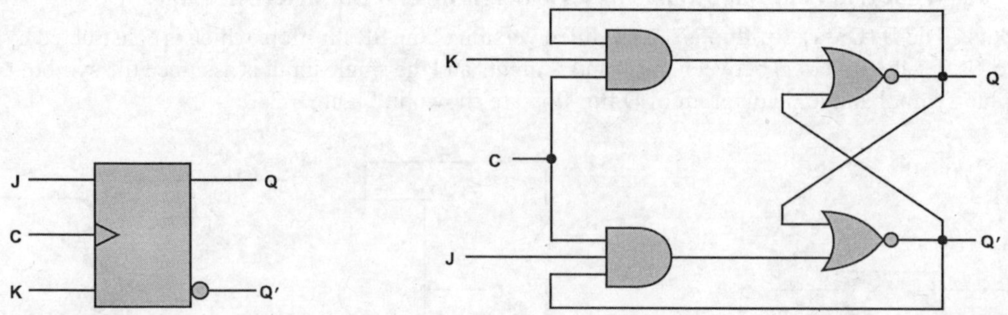

(a) Graphic symbol (b) Logic diagram

J	K	Q_{n+1}
0	0	Q_n (No change)
0	1	0 (Reset)
1	0	1 (Set)
1	1	Q_n' (Complement)

(c) Characteristic table

Figure 3.26 Graphic Symbol, Logic Diagram and Characteristic Table of JK Flip-flop

18. Explain T Flip-flop.

Ans. The **T (Toggle) flip-flop** is the modified version of the JK flip-flop, which is obtained by connecting the inputs J and K to provide a single input indicated by T. The graphic symbol, logic diagram and characteristic table of T flip-flop are shown in Figure 3.27.

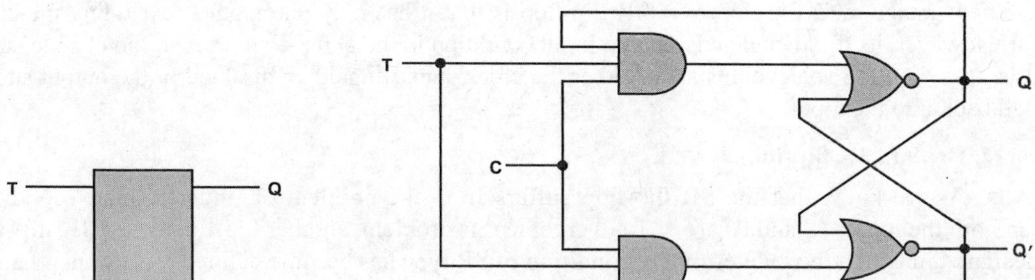

(a) Graphic symbol (b) Logic diagram

T	Q_{n+1}
0	Q_n (No change)
1	Q_n' (Complement)

(c) Characteristic table

Figure 3.27 Graphic Symbol, Logic Diagram and Characteristic Table of T Flip-flop

From the characteristic table, it is clear that that there exist only two conditions in the T flip-flop, which are given as follows:

- When T = 0 (that is, both J and K are equal to 0), a clock transition does not affect the state of the flip-flop and it remains unchanged.
- When T = 1 (that is, both J and K are equal to 1), a clock transition complements the state of the flip-flop.

These conditions can be expressed by the characteristic equation given below:

$$Q_{n+1} = Q_n \oplus T$$

19. Define the following:

(a) Edge-triggered flip-flop

(b) Master-slave flip-flop

Ans. (a) Edge-triggered flip-flop: This is the flip-flop that responds only during the instant the clock pulse transits from one voltage level to another. If the triggering happens on the rising (positive) edge of the clock pulse, then it is termed as **positive-edge triggering**. That is, the positive edge of clock activates the gates and thus, enables data to be recognized On the other hand, some applications require triggering on the falling (negative) edge of the clock pulse, which is termed as **negative-edge triggering**. Here, the gates are activated; and thus, data is allowed to be recognized by the trailing edge of clock pulse.

(b) Master-slave flip-flop: This flip-flop has the same functionality as that of edge-triggered flip-flop; however, this is rarely used. It consists of two flip-flops: the first flip-flop works as a master and responds to the rising edge of the clock cycle and the second flip-flop works as a slave and responds to the falling edge of the clock cycle. As a result, the output also changes during the 1 to 0 clock transition. A master-slave flip-flop can be constructed using two JK, D or SR flip-flops.

20. What is the difference between latch and flip-flop?

Ans. Both latches and flip-flops are the building blocks of sequential circuits where the output depends on current input and current state of the circuit, Which is defined by the contents of memory elements. However, still there are some differences between them which are listed in Table 3.2.

Table 3.2 Differences between Latch and Flip-flop

Latch	Flip-flop
Latches are used as memory elements in asynchronous sequential circuit.	Flip-flops are used as memory elements in synchronous sequential circuit.
Latches are built from the collection of gates.	Flip-flops are usually built from the collection of latches.
A latch is level triggered.	A flip-flop is edge triggered.

21. What are flip-flop excitation tables?

Ans. The characteristic table of a flip-flop defines the next state for a given set of inputs and the present state. However, generally when we design a sequential circuit, we know the possible transitions that can occur from the present state to next state and we are interested in finding out the flip-flop input conditions that will cause those transitions. For this, we require a table that specifies the required input combinations for a given state transition. This table is called **excitation table** of flip-flop.

The excitation tables for the SR, D, JK and T flip-flops are shown in Figure 3.28. Each table lists the possible transitions from the present state (Q_n) to the next state (Q_{n+1}) along with the inputs required to achieve those transitions. The symbol '×' in the tables represents a do not care condition, which implies that it does not matter whether the input is 0 or 1.

Transitions		Input Conditions	
Q_n	Q_{n+1}	S	R
0	0	0	×
0	1	1	0
1	0	0	1
1	1	×	0

(a) SR flip-flop

Transitions		Input Condition
Q_n	Q_{n+1}	D
0	0	0
0	1	1
1	0	0
1	1	1

(b) D flip-flop

Transitions		Input Conditions	
Q_n	Q_{n+1}	J	K
0	0	0	×
0	1	1	×
1	0	×	1
1	1	×	0

(c) JK flip-flop

Transitions		Input Condition
Q_n	Q_{n+1}	T
0	0	0
0	1	1
1	0	1
1	1	0

(d) T flip-flop

Figure 3.28 Excitation Tables for SR, D, JK and T Flip-flops

22. What do you understand by flip-flop input equations? Explain with the help of an example.

Ans. As we know that a sequential circuit consists of a combinational circuit (interconnection of logic gates) and a set of clocked flip-flops. The combinational circuit may have external inputs and the outputs of the flip-flops may also serve as inputs to it. Similarly, the outputs from the combinational circuit may go to the external output and also form the inputs to the flip-flops. The part of the combinational logic circuit that produces the inputs to the flip-flops can be described by a set of Boolean expressions called **flip-flop input equations**. The part of combinational circuit that generates external output can be algebraically expressed by a set of Boolean equations, called output equations.

To understand how the flip-flop input equations can be derived, consider the sequential circuit shown in Figure 3.29. This circuit consists of one input variable A, one output variable B and two clocked D flip-flops. The AND, OR and NOT gates constitute the combinational logic part of the circuit.

For the circuit shown above, we have two flip-flop input equations, denoted by the symbols D_X and D_Y. The first letter in each symbol denotes the flip-flop input (D input in our case), while the subscript letter (that is, X or Y) denotes the output of flip-flop. Since the output of the first OR gate is connected to the D input of the flip-flop X, the first input equation D_X can be written as:

$$D_X = XA + YA$$

Where X and Y are the outputs of the flip-flops and A is the external input.

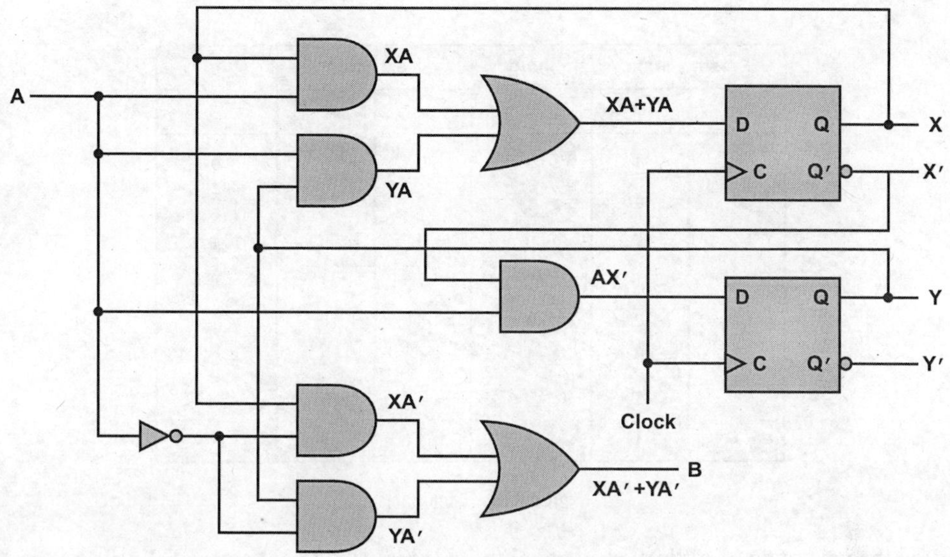

Figure 3.29 Example of a Sequential Circuit

The input to the second D flip-flop is the output from the single AND gate, which has two inputs: X′ and A. Thus, the second flip-flop input equation DY can be written as

$$D_Y = AX'$$

In addition, the circuit shown in Figure 3.29 has an external output B that can be expressed by the following algebraic expression:

$$B = XA' + YA'$$

23. What do you mean by state table and state diagram of a sequential circuit? Draw the state table and state diagram for the circuit shown in Figure 3.29.

Ans.

State table:

A **state table** is a way of specifying a sequential circuit in tabular form representing the outputs and the next states as a function of inputs and the present states. Figure 3.30 shows the state table for the sequential circuit shown in Figure 3.29. Observe that this state table consists of four parts: *present state*, *input*, *next state* and *output*. The **present state** part depicts the states of two flip-flops X and Y at a given time t, the **input** part depicts the values of external input A corresponding to each present state, the **next state** part depicts the state of flip-flops at time t + 1 and the **output** part depicts the values of external output B corresponding to each present state and input combination.

To derive the values in state table, first, all possible binary combinations of the present state and the input variables are listed in the state table. In our case, we have three variables X, Y and A; and thus, there are eight possible combinations from 000 to 111. Then, the values for the next state are determined with the help of logic diagram or input equations. For example, the input equation for the flip-flop X and Y is (see previous question):

$$D_X = XA + YA$$

$$D_Y = AX'$$

Present State		Input	Next State		Output
X	Y	A	X	Y	B
0	0	0	0	0	0
0	0	1	0	1	0
0	1	0	0	0	1
0	1	1	1	1	0
1	0	0	0	0	1
1	0	1	1	0	0
1	1	0	0	0	1
1	1	1	1	0	0

Figure 3.30 State Table

Now, as the next state of a flip-flop is equal to its D input, the next state of flip-flop X will be 1 in the state table if $D_X = 1$, which implies either XA = 1 or YA = 1. There are three possible cases in the state table suiting to this condition. Similarly, the next state of flip-flop Y will be 1 in the state table if $D_Y = 1$, which implies that AX′ = 1, that is, when A = 1 and X = 0. There are two possible cases in the state table suiting to this condition. Finally, the values of the output B can be derived from the output equation:

B = XA′ + YA′

Generally, a sequential circuit with M flip-flops, N input variables and P output variables will have M columns for present state, N columns for inputs, M columns for the next state and P columns for outputs.

State diagram:

A **state diagram** is the graphical representation of a state table. It is made up from a set of circles connected via directed lines; each circle represents a state and a directed line between two circles indicates the transition between those states. Figure 3.31 shows the state diagram corresponding to the state table shown in Figure 3.30. Note that the states are always written inside the circles and each directed line is labelled with two binary numbers that are separated by a slash. The binary number before the slash shows the input value during the present state and the binary number after the slash shows the output value during the present state. For example, the directed line from state 01 to state 11 is labelled with 1/0, which means when the sequential circuit is in present state 01 and the input is 1, the output is 0 and the circuit goes to the next state 11.

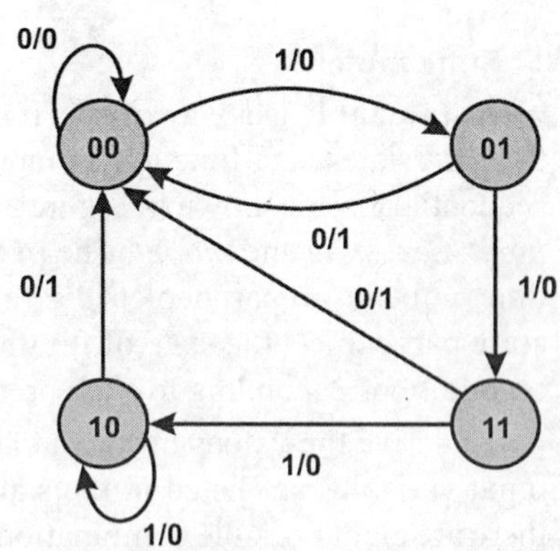

Figure 3.31 State Diagram

24. What is register? Explain 4-bit register.

Ans. An individual flip-flop can hold only one bit of information at a time. However, in machines that handle data consisting of multiple bits, a number of flip-flops can be organized into a structure called **register**. A register with N flip-flops can store N bits of information and a common clock is used to synchronize the operation of all flip-flops. In addition to flip-flops, a register may also include combinational logic gates to perform some data-processing tasks. These gates control when and how the information available at the flip-flop inputs is transferred into the register.

A simple register consists of only flip-flops without any external logic gates. Figure 3.32 shows a simple 4-bit register designed using four D flip-flops. There are four input lines (I_0 to I_3), four output lines (A_0 to A_3) and a common clock signal (C) line tied into all the four flip-flops, which enables their D inputs. The common clock triggers all the flip-flops on the positive edge transition of each clock pulse and the binary information at four inputs to flip-flops is transferred into the 4-bit register. The binary information stored in the register can be obtained at any time by sampling all the four outputs. An additional clear line is also input at a special terminal in each flip-flop, which gives the ability to reset the whole register to all 0's. During normal clocked operation, the clear input must be maintained at 1.

The process of transferring new information into a register is known as **loading** the register. When all the bits of the register are loaded at the same time with a common clock pulse, it is called **parallel loading**. In the register shown in Figure 3.32, when a clock transition is applied at C inputs of the register, all the four inputs I_0, I_1, I_2 and I_3 are loaded in parallel.

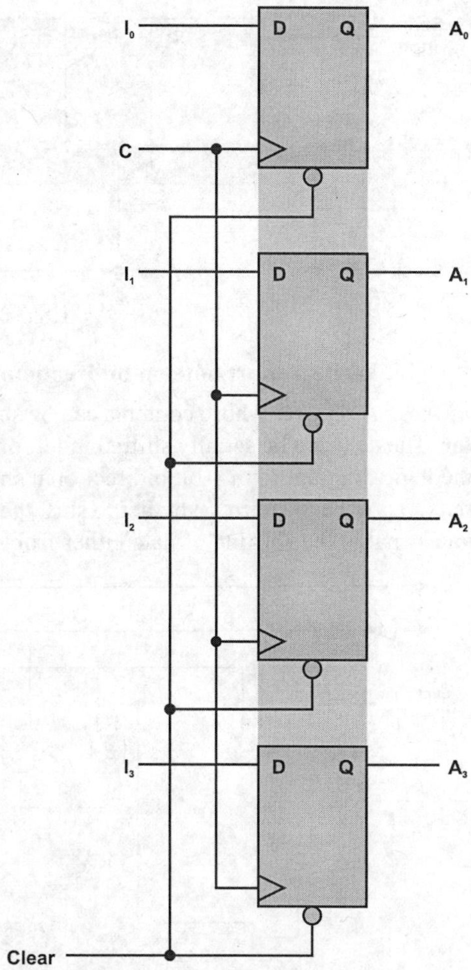

Figure 3.32 A Simple 4-bit Register

25. Write a short note on shift registers.

Ans. A **shift register** is the one whose contents can be shifted in either one (unidirectional shift register) or both directions (bidirectional shift register). It is the combination of flip-flops connected in a cascading manner where the output from one flip-flop is the input to the next flip-flop. A common clock synchronizes the operation of all the flip-flops and each clock pulse initiates the shift operation from one stage to the next. Figure 3.33 shows a simple 4-bit shift register consisting of only flip-flops.

In this shift register, the D flip-flops are connected such that the output of one flip-flop forms the D input of the flip-flop to its right. The **serial input** determines what goes into the flip-flop at the leftmost position, while the **serial output** is accepted from the output of the flip-flop at the rightmost position. With each clock pulse, the contents of a flip-flop F_i are transferred to the flip-flop F_{i+1} causing a right shift, that is, data is shifted serially by one position at a time.

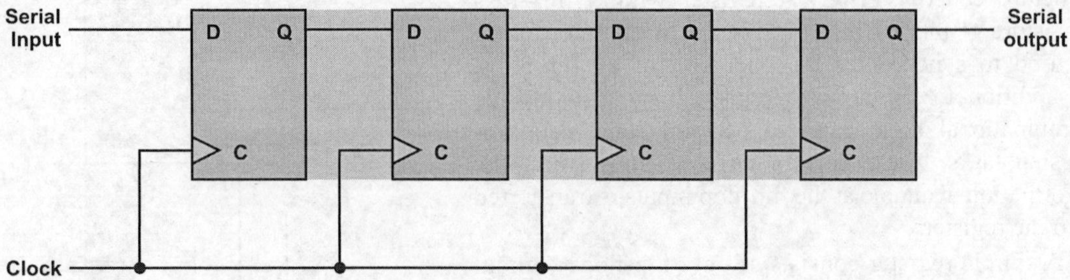

Figure 3.33 A 4-bit Shift Register

26. Write a short note on bidirectional shift register.

Ans. A register whose contents can be shifted in both directions is called **bidirectional shift register**. The data can be serially shifted in left or right direction but not simultaneously. Figure 3.34 shows the logic diagram for a 4-bit bidirectional shift register implemented using logic gates. The control input (M) is used to control whether to shift the data to left or right. Depending on the state of M, the logic gates enable the shifting of data either from left to right or from right to left, with one bit at a time.

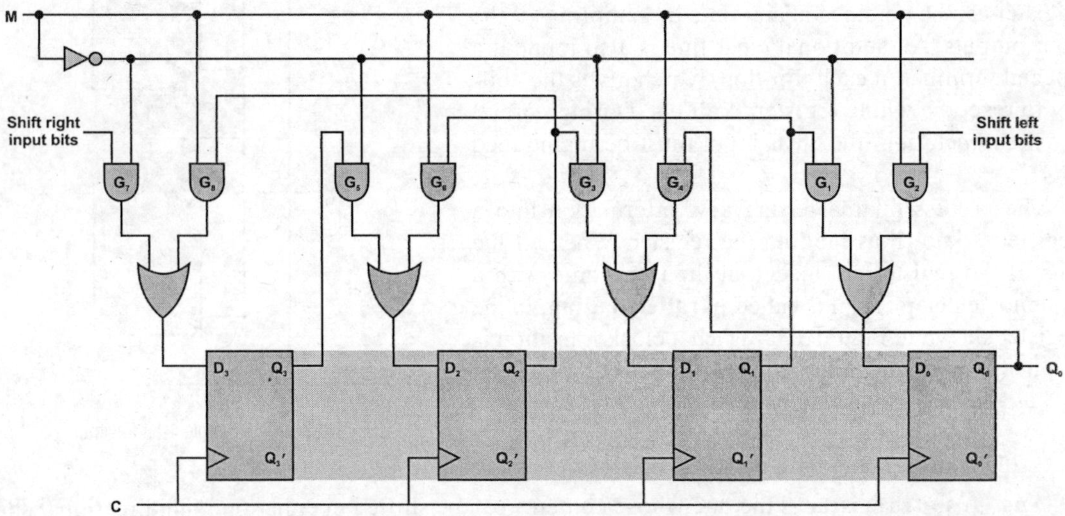

Figure 3.34 A 4-bit Bidirectional Shift Register

When the control input is high (that is, M = 1), the AND gates G_1, G_3, G_5 and G_7 are enabled, while the AND gates G_2, G_4, G_6 and G_8 are disabled. The data input bits move through G_1 to the D_0 input of flip-flop and are shifted to the right with occurrence of each clock pulse. In contrast, when the control input is low (that is, M = 0), the AND gates G_1, G_3, G_5 and G_7 are disabled, while the AND gates G_2, G_4, G_6 and G_8 are enabled. The data input bits move through G_8 to the D_3 input of flip-flop and are shifted to the left with occurrence of each clock pulse.

27. What do you mean by counter? Distinguish between synchronous and asynchronous counter.

Ans. A sequential logic circuit used to count the number of clock pulses that arrive at its input is referred to as **counter**. The clock pulses may arrive at the input either at uniform intervals or at random.

The purpose of a counter is to count the number of times an event occurs. It is different from the register in the sense that a specified set of states appear at the output of a counter.

Counters can be divided into two categories, namely, *synchronous* and *asynchronous* counter. A **synchronous counter** (also known as **parallel counter**) is a circuit where a common clock synchronizes the operation of all flip-flops. That is, all the flip-flops function on the arrival of simultaneous clock pulse. On the other hand, an **asynchronous counter** (also known as **ripple counter**) is a circuit where each flip-flop is clocked by a different clock pulse. The first flip-flop in the circuit is clocked by an external clock pulse and then each successive flip-flop is clocked by the output from the previous flip-flop.

28. Design a half adder as a two-level AND-OR circuit.

Ans. As we know that the simplified Boolean functions for the two outputs (S and C) for a half adder are given as

$$S = x'y + xy'$$
$$C = xy$$

Figure 3.35 shows the two-level AND-OR circuit for the half adder. Here, the combination of two AND gates and one OR gate represents the output S, while the output C is represented through one AND gate.

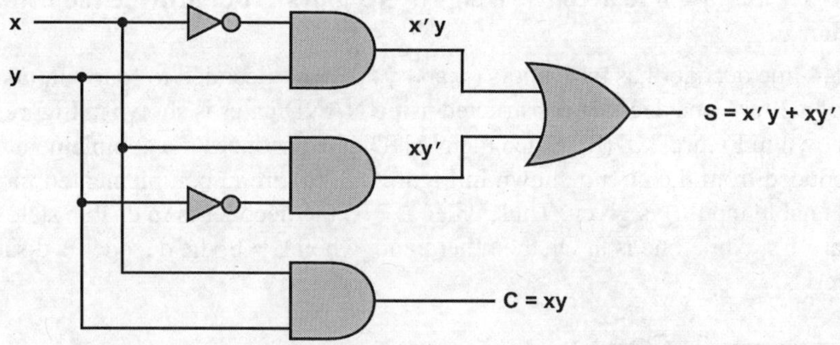

Figure 3.35 Implementation of Half Adder as a Two-level AND-OR Circuit

29. Show how to implement a full adder using two half adders and an external logic gate.

Ans. A full adder can also be implemented with two half adders and an OR gate. As we know that the Boolean function for sum (S) output of full adder is (see Q5):

$$S = x \oplus y \oplus z$$
$$= (x \oplus y) \oplus z, \text{ that is, the XOR of third input and the output of first half adder.}$$

The Boolean function for the carry (C) output of full adder is

$$C = xy + xz + yz$$
$$= xy + xz\ (y + y') + yz\ (x + x')$$
$$= xy + xyz + xy'z + xyz + x'yz$$
$$= xy + xyz + xyz + z\ (x'y + xy')$$
$$= xy + xyz + (x \oplus y)\ z$$
$$= xy\ (1 + z) + (x \oplus y)\ z$$
$$= (x \oplus y)\ z + xy$$

The implementation of full adder combinational circuit with two half adder circuits (XOR plus AND gate) and an external OR gate is shown in Figure 3.36.

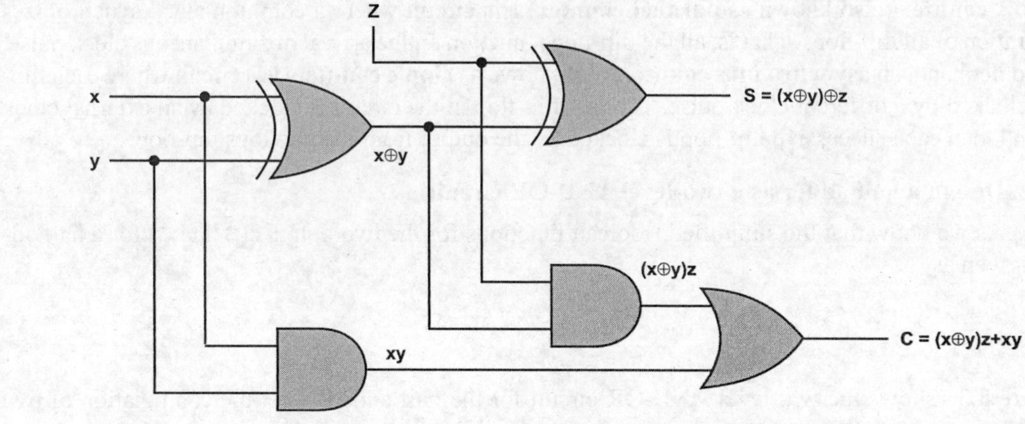

Figure 3.36 Implementation of Full Adder with two Half Adders and an OR Gate

30. Construct a 2-to-4 line decoder using NAND gates. Also, provide the truth table for this decoder.

Ans. A 2-to-4 line decoder has two inputs (x and y) that are decoded to four outputs (Y_0 to Y_4). The logic diagram of a 2-to-4 line decoder constructed using NAND gates is shown in Figure 3.37(a) and the truth table is shown in Figure 3.37(b). Since the NAND gate produces the complement of AND output, the outputs produced from the circuit shown in Figure 3.37(a) are in complemented form and also, the complemented enable input E is given. Thus, when E = 1, the decoder is in enable state and out of four outputs, three are 1's, while one is 0. On the other hand, when E = 0, the decoder is disabled and all the four outputs are 1's.

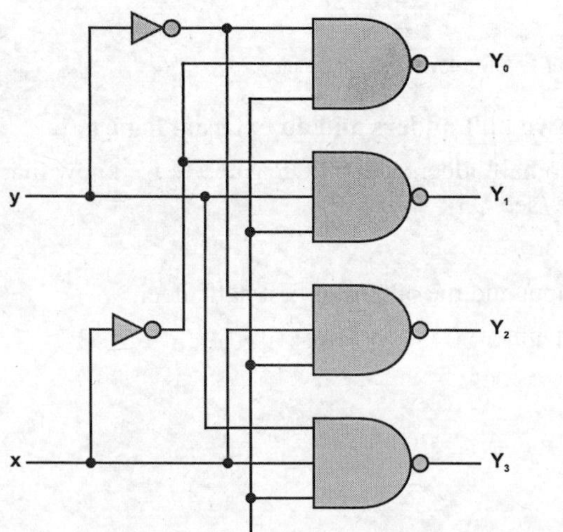

(a) Logic diagram with NAND gates

E	x	y	Y_0	Y_1	Y_2	Y_3
0	0	0	0	1	1	1
0	0	1	1	0	1	1
0	1	0	1	1	0	1
0	1	1	1	1	1	0
1	×	×	1	1	1	1

(b) Truth table

Figure 3.37 Logic Diagram and Truth Table for 2-to-4 Line Decoder

31. Draw a 4 × 16 decoder by using 3 × 8 decoder.

Ans. Sometimes, a particular size decoder is required that is not available but small sizes are available. In such situations, we can construct the required size decoder by combining two or more small size decoders. For example, a 4 × 16 line decoder can be constructed using two 3 × 8 decoders as shown in Figure 3.38. The three least significant bits of the input are connected to both decoders. The most significant bit forms the enable input of one decoder, while its complement forms the enable input of another decoder.

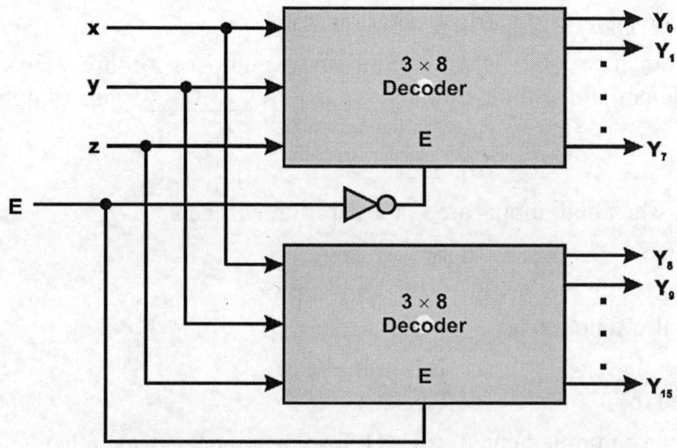

Figure 3.38 A 4 × 16 Decoder Constructed Using Two 3 × 8 Decoders

It is clear from the figure that when E = 1, the upper decoder is in enable state and produces outputs Y_0 through Y_7 depending on the values of inputs x, y and z. However, at that time, the lower decoder is disabled and thus, all its outputs (that is, Y_8 to Y_{15}) are 0's. On the other hand, when E = 0, all the outputs of upper decoder are 0's, while the lower decoder produces outputs Y_8 to Y_{15} depending on the values of inputs x, y and z.

MULTIPLE CHOICE QUESTIONS

1. The time for which the D input of a D-FF must not change after the clock is applied is known as
   (a) Hold time (b) Set-up time
   (c) Transition time (d) Delay time
2. A device/circuit that produces a specified sequence of states as output on applying input pulses is called ________.
   (a) Counter (b) Register
   (c) Flip-flop (d) Decoder
3. A flip-flop is a binary cell capable of storing information consisting of ________.
   (a) Eight bits (b) One bit
   (c) Several bytes (d) None of these
4. Which of the following is the graphical representation of the information available in a state table?
   (a) Transition diagram (b) Characteristic table
   (c) State diagram (d) Data-flow diagram

5. Which of the following tables specifies the required input combinations for a given state transition?

   (a) State table (b) Characteristic table
   (c) Transition table (d) Excitation table

6. Which of the following tables represents the next states and outputs of a sequential circuit as a function of present states and inputs?

   (a) Truth table (b) State table
   (c) Characteristic table (d) Excitation table

7. In the combinational circuit where the input binary number is of three bits and the output binary number is the square of the input number, we require _________ bits of output.

   (a) Three (b) Four
   (c) Eight (d) Six

8. In SR flip-flop, when both inputs are 1, the flip-flop will be in _________ state.

   (a) Indeterminate (b) Set
   (c) Reset (d) None of the above

9. A decoder can also function as

   (a) Multiplexer (b) De-multiplexer
   (c) Both (a) and (b) (d) Register

10. A JK flip-flop can be implemented using D flip-flop connected such that

    (a) $D = J'Q + KQ'$ (b) $D = JQ' + K'Q$
    (c) $D = J'Q' + KQ$ (d) $D = J'Q + K'Q$

Ans. 1. a 2. a 3. b 4. c 5. d 6. b 7. d 8. a 9. c 10. b

4

Data Representation

1. What is a number system? What are its categories?

Ans. A **number system** defines a set of values used to represent *quantity*. The number systems can be classified into two broad categories which are as follows:

- **Non-positional number systems**: In ancient times, people used to count on their fingers. When the fingers became insufficient for counting, stones, pebbles or sticks were used to indicate the values. This method of counting is called the **non-positional number system.** It was very difficult to perform arithmetic with such a number system because it had no symbol for zero. The most common non-positional number system is the Roman Number System in which only a few characters such as I, V, X, L, etc., are used to represent the numbers. These systems are often clumsy, and it is very difficult to perform calculations for large numbers.
- **Positional number systems**: In a positional number system, only a finite number of symbols (called digits) are used to represent the numbers. Such systems have a base (also called **radix**) that determines the number of digits available in the system. The value of each digit in a number depends on the digit itself, the position of digit in the number and the base of the number system. The most popular positional number system being used today is the **decimal** number system. This system is called base 10 system as it uses ten symbols (0, 1, 2,...,9) to represent the numbers. Apart from the decimal number system, there are some other positional number system such as, **binary** number system, **octal** number system and **hexadecimal** number system, each having a radix point of 2, 8 and 16, respectively.

2. Explain different types of positional number systems.

Ans. In a digital system, there are four types of positional number systems, namely, *decimal*, *binary*, *octal* and *hexadecimal*. The important thing about these number systems is that each system is just a different method for representing the quantities. Moreover, the quantities do not change but the symbols used to represent those quantities are changed in each number system. All the types of positional number system are discussed as follows:

Decimal number system

The decimal number system is a base 10 number system. This number system includes 10 digits from 0 to 9. All the digits are assigned weights as follows:

$10^3, 10^2, 10^1, 10^0$

If the number contains a decimal point, then a minus sign is placed in front of each power for the weight of each position after the decimal point as shown here.

$10^3, 10^2, 10^1, 10^0, 10^{-1}, 10^{-2}, 10^{-3}$

For example, the number 9735.45 is formed in decimal as follows:

$$9735.45 = (9 \times 10^3) + (7 \times 10^2) + (3 \times 10^1) + (5 \times 10^0) + (4 \times 10^{-1}) + (5 \times 10^{-2}).$$

Binary number system

The base of the binary number system is 2 and it is represented with the values 0 and 1. In the binary number system with base 2, the weighted values for each position are determined as follows:

2^7	2^6	2^5	2^4	2^3	2^2	2^1	2^0	2^{-1}	2^{-2}
128	64	32	16	8	4	2	1	0.5	0.25

Octal number system

The octal number system with its 8 digits, '0', '1', '2', '3', '4', '5', '6' and '7' is a base 8 system. The following table shows the weights for the octal number system up to 3 decimal places before and 2 decimal places after the octal point (.).

Octal Weights	8^3	8^2	8^1	8^0	.	8^{-1}	8^{-2}
Values	512	64	8	1	.	0.125	0.015625

Hexadecimal number system

Hexadecimal is another number system whose base is 16. Just as the decimal number represents a power of 10, each hexadecimal number represents a power of 16. To represent the decimal numbers, this system uses 0 to 9 numbers and A to F characters to represent 10 to 15, respectively. The following table shows the weights for the hexadecimal number system up to 3 decimal places before and 2 decimal places after the octal point (.).

Hexadecimal Weights	16^3	16^2	16^1	16^0	.	16^{-1}	16^{-2}
Values	4096	256	16	1	.	0.0625	0.003906

3. Write the steps to convert from any number system to decimal number system. Explain with the help of an example.

Ans. The steps to convert a number from binary/octal/hexadecimal number system to decimal number system are as follows:

1. Determine the weight assigned for each position of the number (depending on the number system).
2. Multiply each digit with its associated weight.

3. Add all the products calculated in the previous step. The result obtained is equivalent to the value in decimal number system.

Example: Determine the decimal equivalent of $(1101.11)_2$.

$1 \times 2^3 + 1 \times 2^2 + 0 \times 2^1 + 1 \times 2^0 + 1 \times 2^{-1} + 1 \times 2^{-2}$
$= 8 + 4 + 1 + 0.5 + 0.25$
$= 13.25$

4. How would you convert from decimal number system to any other number system?

Ans. The steps to convert a number (without any decimal point) from decimal number system to any other number system are as follows:

1. Divide the decimal number by the base of the target number system (to which the number is to be converted) until the quotient becomes zero. For example, to convert to binary number system, divide by 2, for octal by 8 and for hexadecimal by 16.
2. Store the remainders that are found. The first remainder becomes the least significant digit (LSD) and the last remainder becomes the most significant digit (MSD) of the number in the target system.
3. Write down the remainders from MSD to LSD to get the target number.

It may often happen that a decimal number contains a decimal point. In such a case, the fractional part is converted by using the following steps.

1. Multiply the fractional part by the base of the target number system.
2. Separate the carry over and the fractional parts.
3. Multiply the fractional part with the base of the target system. Continue multiplication until the fractional part becomes 0.
4. Write down the carry over parts in downward direction to obtain the target number.

Example: Determine the octal equivalent of the decimal number 677.0625.

Conversion of integral part

	Remainder
$677 \div 8 = 84$	5 (LSD)
$84 \div 8 = 10$	4
$10 \div 8 = 1$	2
$1 \div 8 = 0$	1 (MSD)

Conversion of fractional part

	Carry
$0.0625 \times 8 = 0.5000$	0
$0.5 \times 8 = 4.0$	4

Thus, $(677.0625)_{10} = (1245.04)_8$.

5. Explain the conversion from binary to octal and hexadecimal number system.

Ans. The steps to convert from a binary number to octal number are as follows:

1. Divide the binary number into 3-bit groups starting from right to left for the integer part and from left to right for the fractional part. For the integer part, you may add extra zeroes on the left and for the fractional part, you may add extra zeroes to the right in order to complete the grouping.
2. Replace each group with its octal equivalent.

You can convert a binary number to its hexadecimal equivalent using the same procedure as described above except now the binary number is divided into 4-bit groups instead of 3-bit groups.

Example: Determine the octal equivalent of the number $(001011.110)_2$

001	011	110
1	4	6

Thus, $(001011.110)_2 = (13.6)_8$

6. Explain the conversion from octal or hexadecimal to binary number system.

Ans. The steps to convert from octal or hexadecimal number to binary number are as follows:

1. Convert each digit of the given number to its 3-bit (in case the number is octal) or 4-bit (in case the number is hexadecimal) binary equivalent.
2. Combine all the groups to get the equivalent binary number.

Example: Determine the binary equivalent of the hexadecimal number $(B64.84)_{16}$

B	6	4	8	4
1011	0110	0100	1000	0100

Thus, $(B64.84)_{16} = (101101100100.10000100)_2$

7. Write the steps to convert from octal to hexadecimal number system and vice versa.

Ans. The steps to convert from octal to hexadecimal number system are as follows:

1. Convert each octal digit to its 3-bit binary equivalent.
2. Combine all the 3-bit groups to get the binary number.
3. Segregate the binary number into 4-bit groups starting from right to left for the integer part and from left to right for the fractional part.
4. Replace each 4-bit group with its hexadecimal equivalent.

To convert from hexadecimal to octal, you can use the same procedure as described above except that initially, the hexadecimal digits are converted to their 4-bit binary equivalents, which are then combined to form the binary number. The binary number is further segregated into 3-bit groups and finally, each 3-bit group is replaced with its octal equivalent.

Example: Determine the hexadecimal equivalent of the octal number $(674.42)_8$

	6	7	4	.	4	2
Step 1:	110	111	100		100	010
Step 2:	110111100.100010					
Step 3:	0001	1011	1100	.	1000	1000
Step 4:	1BC.88					

8. What are signed and unsigned numbers?

Ans. The binary numbers are represented as either *signed* or *unsigned* numbers. An ***n*-bit signed** binary number consists of two parts: one part denotes the sign of the number and another part denotes the magnitude of the number. The most significant bit (MSB) is always a **sign** bit which denotes the sign of the number and the convention is that 0 and 1 denote '+' and '–', respectively. The remaining $(n-1)$ bits denote the magnitude of the number as shown in Figure 4.1.

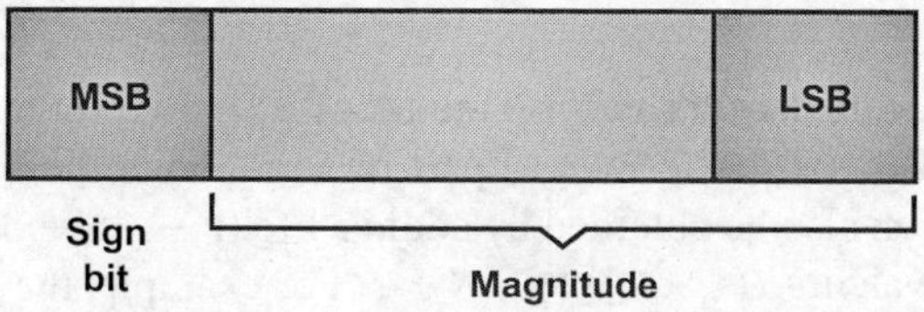

Figure 4.1 Representation of Signed Numbers

In some applications, there is no need to include the sign along with the number while representing the numbers into the computers. The numbers that have no sign associated with them are called **unsigned** numbers. All the bits in an unsigned binary number represent the magnitude of the number as shown in Figure 4.2.

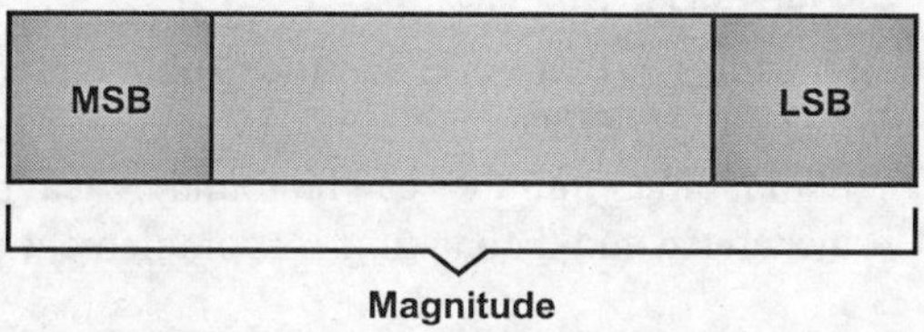

Figure 4.2 Representation of Unsigned Numbers

9. What is the purpose of complements in digital computer? Explain (r - 1)'s and r's complement.

Ans. Complements are used in digital computers to simplify the subtraction and logical manipulation and to represent the negative numbers. For any number system of base *r*, there can be two types of complements: (r – 1)'s and r's. For example, for decimal number system, the two types of complements are 10's and 9's. Similarly, for binary system, two types of complements are 2's and 1's. These complements are discussed as follows:

(r – 1)'s Complement

The (r – 1)'s complement (also known as **diminished complement**) of a positive number (say, N) is defined as $r^n - r^{-m} - N$ where n is the number of digits in integer part of N, m is the number of digits in fractional part of N and r is the base of the system. In case, N is an integer with n digits, then the (r – 1)'s complement of N is $r^n - 1 - N$. For example, the 9's complement of a given integer decimal number (N) is $(10^n - 1) - N$. Here, the number 10^n represents a $(n + 1)$-digit number having a single one followed by n zeroes. Thus, $10^n - 1$ will represent an n-digit number having all 9's. We can observe that, the 9's complement of a decimal number can be obtained by subtracting each digit of number individually from 9. For example, if we want to calculate the 9's complement of 32, then it will be 99 – 32 = 67. Similarly, 1's complement of a binary number can be found by subtracting each bit from 1. But, while performing subtraction operation from binary digit 1, the bits change from either 0 to 1 or 1 to 0. The 1's complement is found by simply changing 1's to 0's and 0's to 1's. For example, the 1's complement of 11001 is 00110.

Similarly, (r – 1)'s complement can also be found for the octal numbers by subtracting each digit of the number from 7 and for hexadecimal numbers by subtracting each digit from F.

r's Complement

The r's complement (also called **radix complement**) of a positive number N is defined as $r^n - N$, where n is the number of digits in the integer part of N and r is the base of the number N. The r's complement of a number can also be obtained by adding 1 to (r – 1)'s complement of the number. This is because $r^n - N$ is equivalent to $(r^n - 1) - N + 1$. For example, the 10's complement of a decimal number can be found by adding 1 to its 9's complement and the 2's complement of a binary number can be found by adding 1 to its 1's complement. An alternate method of finding 10's complement of a decimal number N is as follows:

(i) Leave all the least significant zeros of N unchanged.
(ii) Subtract the first least significant non-zero digit from 10.
(iii) Subtract all the most significant digits from 9.

For example, consider N = 22300. The 10's complement of N can be found by leaving two zeroes (LSBs) unchanged, subtracting 3 from 10 (that is, 7) and then subtracting the other two digits from 9. That is, the 10's complement of 22300 is 77700.

Similarly, the 2's complement of a binary number can be found by leaving the least significant zeros and the first least significant 1 unchanged and then taking 1's complement of all other significant digits.

10. Explain the various ways to represent the signed binary numbers.

or

How are the binary integer numbers represented in computers?

Ans. An integer number is represented by a sign bit and the magnitude bits. For a positive integer, the sign bit is 0 and a positive binary number represents the magnitude bits. However, for a negative integer, the sign bit is 1 and rest of the number can be represented by one of the three possible methods, namely, *signed-magnitude representation, 1's complement representation* and *2's complement representation.* All these methods are discussed as follows:

- **Signed-magnitude representation:** In the signed-magnitude representation, a bit known as the sign bit is used to indicate the sign of the number. For a word containing n bits, the right most n – 1 bits indicate the magnitude of the number and the leftmost indicate the required sign bit. To determine whether a number is positive or negative, two values, 0 and 1, are assigned, which indicate the positive and negative numbers, respectively.

For example, we have to represent –15 using the signed-magnitude method. If we have an 8-bit format, then the signed-magnitude representation of –15 is:

+15 0 0 0 0 1 1 1 1
–15 1 0 0 0 1 1 1 1

- **Signed 1's complement representation:** In this representation, the negative number is represented in 1's complement of its positive value. The 1's complement of a given number is obtained by complementing each digit of the number, that is, replacing the 0's with 1's and the 1's with 0's. Note that the sign bit is also complemented. For example, the signed 1's complement representation of −15 can be found by taking the 1's complement of the binary equivalent of +15 as shown here.

+15	0 0 0 0 1 1 1 1	
−15	1 1 1 1 0 0 0 0	(taking 1's complement)

- **Signed 2's complement representation:** In this representation, the negative number is represented in 2's complement of its positive value. The 2's complement of a given number is calculated by adding 1 to the 1's complement of that number. For example, the signed 2's complement representation of −15 can be found by taking the 2's complement of the binary equivalent of +15 as shown here.

+15	0 0 0 0 1 1 1 1	
−15	1 1 1 1 0 0 0 0	(1's complement)
	+ 1	
	1 1 1 1 0 0 0 1	(2's complement)

Thus, the signed 2's complement representation of −15 is 11110001.

11. Explain the different ways to represent the real numbers.

or

Explain fixed-point and floating-point representation of numbers.

Ans. In addition to sign, a number may also include a radix point, which needs to be stored in the register along with the number. The position of radix point in the register indicates whether the number stored is an integer, a fraction or mixed integer fraction. There are two ways to specify the position of radix points in the register, which are *fixed-point* and *floating-point representation*. Both of them are discussed as follows:

- **Fixed-point representation:** In this representation, the position of radix point is fixed. Generally, it is either stored at the extreme left in the register indicating that the number stored is a fractional number or at the extreme right position indicating that the number stored is an integer. However, in any case, the radix point is not actually stored in the register; its presence is presumed at a specific position in the register depending on whether the number stored in the register is treated as an integer or a fraction. Figure 4.3 shows the fixed-point representation of the binary number +00110101.011001.

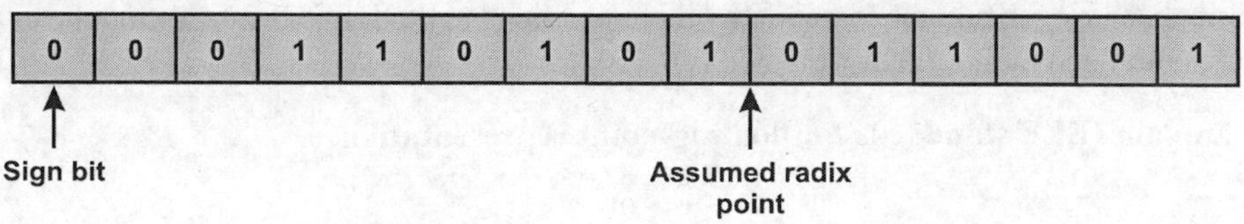

Figure 4.3 Fixed-point Representation

The benefit of fixed-point representation is that it requires simple hardware for being implemented; however, it allows only a limited range of values, which is not adequate even for simple arithmetic calculations.

- **Floating-point representation:** In this representation, the radix point is not assumed to be fixed at a specific position. A separate register is used, which stores a number specifying the position of radix point in the register in which the number (without radix point) is stored. The floating-point representation of a number consists of two parts: *mantissa* (or *fraction*) and *exponent*. The **mantissa** (`m`) represents a signed fixed-point number that can be either an integer or fraction and the **exponent** (`e`) specifies the position of radix point in mantissa. A given number (say, `N`) is represented in the form $m \times r^e$, where `r` is the radix of `N`. For example, the floating-point representation of the floating-point binary number +101.011 (for which $r = 2$) is $+ (0.101011) \times 2^{+3}$.

When floating-point numbers are stored in the register, only the mantissa and exponent including their signs are actually represented, while the radix and the position of radix point are always assumed. For example, if we have 8 bits for fraction (mantissa) and 6 bits for exponent, then the binary number $+(.101011) \times 2^3$ will be represented as shown in Figure 4.4.

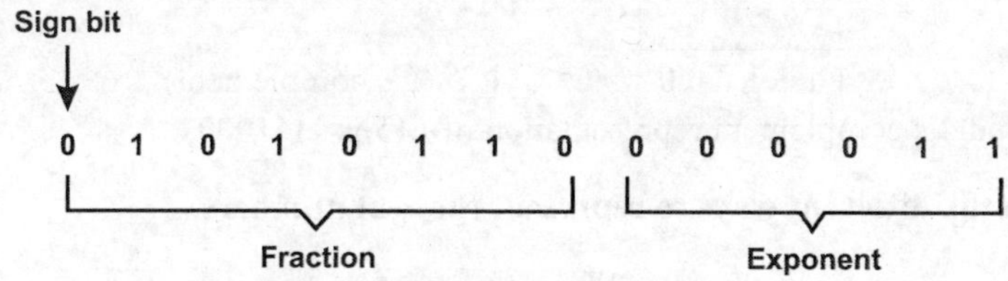

Figure 4.4 Floating-point Representation

Here, the bit 0 at the leftmost position (sign bit) in the fraction indicates the positive number. Following the sign bit of the fraction is the binary point that is assumed but not actually shown in the register. The exponent holds the binary equivalent of +3. The floating-point representation allows a wide range of values as compared to fixed-point representation; however, it requires expensive hardware for being implemented.

12. What is a normalized floating-point number?

Ans. A floating-point number in which the most significant digit of the mantissa is not zero is called **normalized floating-point number**. Examples of normalized floating-point numbers are 450, 11001, etc. A number that is not in normalized form can be converted to the normalized form by shifting the mantissa part to the left discarding the leading zeroes and subtracting the exponent by the number of positions shifted. For example, consider a number 0.000110×2^{-6}, which is not normalized. This number can be normalized by shifting the mantissa by three positions to the left and subtracting the exponent by three. The normalized number thus obtained is 0.110×2^{-9}.

13. Explain IEEE standards for floating-point representation.

or

How are the floating-point numbers represented in single and double precision?

Ans. The Institute of Electrical and Electronics Engineers (IEEE) has specified standards known as IEEE 754 standard for representing the floating-point numbers in 32 bits and 64 bits. In case of 32 bits, the floating-point numbers are said to be in *single precision* format, while in case of 64 bits, they are said to be in *double precision* format.

Single-precision Representation

In single-precision representation, the 32 bits are divided into three groups. The first group consists of a single bit called the sign bit which indicates the sign of the number. The second group consisting of 8 bits is used to specify the exponent part. The exponent part e uses excess −127 representation and stores an unsigned integer value `e'` = `e` + 127. Thus, `e'` lies in the range of 0 to 255. However, the actual exponent lies in the range of −126 to +127. The last group represents the mantissa fraction part (value after decimal point) and contains 23 bits. Notice that radix 2 is used for the fractions. In general, all the components of single precision including sign bit, exponent and mantissa fraction part are substituted in the equation $\pm 1.M \times 2^{(e-127)}$. The single precision format is shown in Figure 4.5.

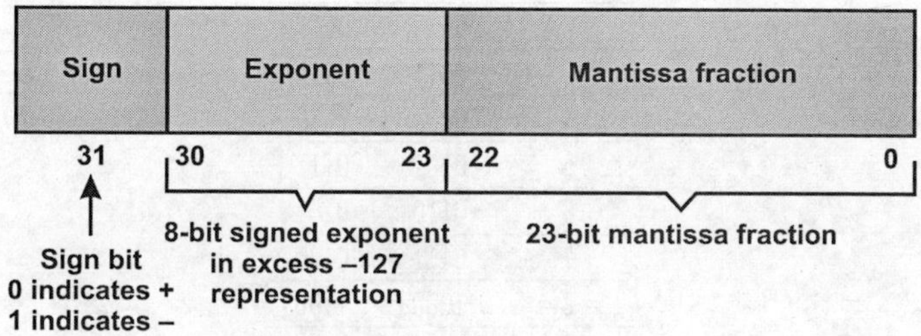

Figure 4.5 Single Precision Format

Double-precision Representation

In the double-precision representation of floating-point numbers, 64-bits are also divided into three groups. The first group consisting of single bit indicates the sign of the number (0 for positive and 1 for negative). However, in this format, the exponent and mantissa parts have higher number of bits and their range is also high. The exponent part e consisting of 11 bits uses excess −1023 representation and thus stores an unsigned integer value `e'`= `e` + 1023. The mantissa fraction part includes 52 bits (value after decimal point) and uses radix 2 for fraction. In general, all the components of double precision including sign bit, exponent and mantissa fraction part are substituted in the equation $\pm 1.M \times 2^{(e-1023)}$. The double precision format is shown in Figure 4.6.

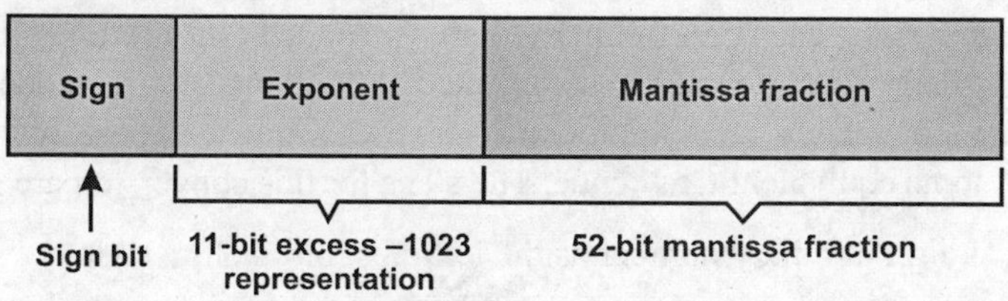

Figure 4.6 Double Precision Format

14. What are Gray codes? Explain how they are represented.

Ans. The digital systems can process data in only digital form, that is, in the form of 0's and 1's. Several physical systems produce analog or continuous output data. Before feeding such data into digital systems, they must be converted into digital format. Sometimes, these converted digital data are represented inside the system using Gray codes. The **Gray code** is an *unweighted* code, which means that the bit positions in Gray code are not associated with specific weights. The advantage of Gray code is that when we jump from one codeword to its immediate next, there is change of only one bit from 0 to 1 or 1 to 0. The Gray codes can have any number of bits similar to the binary numbers. The total number of combinations in Gray code can be 2^N, where N is the number of bits in a code. A 4-bit representation of Gray code with its binary codes is shown in Table 4.1.

Table 4.1 4-bit Gray Code

Decimal	Binary	Gray
0	0000	0000
1	0001	0001
2	0010	0011
3	0011	0010
4	0100	0110
5	0101	0111
6	0110	0101
7	0111	0100
8	1000	1100
9	1001	1101
10	1010	1111
11	1011	1110
12	1100	1010
13	1101	1011
14	1110	1001
15	1111	1000

15. How do we convert binary numbers into Gray codes?

Ans. A binary number is converted to its equivalent Gray code by performing the following steps.

1. The most significant digit of the binary code is included as the MSB of the Gray code.
2. Starting from left to right, each pair of binary digits are added (ORed) to get the next Gray code digit ignoring the carry. This step has to be repeated until all bits of Gray code are obtained.

To understand this conversion technique, consider an example. Suppose we need to convert the binary number 0101 to its equivalent Gray code. The steps for this conversion are shown as follows:

1. Take the leftmost digit of binary number as the left most bit in Gray code.

   0 1 0 1 – Binary
   0 Gray

2. Obtain the next bit in Gray code by adding the leftmost bit in binary number with its adjacent bit as shown here.

   0 + 1 0 1 Binary
   ↓
   0 1 Gray

3. Add the next adjacent pair in the binary number to get the next digit of the Gray code as shown here.

0	1	+	0	1	Binary
			↓		
0	1		1		Gray

4. Add the last adjacent pair in the binary number to get the last bit in the Gray code.

0	1	0	+	1	Binary
				↓	
0	1	1		1	Gray

Thus, the required Gray code number is 0111.

16. What are the BCD codes? What are its advantages?

Ans. Binary Coded Decimal (BCD) is a method of using binary digits to represent the decimal digits 0 to 9. Each decimal digit is represented by four binary digits. The BCD coding is the binary equivalent of the decimal digit. BCD system was developed by the IBM (International Business Machines) corporation. With BCD, each digit of a number is converted into its binary equivalent rather than converting the entire decimal number to its binary form. Similarly, letters and special characters can be coded in the binary form.

The BCD value for the decimal number 5319 is calculated as follows:

5	3	1	9
0101	0011	0001	1001

Table 4.2 lists the BCD code for decimal digits (0 to 9).

Table 4.2 BCD Code

Decimal Code	BCD Digit
0	0000
1	0001
2	0010
3	0011
4	0100
5	0101
6	0110
7	0111
8	1000
9	1001

One of the advantages of the BCD system is that there is no limit to the size of a number. For adding one more digit to a number, a new 4-bit sequence is to be added. In contrast, numbers represented in binary format are generally limited to the largest number, which can be represented by 8, 16, 32 or 64 bits. Moreover, BCD coding is a fast means to convert numbers from decimal to binary. However, it is not sufficient for business purposes as it can represent only 16, that is, 2^4 symbols.

17. What are alphanumeric codes? Also explain their various types.

Ans. The alphanumeric codes are used to represent numbers and alphabetic characters. Generally, if an n-bit binary code is used, then only 2^n elements can be represented using this code. Thus, to represent the numbers (0 to 9) and alphabets (A to Z), 6 bits can be used which is equivalent to $2^6 = 64$ codes. However, usually there are more than 64 characters to be represented including the lower case letters and special symbols. For this, two alphanumeric codes are widely used which are discussed as follows:

ASCII

ASCII (stands for **American Standard Code for Information Interchange**) is one of the standardized codes for representing alphanumeric characters. This code was originally designed as a 7-bit code. Several computer manufacturers cooperated to develop this code for transmitting and processing data. Later on, IBM developed a new version of ASCII, called as ASCII-8. They made use of all eight bits providing 256 symbols. Nevertheless, IBM had not changed the original set of 128 codes so that the original instructions and data could still work with the new character set. ASCII is commonly used in the transmission of data through data communication and is used almost exclusively to represent the data internally in the microcomputers.

EBCDIC

EBCDIC (stands for **Extended Binary Coded Decimal Interchange Code**) uses 8 bits for each character, thus it is possible to represent 256 different characters or bit combinations. This provides a unique code for each decimal value 0 to 9 (for a total of 10), each upper case and lower case letter (for a total of 52) and for a variety of special characters. Since it is an 8-bit code, each group of the eight bits makes up one alphabetic, numeric or special character and is called a **byte**.

In EBCDIC, the bit pattern 1100 is the zone combination (zone and digit) used for the alphabetic characters A through I, 1101 is used for the characters J through R and 1110 is the zone combination used for characters S through Z. The bit pattern 1111 is the zone combination used when representing decimal digits. For example, the code 1100 0001 is equivalent to the letter A; the code 1111 0001 is equivalent to the decimal digit 1. Other zone combinations are used while forming special characters.

18. What are error detection codes?

Ans. When digital information is transmitted through a medium they are exposed to some disturbances like external noise. Due to this exposure, the information may be affected and the bits may change from 1 to 0 or 0 to 1. This results in an error at the receiving end. The codes which are used to detect errors occurred during transmission are known as **error detection codes.** It is to be noted that error detection code can only detect the presence of error in the information but cannot correct it. If errors occur infrequently at random, the information needs to be retransmitted. However, if errors occur too frequently, the system needs to be checked.

In error detection, the emphasis is on finding whether there is an error(s) in the received data irrespective of the number of errors. The sender adds only enough extra (redundant) bits to the data being transmitted which enable the receiver to infer that some error has occurred. Thus, whether there is a single-bit error or burst error, it does not make any difference. Some of the commonly used error-detecting codes include simple parity check, two-dimensional parity check, checksum and cyclic redundancy check (CRC).

19. Explain the parity bit error detection code.

Ans. In the parity bit error detection code, an extra bit called parity bit is included in every binary message that is transmitted from a sender to a receiver. The parity bit helps in the detection of single-bit errors in the message. There are two types of parity, namely, *even parity* and *odd parity*. In **even parity**, a parity bit is chosen such that the sum of all the 1's in the message is even. In **odd parity**, the parity bit is chosen such that the sum of all the 1's in the message is odd.

To handle the parity bit during the transfer of the message, the parity scheme involves the use of *parity generator* at the sender's end and *parity checker* at the receiver's end.

- **Parity generator:** The parity generator is used at the sender's end. Here, the required odd/even parity bit is generated using the exclusive-OR functions.
- **Parity checker:** The parity checker is used at the receiving end. Here, the received bits are passed through the parity checker which checks the odd/even parity using the exclusive-OR of function. An error occurs if the results do not conform to the applied odd/even scheme.

For better understanding, let us take an example of a four bit message 1001 which is to be transmitted. First, the message is generated in the parity generator as follows:

Even parity	**Odd parity**
1^0^0^1 = 0	~ (1^0^0^1) = 1

Next, the messages along with the parity bits generated are transmitted. The transmitted messages are as follows:

Even parity	**Odd parity**
10010	10011

Finally, the respective odd/even messages are checked at the receiver's end by the parity checker.

Even parity	**Odd parity**
1^0^0^1^0 = 0	1^0^0^1^1 = 1

As we get the same parity bits at the sender's and receiver's end, thus, the message is considered to be error free.

20. Explain the checksum error detection method.

Ans. To overcome the limitation of detecting multiple errors in parity checking, checksum was introduced. Checksum method can be used for detecting multiple errors within the same word. With the transmission of a word in a block of data bytes, its contents are added bit by bit to that of its predecessor and the sum is maintained at the sender's side. Similarly, the contents of each successive word are added to the previous sum. After all the words of a block of data bytes have been transmitted, the total sum (called **checksum byte**) up to that time is transmitted. While computing the checksum byte, the carries of the MSB are discarded.

At the receiver's end, the checksum is again computed by adding the bits of received bytes. The newly computed checksum is compared with the checksum transmitted by the sender. If both are found to be same, then it implies no error; otherwise, errors are present in the received block of data. Sometimes, the 2's complement of the checksum is transmitted instead of the checksum. In such a case, the receiver adds the data block of received bytes with 2's complement of the checksum obtained from sender bit by bit. If the sum is zero, then there is no error in data; otherwise, the errors are present. The advantage of checksum method is that it can detect burst errors.

The performance of checksum detection method is better than simple parity checking as it can detect all odd number of errors and most of the even number of errors.

21. How is the number 25 represented in BCD and ASCII code?

Ans. The number 25 can be represented in BCD and ASCII as follows:

BCD representation

The number 25 can be represented in BCD by replacing each decimal digit (2 to 9) with its BCD equivalent as shown here.

2	5
0010	0101

Therefore, the BCD equivalent of 25 is 00100101.

ASCII representation

To represent a decimal number in ASCII code, a 7-bit binary code is used for every decimal digit. The representation of the number 25 in ASCII code is shown as follows:

2	5
0110010	0110101

22. Consider two 8-bit binary numbers A = 01000001 and B = 10000100. Give the decimal equivalent of each number assuming that they are unsigned and they are signed numbers in 2's complement representation.

Ans. Given A = 01000001 and B = 10000100.

(a) A and B are unsigned numbers.

$$\begin{aligned}\text{Decimal equivalent of A} &= 0 \times 2^7 + 1 \times 2^6 + 0 \times 2^5 + 0 \times 2^4 + 0 \times 2^3 + 0 \times 2^2 + 0 \times 2^1 + 1 \times 2^0\\ &= 0 + 64 + 0 + 0 + 0 + 0 + 0 + 1\\ &= 65.\end{aligned}$$

$$\begin{aligned}\text{Decimal equivalent of B} &= 1 \times 2^7 + 0 \times 2^6 + 0 \times 2^5 + 0 \times 2^4 + 0 \times 2^3 + 1 \times 2^2 + 0 \times 2^1 + 0 \times 2^0\\ &= 128 + 0 + 0 + 0 + 0 + 4 + 0 + 0\\ &= 132.\end{aligned}$$

(b) A and B are in signed 2's complement representation.

As the leftmost digit of A is 0, it is a positive number. Thus, we can convert it to binary form in a similar manner as in case of unsigned numbers. That is, the decimal equivalent of A = 65.

As the MSB of B is 1, it is a negative number. Therefore, first we have to calculate the magnitude of the number. To find the magnitude, we again need to find the 2's complement of the given number as follows:

		1	0	0	0	0	1	0	0
(1's complement)	~	0	1	1	1	1	0	1	1
(2's complement by adding 1)	+								1
		0	1	1	1	1	1	0	0

Thus, the magnitude of B is 01111100 = $(124)_{10}$. Since the original binary number was negative, the resultant decimal number is –124.

23. Represent the number –208.1025$_{10}$ in single and double precision.

Ans. To represent the number –208.1025$_{10}$ in single and double precision, the steps involved are as follows:

1. Convert the decimal number into its binary equivalent.

$$-208_{10} = (11010000)_2$$
$$0.1025_{10} = (0.0001)_2$$

Therefore, $-208.1025_{10} = (-11010000.0001)_2$

2. Normalize the number.

   $-11010000.0001 = -1.10100000001 \times 2^7$

3. Now, represent the number in single and double precision as follows:

In case of Single Precision

S = 1 (since it is a negative number)
e = 7
M = 10100000001 (including the values after decimal point)
Bias of single precision is 127
Therefore, e′ = e + 127
= 7 + 127
= 134_{10}
e′ = $(10000110)_2$

Hence, the single precision number is represented as given below:

S	e′	M
1 bit	8 bits	23 bits
1	10000110	10100000001000000000000

In case of double precision

S = 1 (since it is a negative number)
e = 7
M = 10100000001 (including the values after decimal point)
Bias of double precision is 1023.
Therefore, e′ = e + 1023
= 7 + 1023
= 1030_{10}
e′ = $(10000000110)_2$

Hence, the double precision number is represented as given below:

S	e′	M
1 bit	11 bits	52 bits
1	10000000110	1010000000100000000000000000000000000000000000000000

24. Convert the following IEEE single precision floating-point number to their decimal value.

01000100101101101000010000000000

Ans. The single precision number can be converted into its decimal equivalent by following these steps.

1. First separate the given number into its sign bit (S), exponent part (e) and the mantissa part (M).

   S = 0
   e (8 bits) = 10001001 = 137
   M (23 bits) = 01101101000010000000000

2. Find the value of e.

   It is known that e′ = e + 127

   That is, e = e′ − 127

   = 137 − 127

   = 10.

3. The required values are

   S = 0

   e = 10

   M = 0110110100001 (discarding the additional zeroes)

By substituting the above components in the equation $\pm 1.M \times 2^{e}$, we get

$$1.0110110100001 \times 2^{10} = (10110110100.001)_2$$

4. Convert the binary number to its decimal equivalent.

$$(10110110100.001)_2 = (1460.125)_{10}$$

25. Express the number .000021 in floating-point form.

Ans. To express the given decimal number in floating point, we will use the IEEE 754 standard representation. The steps for conversion are as follows:

1. Convert the number into its binary equivalent.

$$(0.000021)_{10} = (0.00000000000000001)_2$$

2. Normalize the number

$$(0.000000000000000001)_2 = 1.0 \times 2^{-18}$$

   e′ = e + 127

   = −18 + 127

   = 109

   = $(1101101)_2$.

3. The required floating-point number is represented as shown below:

S	e′	M
1 bit	8 bits	23 bits
0	01101101	00000000000000000000000

MULTIPLE CHOICE QUESTIONS

1. In signed numbers, which bit denotes the sign of the number?

   (a) LSB (b) MSB
   (c) Carry bit (d) None of these

2. The 2's complement representation of (−24) in a 16-bit microcomputer is:

   (a) 0000 0001 1000 1000 (b) 1111 1111 1110 0111
   (c) 1111 1111 1110 1000 (d) 0001 0001 1111 0011

3. The mantissa and exponent are used to denote which type of numbers?
   (a) 2's complement numbers (b) Fixed-point numbers
   (c) Decimal numbers (d) Floating-point numbers
4. In normalized floating-point numbers, the most significant bit in mantissa part should not be ________.
   (a) 1 (b) 2
   (c) 0 (d) None of these
5. The 10's complement of 7 is ______.
   (a) 5 (b) 3
   (c) 0 (d) 1
6. In BCD system, each decimal digit is represented by ________ bits.
   (a) 3 (b) 2
   (c) 5 (d) 4
7. In single and double precision, _____ bits and ____ bits are used, respectively.
   (a) 8, 16 (b) 32, 64
   (c) 16, 32 (d) 1, 2
8. In Gray code, how many bit positions change when we move from one codeword to its immediate next codeword.
   (a) 0 bits (b) 1 bit
   (c) 3 bits (d) All bits
9. Which codes are used by the BCD method to determine the decimal digits?
   (a) Binary codes (b) Gray codes
   (c) Parity Codes (d) None of these
10. In the parity generator, which logical operator is used to generate the parity bits?
    (a) OR (b) AND
    (c) NOT (d) Exclusive-OR

Ans. 1. b 2. c 3. d 4. c 5. b 6. d 7. b 8. b 9. a 10. d

5

Computer Arithmetic

1. What is the need of computer arithmetic?

Ans. In digital computers, data are manipulated by the arithmetic instructions to produce solution for computational problems. The arithmetic instructions carry out arithmetic operations and other activities for processing the data. Four basic arithmetic operations are addition, subtraction, multiplication and division. From these four basic operations, other mathematical functions can be derived to do complex arithmetic calculations, usually, required for scientific problems. All the arithmetic operations are performed by the **arithmetic processor,** which is a part of the processor.

During the execution of an arithmetic instruction, the data type that is specified in the definition of arithmetic instruction is assumed to reside in the processor registers. An arithmetic instruction may need to perform operation on binary or decimal data. In either case, the data can be in the form of fixed-point (integers or fractions) or floating-point numbers.

Some arithmetic processors have simple instruction set as they include only fixed-point add instruction. Alternatively, arithmetic processor can include instructions for performing all four operations on both binary and decimal data in fixed-point and floating-point form. Such arithmetic processor has a complex instruction set.

2. How addition and subtraction are performed in fixed-point numbers?

Ans. The fixed-point binary data can be represented in signed-magnitude or signed-2's complement form in computers. The addition and subtraction on fixed-point binary numbers represented in both these forms are discussed here.

- **Signed-magnitude data:** The addition and subtraction of signed-magnitude data are done by considering the sign (+ or –) of the numbers. Suppose the magnitudes of the two signed binary numbers are N_1 and N_2. The addition and subtraction on these numbers are performed as follows:

  Addition

  - When both the numbers have same signs (+ or –) then the magnitudes of the numbers are added and the sign of the result is same as that of sign of N_1 and N_2.
  - When both the numbers have different signs then the magnitudes of the two numbers are compared. If N_1 and N_2 are equal, the result will be 0 with a positive sign. Otherwise, the smaller

magnitude is subtracted from the larger one and the sign of the result will be same as that of the larger number.

Subtraction

- When both the numbers have same signs then the magnitudes of the two numbers are compared. If N_1 and N_2 are equal, the result will be 0 with a positive sign. Otherwise, the smaller magnitude is subtracted from the larger one and the sign of the result will be same as that of the larger number.
- When both numbers have different signs then the magnitude of both the numbers will be added and the sign of the result is same as that of N_1.

- **Signed-2's complement data:** Addition and subtraction on the binary numbers in signed-2's complement form is performed as follows:

Addition

- Addition of numbers is performed by adding all the bits (including the sign bit) of two numbers starting with the least significant bits (LSBs). Carry produced by adding two bits is propagated to the next high-order bits. If the result obtained after adding the numbers is negative (the left most bit is 1) then result is in 2's complement form. Notice that when two n digit numbers are added then overflow may occur if the sum occupies n + 1 digit. Overflow can be detected by examining the carry-in to the most significant bit (MSB) and carry-out of it. If they are different, there is an overflow. Some examples of addition are shown in Figure 5.1.

```
+4 00000100        +4 00000100
+3 00000011        -9 11110111
-----------        -----------
+7 00000111        -5 11111011
-----------        -----------
```

Figure 5.1 Addition in 2's Complement

Subtraction

- It is performed by calculating the 2's complement of the subtrahend (the number to be subtracted) and adding it to the minuend (the number from which subtrahend is to be subtracted). Notice that taking 2's complement of a number is same as changing the sign of number. Hence, $N_1 + N' + 1$ is equal to $N_1 - N_2$. Overflow is to be handled in same way as in addition.

3. Discuss the hardware implementation of signed-magnitude addition and subtraction.

Ans. The addition and subtraction operations can be implemented using registers, flip-flops, a parallel adder and a complementer (see Figure 5.2). As subtraction can be performed by the means of complement and addition, parallel subtractor is not required for hardware implementation.

The magnitudes of the two numbers are stored in registers R_1 and R_2 with their signs stored in the flip-flops F_1 and F_2 respectively. The result of the operation can be stored in a third register with its sign stored in a third flip-flop. Alternatively, one of the source registers, say R_1, and flip-flops, say F_1, can be used to hold the result.

The state of mode control M (0 or 1) controls the operation (addition or subtraction) to be performed. Notice that mode control M is passed as an input to the complementer as well as to the parallel adder. When the value of M is 0, the complementer provides the value of R_2 to the parallel adder. In this case, the input carry is also 0 and thus the result of the adder is $R_1 + R_2$. When the value of M is 1, then complementer provides the complements of R_2 to the parallel adder. In this case, the input carry is 1 and thus the parallel adder performs $R_1 + R_2' + 1$ or $R_1 - R_2$.

After performing the required operation, the parallel adder stores the result in register R_1 and the output carry in E, where it is examined to determine the relative magnitudes of the input numbers. The flip-flop AVF is used to indicate the overflow, which can occur when addition is performed.

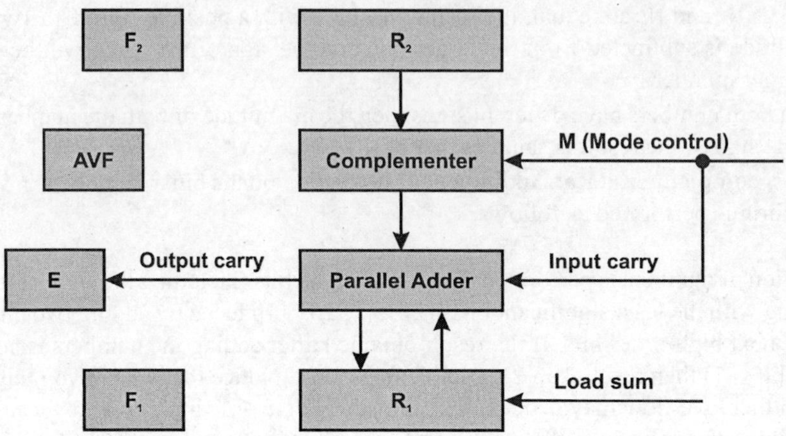

Figure 5.2 Hardware Implementation of Signed-magnitude Addition and Subtraction

4. Provide the hardware implementation for addition and subtraction with signed-2's complement data.

Ans. The hardware required for implementing the addition and subtraction with signed-2's complement data is similar to that of signed-magnitude data. The difference lies in the fact that the sign bits are stored in registers rather than being stored separately in flip-flops. Register R_1 is named BR and register R_2 is named AC and sign of the numbers are represented by the left most bit of BR and AC (see Figure 5.3).

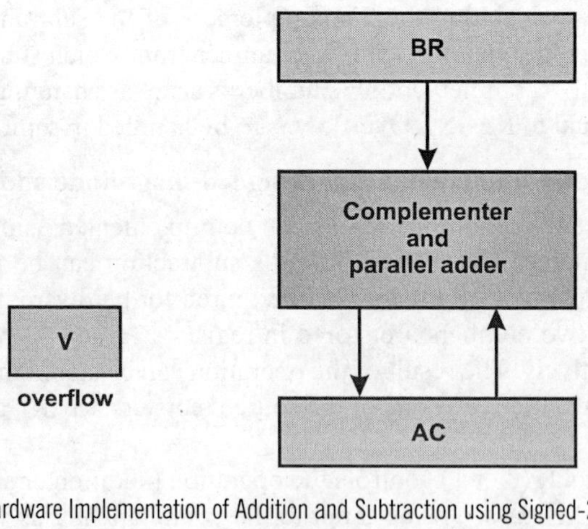

Figure 5.3 Hardware Implementation of Addition and Subtraction using Signed-2's Complement

- **Addition:** Contents of AC and BR are added and the last two carries are passed through the exclusive-OR gate. If the output is 1, the overflow flip-flop V is set to 1 to indicate the overflow. Otherwise, V is set to 0.

- **Subtraction:** Contents of AC are added to the 2's complement of BR. Overflow is detected in the similar manner by passing the last two carries through the exclusive-OR gate and accordingly the overflow flip-flop V is set or reset.

Addition and subtraction operations on numbers are simple when negative numbers are represented in signed-2's complement form. Hence, signed-2's complement form for representing numbers is used in most of the computers.

5. Explain the overflow condition during the addition of numbers.

Ans. During the addition of two numbers, there may arise a case when the sum contains more digits than those of the actual numbers. This situation is known as an **overflow** which is considered to be a problem in computers as the length of a computer register is finite. A register having a length of n bits cannot store the result of n + 1 bits. In such a case, most computers detect overflow and set a corresponding flip-flop, which can be checked by the user. Some conditions to be kept in mind while dealing with overflow are as follows:

- Overflow may occur only when both the numbers being added are either positive or negative.
- Overflow does not occur if the numbers differ in their signs. This is because adding a positive and a negative number results in a number smaller than the larger of the two numbers.

The overflow condition is detected in different ways for signed and unsigned numbers. These ways are as follows:

- In case of unsigned numbers, overflow is detected from the carry out of the MSB.
- In case of signed numbers, overflow is detected by examining the carry-in and carry-out of the sign bit. If both the carries are not equal, overflow occurs.

6. Describe serial adder in brief.

Ans. A **serial adder** can be designed by combining additional circuitry such as full adders and flip-flops with the shift registers. Figure 5.4 shows the logic diagram for a serial adder. It comprises two right shift registers (A and B), a full adder and a D flip-flop. The full adder performs the addition of two bits at a time and stores the generated carry output in the D flip-flop. This carry is used as an input for the addition of the next two higher-order bits.

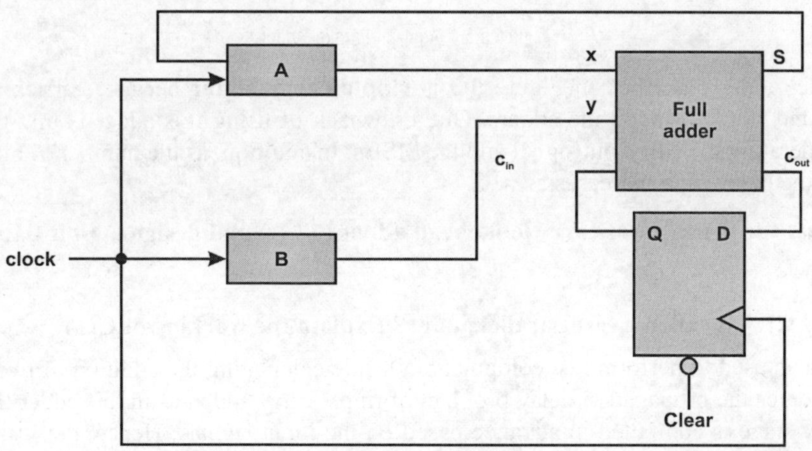

Figure 5.4 Serial Adder

Initially, the numbers to be added are loaded in the shift registers A and B and the D flip-flop is set to 0. The addition starts with the LSBs of both the registers and the carry output is stored in D flip-flop. With each clock pulse, the contents of registers are shifted to the right by one bit and the next two bits are taken from the registers. These two bits along with the carry of previous addition that is stored in D flip-flop become the input to the full adder. The sum and carry bit produced by the full adder are stored in register A and D flip-flop, respectively. As the sum (S) output of the full adder is connected as a serial input to the shift register A, we get the result of serial addition from the shift register A after all the bits have been added. If we want to add another number to the result stored in A, we can do this by loading the new number in register B and repeating the above process.

7. What is parallel adder? Give its block diagram also.

or

Describe ripple carry adder.

Ans. A full adder can add two 1-bit numbers and an input carry at one time. Therefore, to add two n-bit binary numbers, n full adders are to be used. Figure 5.5 shows the block diagram of an n-bit parallel adder which has been constructed by interconnecting n full adder circuits in a way that the carry output of one full adder becomes the carry input for the next full adder in the chain. The sum bit from the full adders generates the required bits.

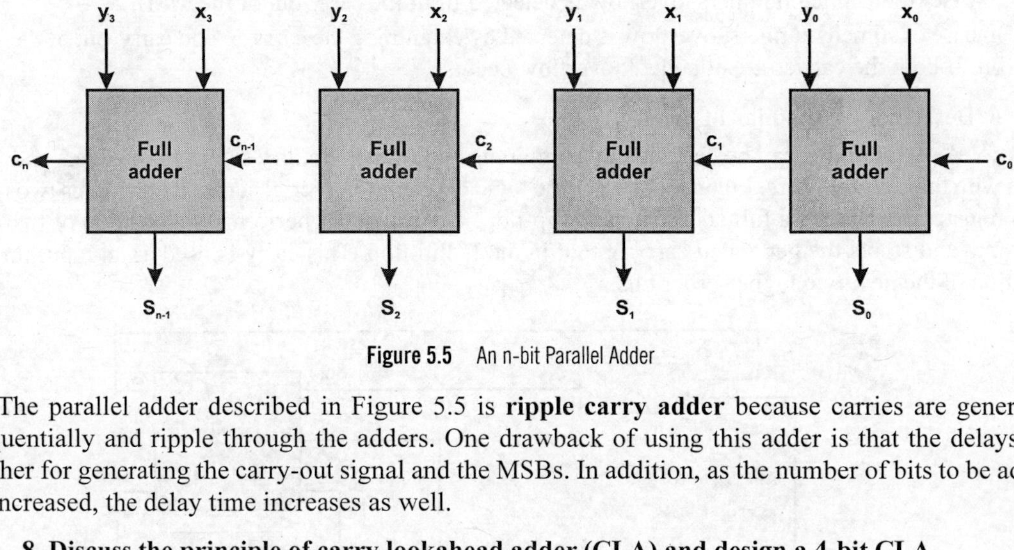

Figure 5.5 An n-bit Parallel Adder

The parallel adder described in Figure 5.5 is **ripple carry adder** because carries are generated sequentially and ripple through the adders. One drawback of using this adder is that the delays are higher for generating the carry-out signal and the MSBs. In addition, as the number of bits to be added is increased, the delay time increases as well.

8. Discuss the principle of carry lookahead adder (CLA) and design a 4-bit CLA.

or

Why CLA is called a fast parallel adder? Explain the working of CLA.

Ans. CLA is used to perform fast computations while calculating the addition of two binary numbers. It overcomes the propagation delay problem of ripple carry added as in this adder the input carry needed at any stage is computed in advance based on the input signals. Hence, the wait time for the supply of carries from one stage to another is reduced.

CLA is also called a **fast parallel adder** because of its capability for calculating carries at fast speed.

At any stage, say i, the carry-out signal c_{i+1} is generated in two cases:

1. When both bits x_i and y_i are 1.
2. When one of the two bits is 1 and the carry-in (c_i) is 1.

These cases can be represented as:

$$c_{i+1} = x_i \cdot y_i + (x_i \oplus y_i) \cdot c_i$$

The above equation can be written in terms of propagating signals p_i denoting carry propagate (carry bit) and g_i denoting the carry generate as shown here.

$$c_{i+1} = g_i + p_i \cdot c_i \quad (1)$$

where,

$$p_i = (x_i \oplus y_i)$$
$$g_i = x_i \cdot y_i$$

Figure 5.6 shows the block diagram of generating p_i and g_i signals using logic gates.

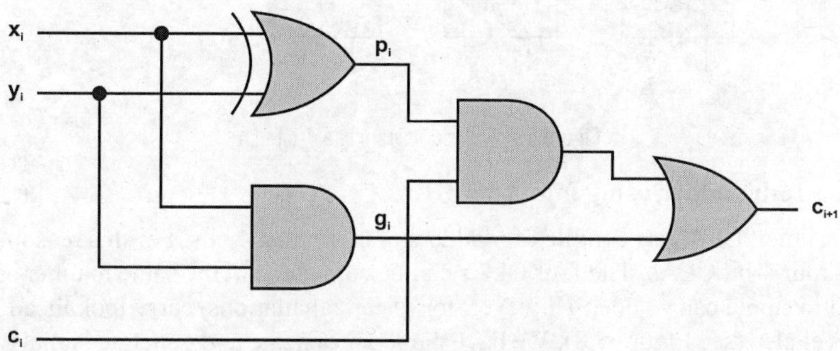

Figure 5.6 Full Adder with p_i and g_i

Figure 5.6 shows that g_i and p_i depend on the input bits x_i and y_i and they will be valid after one and two gate delay, respectively. If the carry signal is calculated using the above expression, the time required to calculate the carry signal will be reduced as the carry will not be rippled through all its previous stages. To design a 4-bit adder, we put i = 0, 1, 2, 3 in Eq. 1 and get the following:

$$c_1 = g_0 + p_0 \cdot c_0 \quad (2)$$

$$c_2 = g_1 + p_1 \cdot c_1 = g_1 + p_1 \cdot g_0 + p_1 \cdot p_0 \cdot c_0 \quad (3)$$

$$c_3 = g_2 + p_2 \cdot g_1 + p_2 \cdot p_1 \cdot g_0 + p_2 \cdot p_1 \cdot p_0 \cdot c_0 \quad (4)$$

$$c_4 = g_3 + p_3 \cdot g_2 + p_3 \cdot p_2 \cdot g_1 + p_3 \cdot p_2 \cdot p_1 \cdot g_0 + p_3 \cdot p_2 \cdot p_1 \cdot p_0 \cdot c_0 \quad (5)$$

Figure 5.7 depicts a 4-bit CLA that is built using four full adders for generating sum bits and carry lookahead logic for generating carry for each stage. The carry lookahead logic is implemented using circuit for generating p_i and g_i signals. Notice that the carry generated by adders (except the one generated from most significant adder) are ignored.

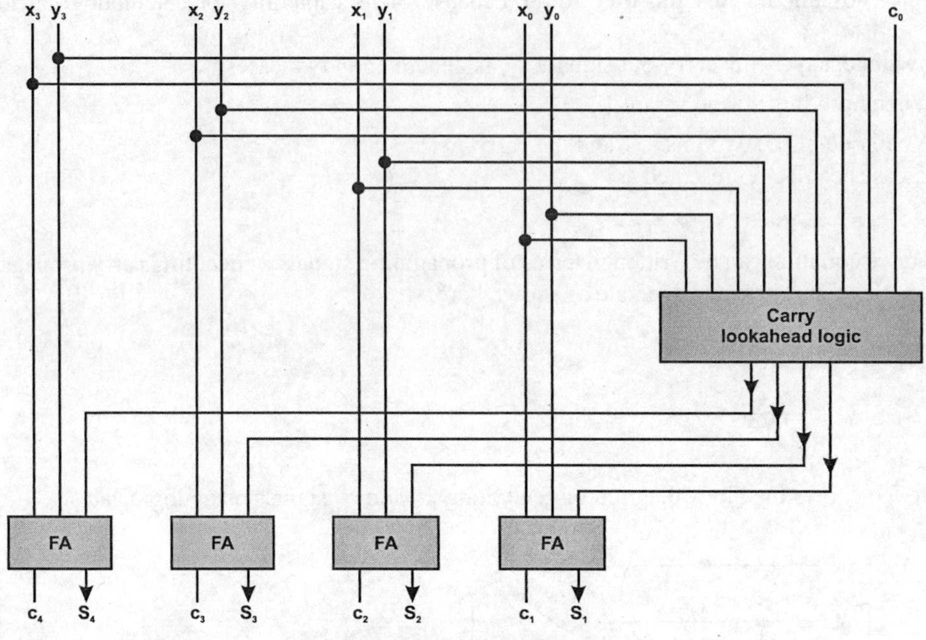

Figure 5.7 Block Diagram of a 4-bit CLA

9. Design a 16-bit adder using four 4-bit CLA.

Ans. The design of CLA gets complex for adders of more than 4 bits. For this reason, 16-bit adder is designed using four 4-bit CLAs. The four CLAs can be connected in the same manner as the adders are connected to form ripple carry adder. However, for faster calculations, carry lookahead logic is needed at the higher level also (see Figure 5.8). We have named propagate and generate signals for this level as super propagate (P) and super generate signals (G).

The super propagate signal P_i is true if all propagate signals of ith CLA propagate a carry. This can be represented as:

$$P_0 = p_3 \cdot p_2 \cdot p_1 \cdot p_0$$
$$P_1 = p_7 \cdot p_6 \cdot p_5 \cdot p_4$$
$$P_2 = p_{11} \cdot p_{10} \cdot p_9 \cdot p_8$$
$$P_3 = p_{15} \cdot p_{14} \cdot p_{13} \cdot p_{12}$$

Similarly, the super generate signal (G_i) is true in the following two cases:

- If generate signal of the MSB of ith adder is true.
- If an earlier generate and all the intermediate propagates are true for i^{th} adder.

These cases can be represented as:

$$G_0 = g_3 + (p_3 \cdot g_2) + (p_3 \cdot p_2 \cdot g_1) + (p_3 \cdot p_2 \cdot p_1 \cdot g_0)$$
$$G_1 = g_7 + (p_7 \cdot g_6) + (p_7 \cdot p_6 \cdot g_5) + (p_7 \cdot p_6 \cdot p_5 \cdot g_4)$$
$$G_2 = g_{11} + (p_{11} \cdot g_{10}) + (p_{11} \cdot p_{10} \cdot g_9) + (p_{11} \cdot p_{10} \cdot p_9 \cdot g_8)$$
$$G_3 = g_{15} + (p_{15} \cdot g_{14}) + (p_{15} \cdot p_{14} \cdot g_{13}) + (p_{15} \cdot p_{14} \cdot p_{13} \cdot g_{12})$$

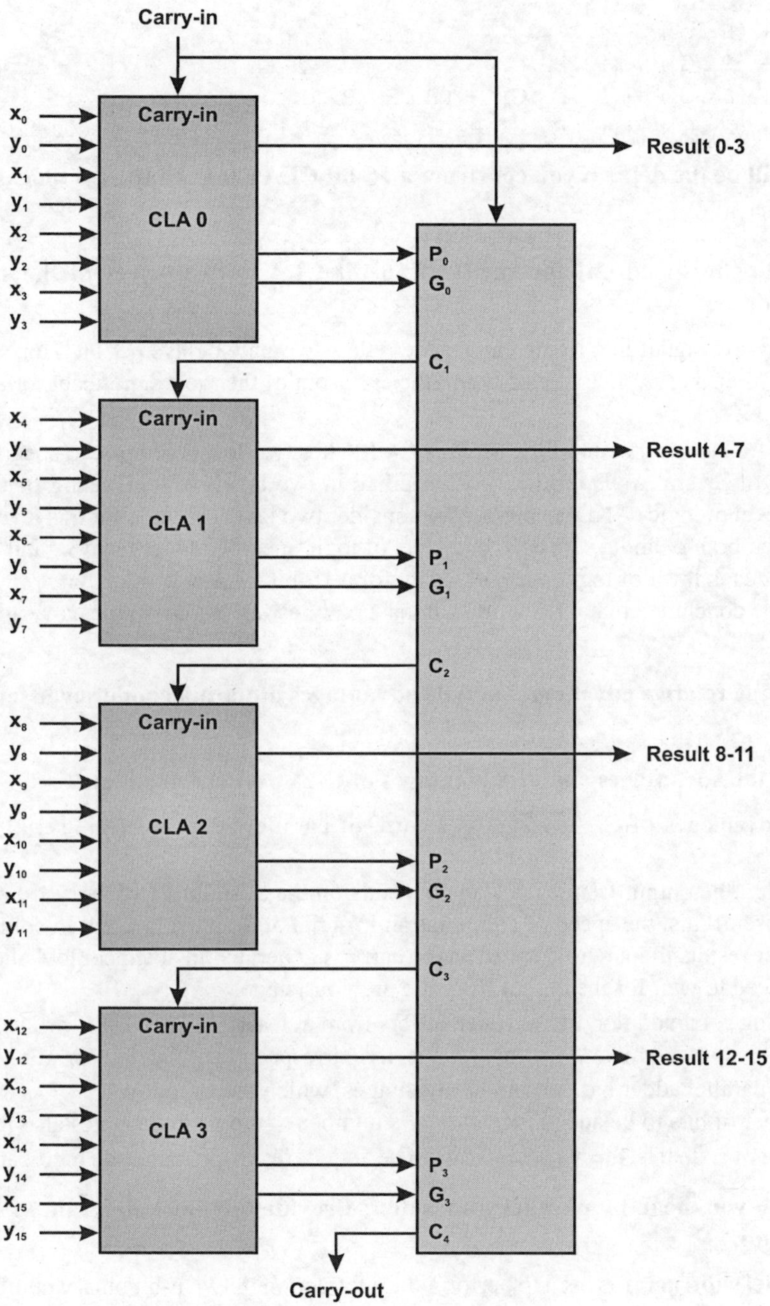

Figure 5.8 16-bit Adder using 4-bit Adders

Similar to super generate and propagate signals, the carry signals propagating to higher level CLA unit are denoted by capital letters as C_1, C_2, C_3 and C_4. Carry-out equations of 16-bit CLA are very similar to carry-out equations for each bit of the 4-bit adder as shown here.

$C_1 = G_1 + (P_0 . c_0)$
$C_2 = G_1 + (P_1 . G_0) + (P_1 . P_0 . c_0)$
$C_3 = G_2 + (P_2 . G_1) + (P_2 . P_1 . G_0) + (P_2 . P_1 . P_0 . c_0)$
$C_4 = G_3 + (P_3 . G_2) + (P_3 . P_2 . G_1) + (P_3 . P_2 . P_1 . G_0) + (P_3 . P_2 . P_1 . P_0 . c_0)$

10. What will be the delay if you construct a 16-bit CLA using 4-bit CLA blocks?

or

Estimate the speed enhancement of 16-bit CLA with respect to the 16-bit ripple carry adder.

Ans. The carry-out signal in a ripple carry adder takes two gate delays per bit. Hence, the number of gate delays between a carry-in to the LSB and the carry-out of the most significant for a 16-bit ripple adder is $16 \times 2 = 32$.

In the 16-bit CLA, the carry-out of the MSB is C_4. It takes two levels of logic to specify C_4 in terms of P_i and G_i (OR of several AND terms). G_i is specified in two levels of logic using p_i and g_i, and P_i depends on one level of logic (AND) using p_i. We consider two levels of logic for this level as this is the worst case. Further, both p_i and g_i are each one level of logic specified in terms of x_i and y_i. Assuming one gate delay for each level of logic, the gate delay for a 16-bit CLA is $2 + 2 + 1 = 5$.

Hence, it can be concluded that CLA works almost six times faster than ripple carry adder for 16-bit addition.

11. Discuss the relative advantages and disadvantages of parallel adder over serial adder.

or

Discuss the advantages and disadvantages of CLA over serial adder.

Ans. Some advantages of CLA, which is a form of parallel adder over the serial adder, are as follows:

- In serial adder, the output from each stage depends on the availability of carry from the previous stage. Because of this, the speed of computation in serial addition is limited. In contrast, the CLA parallel adder results in increased speed as the carry is generated in advance (lookahead) and thus, there is no need to wait for the output from the previous stage.
- For performing n-bit addition, serial adder suffers from at least 2n gate delays, while in parallel adder, gate delay always remains the same (that is, five) irrespective of the number of bits to be added.

Besides, CLA parallel adder has certain disadvantages, which are as follows:

- As the number of bits to be added increases, the number of inputs to the gates also increases.
- A large value of n (that is, the number of bits to be added) results in increased hardware complexity.

12. What do you mean by parallel subtractor? Provide the block diagram of 4-bit parallel subtractor.

Ans. A **parallel subtractor** is used to perform the subtraction of two n-bit binary numbers. In digital computers, the subtraction of two binary numbers can be efficiently performed using 2's complement method. For example, if X and Y are two binary numbers, then X − Y can be determined by taking the 2's complement of Y and adding it to X. The 2's complement of a number can be obtained by adding one to its 1's complement. The 1's complement can be implemented using inverters and one can be added to it through the input carry, thus obtaining the 2's complement. Figure 5.9 shows the block diagram of a 4-bit parallel subtractor.

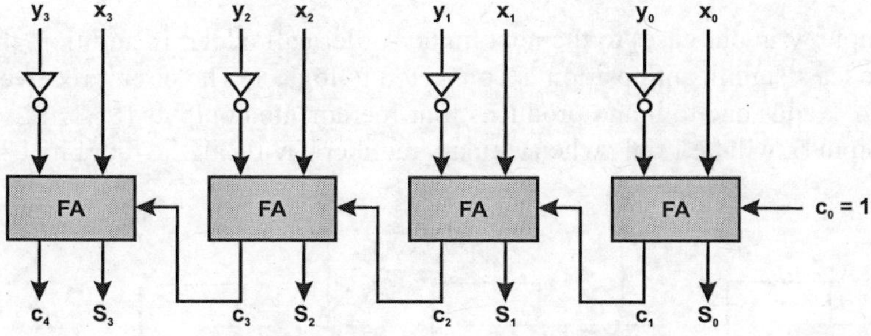

Figure 5.9 4-bit Parallel Subtractor

13. What is adder-subtractor? Design a 4-bit adder-subtractor.

Ans. The addition and subtraction operations can be combined into a single circuit. For this, an XOR gate is to be included in each full adder. Figure 5.10 shows the circuit for a 4-bit adder-subtractor. The operation of the adder-subtractor circuit is controlled with the help of mode input M.

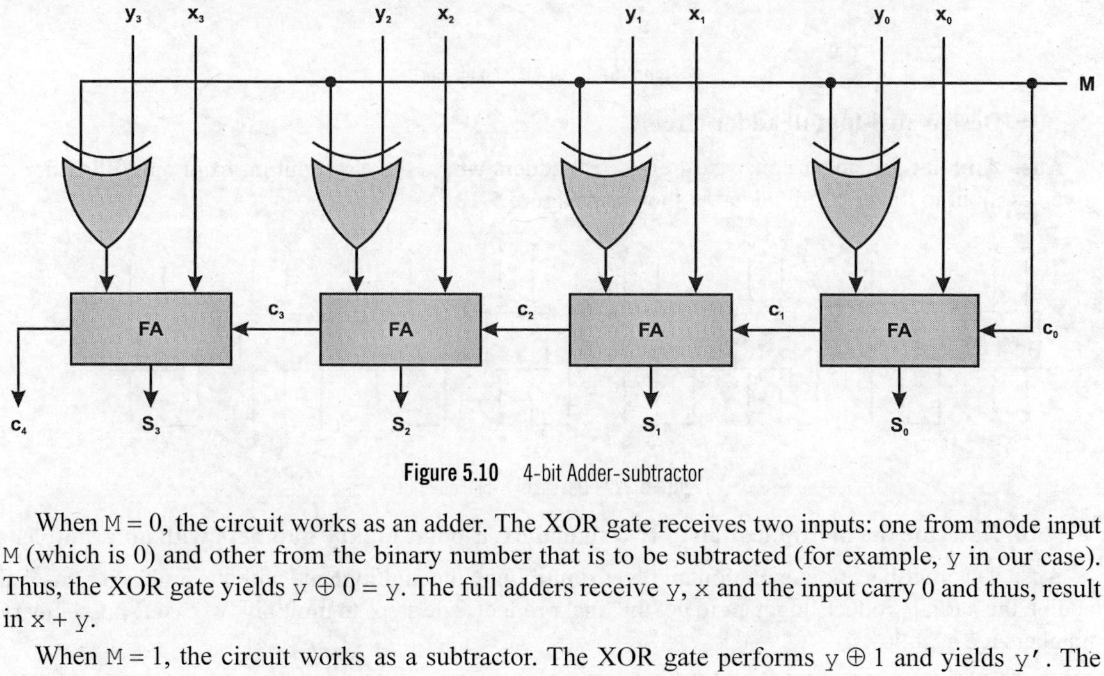

Figure 5.10 4-bit Adder-subtractor

When M = 0, the circuit works as an adder. The XOR gate receives two inputs: one from mode input M (which is 0) and other from the binary number that is to be subtracted (for example, y in our case). Thus, the XOR gate yields $y \oplus 0 = y$. The full adders receive y, x and the input carry 0 and thus, result in $x + y$.

When M = 1, the circuit works as a subtractor. The XOR gate performs $y \oplus 1$ and yields y'. The full adders receive y', x and the input carry 1. The circuit performs the operation $x + y' + 1$, which is equivalent to $x - y$ as $y' + 1$ means 2's complement of y.

14. Design a 4-bit combinational circuit incrementer.

Ans. The increment operation is used to add one to a given binary number. For example, if a binary number A has value 0110, then after incrementing A by one, we get 0111. Figure 5.11 shows the circuit of a 4-bit combinational circuit incrementer. It has been constructed by connecting four half adders in a cascade manner where the carry output from one half adder forms one of the inputs (for example, y in our case) to the next higher-order half adder. In addition, the y input of the half adder in the least significant position is connected to logic 1. The circuit receives four input bits (A_0, A_1, A_2 and A_3), adds one to it and produces four incremented outputs (S_0, S_1, S_2 and S_3). Notice that the carry output c_4 will be 1 only when a binary number having all the four bits 1's is incremented.

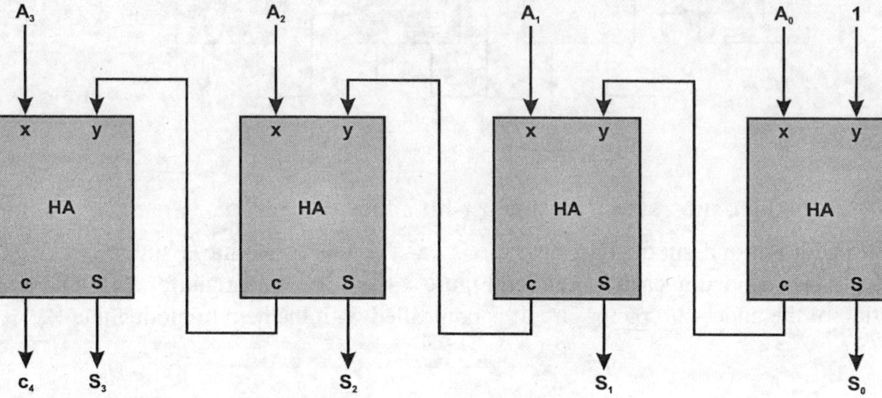

Figure 5.11 4-bit Incrementer

15. Design an 8-bit full adder circuit.

Ans. An 8-bit full adder consists of eight full adders where the carry output from one full adder is given as input to the next full adder as shown in Figure 5.12.

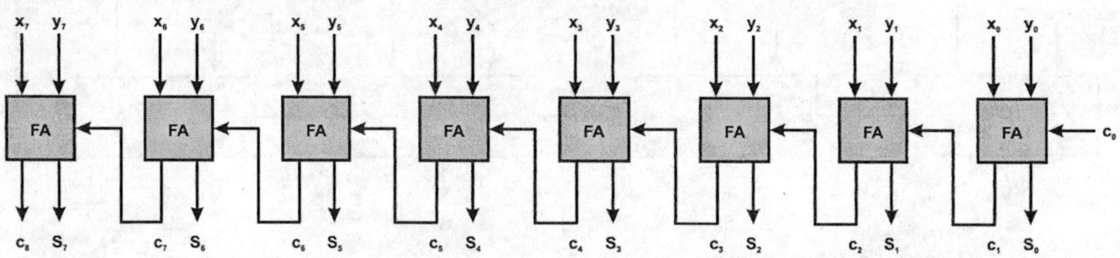

Figure 5.12 Design of 8-bit Full Adder

16. Describe the multiplication of two signed fixed-point binary numbers with an example.

Ans. The multiplication operation involves multiplying the multiplicand with the multiplier bits and adding the partial products together to get the final product. The steps to multiply two fixed-point binary numbers are as follows:

1. Take one digit of multiplier at a time starting from LSB.
2. If the multiplier bit is 0 then partial product will have as many 0s as the bits in the multiplicand.On the other hand, if the multiplier bit is 1, partial product will be same as that of the multiplicand.
3. Place the partial product in the line one position left to the partial product in the previous line.
4. Repeat steps 2 and 3 for all the bits in the multiplier.
5. Add the partial products together to get the final product.
6. Assign the positive sign to the product if the signs of the multiplicand and the multiplier are same. Otherwise, assign the negative sign.

For example, consider the multiplication of 1000 and 1010.

```
Multiplicand (8)        1000
Multiplier (10)        x1010
                        0000
                       1000x
                      0000xx
                     1000xxx
Product (80)         1010000
```

17. Draw and explain the flowchart depicting the multiplication operation using add and shift operations.

Ans. The flowchart for multiplication of two n-bit numbers using add and shift operations is shown in Figure 5.13.

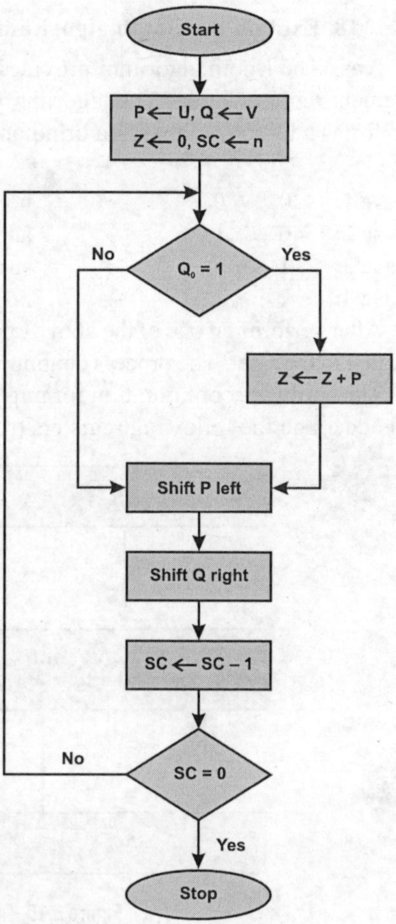

Figure 5.13 Flowchart for Multiplication using Add and Shift Operations

Initially, the multiplicand (U) is loaded into the register P, multiplier (V) is loaded into the register Q, product register (Z) is initialized to 0 and the sequence counter (SC) is initialized to n, the number of bits in multiplier. The decision of whether the multiplicand is to be added to the product register is made by checking the LSB of the multiplier register, which is Q_0. If Q_0 is 1, the multiplicand is added to the product register Z. On the other hand, if Q_0 is 0, nothing is added. In either case, P is shifted to the left and Q is shifted to the right. This process continues until SC becomes 0. For example, consider the multiplication of 4-bit numbers 10 (1010) and 14 (1110). Figure 5.14 shows the value of registers after each iteration of multiplication.

After all the iterations, the result of multiplication, i.e. 01111000 (140) of 1010 × 1100 is stored in the product register Z.

SC	Z (product)	Q (multiplier)	P (multiplicand)	Operation
4	0000 0000	1100	0000 1010	Initialization
3	0000 0000	0110	0001 0100	Left shift P Right shift Q
2	0000 0000	0011	0010 1000	Left shift P Right shift Q
1	0010 1000	0001	0101 0000	Add P to Z Left shift P Right shift Q
0	0111 1000	0000	1010 0000	Add P to Z Left shift P Right shift Q

Figure 5.14 Register Values after Each Iteration of Multiplication Algorithm

18. Explain the Booth algorithm along with its hardware implementation.

Ans. The Booth algorithm provides a technique to multiply two binary numbers in signed-2's complement representation. The algorithm examines the two LSBs of the multiplier, say Q_n and Q_{n+1}, and performs addition, subtraction or no operation on the basis of the following cases.

	Q_n	Q_{n+1}		
Case 1:	0	0	→	no arithmetic operation
Case 2:	0	1	→	add multiplicand to the partial product
Case 3:	1	0	→	subtract multiplicand from the partial product
Case 4:	1	1	→	no arithmetic operation

After performing one of the above operations, the partial product and the multiplier (along with Q_{n+1}) are shifted to the right. The process continues for n times, where n denotes the number of bits in the multiplier.

The hardware configuration for implementing the Booth algorithm includes a complementer, a parallel adder and the following registers (see Figure 5.15):

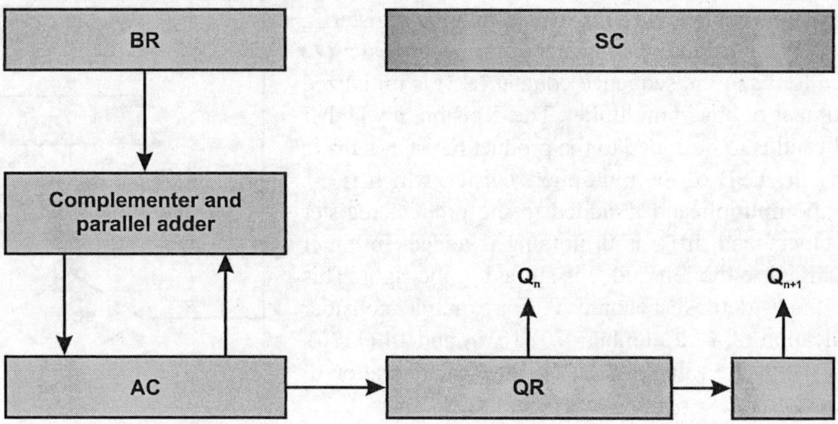

Figure 5.15 Hardware Configuration for Implementing Booth Algorithm

- **AC:** Stores the partial product.
- **BR:** Stores the multiplicand.
- **QR:** Stores the multiplier. Q_n denotes LSB of the multiplier and Q_{n+1} is affixed to QR as an extra flip-flop to store the multiplier's previous LSB. Q_{n+1} is initialized with 0.
- **SC:** Represents the total number of steps to be performed as it is initialized with the number of bits (n) in the multiplier.

19. Write the pseudocode for Booth algorithm.

Ans. The pseudocode for multiplying binary integers, say X and Y, with the help of Booth algorithm is as follows:

1. BR ← X
   QR ← Y
   Q_n ← Y_0
   AC ← 0
   Q_{n+1} ← 0
   SC ← n (number of bits in multiplier)

```
2. If Qn Qn+1 = 01
      AC ← AC + BR
      ashr (AC and QR), SC ← SC – 1
   Else if Qn Qn+1 = 10
      AC ← AC + BR̄ + 1
      ashr (AC and QR), SC ← SC – 1
   Else
      Set ashr (AC and QR)
      Set SC ← SC - 1
   End if
3. Repeat step 2 until SC≠0
4. Stop
```

20. Draw a flowchart for the multiplication of two numbers using Booth algorithm.

Ans. The flowchart for multiplying binary integers, say x and y, using Booth algorithm is depicted in Figure 5.16.

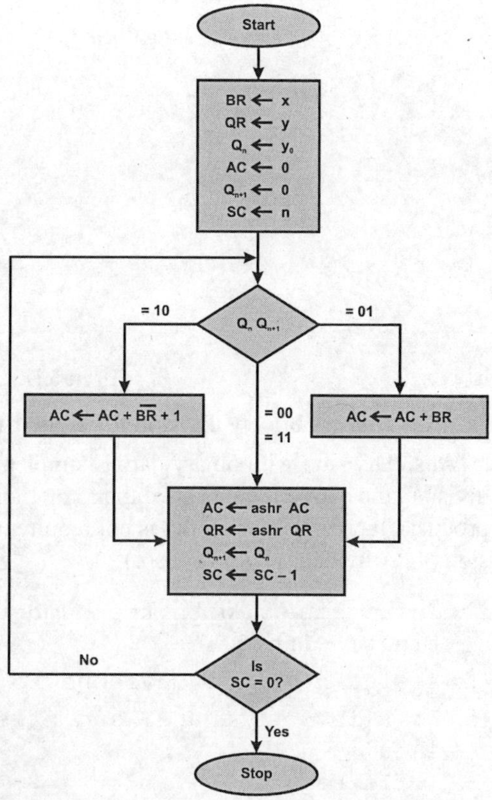

Figure 5.16 Flowchart for Multiplication of Two Signed-2s Numbers Using Booth's Algorithm

21. Explain array multiplier with the help of logic diagram.

Ans. The **array multiplier** is a combinational circuit used to multiply two binary numbers. It consists of gates, and has the capability to form the product bits at once. It provides the fastest means to multiply two binary numbers because it only needs to propagate the signals through the gates, which form the multiplication array.

To understand the working of a 2-bit array multiplier, consider y_1 y_0 as the multiplicand bits, x_1 x_0 as the multiplier bits and $z_3z_2z_1z_0$ as the product bits (see Figure 5.17).

The first partial product is formed by multiplying x_0 with y_1 and y_0. Notice that the product of two bits, say x_0y_0, is 1 if both the bits are 1; otherwise the product is 0. This is same as AND operation of two bits and thus can be implemented using AND gate. The first partial product is formed with the help of two AND gates as shown in figure. This output of the first AND gate forms the LSB of the final product, which is z_0. The second partial product is formed by multiplying x_1 with y_1 and y_0, and shifting the result to left by one position. Now, by using two half adder (HA) circuits, the first and the second partial products are added. The sum output of the first HA forms the product bit z_1, while carry output becomes the carry input to the second HA. The sum and the carry output of the second HA form the product bits z_2 and z_3.

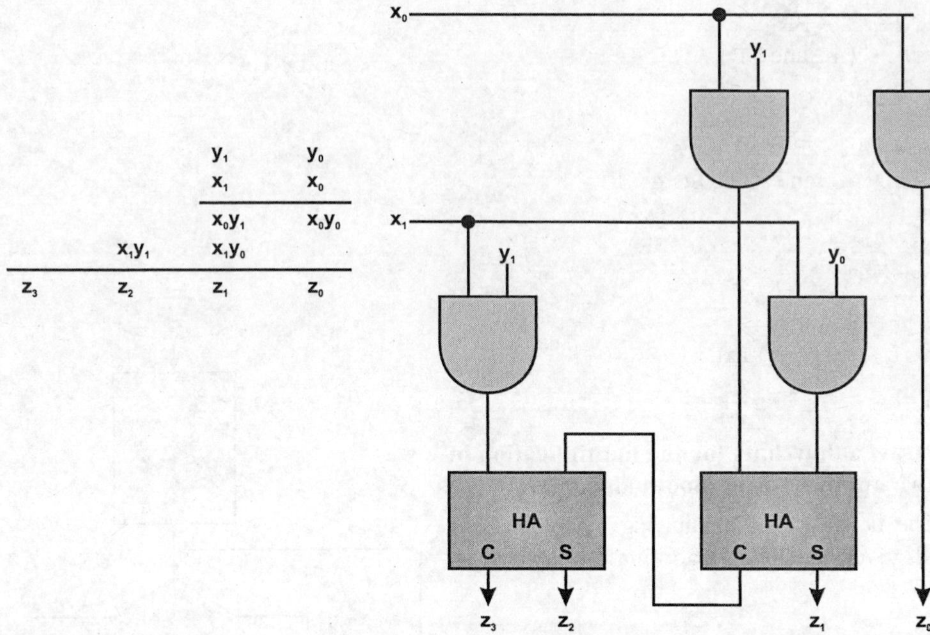

Figure 5.17 2-bit by 2-bit Array Multiplier

22. Discuss binary division for signed-magnitude data with the help of an example.

Ans. Division with binary data is simpler as compared to dividing decimal data because in binary division, the quotient digits are either 0 or 1 and estimating the number of times the dividend (or partial product) fits into the remainder is not required. To understand the process of division, consider the division of `X` (dividend) by `Y` (divisor).

```
1. Initialize n with the number of bits in Y, flag with 0, Q (quo-
   tient) with 0.
2. Assign n MSB of dividend to partial remainder P.
3. If P is less than Y and n is less than the number of bits in X
   then
      If flag = 0
            Increase n by one
            Set flag to 1
            Go to step 2
      Else
            Append 0 to Q
      End if
   Else if P is greater than or equal to Y
      Append 1 to Q
      Subtract Y from P
      Assign the difference to P
      Set flag to 0
```

```
Else
   Go to step 5
End if
```

4. Increase n by one and append n^{th} MSB of X to P, set flag to 1 and go to step 3
5. Q contains the quotient and P contains the remainder.

For example, consider the division of 11001 by 101. Here X = 11001 and Y = 101.

Step 1: n = 3, Q = 0 and flag = 0.

Step 2: P = 110.

Step 3: As P is greater than Y, Q becomes 1, P becomes 001 and flag becomes 1.

Step 4: n becomes 4 and after appending 4th MSB of X (which is 0), P becomes 0010 and flag becomes 1.

Step 5: As P is less than Y and n is less than 5 (number of bits in X), Q becomes 10, n becomes 5 and P becomes 00101.

Step 6: As P is equal to Y, Q becomes 101, P becomes 0 and flag becomes 1.

Step 7: Quotient Q is 101 and remainder P is 0.

The above steps of division are depicted in Figure 5.18.

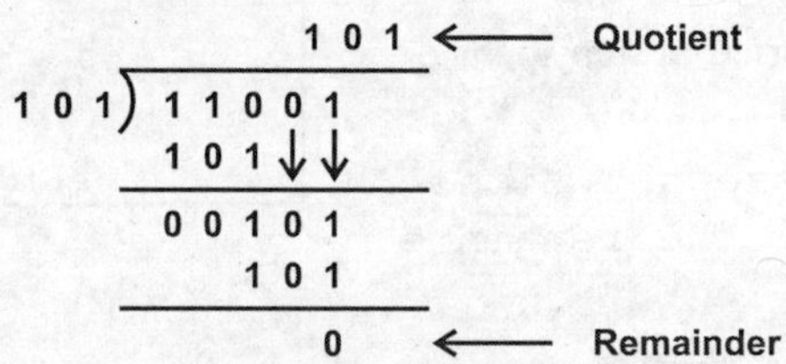

Figure 5.18 Binary Division

Division can be performed using three techniques which are as follows:

- Restoring technique
- Non-restoring technique
- Comparison technique.

23. Discuss restoring technique of division for fixed point numbers.

or

Discuss the hardware implementation of division for signed magnitude data.

Ans. The hardware required for the division of signed-magnitude data is quite similar to that of the multiplication process. The registers required for division algorithm are as follows:

- **X and Q:** These two registers store the double-length dividend. If the dividend is not twice as long as the divisor, it is made so by adding 0's to the left. Registers X and Q store half high-order bits and half low-order bits of the dividend, respectively. Finally, at the end of the algorithm, register X stores the remainder and register Q stores the quotient.
- **Y:** Stores the divisor.

- **E:** Stores the relative magnitude of partial remainder.
- **SC:** Initializes with the number of bits (n) in the divisor and represents the total number of steps to be performed.

After initializing all the registers, following steps are performed in the restoring division algorithm:

```
1. Shift left EXQ
2. If E = 0 then
      Subtract Y from X
      Store result in EX
   Else if E = 1 then
      Subtract Y from X
      Store the result in X
   End if
3. If E = 1 then
      Set Qn bit to 1
   Else
      Add Y to X
      Store the result in EX
      Leave Qn = 0 (inserted in step 1)
   End if
4. Repeat the above steps n times
   after which we get the remainder
   in X and quotient in Y.
```

The flowchart depicting the division operation of signed-magnitude data is shown in figure 5.19

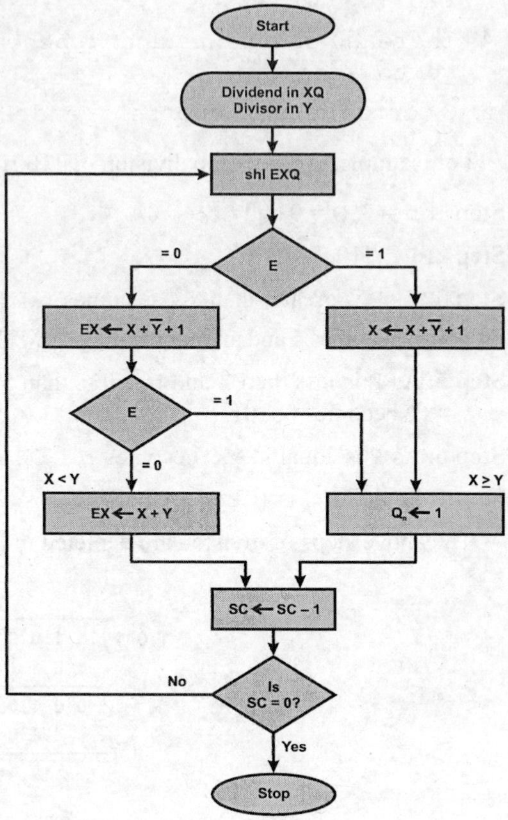

Figure 5.19 Flowchart for Division Operation

24. Draw and explain the flowchart for division of two binary numbers using non-restoring division algorithm.

Ans. The non-restoring division technique skips the restoring step and works with the negative residual. The hardware implementation of this algorithm requires the following four registers.

- Register X for dividend.
- Register Y for divisor.
- Register A for accumulation (Initial value of A must be 0).
- Register SC represents the total number of steps to be performed as it is initialized with the number of bits (n) in the divisor.

The arithmetic actions in register A depends on the following two cases.

Case 1: When A is negative

The register pair (AX) is shifted one bit left.

The contents of register Y and A are added.

If A is negative, the LSB of X is set to 0; otherwise it is set to 1.

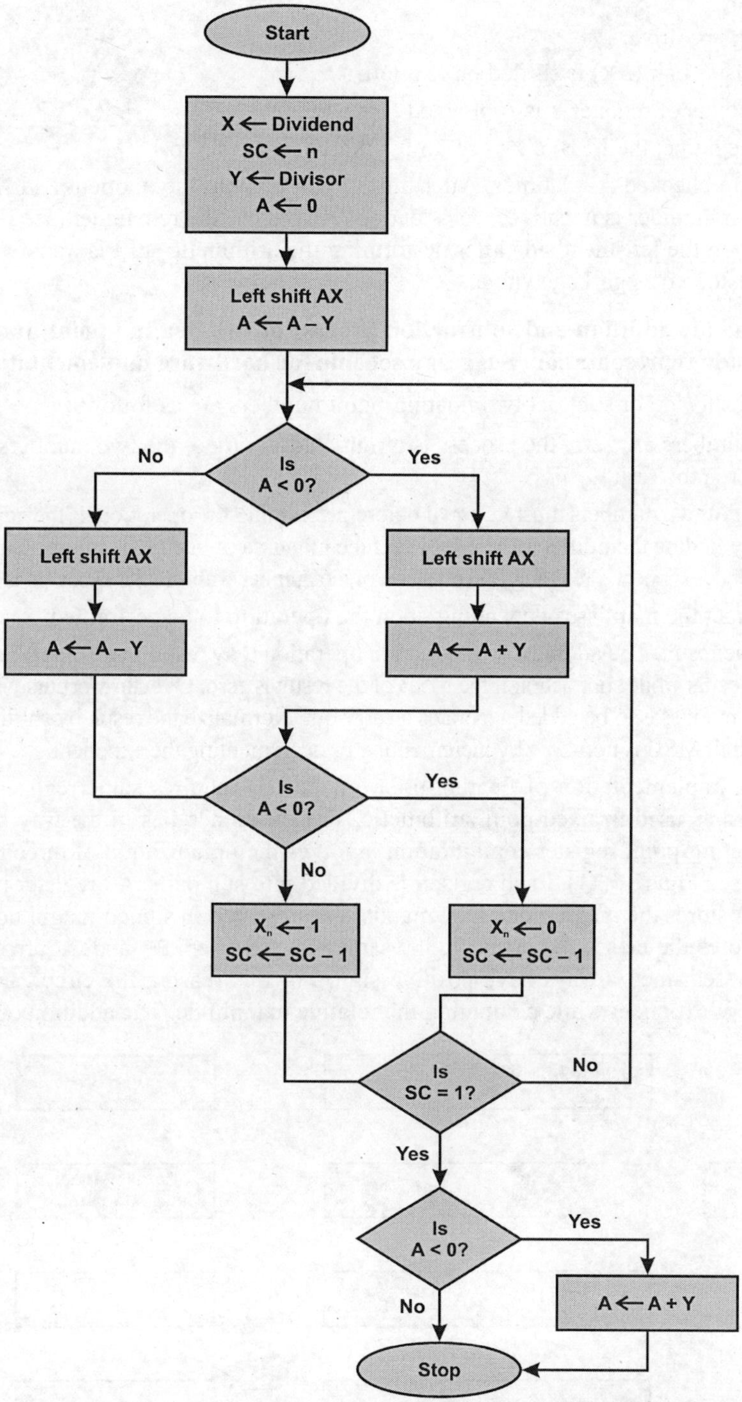

Figure 5.20 Flowchart of Division with Non-restoring Technique

Case 2: When A is positive

The register pair (AX) is shifted one bit left.

The contents of register Y is subtracted form A.

If A is negative, the LSB of X is set to 0; otherwise it is set to 1.

These cases are checked n – 1 times. After this, X will contain the quotient and A will contain the remainder. If the remainder is negative, Y is added to A to restore the remainder (see Figure 5.20). Note that the extra-bit on the left-most side after performing the arithmetic shift is transferred to register E. This value is considered as garbage value.

25. Describe the addition and subtraction process of two floating-point numbers in signed-magnitude representation. Suggest a scheme for hardware implementation.

Ans. The steps to add or subtract two floating-point numbers are as follows:

1. If both the numbers are zero, the process is terminated. If any of the two numbers is zero then, the other number is the result.
2. The exponent of two numbers must be equal before performing the operation. If they are not equal, make them equal by finding their difference and shifting the mantissa of one of the numbers until its exponent is equal to the other exponent. Preferably, the mantissa of the number with smaller exponent is shifted to the right.
3. Add or subtract the mantissas depending upon the operation to be performed.
4. Normalize the result. The addition or subtraction operation may result in an overflow or an underflow. **Underflow** occurs while subtraction if the MSB of the result is zero. **Overflow** occurs while addition if the MSBs of the mantissas to be added generates a carry out. Normalize the result by shifting the mantissa to right or left until MSB is non-zero by incrementing or decrementing the exponent.

The hardware implementation of floating-point operations requires same registers and adders for handling mantissa as used in fixed-point arithmetic. The difference lies in the way the exponents are handled. The floating-point register configuration involves the organization of three registers, namely, AC, BR and QR (see Figure 5.21). Each register is divided into sub parts. AC register is divided into A_s, A and a, where A stores the magnitude of the mantissa represented in signed-magnitude form, A_s stores the sign and a stores the biased exponent. In the same way, registers BR and QR are organized. As the exponents are biased, they always have positive sign. For this reason, the circuit need not take into account the sign of exponent while comparing the relative magnitude. The addition of two mantissas is

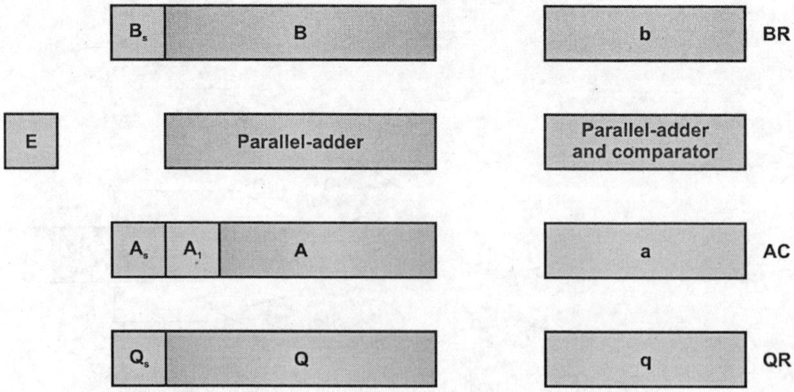

Figure 5.21 Addition and Subtraction of Floating-point Numbers

performed by a parallel-adder and the result is transferred into A. The carry bit (if generated) is transferred to E. A separate parallel adder is used to add the exponents.

26. Perform subtraction with the unsigned binary number by taking 2's complement of the subtrahend 11101101.

Ans. The calculation of 2's complement of 11101101 requires calculating 1's complement and adding 1 to the 1's complement as shown here.

1's complement	00010010
	+ 1
2's complement	00010011
	11101101
	− 00010010
Final answer	11011010

27. Use Booth algorithm to multiply –5 and 2 and also verify your answer.

Ans. Given that –5 is multiplicand and +2 is the multiplier. In signed-2's complement representation, multiplicand and multiplier can be written as 1011 and 0011, respectively. The BR register stores the multiplier and the QR registers stores the multiplicand. The step-by-step execution of Booth algorithm for the multiplication of –5 and +2 is shown in Figure 5.22.

Q_n	Q_{n+1}	BR = 11011 $\overline{BR}$ + 1 = 00101	AC	QR	Q_{n+1}	SC
		Initial	00000	00010	0	5
0	0	ashr	00000	00001	0	4
1	0	Sub BR	00101			
			00101			
0	1	ashr	00010	10000	1	3
		Add BR	11011			
			11101			
		ashr	11110	11000	0	2
0	0	ashr	11111	01100	0	1
0	0	ashr	11111	10110	0	0

Figure 5.22 Multiplication with Booth Algorithm

As SC is 0, the process is completed and the result is stored in AC and QR. The bit Q_{n+1} = 1, indicates that the result in AC and QR is negative and is in 2's complement form. To verify the correctness of answer, we need to take the 2's complement of result, which is 00001010, that is, the binary of 10.

28. Divide 97 by 7 using restoring division algorithm.

Ans. Binary equivalent of 97 = 1100001

Binary equivalent of 7 = 0111

According to restoring division algorithm, the divisor is stored in register Y and double-length dividend is stored in register XQ. For subtraction of Y from X, 2's complement of 0111 (X′+ 1) is required, which is equal to 1001. Therefore, the divisor Y = 1000, Y′ + 1 = 1000 and the dividend XQ = 0110 0001. SC is initialized with the number of bits in the divisor, that is, 4. Figure 5.23 shows the steps of dividing 97 by 7 using the restoring division algorithm.

Operation	E	X	Q	SC
		0110	0001	4
shl EXQ	0	1100	0010	
$E = 0; EX \leftarrow X + \overline{Y} + 1$		1001		
	1	0101		
$E = 1; Q_n \leftarrow 1$			0011	
SC = SC − 1				3
shl EXQ	0	1010	0110	
$E = 0; EX \leftarrow X + \overline{Y} + 1$		1001		
	1	0011		
$E = 1; Q_n \leftarrow 1$			0111	
SC = SC − 1				2
shl EXQ	0	0110	1110	
$E = 0; EX \leftarrow X + \overline{Y} + 1$		1001		
	0	1111		
$E = 0; EX \leftarrow X + Y$		0111		
leave $Q_n = 0$	1	0110		
SC = SC − 1				1
shl EXQ	0	1101	1100	
$E = 0; EX \leftarrow X + \overline{Y} + 1$		1001		
	1	0110		
$E = 1; Q_n \leftarrow 1$			1101	
SC = SC − 1				0

Figure 5.23 Division Using Restoring Division Algorithm

As SC reaches 0, the process is completed with quotient stored in Q (1101) and remainder in X (0110). This can be observed by performing decimal division of 97 by 7, that the quotient is 13 and remainder is 6.

29. Using non-restoring technique, divide 14 by 3.

Ans. Here, the dividend (X) is 14 and divisor (Y) is 3. The 2's complement of divisor is 11101. The steps involved in the division operations are shown in Figure 5.24.

Thus, the quotient is X (0100) and the remainder is A (00010). It can be observed by performing decimal division on 14 by 3, that the quotient is 4 and the remainder is 2.

30. Add two floating-point numbers $1.02541576 \times 10^{15}$ and 3.6541257×10^{12}.

Ans. The mantissa of first number (A) is 1.0254157 and exponent (a) is 15 and the mantissa of second number (B) is 3.6541257 and exponent (b) is 15.

Step 1: Both A and B are non-zero. Thus, proceed to Step 2.

Step 2: Subtract b from a.

$$a - b = 15 - 12 = 3$$

As, B has smaller exponent. Thus, to make a and b equal, shift the mantissa of B three times to the right. After shifting $B = 0.0036541 \times 10^{15}$

Step 3: Add the mantissa.

$$\begin{array}{r} 1.0254157 \\ +\ 0.0036541 \\ \hline 1.0290698 \\ \hline \end{array}$$

A	X	Operation	SC
00000	01110	Divide 14 = 1110 by 3 = 0011. Y register always contains 0011	5
00000	11100	Perform left shift AX	
+ 11101		Subtract Y (add 2's complement of Y)	
11101	11100	A is –ve	
11011	1100	Perform left shift AX	
+ 00011	1100	Add Y	
11110	11000	A is –ve, set quotient bit to 0	
		SC ← SC – 1	4
11101	1000	A is –ve, perform left shift AX	
+ 00011	1000	Add Y	
00000	10001	A is +ve, set quotient bit to 1	
		SC ← SC – 1	3
00001	0001	A is +ve, perform left shift AX	
+ 11101	0001	Subtract Y	
11110	00010	A is –ve, set quotient bit to 0	
		SC ← SC – 1	2
11100	0010	A is –ve, perform left shift AX	
+ 00011	0010	Add Y	
11111	00100	A is –ve, set quotient bit to 0	
		SC ← SC – 1	1
11111	00100	SC = 1, A is –ve	
+ 00011	00100	Restore remainder (Add Y)	
00010	00100		

Figure 5.24 Steps in Division Operation

Step 4: Hence, A + B = 1.0290698×10^{15} whose normalized form is 10.290698×10^{14}.

31. Write down the steps to subtract 110.101101 from 10110.1110.

Ans. The Minuend is 10110.1110 or 101101110×2^{-4} and subtrahend is 110.101101 or 110101101×2^{-6}. Therefore, mantissa of minuend (A) is 101101110 and exponent (a) is –4 and the mantissa of subtrahend (B) is 110101101 and exponent (b) is –6.

Step 1: Both A and B are non-zero. Thus, proceed to Step 2.

Step 2: Subtract b from a.

$a - b = -6 - (-4) = -2$

To make a and b equal, shift the mantissa of B three times to the left and adjust the exponent. After shifting B = 1101011.01×2^{-4}.

Step 3: Subtract the mantissa.

```
  101101110.00
+   1101011.01
  ------------
  100000010.11
```

Step 4: Result = $100000010.11 \times 10^{-4}$

32. Multiply 1.008321×10^{13} and 1.054302×10^{6}.

Ans. Multiplication of two floating-point numbers does not require comparing the exponents and aligning the mantissas. They are multiplied by multiplying their mantissas and adding their exponents.

1.008321×10^{13} and 1.054302×10^{6}
$= (1.008321 \times 1.054302) \times 10^{13+6}$
$= 1.063074 \times 10^{19}$
$= 10.63074 \times 10^{18}$ (normalized).

33. Divide 5.046350×10^{12} by 1.620276×10^{6}.

Ans. The division of two floating-point numbers does not require comparing the exponents and aligning the mantissas. They are divided by dividing their mantissas and subtracting their exponents.

$5.046350 \times 10^{12}/1.620276 \times 10^{6}$

$= (5.046350/1.620276) \times 10^{12-6}$

$= 3.114500 \times 10^{6}$.

MULTIPLE CHOICE QUESTIONS

1. The addition of two signed numbers, represented in 2's complement form generates an overflow if______________, where A and B denote the last two carries.
   (a) $A.B = 0$ (b) $A \oplus B = 1$
   (c) $A \oplus B = 0$ (d) $A + B = 1$
2. Which adder comprises of two right shift registers, a full adder and a flip-flop?
   (a) Parallel adder (b) Serial adder
   (c) Full adder (d) Half adder
3. A ripple carry adder requires time in the order of ____________.
   (a) Linear time (O(N)) (b) (O(Log(N)))
   (c) Constant (d) (O(N Log(N)))
4. If both of the inputs in CLA are 0, the carry is ____________.
   (a) Generated in current bit position (b) Generated from a least significant bit
   (c) Not generated (d) None of these
5. Why is Booth algorithm used for computer arithmetic?
   (a) Multiplication of numbers in signed magnitude form
   (b) Division of numbers in signed magnitude form
   (c) Division of numbers in 2's complement form
   (d) Multiplication of numbers in signed-2's complement form
6. In multiplication of two numbers using Booth algorithm, no arithmetic operation is performed when the LSBs are ______________.
   (a) 00 and 10 (b) 10 and 01
   (c) 11 and 01 (d) 00 and 11

7. How many numbers of adders are required for multiplying (j and k) using array multiplier?

   (a) (j – 1) × k
   (b) j – 1
   (c) j + 1
   (d) 0

8. What would be the result in a restoring division algorithm, if 1 is fixed as low-order bit of a dividend?

   (a) Positive
   (b) Same as the initial one
   (c) Negative
   (d) Double the divisor

9. In non-restoring division algorithm, what is the partial remainder when contents of divisor are subtracted?

   (a) Negative
   (b) Positive
   (c) Equals to 0
   (d) Equals to 1

10. Floating point multiplication can be performed by __________ two mantissas and __________ two exponents.

    (a) Multiplying, multiplying
    (b) Adding, multiplying
    (c) Multiplying, adding
    (d) Multiplying, subtracting

Ans. 1. b 2. b 3. a 4. c 5. d 6. d 7. a 8. a 9. b 10. c

6

Register Transfer Logic

1. What do you understand by microoperation? List various types of microoperations.

Ans. The elementary operations performed on the data stored in one or more CPU registers are known as **microoperations**. For example, count, clear, shift and load are some of the microoperations. The output of a microoperation may be stored in the same register that contained the data, replacing its existing content or may be transferred to some other register.

The microoperations that are most commonly used in digital computers belong to one of the following categories:

- **Register transfer microoperations:** This category includes microoperations that are used for transferring the binary information between the registers.
- **Arithmetic microoperations:** This category includes microoperations that are used for performing arithmetic operations such as add, subtract, increment, decrement and complement on the numeric data stored in the registers.
- **Logic microoperations:** This category includes microoperations that are used for performing logical operations (bit-level manipulation) such as AND, OR and NOT on the non-numeric data stored in the registers.
- **Shift microoperations:** This category includes microoperations that are used for performing shift operations such as logical shift, arithmetic shift and circular shift on the data stored in registers. The bits are shifted either to the left or to the right.

2. What is register transfer language? Explain how registers and register transfers are represented in register transfer language. Also, discuss the hardware implementation for register transfers.

Ans. The internal hardware organization of a digital computer can be precisely described by the set of registers along with their functions, the sequence of microoperations performed on the binary information stored in registers and the control originating the sequence of microoperations. **Register transfer language** (**RTL**) is a system used to specify the sequence of microoperations among the registers in a symbolic form. Here, the term **register transfer** refers to the transfer of binary information between the registers via a common bus. It implies the involvement of hardware logic circuit that executes the microoperations and transfers the result of a microoperation to the same or another register.

Representation of registers: The registers in a digital computer are represented using capital letters (sometimes followed by a numeral) that indicate the function of the register. For example, the program counter register is denoted as `PC` and R_1, R_2, etc., are used for designating processor registers. Each register is represented by a rectangular box containing the name of the register within itself as shown in Figure 6.1(a). The individual bits in the register can also be represented as shown in Figure 6.1(b) with each bit assigned a letter along with a subscript that indicates the bit position. In case of a 16-bit register, the bit numbers can be marked at the top of the box starting from left to right [see Figure 6.1 (c)]. The bits numbered through 0 to 7 are termed as low byte (denoted as `L`) of the register, while the bits numbered through 8 to 15 are termed as high byte (denoted as `H`) of the register as shown in Figure 6.1(d).

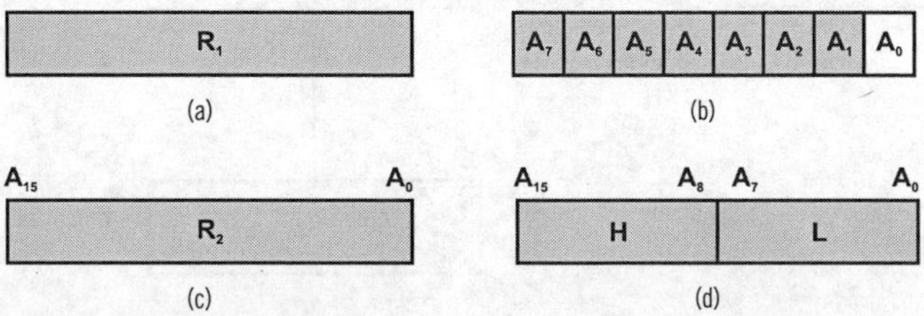

Figure 6.1 Block Diagram of Register

Representation of register transfers: In RTL, the register transfer is indicated with the help of a replacement operator (←) connecting the source and destination registers. For example, the transfer of contents from the register R_1 to the register R_4 can be denoted using the following statement.

$$R_4 \leftarrow R_1$$

On executing this statement, the previous contents of R_4 will be replaced with that of R_1; however, the contents of R_1 will remain intact.

Generally, the register transfer takes place only when certain control condition satisfies. This can be expressed using the *if-then* statement as shown below:

$$\text{if}(P = 1) \text{ then } (R_4 \leftarrow R_1)$$

Here, `P` denotes the control signal generated by the control unit. It is often convenient to distinguish the control condition from the register transfer operation. For this, a **control function**—a Boolean variable equal to 0 or 1—is specified in the register transfer statement as shown here.

$$P: R_4 \leftarrow R_1$$

In this statement, the colon (:) indicates the termination of control condition.

In addition to letters along with numerals (for symbolizing registers), replacement operator (for symbolizing register transfers) and colon (for symbolizing termination of control function), some other symbols are also used in RTL for register transfers. These symbols along with their description and examples are listed in Table 6.1.

Table 6.1 Symbols used for Register Transfers

Symbol	Description	Example
Parentheses ( )	To indicate a portion of the register.	`PC(8-14), PC(H)`
Comma (,)	To separate two or more microoperations that execute simultaneously.	R1 ← R2, R3 ← R2
Subscript	To denote an individual bit of register.	`A2, B7`

Hardware Implementation: Every register transfer statement needs hardware to implement the transfer. Figure 6.2 shows the block diagram for the hardware implementing $P: R_4 \leftarrow R_1$ register transfer statement. In Figure 6.2, the letter n is used to indicate the number of bits in the register. The n outputs of the register R_1 are connected to n inputs of register R_4. In addition, R_4 has a Load input which is directed by the control function P. At the time P activates the Load input, the contents of R_1 are loaded into R_4. Both the control function P and register R_4 are synchronized with the same clock.

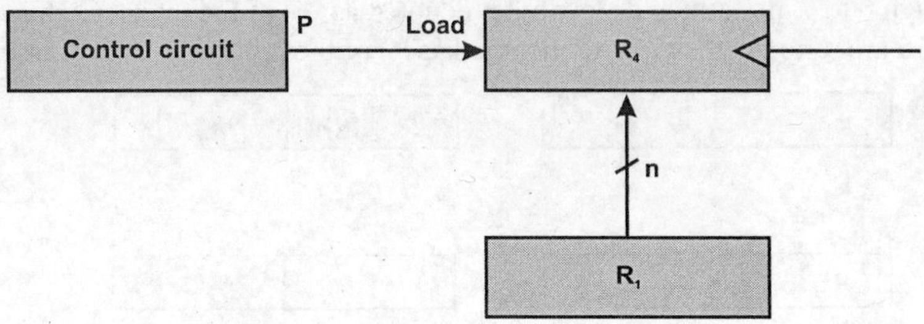

Figure 6.2 Hardware Implementation of $P: R_4 \leftarrow R_1$

3. What is the need of a common bus system? Draw and explain the diagram of bus system constructed using multiplexers.

Ans. A digital computer consists of a number of CPU registers and it is often required to transfer information from one register to another. This necessitates for the data paths through which register transfers could take place. If every register is connected to the other registers via a separate path, the required number of wires will increase significantly. Hence, a common bus system is used for the transfer of information among registers. The **bus system** consists a set of common lines one per each bit of a register through which register transfers take place, one at a time. The register whose information is to be placed onto the bus during a specific register transfer is determined with the help of the control signals generated in the control section. The transfer of information through the common bus is referred to as the **bus transfer**.

A simple means to construct a common bus system is with multiplexers. The role of multiplexers is to select one of the registers whose information is to be put onto the bus (that is, to determine the source register). In general, if we have m registers of n bits each, we need n multiplexers each of size $m \times 1$ to construct an n-line common bus. Each multiplexer multiplexes m data lines (one from each register), forming a line of the bus. Figure 6.3 shows a 4-line common bus system for four registers (R_0, R_1, R_2 and R_3) constructed using four 4×1 multiplexers. Each multiplexer has four data inputs (labelled as 0, 1, 2 and 3), one per each register and two selection inputs (S_0 and S_1). The outputs from each register are connected to the inputs of the multiplexers in such a way that the output 0 of all registers are input to MUX 0, the output 1 of all registers are input to MUX 1 and so on. Notice that all connections are not shown in Figure 6.3 to avoid the complexity; instead the connections have been labelled to indicate the connectivity. The output from each multiplexer forms one line of the 4-line common bus.

Depending on the selection inputs, the four bits of a register are selected and placed onto the common bus. For example, when $S_0 = 0$ and $S_1 = 1$, the input bit 2 of each multiplexer is selected (that is, bits of register R_3) and applied to the outputs forming the bus. Thus, the contents of register R_3 are transferred to the common bus. Figure 6.4 depicts the function table that lists the register selected by the bus for each possible combination of binary values of S_0 and S_1.

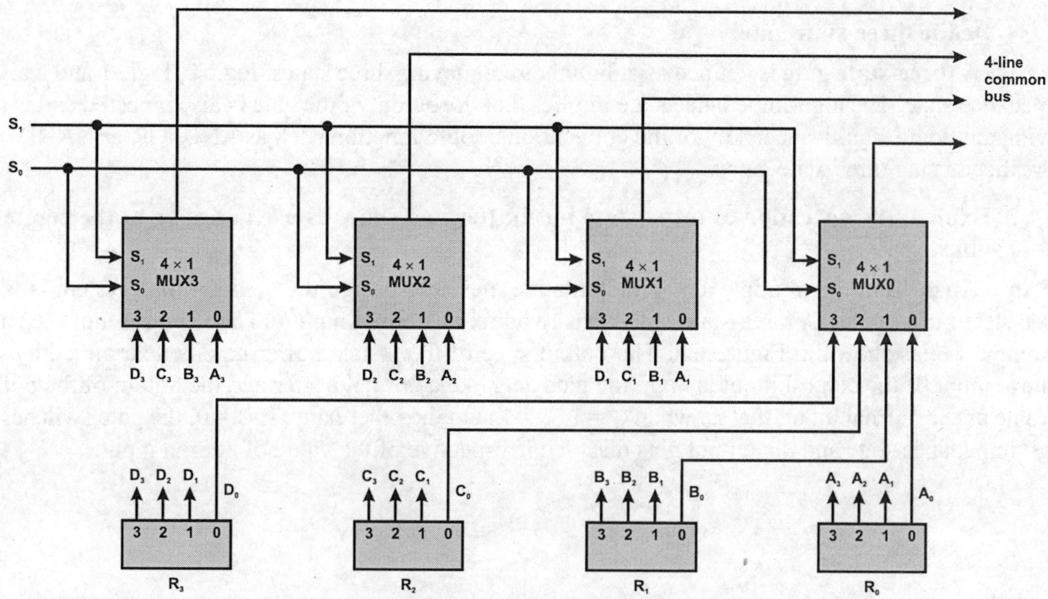

Figure 6.3 A Common Bus System for Four Registers using Multiplexers

Selection inputs		Register selected
S_0	S_1	
0	0	R_0
0	1	R_1
1	0	R_2
1	1	R_3

Figure 6.4 Function Table for Bus

After the information has been placed onto the bus, it needs to be loaded into the desired destination register. To choose one destination from several available registers, the bus lines are connected to the inputs of all destination registers and the load control input of the desired destination register is activated. For example, if we have to transfer information from register R_1 to R_3 via the common bus, first the contents of R_1 are placed onto the bus, and then the contents of the bus are loaded into R_3 by activating its load control input.

The register transfer through the bus can also be represented in symbolic form where the presence of bus may be mentioned or implied in the statement. For example, the bus transfer from register R_1 to R_3 can be symbolized as shown here.

$BUS \leftarrow R_1,\ R_3 \leftarrow BUS$

or

$R_3 \leftarrow R_1$ in case the existence of bus in the system is known.

4. Define three-state gate.

Ans. A **three-state gate** is defined as a digital circuit having three states: logic 0, logic 1 and a high-impedance state. The high-impedance state implies that the output of the gate is disconnected and is not having any logic significance. Any of the conventional logic function such as AND, OR or NAND can be realized using three-state gates.

5. Explain the operation of three-state bus buffer and show its use in design of the common bus.

Ans. Apart from the multiplexers, an alternative means to design the common bus system is with three-state buffer gates. A three-state buffer has two inputs: normal input (`I`) and control input (`C`) and an output (`Y`) as shown in Figure 6.5. The output state of three-state buffer gate is determined by the control input. If the control input is high, the gate acts like a normal buffer and the output of the buffer is same as the normal input, that is, when `C` = 1, `Y` = `I`. On the other hand, if `C` = 0, the gate switches to high-impedance state and the output gets disabled irrespective of the value of normal input.

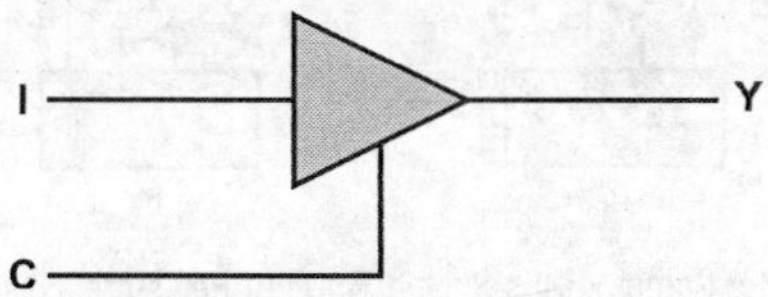

Figure 6.5 Logic Symbol for Three-state Buffer

The high-impedance state of a three-state buffer provides a feature that enables to connect the outputs of a vast number of three-state buffer gates with wires, thus forming a line of the common bus. For example, Figure 6.6 illustrates the construction of a single line of the common bus for four registers

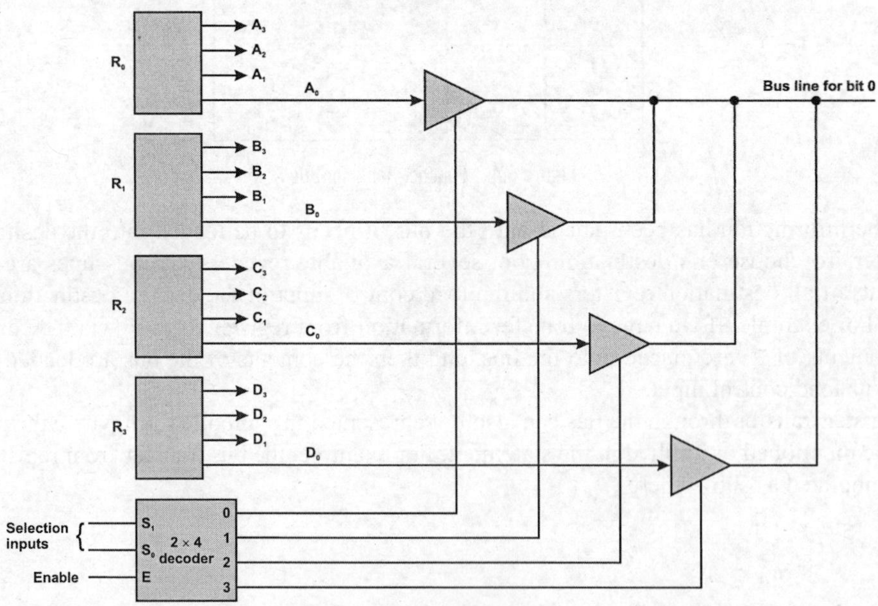

Figure 6.6 Construction of a Single Bus-line using Three-state Buffers

(R_0, R_1, R_2 and R_3) of four bits each using four three-state buffers. One significant bit (the input bit 0 in our case) from each of the four registers form the normal input to a three-state buffer. The outputs of all the four buffers are connected to form one line of the common bus. A 2 × 4 decoder has been used, whose outputs form the control input of the buffers. The decoder enables to select one of the four registers at a specific time, and it ensures that only one buffer will be in active state at a time. Which of the four buffers will be active at a particular time is determined by the enable input (E) of the decoder.

When E = 0, all the four outputs of the decoder are 0's, making all the control inputs 0's. As a result, all the four buffers get disabled and the bus line goes to high-impedance state. On the other hand, if E = 1, one of the four outputs of the decoder is 1 depending on the binary value of selection variables S_0 and S_1. As a result, only one of the four buffers is active and the corresponding normal input communicates with the bus line. Notice that if each of the four registers is of n bits, we need n circuits similar to one shown in Figure 6.6 to construct a common bus using three-state buffers. The common output from each of the n circuits forms one of the n lines of common bus. However, only one decoder is sufficient for choosing among the four registers.

6. How the memory transfer operations are represented in RTL?

Ans. When the information is transferred from a memory word to external environment, it is referred to as a **memory read** operation. On the other hand, when some new information is stored in the memory, it is referred to as **memory write** operation. In RTL, the memory word is generally symbolized with the letter M followed by the square brackets [] that enclose the address of the memory word.

To understand how memory transfers are symbolized in RTL, suppose we have to transfer data from a memory word M whose address is stored in address register (denoted as AR) to the data register (denoted as DR). This memory read operation can be symbolized as:

Read: $DR \leftarrow M[AR]$

Now, suppose we have to transfer data from the register R_1 to the memory word M whose address is stored in address register (denoted as AR). This memory write operation can be symbolized as:

Write: $M[AR] \leftarrow R_1$

7. Describe various arithmetic microoperations.

Ans. The basic set of arithmetic microoperations includes add, subtract, increment and decrement. These operations are described as follows:

- **Add:** This microoperation is used to add the contents of two registers and store the sum in either one of the source registers or in a third register. For example, suppose we have to add the contents of registers R_1 and R_2 and transfer the result into register R_3. This microoperation can be symbolized as:

  $R_3 \leftarrow R_1 + R_2$

  The hardware implementation of the above microoperation requires three registers and a parallel binary adder circuit that performs the addition operation.

- **Subtract:** This microoperation is used to subtract the contents of one register from another and store the result in either one of the source registers or in a third register. The subtraction operation is implemented through complement and addition operation. For example, suppose we have to subtract the contents of register R_2 from register R_1 and transfer the result into register R_3. To implement this microoperation, first we take the 1's complement of the contents of R_2, add one to it and then add it to the contents of R_1. In other words, the 2's complement of the contents of R_2 is added to the contents of R_1. This microoperation can be symbolized as:

$$R_3 \leftarrow R_1 + \overline{R}_2 + 1 \qquad \text{[Equivalent to } R_3 \leftarrow R_1 - R_2\text{]}$$

The hardware implementation of the above microoperation requires three registers, an inverter and a parallel binary adder circuit.

- **Increment:** This microoperation is used to increase the contents of a register by one. For example, the microoperation to increment the contents of register R_1 can be symbolized as:

$$R_1 \leftarrow R_1 + 1$$

This microoperation can be implemented using a combinational circuit or a binary up-down counter.

- **Decrement:** This microoperation is used to decrease the contents of a register by one. For example, the microoperation to decrement the contents of register R_1 can be symbolized as:

$$R_1 \leftarrow R_1 - 1$$

This microoperation can also be implemented using a combinational circuit or a binary up–down counter.

8. What is binary adder?

Ans. A **binary adder** refers to a digital circuit that performs the arithmetic sum of two binary numbers of any length. It can be constructed by connecting the full adder circuits in a cascade manner where the output carry from one full adder is given to the input carry of next full adder. The construction of an n-bit binary adder is similar to an n-bit parallel adder discussed in Chapter 5.

9. Design the arithmetic circuit of a processor. Give the function table also.

or

Explain the hardware implementation of arithmetic circuit.

Ans. All the basic arithmetic microoperations such as add, subtract, increment and decrement can be implemented with the help of a single arithmetic circuit. One of the basic components of such an arithmetic circuit is the parallel adder that results in different arithmetic operations depending on its data inputs. The circuit also employs multiplexers to choose among different operations.

Figure 6.7 depicts a 4-bit arithmetic circuit that comprises a 4-bit parallel adder (made up from four full adders) and four 4 × 1 multiplexers with four data inputs (I_0 to I_3) and two selection inputs S_0 and S_1. The circuit has two 4-bit inputs A and B and one 4-bit output D. The four bits of input A form the x inputs and the outputs from the multiplexers form the y inputs of the parallel adder. The input carry (C_{in}) is connected to the carry input of the full adder in least significant position, that is, to C_0. The carry output from this full adder (which is C_1) becomes the carry input of the full adder in the next higher significant position and so on. The four bits of input B and their complements form the input I_0 and I_1 of the multiplexers, respectively. The inputs I_2 and I_3 of the multiplexers are connected to logic 0 and logic 1, respectively. The output from the multiplexers depends on the selection inputs S_0 and S_1.

The output of the arithmetic circuit shown in Figure 6.7 is calculated from the following arithmetic sum.

$$D = A + y + C_{in}$$

where A is the 4-bit number forming the x inputs of the adder, y is 4-bit number (the outputs from the multiplexers) at the y inputs of the adder and C_{in} (either 0 or 1) is the carry input.

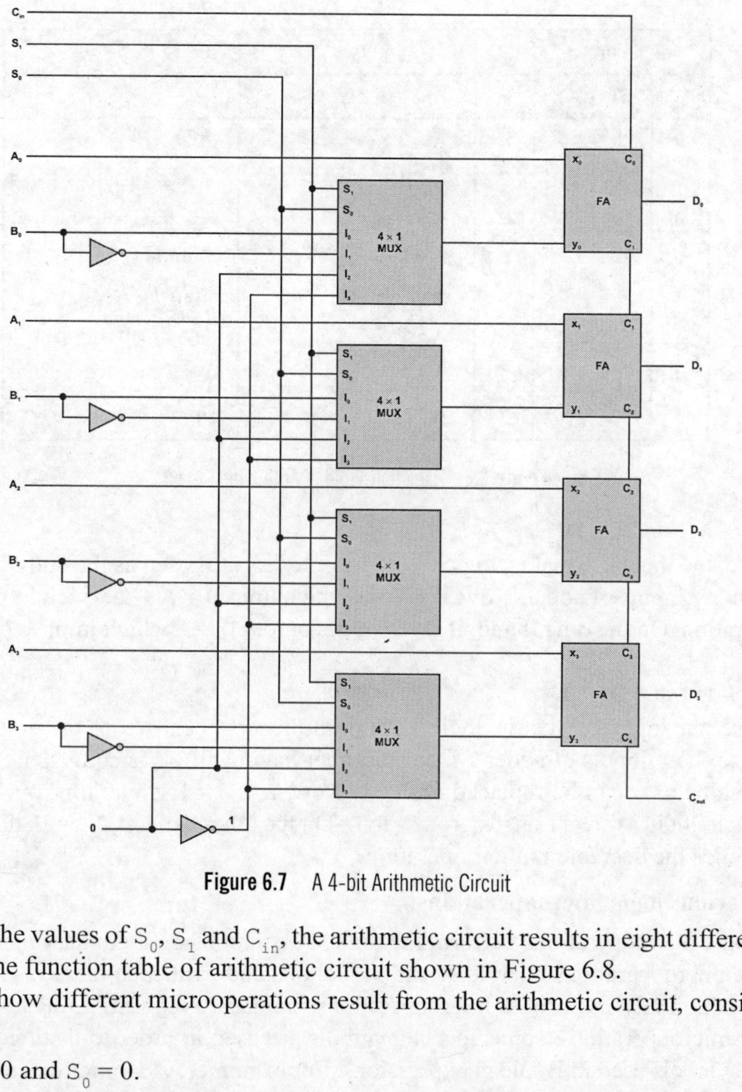

Figure 6.7 A 4-bit Arithmetic Circuit

Depending on the values of S_0, S_1 and C_{in}, the arithmetic circuit results in eight different microoperations as listed in the function table of arithmetic circuit shown in Figure 6.8.

To understand how different microoperations result from the arithmetic circuit, consider the following cases.

- **Case I:** $S_1 = 0$ and $S_0 = 0$.

  In this case, the input I_0 (that is, bits of B) of multiplexers is chosen as the output and as a result, the value of B goes to the y inputs of adder, that is, $y = B$. Now, if $C_{in} = 1$, the output $D = A + B + 1$ and if $C_{in} = 0$, the output $D = A + B$. Thus, in both cases, the arithmetic circuit results in add microoperation.

- **Case II:** $S_1 = 0$ and $S_0 = 1$.

  In this case, the input I_1 (that is, complement of bits of B) of multiplexers is chosen as the output and as a result, the value of $\overline{B}$ goes to the y inputs of adder, that is, $y = \overline{B}$. Now, if $C_{in} = 1$, the output $D = A + \overline{B} + 1$ which is equivalent to $A - B$. On the other hand, if $C_{in} = 0$, the output $D = A + \overline{B}$ which is equivalent to $A - B - 1$. Thus, in both cases, the arithmetic circuit results in subtract microoperation.

Inputs				Outputs	Microoperation
S_1	S_0	C_{in}	y	$D = A + y + C_{in}$	
0	0	0	B	A + B	Add
0	0	1	B	A + B + 1	Add with carry
0	1	0	$\bar{B}$	$A + \bar{B}$ or A – B – 1	Subtract with borrow
0	1	1	$\bar{B}$	$A + \bar{B} + 1$ or A – B	Subtract
1	0	0	0	A	Transfer A
1	0	1	0	A + 1	Increment A
1	1	0	1	A – 1	Decrement A
1	1	1	1	A	Transfer A

Figure 6.8 Function Table of Arithmetic Circuit

- **Case III:** $S_1 = 1$ and $S_0 = 0$.
  In this case, the input I_2 (that is, logic 0) of multiplexers is chosen as the output and as a result, all 0's go to the y inputs of adder. Now, if $C_{in} = 1$, the output $D = A + 1$ which implies the increment microoperation. On the other hand, if $C_{in} = 0$, the output $D = A$ which implies direct transfer from A to D.
- **Case IV:** $S_1 = 1$ and $S_0 = 1$.
  In this case, the input I_3 (that is, logic 1) of multiplexers is chosen as the output and as a result, all 1's go to the y inputs of adder. Since a number having all 1's is equivalent to 2's complement of 1, the value of y can be replaced with −1. Now, if $C_{in} = 1$, the output $D = A - 1 + 1$, that is, $D = A$ which implies direct transfer from A to D. On the other hand, if $C_{in} = 0$, the output $D = A - 1$ which implies the decrement microoperation.

10. List various logic microoperations.

Ans. The logic microoperations perform the logical operations on the binary numbers stored in the registers. These microoperations operate on individual bits and treat each bit as a separate binary variable. The four commonly used logic microoperations include AND, OR, XOR and complement. To represent these microoperations, some special symbols are used in order to distinguish them from the corresponding symbols used in Boolean expressions. For example, AND microoperation is represented with $\wedge$ symbol, OR with $\vee$ and complement with ¯ (bar) symbol.

Let R_1 and R_2 be two registers containing binary numbers, and A and B designate their bits, respectively. When a logic microoperation is performed on R_1 and R_2, A and B are treated as separate binary variables. In general, there are 16 possible logic microoperations that can be performed with two binary variables A and B. Figure 6.9 shows the truth table for the 16 microoperations of A and B which designate the bits of the numbers stored in registers R_1 and R_2, respectively. Each column except the first two in the truth table represents one of the 16 possible Boolean functions of variables A and B.

Table 6.2 lists the 16 possible logic microoperations derived from the 16 Boolean functions (F_0 to F_{15}). The first column of the table shows the simplified Boolean functions expressed in algebraic form as a function of variables A and B. The second column shows the corresponding microoperation that is obtained on replacing variable A with contents of register R_1 and B with contents of register R_2. The last column describes the microoperations.

A	B	F_0	F_1	F_2	F_3	F_4	F_5	F_6	F_7	F_8	F_9	F_{10}	F_{11}	F_{12}	F_{13}	F_{14}	F_{15}
0	0	0	0	0	0	0	0	0	0	1	1	1	1	1	1	1	1
0	1	0	0	0	0	1	1	1	1	0	0	0	0	1	1	1	1
1	0	0	0	1	1	0	0	1	1	0	0	1	1	0	0	1	1
1	1	0	1	0	1	0	1	0	1	0	1	0	1	0	1	0	1

Figure 6.9 Truth Table for 16 Boolean Functions of two Variables

Table 6.2 Sixteen Logic Microoperations

Boolean Function	Logic Microoperation	Description
$F_0 = 0$	$F \leftarrow 0$	Clear
$F_1 = AB$	$F_1 \leftarrow R_1 \wedge R_2$	AND
$F_2 = AB'$	$F_2 \leftarrow R_1 \wedge \bar{R}_2$	
$F_3 = A$	$F \leftarrow R_1$	Transfer contents of R_1
$F_4 = A'B$	$F \leftarrow \bar{R}_1 \wedge R_2$	
$F_5 = B$	$F \leftarrow R_2$	Transfer contents of R_2
$F_6 = A \oplus B$	$F \leftarrow R_1 \oplus R_2$	Exclusive-OR
$F_7 = A + B$	$F \leftarrow R_1 \vee R_2$	OR
$F_8 = (A + B)'$	$F \leftarrow \overline{R_1 \vee R_2}$	NOR
$F_9 = (A \oplus B)'$	$F \leftarrow \overline{R_1 \oplus R_2}$	Exclusive-NOR
$F_{10} = B'$	$F \leftarrow \bar{R}_2$	Complement R_2
$F_{11} = A + B'$	$F \leftarrow R_1 \vee \bar{R}_2$	
$F_{12} = A'$	$F \leftarrow \bar{R}_1$	Complement R_1
$F_{13} = A' + B$	$F \leftarrow \bar{R}_1 \vee R_2$	
$F_{14} = (AB)'$	$F \leftarrow \overline{R_1 \wedge R_2}$	NAND
$F_{15} = 1$	$F \leftarrow$ all 1's	Set to all 1's

11. Design the logic circuit of a processor. Give the function table also.

or

Discuss the hardware implementation of logic microoperations.

Ans. As the logic microoperations operate at bit-level, their hardware implementation demands for inserting logic gates for every bit or pair of bits in the registers so that the desired logic function could be performed. Though there are 16 logic microoperations in total, generally only four microoperations including AND, OR, XOR and complement are used and the rest operations can be derived from them.

Figure 6.10 depicts the hardware implementation for four common logic microoperations. It consists of a 4 × 1 multiplexer with four data inputs (I_0 to I_3) and two selection inputs (S_0 and S_1). Four logic gates are also employed to perform one of the four logic operations. Each gate (except the NOT gate)

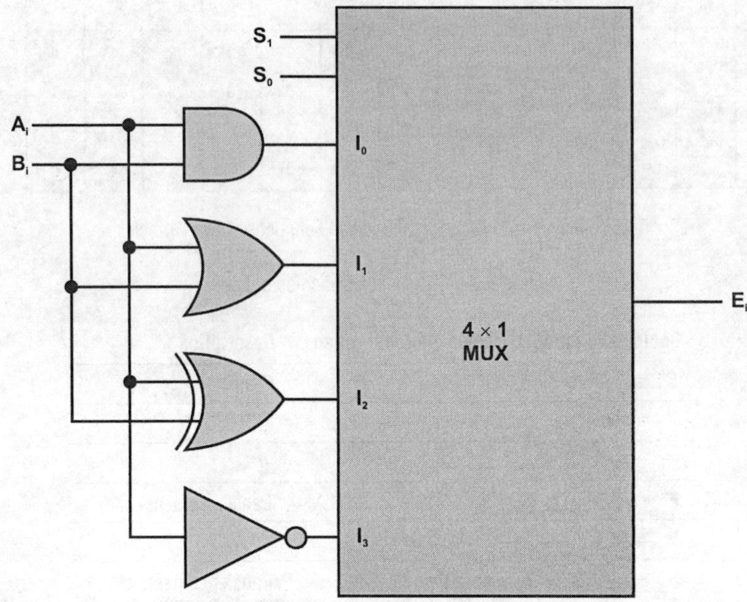

Figure 6.10 A Single Stage of Logic Circuit

has two inputs (say, A_i and B_i that designate the ith bits of two registers storing the binary numbers). The NOT gate has only one input A_i. The output from each gate is connected to one of the data inputs of the multiplexer.

The selection inputs S_0 and S_1 enable to choose one among the four data inputs of the multiplexer and direct it as output E_i, resulting in one of four logic microoperations as shown in the function table depicted in Figure 6.11.

Selection inputs		Output	Microoperation
S_1	S_0	E	
0	0	$A \wedge B$	AND
0	1	$A \vee B$	OR
1	0	$A \oplus B$	XOR
1	1	$\bar{A}$	Complement

Figure 6.11 Function Table

Notice that for simplicity, we have shown only one stage of logic circuit for two bits designated as A_i and B_i. In case of n bits, the logic circuit will comprise n such stages and the same selection variables (that is S_0 and S_1) will be input to the multiplexer in each stage.

12. Discuss some applications of logic microoperations.

Ans. The logic microoperations can be used to set the selected bits to 1's, clear the selected bits to 0's, delete a group of bits, insert new bits, etc. Following are the some common applications of logic microoperations. To understand these applications, consider R_1 as a processor register, register R_2 stores a logic operand retrieved from the memory and the result of the operation is to be stored in R_1 itself.

- **Selective-set:** This operation sets those bits in R_1 to 1 where there are corresponding 1's in R_2. The bit positions in R_2 having a 0 are not considered. For example, if R_1 = 1100 and R_2 = 0110 before operation, then the contents of R_1 after the selective-set operation will be 1110. This implies the OR logic microoperation of previous value of R_1 and bits in R_2 which can be symbolized as: $R_1 \leftarrow R_1 \vee R_2$.
- **Selective-clear:** This operation clears those bits in R_1 to 0 where there are corresponding 1's in R_2. For example, if R_1 = 1100 and R_2 = 0110 before operation, then the contents of R_1 after the selective-clear operation will be 1000. This implies the AND logic microoperation of previous value of R_1 and complement of bits in R_2 which can be symbolized as: $R_1 \leftarrow R_1 \wedge \overline{R}_2$.
- **Selective-complement:** This operation complements those bits in R_1 where there are corresponding 1's in R_2. For example, if R_1 = 1100 and R_2 = 0110 before operation, then the contents of R_1 after the selective-complement operation will be 1010. This implies the XOR logic microoperation of previous value of R_1 and bits in R_2 which can be symbolized as:$R_1 \leftarrow R_1 \oplus R_2$.
- **Mask:** This operation clears those bits in R_1 to 0 where there are corresponding 0's in R_2. For example, if R_1 = 1100 and R_2 = 0110 before operation, then the contents of R_1 after the mask operation will be 0100. This implies the AND logic microoperation of previous value of R_1 and bits in R_2 which can be symbolized as: $R_1 \leftarrow R_1 \wedge R_2$.
- **Insert:** This operation inserts new values in a group of bits in a register. To perform this, first the unwanted bits of the register are masked and then, ORed with the desired value. For example, suppose R_1 = 1100 0110 and we want to insert a value 1100 in the rightmost four bits of R_1. For this, first we mask the four rightmost bits of R_1 by ANDing its contents with value 1111 0000. After the mask operation, we get R_1 = 1100 0000. Now, the contents of R_1 are ORed with the desired value (that is, 0000 1100), after which we get R_1 = 1100 1100.
- **Clear:** This operation compares the contents of register R_1 with that of R_2 and results in all 0's if the contents of both are same. For example, if R_1 = 1100 and R_2 = 1100 before operation, then the contents of R_1 after the clear operation will be 0000. This implies the XOR logic microoperation of previous value of R_1 and bits in R_2 which can be symbolized as: $R_1 \leftarrow R_1 \oplus R_2$. Thus, the XOR operation can be used to determine whether the two binary numbers are equal.

13. What are shift microoperations? Explain their hardware implementation also.

Ans. The shift microoperations move the bits of the binary word stored in the register to the left or right. They are used for serial transfer of data. When shifting takes place in left direction, the serial input transfers a bit into the rightmost position. On the other hand, when shifting takes place in right direction, the serial input transfers a bit into the leftmost position. There are three types of shifts: *logical*, *arithmetic* and *circular* shifts. All these types are discussed here.

- **Logical shift:** This microoperation moves the bits to the right or left and transfers 0's through the serial input. In logical shift-left operation, the bits are shifted to the left and a 0 is inserted at the rightmost bit position. In logical shift-right operation, the bits are shifted to the right and a 0 is inserted at the leftmost bit position. These microoperations can be symbolized as:

  $R_1 \leftarrow \text{shl } R_1$ [1-bit shift-left the contents of R_1]

  $R_1 \leftarrow \text{shr } R_1$ [1-bit shift-right the contents of R_1]

- **Arithmetic shift:** This microoperation shifts a signed binary number to the left or right, leaving the sign bit unchanged. The leftmost position in the number represents the sign bit, while the rest bits represent the magnitude. The sign bit is 0 for positive numbers and 1 for negative numbers. The negative numbers are represented in 2's complement form. To understand how arithmetic operations are performed, let us assume that b_0, b_1,..., b_{n-2}, b_{n-1} denote bits of an n-bit signed binary number. The bit b_{n-1} denotes the sign bit of the number, b_{n-2} denotes the most significant bit (MSB) and b_0 denotes the least significant bit (LSB).

In arithmetic shift-right operation, the sign bit remains unchanged; all the bits including the sign bit are shifted to the right, losing the rightmost bit. That is, bit b_{n-1} remains as it is, b_{n-2} is replaced with b_{n-1}, b_{n-3} is replaced with b_{n-2} and so on and eventually, the bit b_0 is lost. On the other hand, during arithmetic shift-left operation, a 0 is inserted into bit b_0 and all other bits are shifted to the left. The original value of bit b_{n-1} is lost and replaced with b_{n-2}, b_{n-2} is replaced with b_{n-3} and so on. If after the shift, the value of b_{n-1} changes, a sign reversal occurs. This happens because of the overflow that occurs after shift, if before the shifting operation, $b_{n-1} \neq b_{n-2}$. We can check whether or not the arithmetic left-shift operation will cause an overflow by determining the XOR of bit b_{n-1} with b_{n-2}. If it results in 1, an overflow occurs; otherwise, there is no overflow. The arithmetic shift microoperations can be symbolized as:

$R_1 \leftarrow \texttt{ashl}\ R_1$ [1-bit arithmetic shift-left the contents of R_1]

$R_1 \leftarrow \texttt{ashr}\ R_1$ [1-bit arithmetic shift-right the contents of R_1]

- **Circular shift:** This microoperation causes a circular shift. The bits shifted out at one end are circulated back to the other end and thus, no information is lost. To accomplish circular shift, the serial output from the shift register is connected back to the serial input. The circular left and circular right shift can be symbolized as:

$R_1 \leftarrow \texttt{cil}\ R_1$ [1-bit circular shift-left the contents of R_1]

$R_1 \leftarrow \texttt{cir}\ R_1$ [1-bit circular shift-right the contents of R_1]

Hardware implementation

The shift microoperations can be implemented with the help of a combinational circuit shifter. Figure 6.12 shows a 4-bit combinational circuit shifter, which consists of four 2 × 1 multiplexers having two data inputs and one selection input (S). The shifter has four data inputs (I_0, I_1, I_2 and I_3) and four

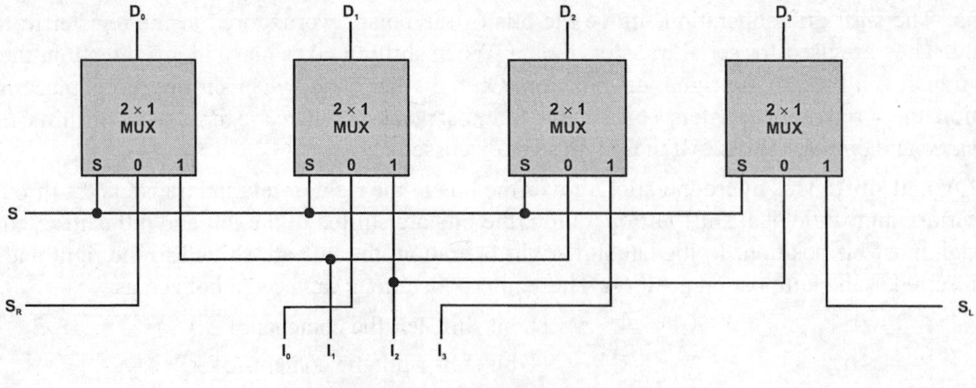

Figure 6.12 A 4-bit Combinational Shifter

outputs (D_0, D_1, D_2 and D_3). In addition, it has two serial inputs: S_L indicating left-shift and S_R indicating right-shift.

The selection input S of the multiplexers determines whether the data should be shifted to left or right. When S = 0, the input S_R is active and thus, data are shifted to the right. On the other hand, when S = 1, the input S_L is active and thus, data are shifted to the left. Which input goes to each output after the shift is demonstrated in the function table shown in Figure 6.13.

Selection input	Outputs			
S	D_0	D_1	D_2	D_3
0	S_R	I_0	I_1	I_2
1	I_1	I_2	I_3	S_L

Figure 6.13 Function Table for 4-bit Shifter

14. Explain the hardware implementation of arithmetic logic shift unit.

Ans. The arithmetic and logic circuits required to perform arithmetic and logic microoperations can be combined to form a common operational unit called **arithmetic logic unit (ALU)**. Whenever a microoperation is to be performed, the contents of registers are input to the common ALU, which then performs the desired microoperation and transfers the result to the destination register. Generally, the shift microoperations are performed in a different unit; however, sometimes the shift circuit also forms a part of ALU.

The arithmetic, logic and shift circuits can be combined into one ALU with common selection variables. Figure 6.14 depicts one typical stage (designated by i) of arithmetic logic shift unit. It comprises one stage of arithmetic circuit (shown in Figure 6.7) and one stage of logic circuit (shown in Figure 6.10) with common selection inputs S_0 and S_1 that select a specific microoperation. The arithmetic, logic and shift operations are to be performed on the contents of registers A and B. The inputs A_i (i^{th} bit of A) and B_i (i^{th} bit of B) are given to both arithmetic and logic circuit. The output carry (C_{i+1}) of the given arithmetic stage is connected to the input carry (C_i) of the next stage in sequence. In addition, the input carry to the first stage is C_{in} which selects among the arithmetic operations.

The circuit also employs a 4 × 1 multiplexer having four data inputs (I_0 to I_3) and two selection inputs S_2 and S_3. The outputs D_i and E_i from the arithmetic and logic circuit, respectively, form the two data inputs I_0 and I_1 of the multiplexer. The data inputs I_2 and I_3 of the multiplexer come from A_{i-1} for shift-right operation and A_{i+1} for shift-left operation, respectively. The inputs S_2 and S_3 select among the arithmetic, logic, shift-right and shift-left operations and direct it to the output F_i. Note that Figure 6.14 shows only one stage of the arithmetic logic shift unit. For n bits, this circuit needs to be repeated n times.

The single stage of arithmetic logic shift unit shown in Figure 6.14 results in eight arithmetic, four logic and two shift operations that are demonstrated in the function table depicted in Figure 6.15. There are totally five selection inputs, S_0, S_1, S_2, S_3 and C_{in}, to choose among the fourteen operations. Note that C_{in} is used to select the arithmetic operations only.

When S_3S_2 = 00, one out of the eight arithmetic operations is selected depending on the values of S_1, S_0 and C_{in}. When S_3S_2 = 01, one out of the four logic operations is selected depending on the values of S_1 and S_0. When S_3S_2 = 10 and S_3S_2 = 11, the shift-right and shift-left operations are selected, respectively, regardless of the values of S_1, S_0 and C_{in}. Since C_{in} does not play any role while choosing the logic and shift operations, it is marked with ×'s (don't care conditions) for these operations.

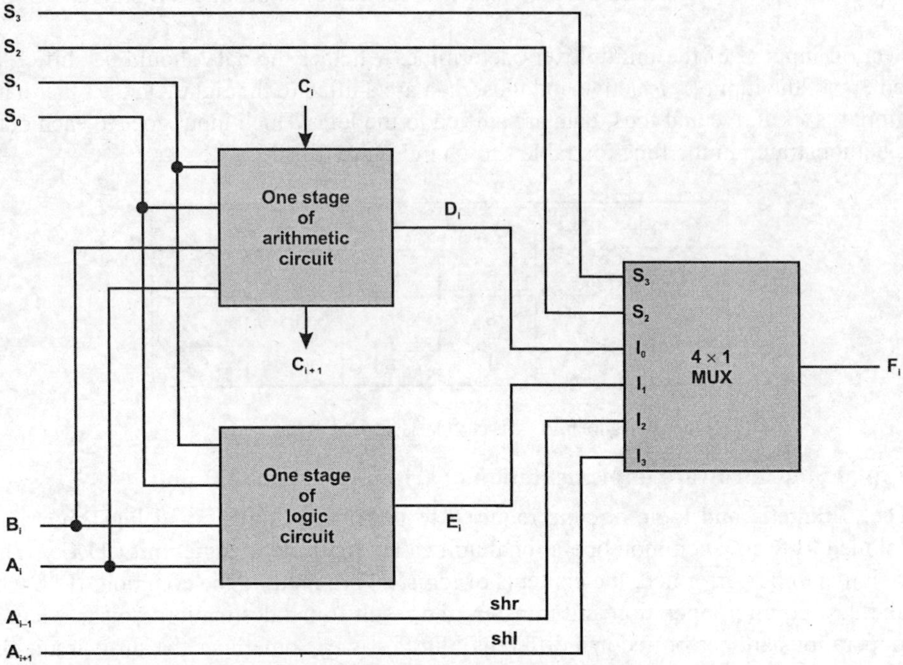

Figure 6.14 One Stage of Arithmetic Logic Shift Unit

Selection inputs					Output	Description
S_3	S_2	S_1	S_0	C_{in}	F	
0	0	0	0	0	A	Transfer A
0	0	0	0	1	A + 1	Increment A
0	0	0	1	0	A + B	Add
0	0	0	1	1	A + B + 1	Add with carry
0	0	1	0	0	$A + \bar{B}$	Subtract with borrow
0	0	1	0	1	$A + \bar{B} + 1$	Subtract
0	0	1	1	0	A − 1	Decrement A
0	0	1	1	1	A	Transfer A
0	1	0	0	×	$A \wedge B$	AND
0	1	0	1	×	$A \vee B$	OR
0	1	1	0	×	$A \oplus B$	XOR
0	1	1	1	×	$\bar{A}$	Complement A
1	0	×	×	×	shr A	Shift-right A
1	1	×	×	×	shl A	Shift-left A

Figure 6.15 Function Table for Arithmetic Logic Shift Unit

Similarly, the inputs S_2 and S_1 do not affect the shift operations and thus, have been marked with x's in the corresponding columns.

15. Define macrooperation.

Ans. Sometimes, it is convenient to specify a sequence of microoperations with a single statement. The statement that needs a sequence of microoperations for its execution is referred to as a **macrooperation**. For example, consider the following statement.

$R \leftarrow$ operand

This statement is a macrooperation as it requires a sequence of microoperations for its execution such as reading the operation code, transferring it to the control register, decoding and recognizing it and finally, transferring the operand to register R.

16. Show the block diagram to execute the following statement.
xT_3: $A \leftarrow B, B \leftarrow A$

Ans. The block diagram to execute the given register transfer statement is shown in Figure 6.16.

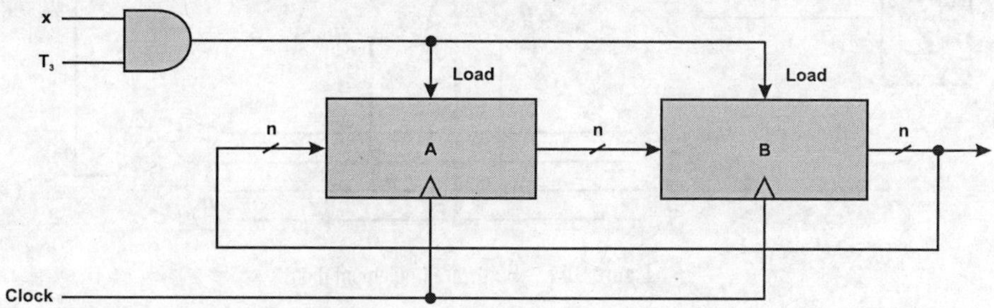

Figure 6.16 Block Diagram for xT_3: $A \leftarrow B$, $B \leftarrow A$

17. Represent the following conditional control statement by two register transfer statements with control functions.
if (P = 1) then ($R_1 \leftarrow R_2$) else if (Q = 1) then ($R_1 \leftarrow R_3$).

Ans. The given conditional control statement specifies that if P = 1, then the contents of register R_2 are to be transferred to register R_1. Else, if this condition fails (that is, $P \neq 1$) and Q = 1, then contents of register R_3 are to be transferred to register R_1. These two statements can be expressed by the following two register transfer statements:

$P: R_1 \leftarrow R_2$
$\bar{P}Q: R_1 \leftarrow R_3$

18. Show the hardware implementation of the following statements. The registers are 4 bits in length.
T_0: $A \leftarrow R_0$
T_1: $A \leftarrow R_1$
T_2: $A \leftarrow R_2$
T_3: $A \leftarrow R_3$

Ans. The hardware implementation of the given statements is shown in Figure 6.17.

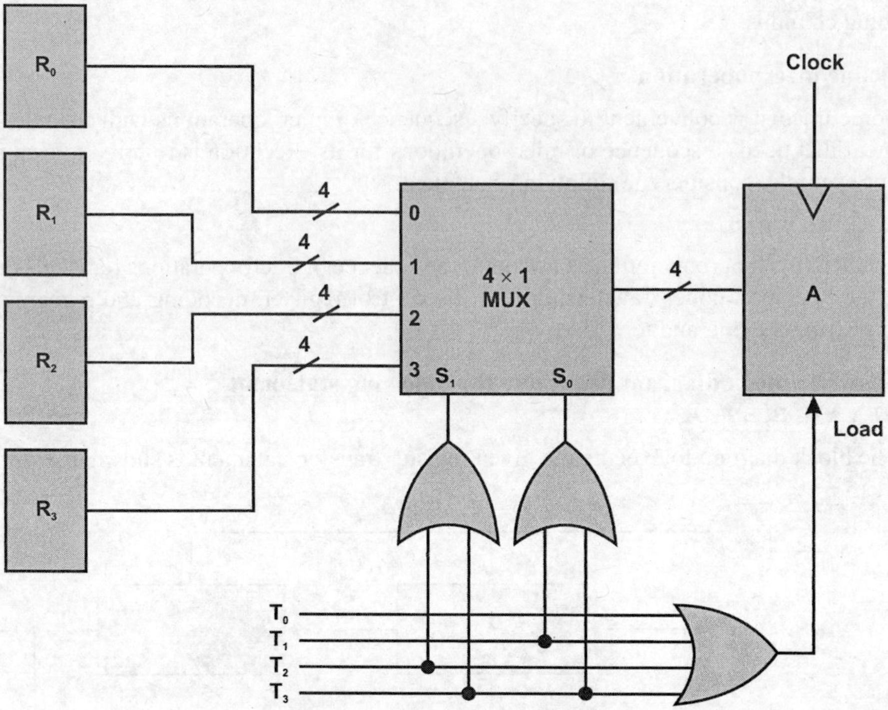

Figure 6.17 Hardware Implementation

19. A digital computer has a common bus system for 16 registers of 32 bits each. The bus is constructed with multiplexers.

(a) How many multiplexers are there in the bus?

(b) What size of multiplexers are needed?

(c) How many selection inputs are there in each multiplexer?

Ans. As we have 16 registers of 32 bits each, we need a 32-line common bus.

(a) The number of multiplexers required to construct a 32-line common bus is 32, one for each bit of registers.

(b) The required size of each multiplexer is 16 × 1.

(c) We need four selection inputs to select one of the 16 registers.

20. What does the following transfer statement indicate?

$R_5 \leftarrow M[R_5]$

Ans. The given statement specifies to read a memory word at the address stored in register R_5 and then transfer the content to register R_5, overwriting its previous contents.

21. Register A holds the 8-bit binary value 11011001. Determine the B operand and the logic microoperation to be performed in order to change the value of A to 01101101.

Ans. Given A = 11011001. If we take the XOR of value of A with 10110100, we get 01101101 that is the desired result. Hence B = 10110100, and the logic microoperation is XOR.

MULTIPLE CHOICE QUESTIONS

1 The operation executed on data stored in registers is called ________.

(a) Macrooperation
(b) Bit operation
(c) Microoperation
(d) Byte operation

2. A common bus system can be constructed using:

(a) Multiplexers
(b) Decoders
(c) Registers
(d) None of these

3. The content of an 8-bit register is initially 10011100. What is the content of the register after an arithmetic shift-right operation?

(a) 11001110
(b) 01001110
(c) 11001111
(d) 11001101

4. The symbolic notation used to describe the microoperations transfer among registers is called ________.

(a) Symbolic microoperation
(b) Register transfer language
(c) Symbolic language
(d) None of these

5. Which of the following register transfer statements is/are correct?

(a) $P, R_1 \leftarrow R_2$
(b) $P: R_1 \leftarrow R_2: R_3 \leftarrow R_4$
(c) $P: R_1 \leftarrow R_2, R_3 \leftarrow R_4$
(d) All of these

6. Two 8-bit registers R_1 and R_2 have values 11110010 and 11111111, respectively. What will be the value in register R_1 after the execution of $R_1 \leftarrow R_1 + R_2$ and $R_1 \leftarrow R_1 + 1$ microoperations in sequence?

(a) 11110011
(b) 01001110
(c) 00000000
(d) 11110010

Ans. 1. c 2. a 3. a 4. b 5. c 6. d

7

Basic Computer Organization and Design

1. Define the following:

(a) Instruction

(b) Program

Ans. (a) A computer system, in general, executes various microoperations. It can also be instructed to perform a specific sequence of microoperations by means of instructions. An **instruction** is a binary code (group of bits) that describes a sequence of microoperations to be performed by the computer.

(b) A **program** refers to a set of instructions that specify the operations and the operands on which operations are to be performed. During the execution of a program, each instruction is read from the memory and placed in the control register. Then, the control decodes the binary code of the instruction and issues a specific sequence of microoperations for executing the instruction.

2. What do you mean by an instruction code? Briefly discuss the various fields of instruction code. How instructions are stored in memory?

Ans. The computer is instructed to perform a specific operation through a group of bits called **instruction code**. As the operations are performed on some operands, which can be stored either in memory or processor registers, the instruction code also specifies the memory words or the registers where operands are stored. In addition, the register or the memory word where the result of operation should be stored is also specified by the instruction code. The binary code of instructions can be arranged in several ways, resulting in a particular format. Each computer employs its own instruction code format (or simply called **instruction format**) as per the computer architecture. A typical instruction code format consists of three fields: *mode*, *operation code* and *address* (see Figure 7.1).

Figure 7.1 Instruction Code Format

The description of the fields included in instruction format is as follows:

- **Operation code (opcode):** The opcode is the vital part of an instruction code as it specifies the operation to be performed. It comprises a number of bits together that define one of the available operations in the computer such as add, subtract, multiply, shift, complement, etc. The number of bits in the opcode may vary depending upon the total number of available operations. For 2^m distinct operations available in computer, the opcode must have at least m bits. For example, an opcode field should have at least five bits to perform 32 distinct operations as $2^5 = 32$.
- **Address:** This part of the instruction code specifies the operands on which the operation is to be performed. If the required operand is stored in a processor register, the instruction code includes n bits to indicate one of the 2^n processor registers. On the other hand, if the required operand is stored in a memory word, the address field specifies a memory address. In case the address field specifies the effective address (actual memory address) of the operand, the instruction is said to have a **direct address**. In contrast, if the address field specifies the address of a memory location where the effective address of the operand is stored, the instruction is said to have an **indirect address**. Sometimes, the address part of an instruction contains the actual operand rather than a memory address. In such a case, the instruction is said to have an **immediate operand**.

Note that in certain instructions, the operation does not require any operand from memory. For example, the operations such as complement AC, increment AC and clear AC operate on the contents of AC only and do not require any operand from memory. For such instructions, the address field of the instruction code is not needed at all and thus, the bits of address field can be used for other purposes.

- **Mode:** This part of the instruction code is used to indicate whether the address specified by the address field is direct or indirect.

3. Distinguish between the direct and indirect address instructions with the help of an example. How many memory references are needed to fetch the operand in each case?

Ans. An instruction is said to be a **direct address instruction** if the address part of the instruction specifies the memory address of the operand. On the other hand, if the address part of the instruction refers to a memory location that contains the address of the operand, the instruction is said to be an **indirect address instruction**. The mode bit of the instruction code distinguishes between the two types. To indicate direct address, the mode bit stores 0, while for indirect address, it stores 1.

To understand the difference, consider the 16-bit instruction code format shown in Figure 7.2(a). It consists of a 12-bit address field, 3-bit operation code and a mode bit (denoted by I). Now, consider the direct and indirect address instructions stored in memory as shown in Figure 7.2(b) and 7.2(c), respectively. In the direct address instruction stored at address 40 in memory, the I bit is 0, the opcode specifies the add operation and address part is the binary equivalent of 345. This instructs the control to go to memory address 345 to find the operand and add it to the content of AC. In the indirect address instruction stored at address 32 in memory, the I bit is 1, the opcode specifies the add operation and address part is the binary equivalent of 150. This instructs the control to go to memory address 150 to find the address of the operand, which is 1440 in our case. The control then goes to memory address 1440 to find the operand and add it to the content of AC.

Thus, it is clear that the memory needs to be referenced twice in case of indirect address instructions: first for the address of the operand and second for the operand itself. In contrast, a direct address instruction needs only a single memory reference.

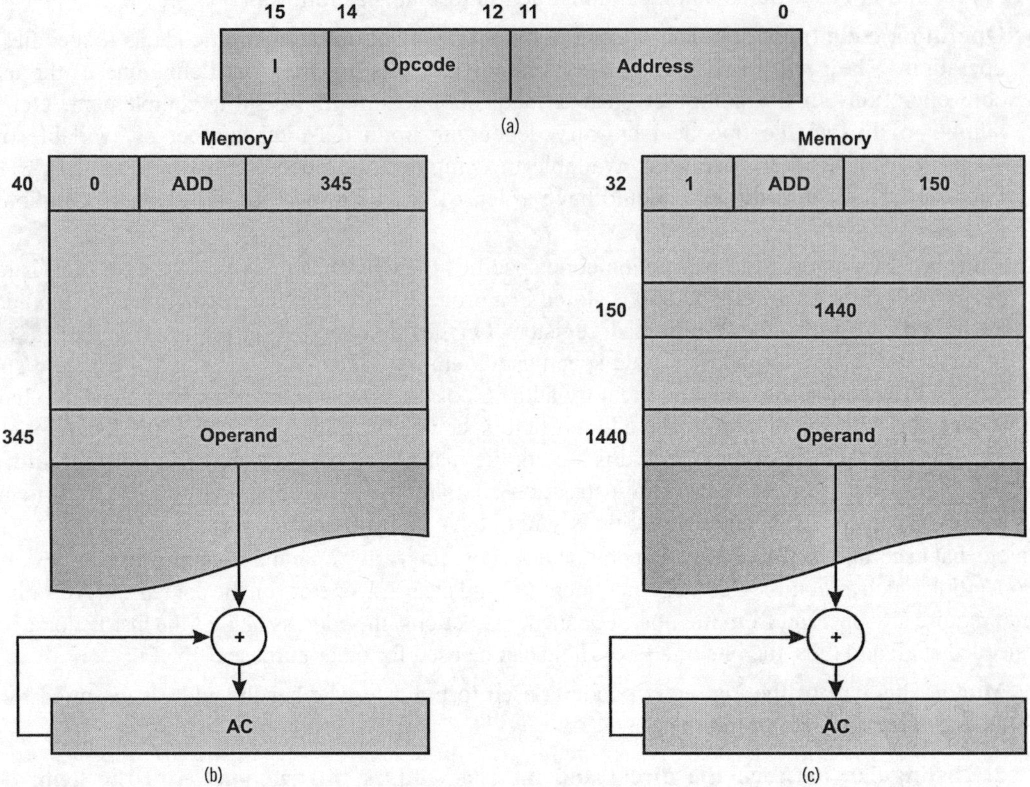

Figure 7.2 Direct and Indirect Address Instruction

4. What are computer registers? Explain the role of following registers in a basic computer: PC, AR, DR, IR, AC, TR, INPR and OUTR registers.

Ans. Registers are the temporary storage units of a computer used to store data, instructions, addresses and results of recent calculations. A basic computer employs certain processor registers for manipulating data and several other registers such as data register, instruction register, program counter, etc., with each having a distinct function.

Before describing the computer registers, consider a basic computer having a capacity of 4096 words, where each word stores 16 bits. This implies that each address in the memory is of 12 bits (as $4096 = 2^{12}$). Thus, the 12 bits (0 to 11) of each 16-bit instruction specify the memory address, opcode is 3 bits long (12 to 14) and one mode bit (15th bit) to indicate direct or indirect address. Figure 7.3 depicts the register organization and the memory in a basic computer.

The description of each register in a basic computer is as follows:

- **Program counter (PC):** It is a 12-bit register that is used to hold the address of the next instruction to be executed. In other words, it is just like a pointer that points to the memory location where the next instruction is stored.
- **Address register (AR):** It is a 12-bit register that is used to hold the address of the memory location where the data is to be read from or written to. AR comprises 12-bits because it is the width for a memory address.

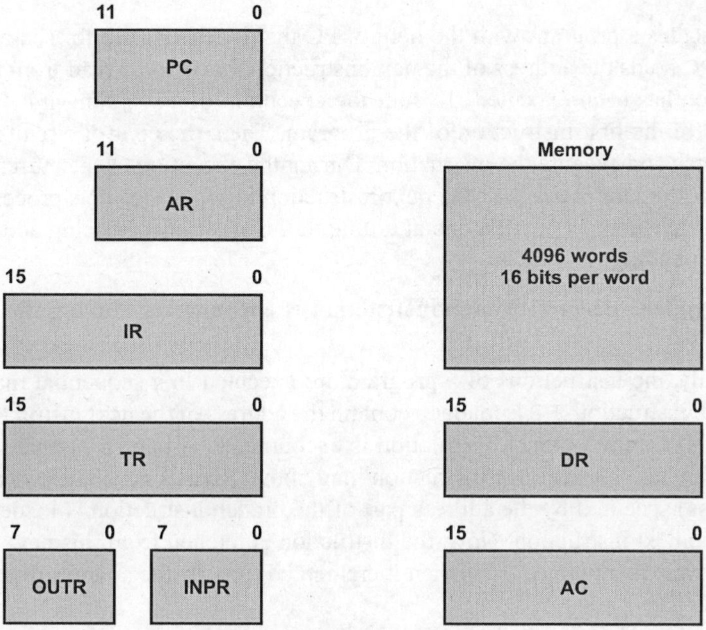

Figure 7.3 Register Organization and Memory in a Basic Computer

- **Data register (DR):** It is a 16-bit register that is used to hold the data to be read from or written to the memory.
- **Accumulator register (AC):** It is a 16-bit register that is used to perform the various operations. It is also termed as general-purpose processor register.
- **Instruction register (IR):** It is a 16-bit register that is used to hold the instruction read from the memory that is currently being executed.
- **Input register (INPR):** It is an 8-bit register that is used to hold the input character received from an input device.
- **Output register (OUTR):** It is an 8-bit register that is used to hold the character for an output device.
- **Temporary register (TR):** It is a 16-bit register that is used to hold the data generated during the execution of an operation.

5. What do you mean by data path?

Ans. The CPU can be categorized into two sections according to the functionality performed, namely, *data section* and *control section*. The **data section** of CPU is termed as **data path**. It contains the registers and ALU, and performs various operations on the data. The **control section** is essentially the control units (CUs) that direct the control signals to the data path.

6. What do you mean by instruction sequencing? Define straight line sequencing.

Ans. To perform a specific task on the computer, the programmer has to choose and write the appropriate instructions one after the other in a proper sequence. The job of writing the instructions in a proper sequence in order to execute a particular task is referred to as **instruction sequencing**. The set of instructions written in a sequence to perform a specific task constitute a program.

The CPU executes a program with the help of PC that is responsible for sequencing the control of execution. The PC holds the address of the next instruction that is to be read from the memory after the current instruction has been executed. To start the execution of a program, initially, the PC is loaded with the address of the first instruction of the program. Then, the control circuits in CPU use the address in PC to fetch and execute the instruction. During the execution of the current instruction, the PC is incremented to store the address of the next instruction in sequence. This process continues, and the instructions are fetched and executed one at a time in the order of increasing addresses. This is called **straight line sequencing.**

7. What happens when a branch instruction is encountered during the execution of a program?

Ans. Generally, the instructions of a program are executed in a sequential manner and during the execution of each instruction, PC is made to contain the address of the next instruction in sequence. This approach works fine until a branch instruction is encountered. A branch instruction causes to transfer the control to some non-consecutive instruction in memory. Thus, a new address (called **branch target** or **target address**) specified by the address part of the branch instruction is loaded into PC to become the address of the next instruction. Now, the instruction is fetched from this new memory address and a memory read cycle is initiated. PC is then incremented to store the address of the next instruction in sequence.

8. What is interconnection structure? Explain bus interconnection structure.

or

Explain the functional groups of system bus.

Ans. A computer system employs various hardware components such as CPU, memory unit and I/O devices. All these modules work together, communicating with each other by the means of paths. The internal data paths are needed for moving the data from one register to another or between the ALU and CPU; whereas for transferring the data from registers to memory or I/O devices, the external data paths are required. The collection of different paths that connect all the modules of a system is called the **interconnection structure**. The design of the interconnection structure depends on the requirements of exchange to be made between modules. A variety of interconnection structures have been used over the years. However, the most common is the bus and several multiple-bus structures.

To enable the communication between modules, signals are provided by the **bus**—a communication pathway that interconnects two or more devices. A bus consists of multiple lines where each line can transmit signals representing 0 or 1. Thus, to transmit multiple bits in parallel, multiple lines of bus are to be used together. A computer system may contain a number of buses that provide interconnections between components at different levels of computer system hierarchy. A bus which connects the major components of computer including CPU, memory and I/O modules is referred to as **system bus**.

Bus Interconnection Structure

A system bus comprises from 50 to hundreds of separate lines with each line having a specific function. These lines can be categorized into three functional groups: *data*, *address* and *control* lines (see Figure 7.4).

- **Data lines:** These lines are used for transferring data between different system modules and are collectively known as **data bus**. A data bus may consist from 32 to hundreds of separate data lines. The number of lines present in the data bus is called the **width** of data bus. Since each line can carry one bit at a time, the width of data bus indicates the number of bits that can be transferred simultaneously between two modules. The width of data bus is a key factor in measuring the overall performance of a computer system.

- **Address lines:** These lines are used to carry the address of the source or destination of data on the data bus. For example, if the processor wants to store some data in memory, then it puts the address of the memory location where the data are to be written to on the address lines. The set of address lines is collectively known as **address bus**. The width of address bus specifies the maximum possible memory supported by a system. For example, if a system has 16-bit wide address bus, it can support memory size equal to 2^{16} (or 65536) bytes. The address bus can also be used to address the source or destination I/O ports.
- **Control lines:** These lines are used to control the access and use of data and address bus. The access control is required since both the data and address lines are shared among different components. The control lines are collectively called **control bus**. These lines are used for the transmission of commands and timing signals (which validate data and address) between the system modules. The command signals specify which operations are to be performed and the timing signals indicate whether the data and address information are valid. Some of the typical control lines are listed as follows:
  - **Bus request:** It indicates that some module wants to gain control of the bus.
  - **Bus grant:** It indicates that the bus request from the requesting module has been granted.
  - **I/O read:** It indicates to transfer the data from the addressed I/O port to the data bus.
  - **I/O write:** It indicates to transfer the data present on the data bus to the addressed I/O port.
  - **Transfer ACK:** It indicates that the data has been taken from or placed on the data bus.
  - **Interrupt request:** It indicates a pending interrupt.
  - **Interrupt acknowledgement:** It indicates an acknowledgement to the pending interrupt.
  - **Memory read:** It indicates to place the data from the memory location whose address is specified on the address bus onto the data bus.
  - **Memory write:** It indicates to store the data placed on data bus into the memory location whose address is specified on the address bus.

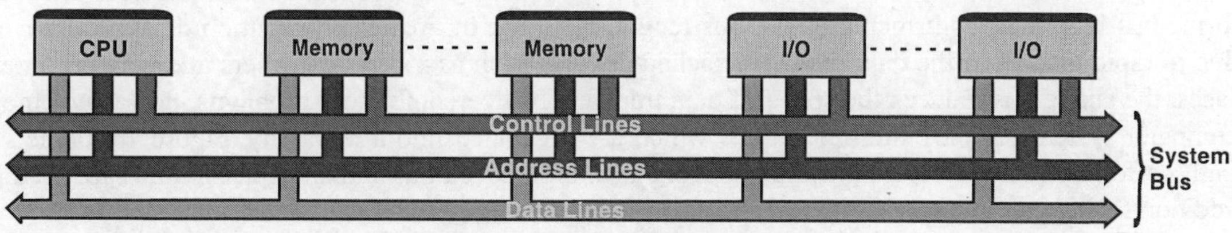

Figure 7.4 Bus Interconnection Structure

9. Explain single-bus structure. What are its advantages and disadvantages?

Ans. An alternative way to represent the bus interconnection structure is to combine the data, address and control bus into a single common bus (system bus) as shown in Figure 7.5. Such an interconnection structure is termed as **single-bus structure**. In this structure, all the modules such as processor, memory and I/O are connected to the system bus. When one module wants to send data to another module, it first obtains the use of bus and then transfers data through the bus. Similarly, when a new module wants to receive data from another module, it has to first obtain the use of bus and then transfers a request to the desired module through the bus. With a single-bus structure, only two devices can communicate at a time. In case multiple requests for the use of bus arrive at the same time, the control lines of the bus are used to decide which request is to be granted.

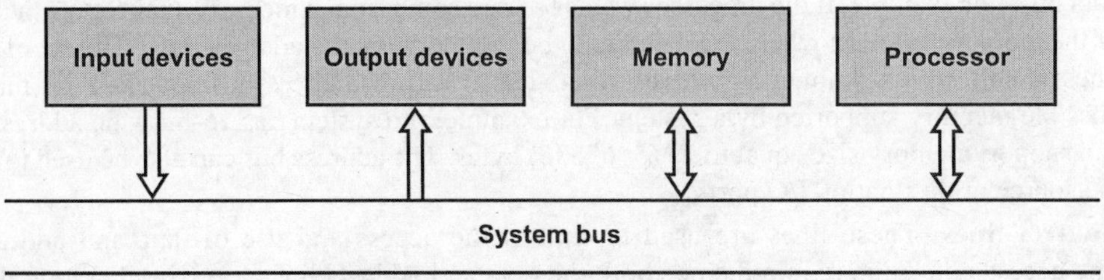

Figure 7.5 Single-bus Structure

Advantages:

- It is cost effective since it employs common data signalling paths for multiple devices instead of having separate paths for communication between each set of devices.
- Since all the modules are connected to a shared transmission medium, each module can receive signals transmitted by any other module connected to the bus.
- It is a flexible organization as new modules can be attached very easily.

Disadvantages:

- As all the data transfer is managed via a common bus, it results in a slow speed.
- The control over the bus can become complicated when more than one module attempt to use the single bus.
- The performance of the single bus structure degrades when a large number of devices are connected to the bus.

10. Explain multiple-bus structure. What are its advantages and disadvantages?

Ans. The single-bus structure does not prove much efficient when the number of devices attached to the bus increases, as it increases the bus length, resulting in greater propagation delay. Moreover, due to rapid growth in the data rates of attached devices such as video controllers and network interfaces, the single bus reduces the speed of data transfer. To overcome these problems, nowadays, most computer systems employ multiple buses, which are organized into a hierarchy. Figure 7.6 depicts a high-performance architecture in which a local bus, a high-speed bus and an expansion bus are used in addition to the system bus.

The **local bus** provides the interconnection between processor and cache memory. It may support one or more local devices. It is connected to a cache controller integrated into a bridge which connects the local bus to the system bus to which main memory is attached. The cache/bridge also connects the local bus to the **high-speed bus** to which video and graphic controllers, high-speed LANs and interface controllers such as SCSI and FireWire are attached. An **expansion bus** supports connections to low-speed devices such as modem, fax and other serial devices. The expansion bus is connected to the high-speed bus via expansion bus interface which buffers the traffic between the expansion and high-speed bus. Though the inclusion of high-speed bus closely integrates the high-demand devices with the processor, it still does not interfere with the processor's activity. Thus, any change in the high-speed bus does not affect the processor's architecture and vice versa.

Advantages:

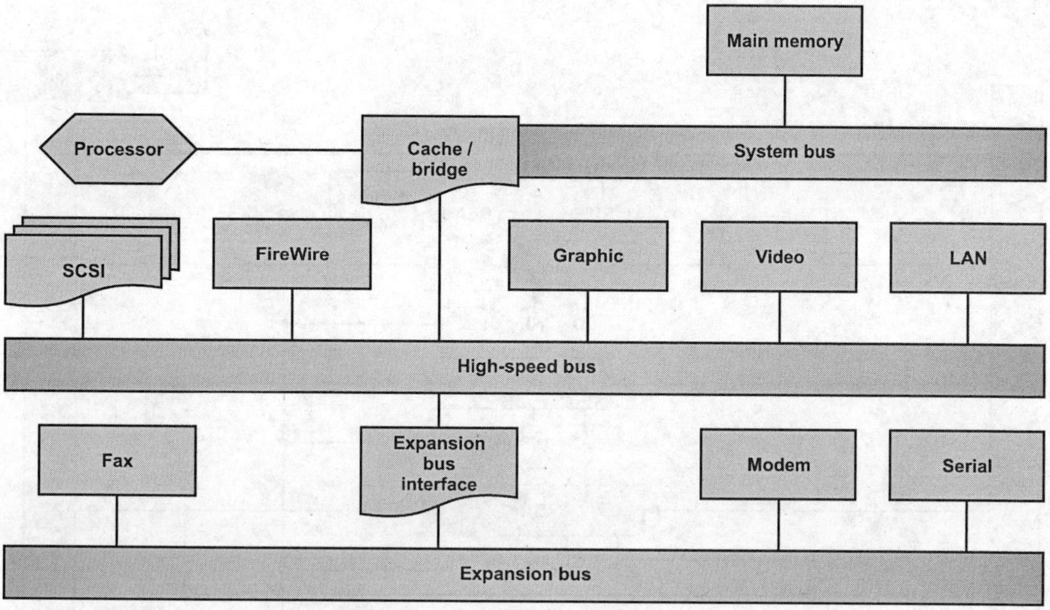

Figure 7.6 High-performance Multiple-bus Structure

- It speeds up the data transfer process. Multiple-bus structure enables to transfer twice as much as the single-bus structure.
- It increases the efficiency and performance of the computer system.
- Each bus is dedicated to a single type of device, thus, providing a flexible communication between processor and devices.

Disadvantages:

- It is costly as compared to single-bus system.
- It requires multiple interfaces to control multiple connections of buses.

11. How the basic computer can be connected to a common bus system?

or

Explain the common bus architecture to exchange the data between registers?

Ans. A basic computer structure consists of several components such as eight registers, a memory unit and a CU. They need a path to exchange the information between registers or between memory and registers. The most efficient way to transfer the information is through the use of a common bus. Figure 7.7 shows the connection of memory and registers of a basic computer to the common bus.

The 16 lines of 16-bit common bus are connected to the inputs of six registers (AR, PC, DR, IR, TR and OUTR) and memory unit. The bus receives outputs from the six registers (AR, PC, DR, AC, IR and TR) and memory unit as shown by numerals (1 to 7) in Figure 7.7. The specific outputs are selected for the bus with the help of three selection variables: S_0, S_1 and S_2. For example if $S_2S_1S_0 = 101$, the output of IR is placed on the bus.

Five registers (AR, PC, DR, AC and TR) have three control inputs: load (LD), increment (INR) and clear (CLR), while two registers (IR and OUTR) have only one control input: LD. When the LD input of any register is enabled, the register receives data from the bus during the transition of next clock pulse.

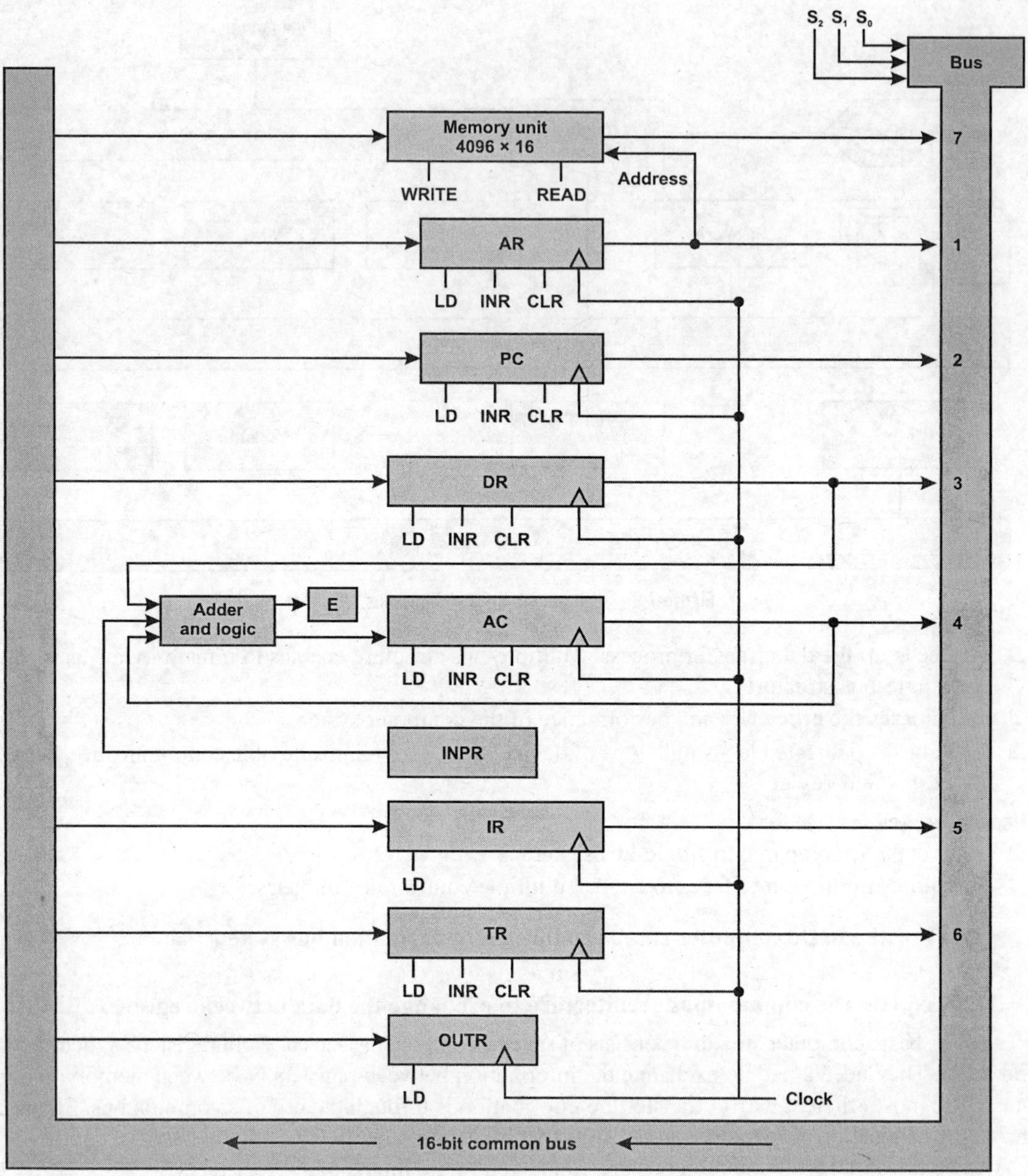

Figure 7.7 Basic Computer Registers connected to a Common Bus

The memory unit contains 4096 16-bit words. The memory unit receives 16-bit word from the bus for storing in the memory when its `WRITE` input is enabled and supplies 16-bit word to the bus when its `READ` input is enabled.

Four registers including `DR`, `IR`, `TR`, and `AC` are of 16-bits each. Two registers, `AR` and `PC`, are of 12 bits, since they hold the memory address, which is of 12 bits (as $4096 = 2^{12}$). Therefore, when either `AR` or `PC` provides 12-bit output from the bus, the four most significant bits are set to 0's to make it 16-bit long. Similarly, when either AR or PC receives 16-bit input from the bus, only the 12 least significant bits are transferred into the registers.

Since, the INPR and OUTR are of eight bits each, both communicate with only eight least significant bits of the bus. The INPR can only give information to bus, whereas the OUTR can only receive information from the bus. The AC register receives its 16-bit input from AC, a 16-bit input from DR and an 8-bit input from INPR. The arithmetic or logic microoperations are performed on the inputs from AC and DR, and the result of operation is stored in AC and an end carry in E flip-flop.

12. List down the types of computer instruction formats in a basic computer. Explain in brief.

Ans. The basic computer consists of three instruction code formats with each format consisting of 16 bits. In each instruction format, three bits are kept reserved for opcode, one bit for mode and the remaining 13 bits depend on the opcode. The type of instruction can be determined by the computer from the bit positions 12 to 15 of the instruction. The types of computer instructions used in a basic computer are as follows:

- **Memory-reference instruction:** In this instruction, the address part of the instruction specifies a memory address. Thus, the bits 0 to 11 of the instruction are used to specify a memory address and the 15th bit (I) is used to specify the addressing mode. The bit I is set to 1 for indirect address and 0 for direct address (see Figure 7.8). The 3-bit opcode of memory-reference instructions varies from 000 through 110.

Figure 7.8 Format of Memory-reference Instructions

Table 7.1 lists the memory-reference instructions in a basic computer.

Table 7.1 Memory-reference Instructions

Symbol	Description
AND	AND memory word to AC
ADD	Add memory word to AC
LDA	Load memory word to AC
STA	Store content of AC in memory
BUN	Branch unconditionally
BSA	Branch and save return address
ISZ	Increment and skip if zero

- **Register-reference instruction:** In this instruction, the 3-bit opcode is 111 and I = 0 (see Figure 7.9). This instruction specifies an operation or a test on AC register. Since an operand from memory is not required, the remaining 12 bits (0 to 11) are used to determine the operations or the text that is to be executed.

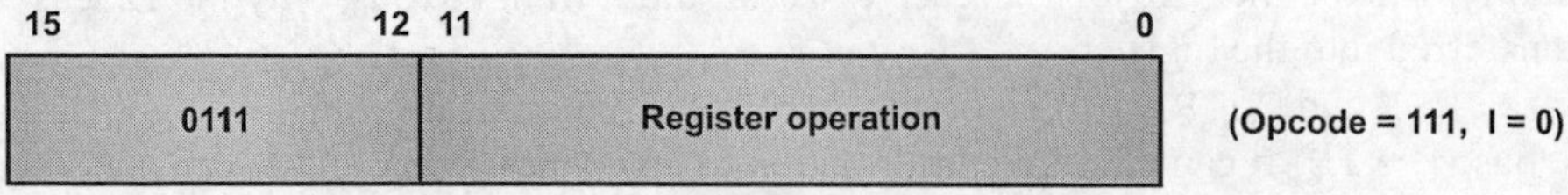

Figure 7.9 Format of Register-reference Instructions

Table 7.2 lists the register-reference instructions in a basic computer.

Table 7.2 Register-reference Instructions

Symbol	Description
CLE	Clear E
CLA	Clear AC
CMA	Complement AC
CME	Complement E
CIR	Circulate right AC and E
CIL	Circulate left AC and E
INC	Increment AC
SPA	Skip next instruction if AC is positive
SNA	Skip next instruction if AC is negative
SZA	Skip next instruction if AC is 0
SZE	Skip next instruction if E is 0
HLT	Halt computer

- **Input/output instruction:** Like register-reference instruction, the 3-bit opcode of an input/output instruction is also 111. One bit that distinguishes between the two is the mode bit `I`, which is 1 for the input/output instruction. The rest 12 bits (0 to 11) of the instruction specify the type of input/output operation (see Figure 7.10).

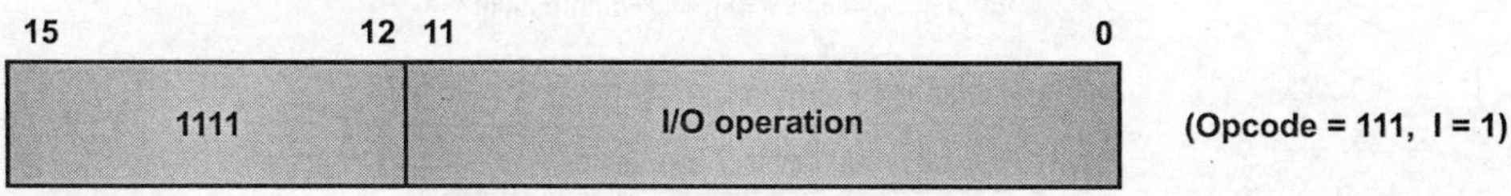

Figure 7.10 Format of Input/Output instructions

Table 7.3 lists the input/output instructions in a basic computer.

Table 7.3 Input/Output Instructions

Symbol	Description
INP	Input character to AC
OUT	Output character from AC
SKI	Skip on input flag
SKO	Skip on output flag
ION	Interrupt enable on
IOF	Interrupt enable off

13. What do you mean by completeness of instruction set? Give the reasons to choose instruction in each category.

Ans. The computer uses a variety of instructions so that the user can construct programs to evaluate any computable function. A set of instructions is considered complete if the computer system includes a sufficient number of instructions in each of the following categories:

- **Arithmetic, logic and shift instructions:** This category of instructions provides the computation capabilities to process the type of data provided by the user. The arithmetic instructions enable to perform computations on the numeric data. Three arithmetic instructions of a basic computer include `ADD`, `CMA` and `INC`. With the help of these three instructions, the binary numbers can be added and subtracted when negative numbers are represented in 2's complement form. The logic and shift instructions, on the other hand, allow to operate on the bits of a word, thus enabling to process any other type of data employed by the user. An example of logic instruction is `AND` which when used in combination with `CMA` instruction produces NAND operation. The NAND operation further enables to implement all other logic operations. Two circulate instructions, `CIR` and `CIL`, can be used to produce arithmetic and any other type of shifts.
- **Data transfer instructions:** This category of instructions is used to move the data between memory and registers. Since most of the data in computer are stored in memory in binary form and the operations on the data are primarily performed in processor registers, it becomes necessary to bring the required data from the memory to the processor registers. The `LDA` instruction serves this purpose and transfers the data from memory to `AC`. After performing the operation, the result may need to be stored back in memory. This is achieved by using the `STA` instruction.
- **Program control and status check instructions:** This category of instructions is used to change the sequence of program execution and check the status conditions. Branch instructions such as `BUN`, `BSA` and `ISZ` used together with four skip instructions (`SPA`, `SNA`, `SZA` and `SZE`) enable to control the program sequence and check the status conditions.
- **Input and output instructions:** This category of instructions is used to provide the communication between the user and the computer. The data and programs provided by the user must be transferred to the memory for processing. To achieve this, the input instruction `INP` is used. Similarly, the result of computation must be transferred back to the user. For this purpose, the output instruction `OUT` is used.

14. What do you mean by instruction cycle? Explain all its phases.

Ans. An **instruction cycle** is the basic operation cycle of computer in which an instruction is retrieved from memory, the sequence of actions to be carried out is determined and the desired actions are performed. The memory unit of the computer stores a program consisting of a sequence of instructions; and each instruction goes through a cycle to execute the program. An instruction cycle consists of a sequence of subcycles (termed as **phases**) which are *fetch*, *decode*, *read* and *execute*. To start with instruction cycle, initially `PC` is loaded with the address of first instruction of the program. The phases involved in instruction cycle are described as follows:

- **Fetch:** During this phase, the address specified in the `PC` is loaded into `AR`. The processor fetches the instruction at the address specified in `AR` from the memory and places it into `TR`. At the same time, `PC` is incremented by one so as to store the address of the instruction that is to be executed next in the program.
- **Decode:** The decoder decodes the bits in opcode part of instruction from the memory into `AR` and determines the sequence of actions that should take place for executing the instructions.

- **Read:** In this phase, one or more operands are fetched from the memory if the instruction is a memory-reference instruction. In case the address part of the instruction specifies a direct address, the data are fetched directly from the location specified by 12 bits (0-11) of `IR` and loaded into `DR`. In case of indirect instruction, first the effective address is read from the memory and loaded into `AR` and then the required data are fetched from the memory and placed into `DR`. However, if the instruction in `IR` is a register-reference or an input/output instruction, this phase is not needed.
- **Execute:** In this phase, CU generates a sequence of control signals corresponding to decoded information and passes the control signals to the relevant functional units of CPU for performing required actions. After executing the instructions, the result is stored into the memory or presented to some output device.

This cycle is then repeated for the next instruction and the process continues until a `HALT` instruction is encountered.

15. What is interrupt and interrupt handler? How an interrupt is handled?

Ans. The term **interrupt** refers to some exceptional event that causes the CPU to temporarily halt its current program execution to carry out some specific task. The program that handles such an event is called an **interrupt handler**, also called an **interrupt service routine (ISR).** It is a subroutine that gets executed whenever an interrupt is generated.

When the CPU receives an interrupt, it stops executing the current program, saves the status of various registers in stack and branches to the corresponding ISR to perform the task requested by the interrupt. After performing the task, the control is returned to the instruction, the CPU was executing at the time the interrupt occurred.

16. Draw and discuss the flowchart of the instruction cycle along with interrupt cycle for the basic computer.

Ans. During the instruction execution, an interrupt may occur which causes the CPU to suspend the execution of the current program and handle the interrupt. To accommodate the interrupts during instruction execution, an interrupt cycle can be added to the instruction cycle. Figure 7.11 depicts the flowchart of instruction cycle along with interrupt cycle in a basic computer.

The computer has an interrupt flip-flop `R` that contains the value 1 to indicate a pending interrupt; otherwise, 0. If `R` = 0, the control is transferred to the instruction cycle. At first, the instruction is fetched and decoded. Now, when the instruction is being executed, the control checks the interrupt enable flip-flop (IEN). If `IEN` = 0, it indicates that the interrupt cannot be generated by the programmer and hence, the control continues with the next instruction cycle. On the other hand, if `IEN` = 1, the control checks the input flag (FGI) and output flag (FGO). In case both the flags have 0 values, it means that both the input and output registers are not ready for data and thus, the control continues with the next instruction cycle. In case either of the flag is set, `R` is set to 1. After the completion of execute phase, the value of `R` flip-flop is again checked by the control. If it is found equal to 1, the interrupt cycle is performed instead of an instruction cycle.

During interrupt cycle, the return address present in `PC` is stored at a specific location such as memory, memory stack or some processor register. This is required so that the control could return to the instruction that was interrupted. For example, in our flowchart we have chosen the location as address 1 in memory. After saving the return address, control branches to the address 1 by saving this address in `PC`. Along with this, it clears the IEN and R flip-flops so that no further interruption could occur until the current interrupt has been serviced.

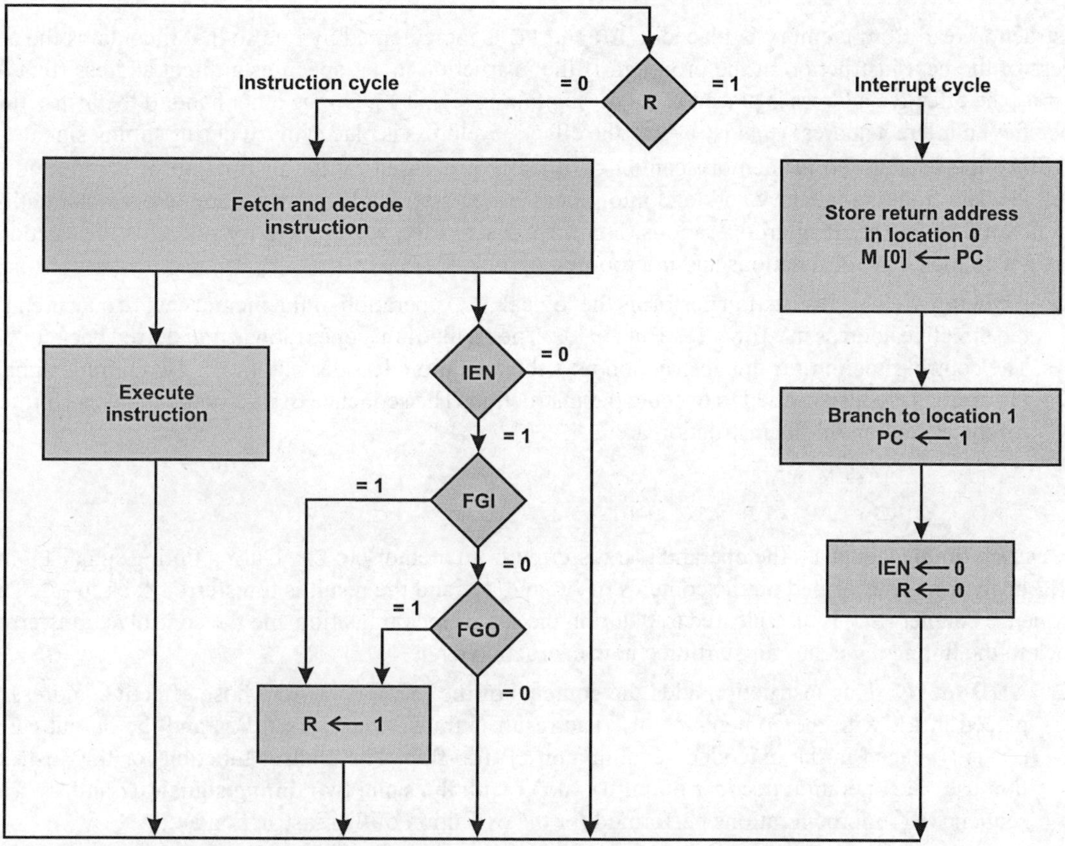

Figure 7.11 Flowchart for Instruction Cycle along with Interrupt Cycle

17. List the hardware components that are used in designing the basic computer.

Ans. A basic computer consists of several hardware components, which are listed as follows:

- A memory unit capable of storing 4096 words with each word having 16 bits.
- Nine registers including `AR`, `PC`, `DR`, `AC`, `IR`, `TR`, `OUTR`, `INPR` and `SC`.
- Seven flip-flops including `I`, `S`, `E`, `R`, `IEN`, `FGI` and `FGO`.
- A 16-bit wide common bus.
- Control logic gates.
- Adder and logic circuit connected to the input of `AC`.
- A 3 × 8 operation decoder that produces eight outputs from D_0 to D_7.
- A 4 × 16 timing decoder that produces 16 timing signals from T_0 to T_{15}.

18. Explain the function of memory-reference instructions in a basic computer by means of register transfer notation.

Ans. In a basic computer, there are seven memory-reference instructions and with each instruction, a specific output from the eight outputs of 3 × 8 operation decoder is associated. During the timing signal T_0, the address of the instruction is transferred from `PC` to `AR`. During the timing signal T_1, the instruction read from memory is placed in AR and PC is incremented by one so that it contains the address of the next instruction in the program. If the instruction in IR specifies a direct address (that is, I = 0), the effective address is placed in AR during timing signal T_2. On the other hand, if the instruction specifies an indirect address (that is, I = 1), the effective address is placed in AR during timing signal T_3.

Since the data stored in memory cannot be directly processed by the instruction, it is required to read the data from the memory and load into processor register. Thus, the execution of each instruction results in a sequence of microoperations. Here, we discuss the seven memory-reference instructions along with their control functions and microoprerations.

- **AND to AC:** This instruction performs the logical AND operation of the memory word specified by the effective address in AR with the bits in AC. The result of this operation is transferred back to AC. The control function for this instruction uses the operation decoder output D_0. Two timing signals (T_4 and T_5) are also needed to execute the instruction. The sequence of microoperations performed for the execution of this instruction are:

$$D_0T_4\text{: } DR \leftarrow M\,[AR]$$
$$D_0T_5\text{: } AC \leftarrow AC \wedge DR,\quad SC \leftarrow 0$$

During timing signal T_4, the operand is transferred from memory to DR. During timing signal T_5, the AND operation is performed on the contents of AC and DR, and the result is transferred back to AC. The sequence counter (SC) is also cleared to 0 during the same clock transition and the control is transferred back to the timing signal T_0 for starting a new instruction cycle.

- **ADD to AC:** This instruction adds the contents of the memory word whose effective address is placed in AR with the contents of AC. The result is transferred back to AC and the output carry (C_{out}) is placed in the extended accumulator (E) flip-flop. The control function for this instruction uses the operation decoder output D_1 along with the same two timing signals T_4 and T_5. The sequence of microoperations performed for the execution of this instruction are:

$$D_1T_4\text{: } DR \leftarrow M\,[AR]$$
$$D_1T_5\text{: } AC \leftarrow AC + DR,\quad E \leftarrow C_{out},\quad SC \leftarrow 0$$

During timing signal T_4, the operand is transferred from memory to DR. During timing signal T_5, the contents of AC and DR are added, the sum is transferred back to AC and the carry output (C_{out}) generated is transferred to E flip-flop. The sequence counter (SC) is also cleared to 0 during the same clock transition and the control is transferred back to the timing signal T_0 for starting a new instruction cycle.

- **Load to AC (LDA):** This instruction loads the memory word specified by AR into AC. The control function for this instruction uses operation decoder output D_2 and same two timing signals T_4 and T_5. Since there is no direct path from the common bus to AC (see Figure 7.7), the memory word is first transferred from bus to DR during timing signal T_4. Then from DR, it is transferred to AC through the adder and logic circuit during timing signal T_5. The sequence of microoperations performed for the execution of this instruction are:

$$D_2T_4\text{: } DR \leftarrow M\,[AR]$$
$$D_2T_5\text{: } AC \leftarrow DR,\quad SC \leftarrow 0$$

- **Store AC (STA):** This instruction is used to store the contents of AC in the memory word whose effective address is specified in AR. As the output of AC and the read (RD) input of memory unit are directly connected to the bus (see Figure 7.7), a single microoperation is needed to execute this instruction. The control function for this instruction uses operation decoder output D_3 and a timing signal T_4. The microoperation performed for the execution of this instruction is:

D_3T_4: M [AR] ← AC, SC ← 0

- **Branch unconditionally (BUN):** This instruction causes the control of the program to be transferred unconditionally to the instruction specified by the effective address in AR. Since the instruction to be read from the memory during the next instruction cycle is stored in PC (which is incremented at time T_1), the effective address in AR needs to be transferred to PC. The control function for this instruction uses the operation decoder output D_4 along with the timing signal T_4. The single microoperation performed for the execution of this instruction is:

  D_4T_4: PC ← AR, SC ← 0

- **Branch and save return address (BSA):** This instruction causes the control to branch to a portion of the program called subroutine or procedure. The execution of this instruction requires to store the contents of PC (that is, the address of the next instruction in sequence) in a memory location specified by the effective address in AR. Then, the contents of AR plus one are transferred to PC to make it to point to the first instruction in the subroutine. In a basic computer, it is not possible to perform the BSA function in a single clock cycle. Instead, two timing signals (T_4 and T_5) are needed to accomplish the function of BSA instruction. The control function for this instruction uses the operation decoder output D_5. The microoperations performed for the execution of this instruction are:

  D_5T_4: M [AR] ← PC, AR ← AR + 1
  D_5T_5: PC ← AR, SC ← 0

During the timing signal T_4, the content of PC is transferred to the memory location specified by the effective address in AR, and AR is incremented by one. During the timing signal T_5, the content of AR is transferred to PC.

- **Increment and Skip if zero (ISZ):** This instruction increments the memory word specified by the effective address in AR and if the value after increment is 0, PC is incremented by one. Usually, a negative number is stored in a memory word in 2's complement form by the programmer. On incrementing this number continuously, it eventually reaches 0. At that time, PC is incremented by one to skip the next instruction of the program.

As the memory word cannot be incremented inside the memory, it is first transferred from memory to DR via bus during the timing signal T_4, then incremented by one during the timing signal T_5 and finally, transferred back to memory during the timing signal T_6. The control function for this instruction uses operation decoder output D_6. The sequence of microoperations performed for the execution of this instruction is:

D_6T_4: DR ← M [AR]
D_6T_5: DR ← DR + 1
D_6T_6: M [AR] ← DR, if (DR = 0) then (PC ← PC + 1), SC ← 0

19. Explain the functions of different input/output instructions in a basic computer.

Ans. The input/output instructions are needed to exchange the information with AC, to check the flag bits and to control the interrupt facility. Some of the input/output instructions are discussed as follows:

- **INP:** This instruction is used to accept the input character from INPR. It transfers the contents of INPR to the eight least significant bits of AC and clears FGI to 0 as well.
- **OUT:** This instruction is used to provide the output character to OUTR. It transfers the eight least significant bits of AC to OUTR and clears FGO to 0 as well.
- **SKI and SKO:** These two instructions determine the status of FGI and FGO, respectively, and if the flag is found set, it causes to skip the next instruction by incrementing the contents of PC by 1.
- **ION and IOF instructions:** These two instructions are used for setting and clearing the IEN flip-flop, respectively. The IOF instruction clears the IEN flip-flop to 0, which means interrupt cannot be generated now. The ION instruction sets the IEN to 1, which means computer is now ready to be interrupted.

MULTIPLE CHOICE QUESTIONS

1. The _______ part of the instruction code specifies the operation to be performed.
   (a) Mode (b) Operation code
   (c) Address (d) None of these
2. Which register holds the instruction read from memory?
   (a) Accumulator (b) Data register
   (c) Instruction register (d) Address register
3. Which instruction is used for changing the sequence of the executing program?
   (a) Circulate instruction (b) Branch instruction
   (c) Input/output instruction (d) All of these
4. The read phase of the instruction cycle is not required to be performed in case of _________ instructions.
   (a) Memory-reference (b) Register-reference
   (c) Input/output (d) Both (b) and (c)
5. Which type of instruction has the 111 value as its operation code?
   (a) Input/output instruction (b) Register-reference instruction
   (c) Memory-reference instruction (d) None of these
6. The load instruction is mostly used to designate a transfer from memory to the _________.
   (a) Instruction register (b) Accumulator
   (c) Program counter (d) Memory address register

Ans. 1. b 2. c 3. b 4. d 5. a 6. b

8

Control Unit

1. What is a control unit?

Ans. The **control unit** is the main component of the CPU which directs the entire system operations by issuing control signals to the data path. These signals control the flow of data inside the CPU and between the CPU and memory or I/O units. The control signals between the control unit and other external units are generally carried by the control buses in a clock-driven manner.

2. List the basic tasks performed by the control unit.

or

Define the functional requirement for the control unit.

Ans. The execution of an instruction involves the execution of various subtasks called **cycles** such as fetch, decode and execute. Each of these cycles is made up of a specific sequence of microoperations. It is the duty of the control unit to initiate the desired sequence of microoperations. The control unit performs two basic tasks which are as follows:

- **Sequencing:** The control unit makes the processor to move through the microoperations in a proper sequence depending on the program being executed.
- **Execution:** The control unit causes the execution of microoperation by generating control signals that are required for opening of gates to let data pass, performing ALU operation and closing of gates.

3. Draw and explain the general model of the control unit.

Ans. To perform its tasks, the control unit must have inputs that enable it to identify the state of the system and outputs that enable it to control the function of the entire system. In addition, internally, the control unit must comprise the logic required to perform the sequencing and execution functions. Figure 8.1 depicts the general model of a control unit. It consists of four inputs: *clock, instruction register*, *flags* and the *control signals from system bus*. It has two outputs: *control signals within CPU* and *control signals to system bus*.

The inputs of the control unit are described as follows:

- **Clock:** The control unit uses a clock to keep track of the time. For each clock pulse, the control unit causes one microoperation or a set of concurrent microoperations to be executed. This is what is referred to as **clock cycle time** or **processor cycle time**.

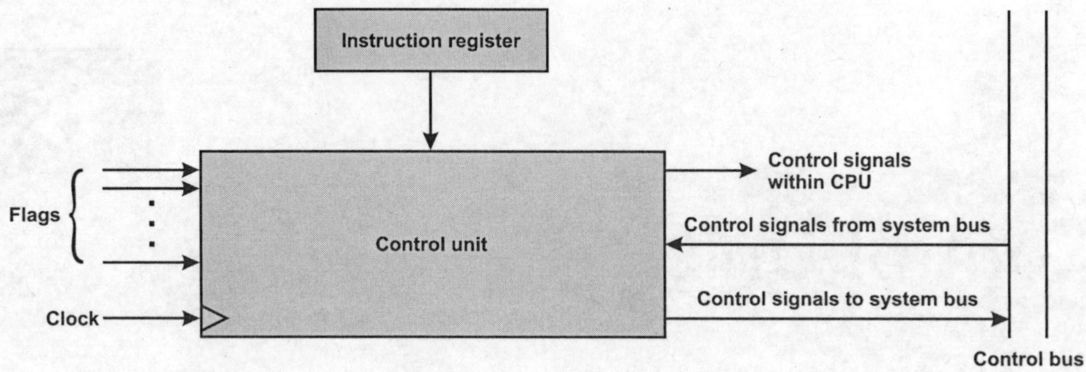

Figure 8.1 General Model of Control Unit

- **Instruction register (IR):** The control unit uses the opcode of the instruction placed in IR to identify the microoperation to be executed.
- **Flags:** A processor includes certain bits (referred to as **flags**) that indicate the current state of the processor and the result of recent ALU operations to the control unit.
- **Control signals from system bus:** The control unit receives signals such as interrupt signals and acknowledgement from the control bus part of the system bus.

The outputs of the control unit are described as follows:

- **Control signals within CPU:** There are two types of control signals that generate within the CPU. One of these causes the register transfers, while the other activates the specific functions of ALU.
- **Control signals to system bus:** The control unit sends two types of control signals out onto the control lines of the system bus: one goes to the I/O modules and the other to the memory.

4. What are the two alternatives to design the control unit?

Ans. The control unit of a digital computer can be designed/implemented in two different ways: *hardwired* and *microprogrammed* implementation. In **hardwired implementation**, the control unit is essentially a combinational circuit that employs logic gates, decoders, flip-flops and other digital circuits to generate the control signals. On the other hand, in **microprogrammed implementation**, the control information is stored in a memory (that is, a part of the control unit) called **control memory**, which is programmed in such a way that the required sequence of microoperations could be initiated.

5. Explain the hardwired control unit. Give the advantages and disadvantages of hardwired implementation.

or

Draw the circuit for control unit of basic computer and explain its working.

Ans. The control unit is said to be hardwired if the control signals are generated by the hardware using conventional logic design techniques. Figure 8.2 shows the block diagram of a hardwired control unit, which consists of a flip-flop, a 3 × 8 decoder, a 4 × 16 decoder, a 4-bit sequence counter (`SC`) and a number of control logic gates.

The instruction to be executed is read from the memory and placed in `IR`. The 16 bits of instruction placed in `IR` are divided into three groups: mode bit (indicated by the 15th bit), operation code (indicated by the bits 12-14) and rest 12 bits (0 through 11). The mode bit is input to the flip-flop

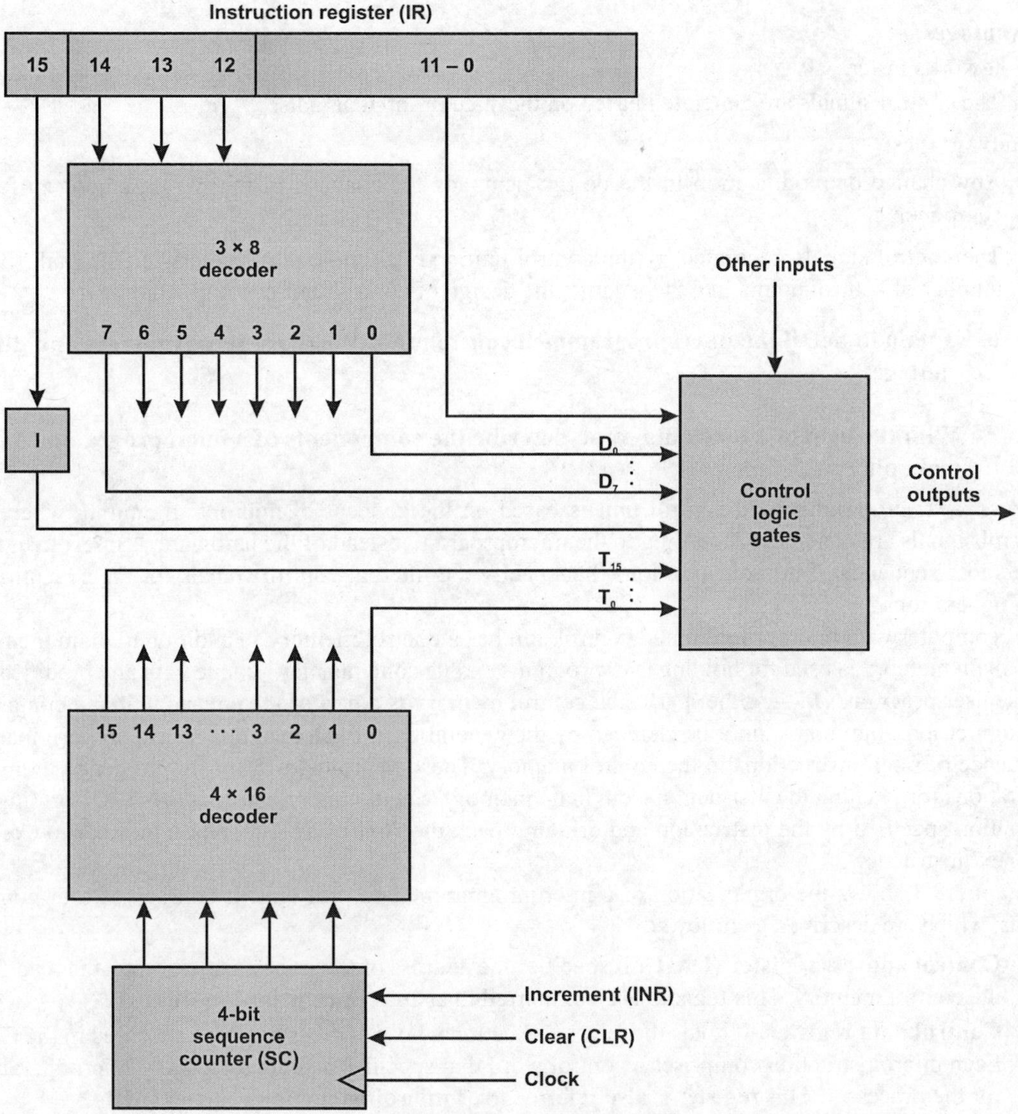

Figure 8.2 Hardwired Control Unit

(designated by I) and the output from the flip-flop is applied to the control logic gates. The three bits of opcode are decoded with the 3 × 8 decoder, which generates eight outputs (D_0 to D_7). These eight outputs are applied to the control logic gates. The bits 0 through 11 of the instruction are directly applied to the control logic gates. The 4-bit SC is capable of counting in binary from 0 through 15. The four outputs of SC are decoded with the 4 × 16 decoder, producing 16 timing signals (T_0 to T_{15}). All these timing signals are applied to the control logic gates. Generally, SC is incremented to generate the sequence of timing signals; however, sometimes it may need to be cleared to 0. Depending on all the inputs to the control logic gates, appropriate output signals (control signals) are generated as a function of input signals.

Advantages:

- It works faster.
- The control signals are generated based on the state of input signals.

Disadvantages:

- Any change or modification in the design demands for changes in the wiring among different components.
- The control signals generated by the control unit activate the control points in data path. If the number of control points in CPU is large, the design of control unit becomes complex.

6. Explain in detail the microprogrammed control unit. What are its advantages and disadvantages?

or

With the help of a block diagram, describe the components of a microprogrammed control unit.

Ans. A microprogrammed control unit is based on the concept of microprogramming where the control signals are generated according to the microprogram instead of the hardware. A **microprogram** refers to a sequence of microinstructions that specify the internal control signals for the execution of microoperations.

A computer with microprogrammed control unit has a control memory in addition to main memory. The main memory is used for holding user programs and its contents may change with any modification in the user program. On the other hand, the control memory is a part of the control unit and contains a fixed microprogram that cannot be changed by the general user. Each machine instruction originates a sequence of microinstructions in the control memory. These microinstructions in turn generate microoperations for fetching the instruction from main memory, calculating effective address, performing the operation specified by the instruction and bringing back the control to fetch phase in order to execute the next instruction.

Figure 8.3 shows the organization of a microprogrammed control unit. It consists of four components, which are described as follows:

- **Control address register (CAR):** It specifies the address of the microinstruction that is read from the control memory. This register is also referred to as **microprogram counter (μPC)**.
- **Control data register:** It holds the microinstruction whose address has been specified in the CAR. Each microinstruction comprises a control word that specifies a single or a set of microoperations for the processor. This register is also referred to as **microinstruction register (μIR)**.
- **Control memory:** It holds all the microinstructions corresponding to the instruction being executed. The control memory can be read only memory (ROM) because once the control unit is under operation, changes in the microprogram are not required.
- **Next-address generator (sequencer):** After all the microoperations specified by the current microinstruction have been executed, it is required to determine the address of the next microinstruction to be read from the control memory. The next microinstruction can be the immediate next to the present microinstruction or may be stored elsewhere in the control memory. The address of the next microinstruction may also be determined from the external inputs. Therefore, some bits of the current microinstruction are used to specify how to generate the address of the next microinstruction. The next address is computed in the next-address generator (also called **microprogram sequencer**) while the microoperations specified by the control word of current microinstruction

are being executed. After computing, the next address is transferred to CAR so that the next instruction could be read from the control memory.

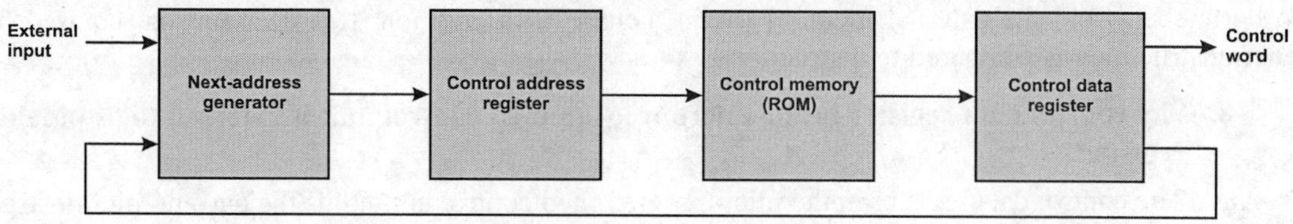

Figure 8.3 Microprogrammed Control Unit

Advantages:

- The design of a microprogrammed control unit is less complex. It is cheaper and less error prone to implement.
- It provides flexibility as it is not required to change the hardware configuration for different operations. A different control sequence can be specified for the system by simply changing the microprogram residing in the control memory.
- Debugging and maintenance of a microprogrammed control unit is easier.
- The complex function such as floating-point arithmetic can be efficiently realized.

DisAdvantages:

- It works with slow speed.
- It costs too much if we are to design a small CPU with limited hardware resources.
- Flexibility is achieved at some extra hardware cost due to the control memory and its access circuitry.

7. Describe in brief the microinstruction execution.

Ans. A microprogrammed control unit has two separate levels of control: *instruction level* and *microinstruction level*. At the **instruction level**, the processor executes the instruction cycles continuously. To start with, an initial address (the address of the first instruction of the program) is loaded into PC. Each instruction cycle involves the following steps:

1. The CPU fetches the instruction whose address is stored in PC from the main memory.
2. The opcode part of the fetched instruction is loaded into IR and the operation specified by IR is then decoded and executed.
3. PC is modified to point to the next instruction that is to be fetched from the main memory.

At the lower **microinstruction level**, the processor executes microinstruction cycles continuously. To start with, an initial address (generally, the address of the first microinstruction in sequence) is loaded into CAR. Each microinstruction cycle involves the following steps:

1. The microprogram sequencer fetches the microinstruction whose address is specified in CAR from the control memory.
2. The fetched microinstruction is loaded into the control data register and is decoded to generate the required control signals.
3. The microprogram sequencer determines the address of the next microinstruction to be fetched from the control memory and CAR is modified to point to that new microinstruction.

The execution of a microinstruction cycle is faster than an instruction cycle. This is because the microinstructions are stored in the control memory which lies inside the CPU and thus, nothing needs to be fetched from the external memory (main memory). In addition, less decoding is required for microinstructions as compared to instructions.

8. Why control data register in the microprogrammed control unit is referred to as pipeline register?

Ans. The control data register in the microprogrammed control unit holds the current microinstruction, while the address of the next microinstruction is computed and read from the control memory. This register is sometimes referred to as **pipeline register** because it allows the microoperations specified by the control word of the current microinstruction to be executed simultaneously with the generation of next microinstruction.

9. Differentiate between hardwired and microprogrammed control unit.

Ans. Some differences between hardwired and microprogrammed control unit are listed in Table 8.1.

Table 8.1 Differences between Hardwired and Microprogrammed Control Unit

Hardwired Control Unit	Microprogrammed Control Unit
It works fast.	It operates at comparatively slow speed. Fetching a microinstruction from the control memory takes more time than generating control signals using hardware circuits.
The control signals are generated using the hardware.	Control functions are implemented in software rather than hardware.
It provides no flexibility since any change or modification in the design demands for changes in the wiring among different components.	It provides flexibility as changes in design can be made easily only by changing the microprogram placed in the control memory.
It is somewhat difficult to handle large or complex instruction sets with hardwired control unit.	It is relatively easier to handle large or complex instruction sets with microprogrammed control unit.
It does not require any memory for the operations; all operations are performed within registers only.	It employs control memory that can be RAM or ROM.
The design process becomes difficult if more operations are to be implemented.	The design process is easy for any number of operations.

10. Define the following terms:

(a) Microinstruction

(b) Microprogram

(c) Control word

(d) Microprogram routine

Ans.

a. **Microinstruction:** An instruction that controls the data flow and sequencing in a processor at a more elementary level than machine instruction is referred to as microinstruction.

b. Microprogram: A series of microinstructions that perform various microoperations together form a microprogram. Each line in a microprogram is a microinstruction that describes the microoperations occurring at one time.

c. Control word: It refers to a binary string consisting of 0's and 1's, where each bit represents one control line emanating from the control unit. Each microoperation is represented by a different pattern of 1's and 0's in the control word.

d. Microprogram routine: In the control memory, the microinstructions are stored in groups, where each group specifies a routine. Each computer instruction is associated with its own microprogram routine stored in the control memory, which generates the microoperations required to execute the instruction.

11. How the instruction code bits are mapped to an address in the control memory?

Ans. We know that a microprogram routine exists in the control memory corresponding to each instruction. For a specific instruction, the location of its microprogram routine in control memory is determined using the **mapping process** which transforms the 4-bit opcode of the instruction to a 7-bit address in the control memory. To accomplish the conversion, the mapping process involves the following steps:

1. Place a 0 in the most significant bit (MSB) position in 7-bit address.
2. Transfer the four bits of opcode into next four bit positions in 7-bit address.
3. Clear the two least significant bit (LSB) positions in 7-bit address to 0.

12. Describe the microinstruction format.

Ans. The format of a 20-bit microinstruction for the control memory is shown in Figure 8.4. It consists of four functional parts: microoperation fields (denoted by F_1, F_2 and F_3) of 3 bits each, 2-bit condition for branching (CD) field, 2-bit branch field (BR) and 7-bit address field (AD).

3 bits	3 bits	3 bits	2 bits	2 bits	7 bits
F_1	F_2	F_3	CD	BR	AD

Figure 8.4 Microinstruction Format

These fields are described as follows:

Microoperation fields: The nine bits of these fields specify the microoperations to be performed. The three bits of each field are individually encoded into seven microoperations, thus giving a total of 21 microoperations listed in Table 8.2. The table also lists the register transfer statement for each microoperation and the symbol assigned for use in microprogram.

Depending on the values of bits in F_1, F_2 and F_3, three microoperations are selected, one from each field. This implies that any microinstruction cannot have more than three microoperations. If less than three microoperations are specified for a microinstruction, it means that one or two of the three fields have the binary value 000 indicating no operation. For example, consider a microinstruction that specifies two simultaneous microoperations AR ← PC and DR ← AC from F_1 and F_2, respectively, but none from F_3. For this microinstruction, the nine bits of microoperation fields will be 110 101 000. Here, it is important to note that no two conflicting microoperations can be specified together. For example, the microoperation fields having content 010 001 000 specify to clear the content of AC to zero and subtract the contents of DR from that of AC at the same time and thus, have no meaning.

Table 8.2 Microoperation Fields

Microoperation Field	Binary value	Microoperation	Symbol
	000	No operation	NOP
	001	AC ← AC + DR	ADD
	010	AC ← 0	CLRAC
F_1	011	AC ← AC + 1	INCAC
	100	AC ← DR	DRTAC
	101	AR ← DR(0–10)	DRTAR
	110	AR ← PC	PCTAR
	111	M[AR] ← DR	WRITE
	000	No operation	NOP
	001	AC ← AC − DR	SUB
	010	AC ← AC ∨ DR	OR
F_2	011	AC ← AC ∧ DR	AND
	100	DR ← M[AR]	READ
	101	DR ← AC	ACTDR
	110	DR ← DR + 1	INCDR
	111	DR(0–10) ← PC	PCTDR
	000	No operation	NOP
	001	AC ← AC ⊕ DR	XOR
	010	AC ← $\overline{AC}$	COM
F_3	011	AC ← shl AC	SHL
	100	AC ← shr AC	SHR
	101	PC ← PC + 1	INCPC
	110	PC ← AR	ARTPC
	111	Reserved	

Condition for branching (CD): This field consists of two bits, which together specify four status bits (symbolized as U, I, S and Z) as shown in Table 8.3.

Table 8.3 Condition for Branching Field

CD	Condition	Symbol	Description
00	Always 1	U	Unconditional branch
01	DR(15)	I	Indirect address bit
10	AC(15)	S	Sign bit of AC
11	AC = 0	Z	Zero value in AC

Observe from Table 8.3 that when CD = 00 (symbolized as U), the condition is always 1, indicating that the condition is always true. When this condition is used along with BR field, it indicates unconditional branch operation. After the instruction has been read from the memory, the 15th bit of DR provides the value for indirect address bit (I). The next status bit S is obtained from the sign bit of AC. The zero (Z) status bit is set to 1 if all bits in AC are 0's.

Branch (BR) field: This field contains two bits and specifies the type of branch to be used. This field is used along with the 7-bit address (AD) field for selecting the address of the next microinstruction. When BR = 00, a jump (symbolized as JMP) operation is performed and when BR = 01, a call to subroutine (symbolized as CALL) operation is performed as shown in Table 8.4. Both these operations are functionally similar except that the call operation requires a return address to be stored in subroutine register (SBR). When BR = 10, a return from subroutine (symbolized as RET) operation is performed and when BR = 11, the mapping (symbolized as MAP) from instruction opcode bits to the address in CAR is performed.

Table 8.4 Branch Field

BR	Symbol	Description
00	JMP	CAR ← AD if condition = 1
		CAR ← CAR + 1 if condition = 0
01	CALL	CAR ← AD, SBR ← CAR + 1 if condition = 1
		CAR ← CAR + 1 if condition = 0
10	RET	CAR ← SBR
11	MAP	CAR(2-5) ← DR(11-14), CAR(0,1,6) ← 0

Address (AD) field: This field consists of seven bits that specify the branch address.

13. What do you mean by horizontal and vertical microinstruction? What are their relative merits and demerits?

Ans. A microinstruction contains various control signals. The microinstructions can be structured in two ways: *horizontal* and *vertical*.

- **Horizontal microinstruction:** In this microinstruction, each individual bit corresponds to an individual control signal required in the CPU. For example, if a CPU needs 32 control signals, then at least 32 bits are required in each horizontal microinstruction.

Merits:

- Since each bit controls a separate control line, a high degree of parallelism can be achieved.
- They provide higher operating speed.
- Decoding is not needed.

Demerits:

- These microinstructions are longer and thus, take more space.
- **Vertical microinstruction:** In this microinstruction, the control lines are grouped (encoded) into specific fields within a microinstruction, with each field containing those control signals that cannot be activated simultaneously. This reduces the length of microinstructions. However, decoders are required to map an n-bit field to one of 2^n possible combinations of control lines. For example, a 4-bit field in vertical microinstruction can be decoded to specify any one of the 16 control lines.

Merits:

- These microinstructions are short and thus, take less space.

Demerits:

- A limited degree of parallelism can be achieved.
- They provide slow operating speed.
- Decoding is necessary.

14. What is a microprogram sequencer? Explain its hardware implementation.

Ans. In the microprogrammed control unit, there are two basic components: the control memory and the circuits that choose the address of next microinstruction in the control memory. The latter component is referred to as a **microprogram sequencer**. The role of the microprogram sequencer is to provide an address to the control memory so that a microinstruction can be read and executed. Figure 8.5 shows the block diagram of a microprogram sequencer. The figure also includes control memory for showing the interactions between the sequencer and the memory attached to it. Two multiplexers (MUX A and MUX B) and input logic are also used.

MUX A has four input lines and two selection inputs (S_0 and S_1). All the four inputs as well as the output of MUX A contain a 7-bit address. The output from MUX A (which is one of the source

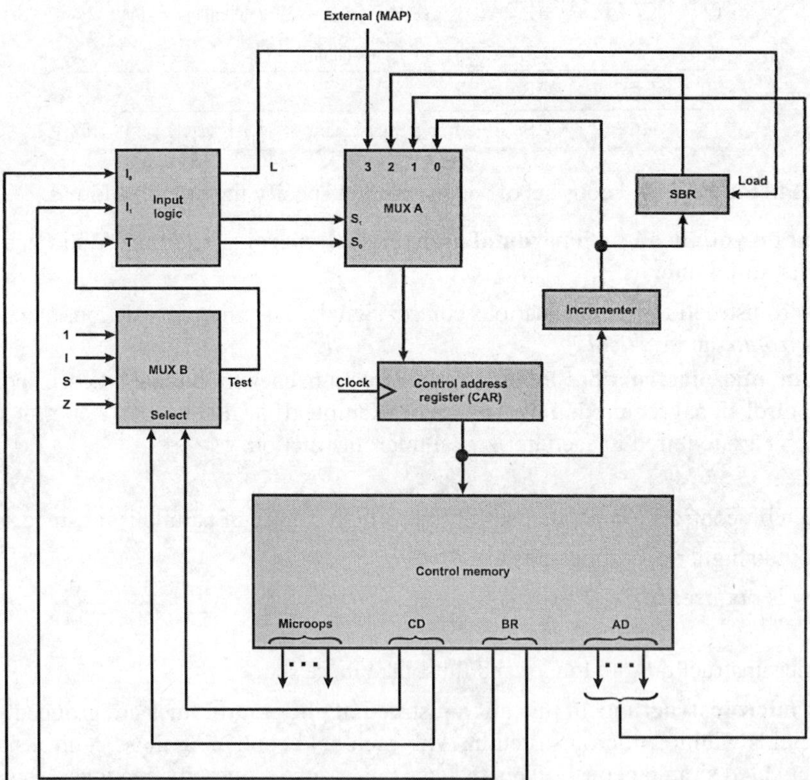

Figure 8.5 Microprogram Sequencer for Control Memory

addresses) is loaded into CAR and the output from CAR specifies the address for control memory. After the address has been provided, the content of CAR is incremented by one by the **incrementer** and is applied to input 0 of MUX A as well as to SBR. The AD field of the present microinstruction in the control memory forms the input 1 and the output from SBR forms the input 2 of MUX A. The input 3 of MUX A comes from an external source that maps the instruction.

MUX B has four status bits (1, I, S and Z) as inputs and the two bits of CD field of the present microinstruction in the control memory form its selection inputs. The output from MUX B forms the T input of the input logic. Depending on the selection inputs of MUX B, one of the status bit is selected as output. If the selected status bit is set, the T input is 1, otherwise 0.

The **input logic** circuit determines the type of operations available in the control unit such as branch/jump, call to a subroutine, push or pop the stack, etc. Besides T input, it has two more inputs, I_0 and I_1, which come from the BR field of the present microinstruction. It produces three outputs, one of which (L) enables the Load input of SBR, while other two (S_0 and S_1) form the selection inputs of MUX A. The binary values of S_0 and S_1 choose one of the source addresses of MUX A for CAR. For example, if $S_1S_0 = 01$, the input 1 of MUX A is selected, which specifies a transfer path from AD field of the present microinstruction to CAR.

The truth table for the input logic circuit is shown in Figure 8.6. The inputs I_0 and I_2 are same as binary values of BR field. The binary values of S_0 and S_1 determine the path in MUX A, specifying the required transfer. The incremented value of CAR is loaded into SBR only during a call microinstruction when status bit condition, that is, T = 1.

BR field		Input			MUX A		Load SBR
		I_1	I_0	T	S_1	S_0	L
0	0	0	0	0	0	0	0
0	0	0	0	1	0	1	0
0	1	0	1	0	0	0	0
0	1	0	1	1	0	1	1
1	0	1	0	×	1	0	0
1	1	1	1	×	1	1	0

Figure 8.6 Truth Table for Input Logic Circuit

15. Write a short note on wide branch addressing.

Ans. Whenever a branch microinstruction that is conditioned on the status of the mode bits of instruction is executed, the effective address computation routine is called from the control memory to generate the effective address of branch (that is, branch address). The computed branch address is then loaded into CAR and the control is transferred to the specified branch address. After executing the current microinstruction, it is required to compute the address of next microinstruction that is to be read from the control memory. If the next microinstruction also involves branching, the same process needs to be repeated and the branch address is to be generated. Generating the branch addresses becomes more difficult with increase in the number of branches.

A simple and inexpensive way of generating branch addresses is **wide branch addressing** that uses a programmable logic array (PLA) to generate the required branch addresses. In this method, the opcode bits of the instruction are translated into the starting address of the corresponding microroutine. To achieve this, the opcode bits are connected to the inputs of PLA which acts as a decoder. The output from PLA is the address of the desired microroutine.

16. Write the steps performed by the processor to fetch a word from the memory.

Ans. To fetch a word from the memory, the processor specifies the address of the memory location where the desired data is stored on the address bus. The processor loads the desired address into AR whose output is connected to the address lines of memory bus. At the same time, it issues a read signal indicating that the word at memory address specified by AR is to be read into DR. Once the desired data have been transferred to DR, they can be loaded into any of the processor registers.

Let the memory address from which data is to be read is specified in register R_1 and the data is to be read into register R_2. To accomplish this operation, the following sequence of steps is performed.

1. AR ← [R_1].
2. Activate the control signal to indicate read operation.
3. Wait for the control signal response.
4. Load the contents at address specified by AR into DR. That is, DR ← M[AR].
5. Transfer the contents of DR to the register R_2. That is, R_2 ← DR.

17. Write the steps performed by the processor to store a word into memory.

Ans. To store a word in a memory location, the processor loads the address of the memory location where the data is to be written into AR and the data to be written into DR. Then, the processor issues a write signal indicating to write the word stored in DR to the memory address specified by AR.

Let the data to be written to the memory be stored in register R_1 and the desired memory address specified in register R_2. To accomplish this operation, the following sequence of steps is performed.

1. AR ← [R_2].
2. DR ← [R_1].
3. Activate the control signal to indicate write operation and wait for the control signal response.
4. Load the contents stored in DR into the memory location specified by AR. That is, M[AR] ← DR.

18. Under what situations the microprogram counter is not incremented after a new instruction is fetched from the microprogram memory?

Ans. Each time a new microinstruction is fetched from the control memory, the microprogram counter is incremented. However, there are certain situations which do not demand for incrementing the microprogram counter. These situations are described as follows:

- When a new instruction is loaded into IR, the microprogram counter is loaded with the starting address of the microroutine for that instruction.
- When a branch microinstruction occurs and the branch condition is satisfied, the microprogram counter is loaded with the branch address.
- When the end instruction occurs, the microprogram counter is loaded with the address of the first control word in the microroutine for fetch cycle of instruction.

19. A CPU has 16 registers, an ALU with 32 operations and a shifter with 8 operations, all connected with a common bus system.

(a). Formulate a control word for a microoperation.

(b). Specify the number of bits in each field of control word.

(c). Show the bits of the control word that specify the microoperation $R_4 \leftarrow R_5 + R_6$.

Ans.

(a). The control word consists of control bits for source register 1, source register 2, destination register, ALU and shift operations.

(b). The number of control bits assigned to each field depends on the number of CPU registers and ALU operations. In our case, 16 CPU registers need four bits (as $16 = 2^4$), ALU needs five bits (as $32 = 2^5$) and the shifter needs three bits (as $8 = 2^3$) to encode all the operations. Thus, total 20 bits will be required in the control word as shown here.

4 bits	4 bits	4 bits	5 bits	3 bits
SRC 1	SRC 2	DEST	ALU	Shift

(c). The contents of the control word for the given microoperation are shown here.

0101	0110	0100	00010	000

Notice that for the bits of ALU, you can refer Table 9.2 of Chapter 9 'Processor Organization'.

MULTIPLE CHOICE QUESTIONS

1. Microinstructions reside in __________.

   (a) Main memory   (b) Control memory
   (c) Cache   (d) None of these

2. The control unit uses the opcode of the instruction placed in _________ to identify the microoperation to be executed.

   (a) PC   (b) Control memory
   (c) Main memory   (d) IR

3. Which of the following registers specifies the address of the microinstruction that is read from the control memory?

   (a) Microprogram counter   (b) Control data register
   (c) Microprogram sequencer   (d) None of these

4. Which of the following operations is performed when BR = 00?
   (a) Jump (b) Call to subroutine
   (c) Return from subroutine (d) Mapping
5. In __________ microinstruction, each bit corresponds to an individual control signal.
   (a) Vertical (b) Horizontal
   (c) Structured (d) None of these
6. ________ field in a microinstruction stores the branch address.
   (a) BR (b) Microoperation
   (c) AD (d) CD

Ans. 1. b 2. d 3. a 4. a 5. b 6. c

9

Processor Organization

1. Discuss various components of CPU.

Ans. The **central processing unit (CPU),** more commonly called as the **processor,** refers to the part of computer system that is responsible for performing the bulk of data processing operations. It comprises three major parts including *arithmetic logic unit* (*ALU*), *control unit* (*CU*) and a set of *registers*. **ALU** contains the electronic circuitry that executes all arithmetic and logical operations on the data made available to it, **CU** contains circuitry that uses electrical signals to direct the entire computer system to carry out, or execute, stored program instructions and **registers** are used to hold the intermediate results produced during the execution.

Components of CPU

A processor is built upon some general components that are discussed below:

- **Buses:** A bus is the communication pathway that interconnects two or more components/devices of the computer system such as CPU, memory unit and I/O devices. For detailed description of bus, refer Chapter 7.
- **Registers:** CPU contains a variety of registers such as data register (DR), address register (AR) and program counter (PC). For the description of these registers, refer Chapter 7.
- **Flag:** A flag is an indicator that describes the status of the processor. There exist a number of flags in the processor, which are organized into a single register referred to as **flag register** or **processor status register**. Each flag can store one bit (0 or 1) and most flags store the outcomes of the most recent arithmetic or logical operations. The flag registers are connected to the mathematical unit of the processor.
- **Stacks:** A stack refers to a block of memory, which is used to temporarily store different data values during the execution of an operation so that the processor can use them when required. Though a processor has registers to temporarily store data, the processor needs temporary memory (stack) many times because the number of processor registers is finite. If some application requires more registers than available, the processor stores the register values that are not in immediate use in stack and retrieves them later. Moreover, during execution, when the processor has to jump to some

function/routine, it needs to keep track of the address of the instruction from where it jumped so that it could return to the same place after the completion of routine. The processor uses stack to store the return address.

An important characteristic of stack is that data can be added or removed only at one end called the **top** of the stack. When some data is put on the top of the stack, the data below it cannot be removed until data above it is removed. This implies that the last data value added to the stack will be the first one to be removed. Therefore, the stack is known as **last-in-first-out (LIFO)** structure. There are two operations associated with a stack, namely, *PUSH* and *POP*. **PUSH** refers to insertion of data in the stack, whereas **POP** refers to removal of data from the stack.

- **Input/output (I/O) ports:** The I/O ports refer to the connections between processor and external devices such as keyboard and printer. The processor issues commands, send/retrieve data to various I/O devices using the ports through which they are connected to the processor. Some I/O devices are directly connected to the memory bus. In case of such devices, the processor sends data to the port by placing it in a memory address, while retrieves data from a port by reading from a memory address.

2. Draw and explain the block diagram of a complete processor.

Ans. The block diagram of a complete processor is shown in Figure 9.1. It consists of *instruction unit*, *caches*, *processing units* and *bus interface unit*. The role of **instruction unit** is to fetch the instructions from the instruction cache. In case the required instruction is not available in instruction cache, the instruction unit fetches it from the main memory. A processor provides **instruction cache** and **data cache** for storing instructions and data, respectively. Though nowadays many processors employ separate caches

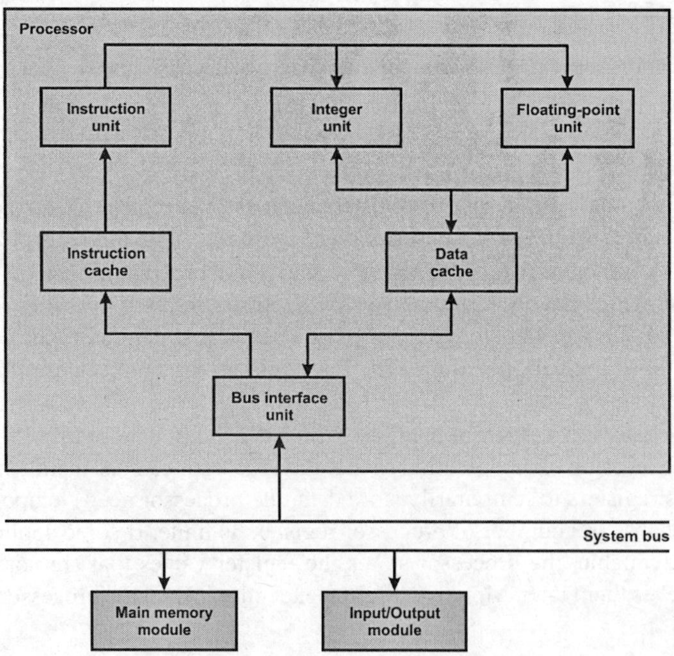

Figure 9.1 Block Diagram of a Complete Processor

for instructions and data, some processors use a common single cache for storing both instructions and data. There are two processing units provided by the processor: **integer unit** to process the integer data and **floating-point unit** to process floating-point data. Both the processing units receive the respective data from the data cache. The **bus interface unit** is responsible for controlling the interface of processor to system bus, main memory module and I/O module.

3. Name the different CPU organizations a computer can have.

Ans. Depending on the internal architecture/organization of registers in a processor, most computers fall under one of the following CPU organizations:

- Single accumulator organization
- General register organization
- Stack organization.

In addition, some computers may also have the combined features of more than one of the above-mentioned organizations.

4. Explain the general register organization of CPU with the help of a block diagram.

Ans. The registers in CPU are used to hold the intermediate results during instruction execution in order to avoid the time-consuming memory access operations. In case a number of registers are included in the CPU, they are connected via a common bus system to make them more efficient. This is also desired because registers need to communicate with each other for data transfer as well as for performing various microoperations. Therefore, a common unit is required in the processor to perform arithmetic, logic and shift microoperations.

Figure 9.2 shows the general register organization of CPU. In this organization, there is a set of seven CPU registers R_1 to R_7, which are connected to a common ALU. The output from each register is input to two multiplexers, forming two buses `A` and `B`. The selection inputs `SELA` and `SELB` in multiplexers `A` and `B`, respectively, determine which register output or the external input should be selected as input for a specific bus. The buses `A` and `B` are attached to the common ALU. The operation (`OPR`) selected in ALU defines the microoperation (arithmetic or logic) to be performed and the output of this microoperation is available for output data and also serves as input for all the registers. The destination register that should receive the information from the output bus is determined by the decoder. Depending on the selection inputs (`SELD`), the decoder activates one of the registers load inputs, thus, providing a path for data transfer between the output bus and the selected register. The control unit directs the entire flow of information through ALU and registers.

To understand how this CPU organization works, let the microoperation to be performed is:

$$R_1 \leftarrow R_2 - R_3$$

To perform this microoperation, four control variables including `SELA`, `SELB`, `OPR` and `SELD` are generated in the control unit. The purpose of each control variable is described as follows:

- **MUX A selector (`SELA`):** To place the contents of R_2 into bus `A`.
- **MUX B selector (`SELB`):** To place the contents of R_3 into bus `B`.
- **ALU operation selector (`OPR`):** To perform the arithmetic subtraction `A-B`.
- **Decoder destination selector (`SELD`):** To transfer the content of the output bus into R_1.

All these control variables must be available in the control unit in the beginning of the clock cycle. The data from source registers R_2 and R_3, going through the multiplexers and ALU, reaches to the output

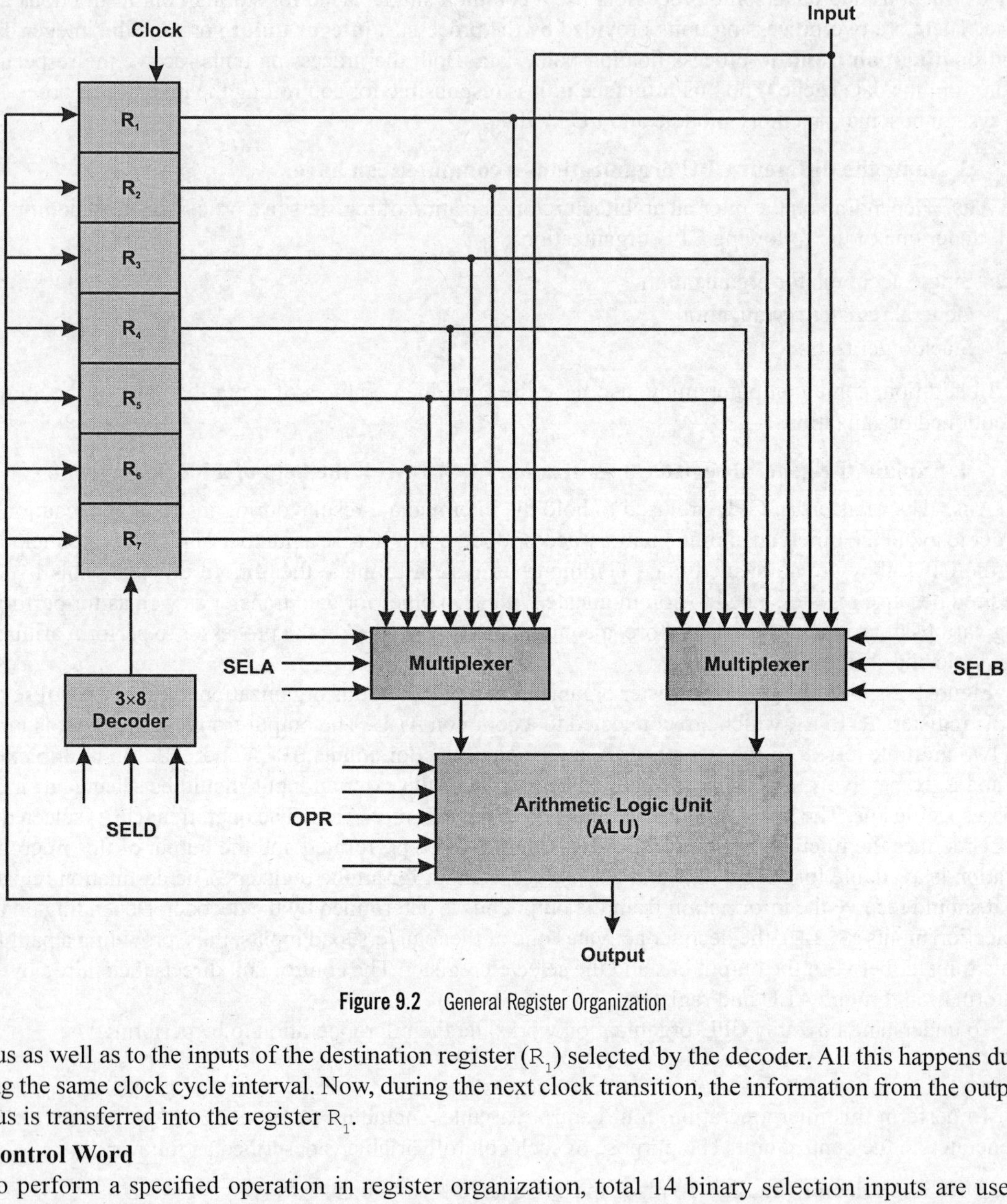

Figure 9.2 General Register Organization

bus as well as to the inputs of the destination register (R_1) selected by the decoder. All this happens during the same clock cycle interval. Now, during the next clock transition, the information from the output bus is transferred into the register R_1.

Control Word

To perform a specified operation in register organization, total 14 binary selection inputs are used. The combined value of these 14 bits specifies the control word of CPU. As shown in Figure 9.3, the 14-bit control word consists of four parts: SELA (3 bits), SELB (3 bits), SELD (3 bits) and OPR (5 bits). The three bits of SELA and SELB in the control word determine the registers to hold A and B inputs of ALU, respectively. The three bits of SELD determine the destination register in which the output is to be stored. The last five bits (OPR) of the control word determine one of the operations available in ALU.

3 bits	3 bits	3 bits	5 bits
SELA	SELB	SELD	OPR

Figure 9.3 Control Word

Table 9.1 specifies the binary encoding of register selection fields (SELA, SELB and SELD).

Table 9.1 Encoding of the SELA, SELB and SELD

Binary code	SELA	SELB	SELD
000	External input	External input	No destination
001	R_1	R_1	R_1
010	R_2	R_2	R_2
011	R_3	R_3	R_3
100	R_4	R_4	R_4
101	R_5	R_5	R_5
110	R_6	R_6	R_6
111	R_7	R_7	R_7

Notice that when the binary code for the selectors SELA or SELB is 000, the multiplexer selects the external input and when the binary code for the selector SELD is 000, then destination register is not selected and the data of the output bus is available to the external output.

Table 9.2 specifies the binary encoding of ALU operation (OPR), where each operation is assigned a symbolic name.

Table 9.2 Encoding of ALU Operation

OPR	Operation	Symbol
00000	Transfer A	TSFA
00001	Increment A	INCA
00010	Addition	ADD
00101	Subtraction	SUB
00110	Decrement A	DECA
01000	AND A and B	AND
01010	OR A and B	OR
01100	XOR A and B	XOR
01110	Complement A	COMA
10000	Shift right A	SHRA
11000	Shift left A	SHLA

For example, let a microoperation be $R_1 \leftarrow R_2$ AND R_3

This expression specifies the registers R_2 and R_3 to hold A and B inputs of ALU, respectively, and register R_1 as the destination register to hold the value of the ALU operation AND. Thus, the 14-bit control word for the above microoperation can be determined using the Tables 9.1 and 9.2 as shown in Table 9.3.

Table 9.3 14-bit Control Word

Fields	SELA	SELB	SELD	OPR
Symbol	R_2	R_3	R_1	AND
Control word	010	011	001	01000

5. Define stack. Explain the stack organization of CPU.

Ans. Stack, also known as **LIFO list**, is a storage device used to temporarily store information in such a manner that the last item inserted into stack is the first one to be removed. The insertion and deletion of items can occur at only one end in the stack that is the top of the stack. In digital computers, a stack is a memory unit associated with an address register, called **stack pointer (SP)**, which holds the address of the item currently at the top of the stack. Two common operations related with stack include PUSH (inserting an item into stack) and POP (deleting an item from the stack). These operations are performed by incrementing and decrementing the SP, respectively.

A stack can be implemented either as a set of registers (*register stack*) or in the random access memory (RAM) attached with the CPU (*memory stack*).

Register Stack

A stack can be organized as a finite number of registers or memory words. The SP holds a binary number whose value is equivalent to the address of the item currently on the top of the stack. The block diagram of a 32-word register stack is shown in Figure 9.4.

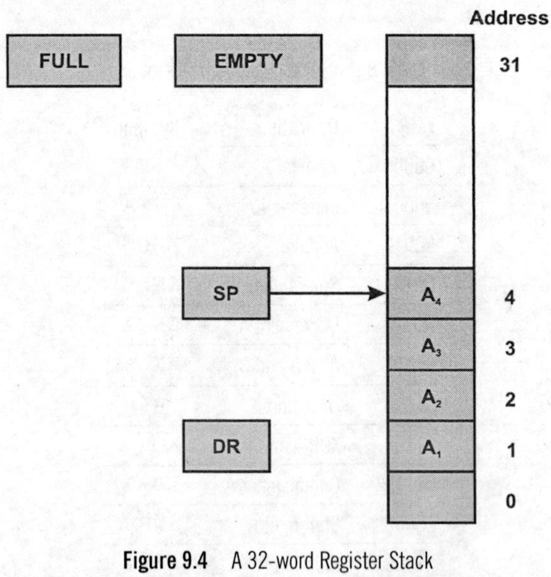

Figure 9.4 A 32-word Register Stack

As shown in Figure 9.4, currently there are four items (A_1, A_2, A_3 and A_4) in the stack at address 1, 2, 3 and 4, respectively. The SP points to A_4 (the item at the top of stack) and thus, its content is 4. Two single bit registers FULL and EMPTY indicate the status of stack at any instant of time. The FULL register is set to 1 when stack is full (**overflow**) and the EMPTY register is set to 1 when the stack is empty (**underflow**). The data register (DR) stores the binary value that is to be written into or read from the stack.

To delete the item at the top of the stack (that is, A_4), first the memory word at address 4 is read and then SP is decremented. Since after decrementing, the new content of SP is 3, the item A_3 is now at the top of the stack. On the other hand, to push a new item at the top of the stack, first the SP is incremented and then the item is inserted at the position specified by SP.

With a 32-word stack, the SP can store a 5-bit value ($2^5 = 32$) and thus, the maximum and minimum values that SP can store are 11111 (decimal 31) and 00000 (decimal 0), respectively. When SP = 11111 and we increment it by one to insert a new item, we get 100000. Since SP can store only five bits, only the five least significant bits of 100000 are stored in SP, that is, SP = 00000. This indicates that the stack is full now and no more items can be inserted into it. Thus, the FULL is set to 1. Similarly, when SP = 00000 and we decrement it by one, we get 111111, which implies SP = 11111. This indicates that the stack is empty now and there are no more items to be deleted. Thus, the EMPTY register is set to 1.

- **PUSH operation:** Initially, SP is cleared to 0 indicating that it points to the memory word at address 0. Along with this, EMPTY is set to 1 and FULL is set to 0. A value 0 in FULL confirms that a new item can be inserted into the stack using the PUSH operation, which is implemented with the following sequence of microoperations:

  1. SP ← SP + 1 [increment the stack pointer]
  2. M[SP] ← DR [write the item from data register to the memory stack pointer]
  3. if (SP = 0) [check if stack is full]
then (FULL ← 1)
  4. EMPTY ← 0 [mark the stack not empty].

- **POP operation:** When EMPTY = 0, an item can be deleted from the stack using the POP operation, which is implemented with the following sequence of microoperations:

  1. DR ← M [SP] [read the item from the top of stack]
  2. SP ← SP - 1 [decrement the stack pointer]
  3. if (SP = 0) [check if stack is empty]
then (EMPTY ← 1)
  4. FULL ← 0 [mark the stack not full].

Memory Stack

A stack is implemented in the processor by assigning a part of the main memory for the stack operations and using one of the processor registers as the stack pointer SP. Figure 9.5 illustrates a portion of RAM divided into three sections: *program*, *data* and *stack*. In the **program** section, the program counter (PC) register points to the next instruction to be executed, in the **data** section, the address register (AR) points to an array containing data and in **stack** section, SP register points to the top of the stack. All the three registers are attached to a common address bus and any of them can give a memory address onto the bus. While an instruction is being executed, PC provides the address of the instruction to be read on the bus

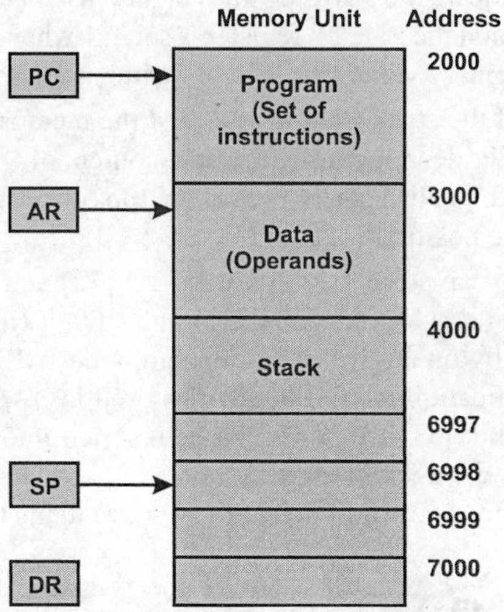

Figure 9.5 A Portion of RAM with Three Sections

during the fetch phase and AR provides the address of the operand on the bus during the execute phase. SP provides the address of the item to be pushed on or popped from the stack. The data register (DR) stores the binary value that is to be written into or read from the stack.

Initially, SP pointed to the memory address 7000. As items were inserted, the stack grew with decreasing memory addresses. This means the first item is stored at address 7000, second at 6999 and so on until the last address that can be used for the stack. Currently, SP points to 6998 as shown in the figure.

- **PUSH operation:** A new item is inserted at the top of the stack using the PUSH operation, which is implemented with the following sequence of microoperations:

  1. $SP \leftarrow SP - 1$ [decrement the stack pointer]
  2. $M[SP] \leftarrow DR$ [write item from the data register to the memory stack pointer].

- **POP operation:** An item can be deleted from the stack using the POP operation, which is implemented with the following sequence of microoperations:

  1. $DR \leftarrow M[SP]$ [read the item from the top of the stack]
  2. $SP \leftarrow SP + 1$ [increment the stack pointer SP]

Notice that if the stack is organized into RAM in such a way that it grows (on inserting items) with increasing memory addresses, SP is incremented in case of PUSH operation, while it is decremented in case of POP operation.

6. What do you mean by reverse Polish notation? How an arithmetic expression is evaluated using stacks?

Ans. Generally, the arithmetic expressions are written in the **infix notation**, where the operator is written between the operands. The Polish mathematician Lukasiewicz presented an alternative notation to represent arithmetic expressions in which the operator is written before the operands. This notation has been given the name the **prefix notation** (also called **Polish notation**). There is one more notation called the **postfix notation** or the **reverse Polish notation (RPN)** in which the operators are written after the operands. For example, consider an arithmetic expression with two operands A, B and a '+' operator. This expression can be written in three notations as shown here.

A + B	[Infix notation]
+AB	[Prefix or Polish notation]
AB+	[Postfix or reverse Polish notation]

An arithmetic expression written in infix notation can be easily converted into RPN. This conversion is performed in accordance with the operators' precedence followed for the infix notation. First, the arithmetic operations inside the inner parentheses and then in the outer parentheses are performed. Also, the multiplication and division operations are performed before the addition and subtraction operations.

Evaluation of Arithmetic Expressions

The arithmetic expressions can be efficiently evaluated using register stack organization. However before evaluation, the expressions must be represented into reverse Polish notation. This is because it is always more efficient to evaluate an arithmetic expression presented in reverse Polish notation. An arithmetic expression presented in reverse Polish notation can be evaluated using stack by following the steps given below:

1. Scan the expression from left to right.
2. If an operand occurs, push it onto the stack.
3. If an operator occurs, then perform the following:
   a. Pop the two top elements from the stack.
   b. Perform the operation involving the operator on the popped operands.
   c. Push the result back onto the stack.
4. Continue scanning the expression and repeat steps 2 and 3 for each element of expression until there are no more operators.
5. After performing all these steps, the value at the top of the stack is the result of the expression.

The above procedure can be better explained with the help of an example. Suppose the arithmetic expression that is to be evaluated using stack organization is:

(4*5) + (5*6)

The reverse Polish notation for the given expression is:

4 5 * 5 6 * +

Now, the expression can be evaluated as illustrated in Figure 9.6.

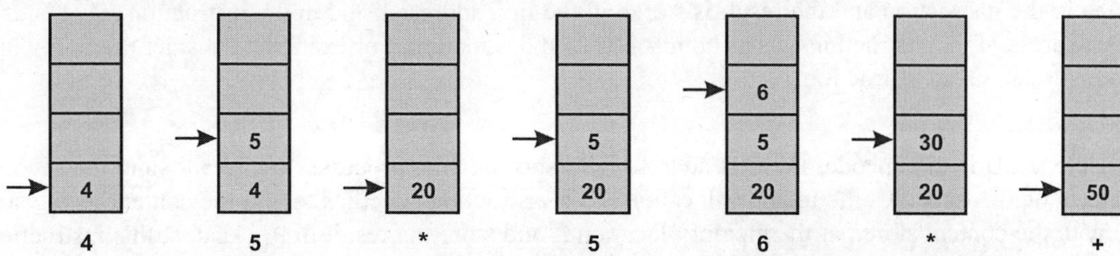

Figure 9.6 Stack Operations to Evaluate the Arithmetic Expression (4 * 5) + (5 * 6)

7. Define instruction and instruction format. Explain the instruction formats for different types of CPU organization.

Ans. An **instruction** can be defined as a command given to the computer for performing a specified function on the given set of data. The format or the way in which the instruction is written is called the **instruction format**. The instruction format is usually represented in the form of a rectangular box, which represents the bits of instructions in the same way as they seem in control register or memory words. The bits of an instruction are divided into various fields out of which the three most common fields are as follows:

- **Operation code (opcode):** This field specifies the operation to be performed such as `ADD`, `MUL` and `SHIFT`.
- **Address:** This field indicates some memory address (such as `M[X]` and `M[Y]`) or a processor register (such as R_0 and R_1).
- **Mode:** This field specifies the way of determining the operands or the **effective address** (address of the operand) in the given instruction.

The instructions in a computer may differ from one another in terms of length and the number of addresses involved in the instructions. The number of address fields in an instruction format depends on the CPU organization of the computer system. There are three types of CPU organizations in a computer, including single accumulator, general register and stack organization.

In single accumulator organization, all the operations are performed with the implied accumulator (AC) register. Thus, only one-address field is used in the instruction format of this type of computer. In general register organization, either two or three addresses fields are used in the instruction format and the computers with stack organization employ one or zero address fields in their instruction format. The instruction formats with one, two, three and zero address fields are discussed as follows:

One-address instruction: This type of instruction format uses only one address field. All the operations are performed with the implied `AC` register and the result is stored in the `AC` itself. For example, consider the following assembly language instruction.

```
ADD A
```

Here, `ADD` is the opcode and `A` is the memory address of the operand. This instruction specifies to add the content stored at the memory location `A` (that is, `M[A]`) with the content stored in `AC` and store the result in `AC`, overriding its previous content. That is, this instruction results in the operation given below:

$$AC \leftarrow AC + M[A]$$

Two-address instruction: This type of instruction format uses two address fields and each address can refer to a memory location or a processor register. The operation is performed on the two addresses listed in the instruction and the result is stored in the first address listed in the instruction. That is, the first address of the instruction acts as both source and destination. For example, consider the following assembly language instruction.

$$ADD\ R_1,\ A$$

Here, `ADD` is the opcode, the first address field specifies the processor register R_1 and the second address field `A` specifies the memory location. This instruction specifies to add the content of register R_1 with the content stored at the memory location `A` and store the result in R_1. That is, this instruction results in the operation given below:

$$R_1 \leftarrow R_1 + M[A]$$

The two-address instruction format is generally used for transfer-type instructions (such as `MOV`) where one address field specifies the source and other specifies the destination. For example, the instruction `MOV` R_1, `A` results in the operation $R_1 \leftarrow M[A]$.

Three-address instruction: This type of instruction format uses three address fields and each address can refer to a memory location or a processor register. The last two addresses listed in the instruction designate the sources on which operation is to be performed and the first address in the instruction designate the destination in which the result is to be stored. For example, consider the following assembly language instruction.

```
ADD A, R1, R2
```

Here, `ADD` is the opcode and A, R_1, R_2 are the three address fields. This instruction specifies to add the contents stored in registers R_1 and R_2 and store the result at the memory address symbolized by A. That is, this instruction results in the operation given below:

$$M[A] \leftarrow R_1 + R_2$$

Notice that a three-address instruction can be easily reduced to a two-address instruction in case the destination address is same as one of the source addresses.

Zero-address instruction: This type of instruction format does not employ any address field for the instructions. It is used in stack-organized computers for instructions like `ADD` and `MUL`. Such an instruction specifies to automatically pop two operands from the `TOS` (top of stack), performs the specified operation on them and then pushes the result back onto the `TOS`.

In contrast, the `PUSH` and `POP` instructions in stack-organized computers require an address field to specify the operand that will communicate with the stack. For example, consider the following assembly language instructions.

```
PUSH A
POP A
```

The first instruction specifies to insert the word at the memory address A on the top of the stack, while the second instruction specifies to retrieve the item from the top of the stack and store it at the memory address A. That is, these instructions result in the operations given below:

$$TOS \leftarrow M[A]$$
$$M[A] \leftarrow TOS$$

8. Write an advantage and disadvantage of three-address instruction format.

Ans. An advantage of three-address instruction format is that it results in short programs for the evaluation of arithmetic expressions. However, its disadvantage is that too many bits are needed for specifying three addresses in each binary-coded instruction.

9. What do you mean by addressing mode? Why the addressing mode is used in the computer?

Ans. Addressing mode refers to the methods used for specifying the operands in an instruction. An instruction may have more than one address field and each field may have its own addressing mode. However, there are two modes including implied and immediate mode that do not require any address field. The addressing mode is used in computers because of one or both of the following reasons:

- It offers the programmers various facilities like counters for loop control, pointers to memory and indexing of data thereby enabling them to write more efficient programs.
- It tends to decrease the number of bits in the address fields of the instruction.

10. Explain various addressing modes that are used in the computers.

Ans. There exists a variety of addressing modes that are used in computers. These modes are discussed as follows:

- **Implied addressing mode:** In this mode, the operands are implicitly specified in the definition of the instruction. Therefore, it is also known as **implicit** or **inherent** addressing mode. An example of implied-mode instruction is `Rotate Accumulator` where the operand in the accumulator is implied in the definition of the instruction itself. All the register reference instructions that use an accumulator are the implied-mode instructions. Moreover, the zero-address instructions in stack-organized computer are implied-mode instructions as in these instructions the operands are implicitly specified to be on top of the stack.
- **Immediate addressing mode:** In this mode, the actual operand (rather than an address) is specified in the instruction itself. This eliminates the need of fetching the operand from the memory. An immediate-mode instruction has an operand field in place of address field.

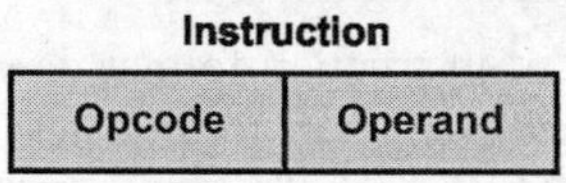

For example, consider the following instruction:

```
ADD 06
```

This instruction directs to add the value 06 with the content of accumulator. Here, the actual operand (that is, 06) to be used in the operation has been specified in the instruction itself. Thus, this instruction is said to be in immediate addressing mode.

The immediate addressing mode is useful when the registers are to be initialized with some constant value. The main advantage of this mode is that the execution of instruction is faster because the operand is available as soon as the instruction is fetched. However, the value of operand is restricted by the length of the operand field.

- **Direct addressing mode:** In this mode, the address field of the instruction specifies the effective address of the operand. The operand is stored in memory and its address is determined directly from the address field of the instruction. An example of direct-mode instruction is `LOAD A`, which results in the operation `AC` $\leftarrow$ `M[A]`. This instruction specifies that the data item having effective address `A` is to be stored in the accumulator. The direct addressing mode is also known as **absolute** addressing mode.

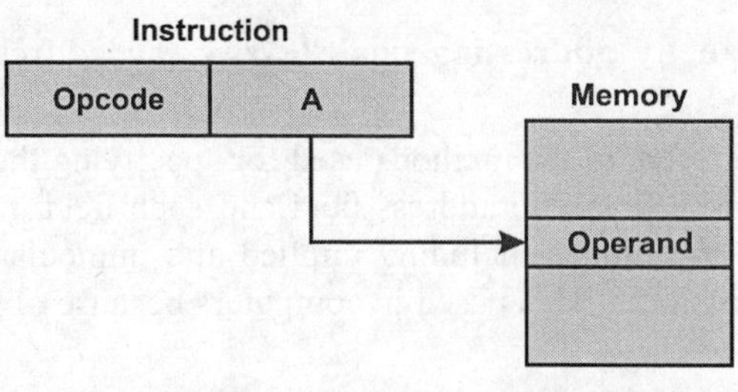

The advantage of direct addressing mode is that the instructions execute much faster since it is not required to determine the effective address of the operand; it is known from the instruction itself.

In addition, only a single memory access is needed to fetch the operand. However, this addressing mode provides limited number of bits for specifying the address of the operand.

- **Indirect addressing mode:** In this mode, the address field of the instruction specifies a memory address, which further stores the effective address of the operand in memory. For example, the instruction `LOAD @ A` is an indirect-mode instruction, which results in the operation `AC` $\leftarrow$ `M[M[A]]`.

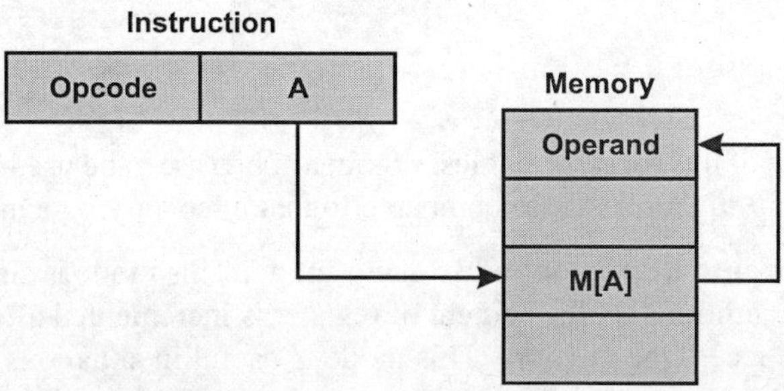

The indirect addressing mode is helpful in implementing the concept of pointers. The advantage of this mode is that the instruction can have a full length address of the operand. However, the instruction cycle time for this mode is higher because two memory accesses are needed even for a single instruction, one for the address specified in the instruction and the other for the operand.

- **Register addressing mode:** In this mode, the address field of the instruction refers to a processor register that contains the operand itself. The register number storing the operand is specified in the instruction. An example of register-mode instruction is `ADD` R_1, R_2, which specifies that the operands to be added are stored in processor registers R_1 and R_2.

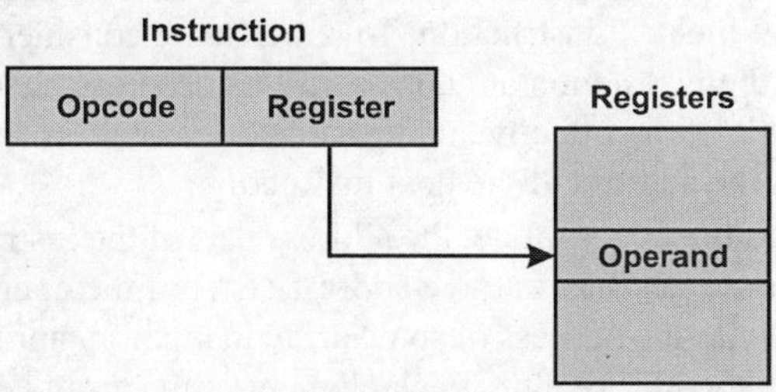

The main advantage of this addressing mode is that the operands are fetched very fast because the memory needs not be accessed. However, since there are only a limited number of processor registers, they must be utilized carefully.

- **Register indirect addressing mode:** In this mode, the address field of the instruction refers to a processor register that contains the memory address of the operand instead of the actual operand. That is, the register in this mode acts as a memory address register. An example of register-indirect mode instruction is `LD`(R_1), which results in the operation `AC` $\leftarrow$ `M[`R_1`]`. Before using this addressing mode, it must be ensured that the memory address of the operand has already been stored in the register.

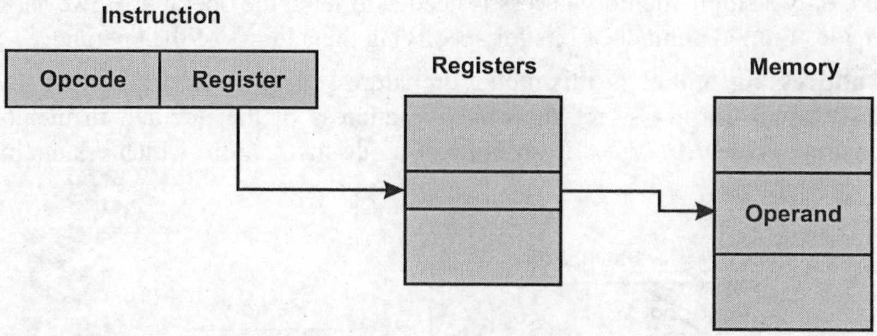

The main advantage of this mode is that less number of bits are to be used in the address field of the instruction for specifying a register as compared to that of specifying a memory address.

- **Auto increment or auto decrement addressing mode:** This mode is similar to the register indirect mode with the addition that the content of register is incremented after or decremented before its value is used to access the memory. This mode is useful in situations when the address stored in the register refers to some table in memory as in such situations, it is required to increment or decrement the address after each table access in order to refer to consecutive locations in the table. Notice that this can also be accomplished by using the increment or decrement instruction explicitly after each access. However, certain computers generally employ a special mode to automatically increment or decrement the register content after data access.
- **Relative addressing mode:** In this mode, the address field of the instruction specifies an offset that needs to be added with the contents of program counter (PC) to get the effective address of the operand in memory. The offset can be either positive or negative number in signed 2's complement representation. Since PC stores the address of next instruction to be executed, therefore, the position of the effective address (produced after addition of PC content and offset) in memory is relative to the address of the next instruction. To understand, consider the content of PC is 750 and the offset is +7. When the instruction at address 750 has been fetched during the fetch phase, the PC is updated to 751. Now, the effective address that we obtain is 758 (751 + 7), which is seven locations forward from the address of the next instruction.
- **Indexed addressing mode:** In this mode, the address part of the instruction is added with the content of the index register to get the effective address (EA) of the operand. The address field of the instruction specifies the starting address of some array in memory and the index register is a special CPU register that stores the index value. Each element of the array is stored in memory relative to the starting address of array and the distance between the position of an operand in memory and the starting address defines the index value contained in the index register. Thus, for accessing each successive element in array, the index register can be incremented.
- **Base register addressing mode:** In this mode, the address part of the instruction is added with the content of the base register to get the effective address (EA) of the operand. This mode functions similarly to indexed addressing mode except the way it is used. In base register addressing mode, the starting address (referred to as **base address**) of the array is stored in base register and the address field of the instruction specifies a displacement relative to this base address. In contrast, in indexed addressing mode, the index value specifies the displacement relative to the starting address specified by the address part of the instruction.

11. Mention three categories of computer instructions.

Ans. In general, the computer instructions fall under three broad categories, namely, *data transfer, data manipulation* and *program control* instructions.

- **Data transfer instructions:** The instructions that specify the transfer of data from one location to another in the computer fall under this category.
- **Data manipulation instructions:** The instructions that carry out arithmetic, logic and shift operations to manipulate the data fall under this category.
- **Program control instructions:** The instructions that change the flow of control of the program being executed fall under this category.

12. Explain data transfer instructions.

Ans. The data transfer instructions are used for moving the data within the computer without modifying the binary content of data. The transfer generally takes place between two processor registers, between processor registers and memory or between processor registers and I/O devices. Table 9.4 lists some data transfer instructions along with their names, mnemonics (symbolic name for the machine language instruction) and functions. Notice that different mnemonics are used for the same instructions in different computers.

Table 9.4 Data Transfer Instructions

Name	Mnemonic	Function
Load	LD	Transfers data from memory to processor register (usually an accumulator).
Store	ST	Transfers data from a processor register to some memory location.
Move	MOV	Transfers data content from one processor register to another.
Exchange	XCH	Swaps data between two processor registers or between a processor register and a memory location.
Input	IN	Transfers data between processor registers and input terminals.
Output	OUT	Transfers data between processor registers and output terminals.
Push	PUSH	Pushes data from processor registers onto the memory stack.
Pop	POP	Pops data from memory stack and places in the processor registers.

Each instruction is usually associated with a number of addressing modes and to distinguish among these different modes, some assembly language conventions use different mnemonic. Table 9.5 lists the mnemonics and the register transfer operation for the 'Load' instruction when used with eight different addressing modes.

Table 9.5 Addressing Modes for Load Instruction

Addressing mode	Instruction	Register transfer
Immediate	LD #NUM	AC ← NUM
Direct	LD ADR	AC ← M[ADR]

Continued...

Table 9.5 (Continued)

Addressing mode	Instruction	Register transfer
Indirect	LD @ADR	AC ← M[M[ADR]]
Register	LD R_1	AC ← R_1
Register indirect	LD (R_1)	AC ← M[R_1]
Relative	LD $ADR	AC ← M[PC + ADR]
Index	LD ADR(A)	AC ← M[ADR + AR]
Auto increment	LD (R_1)+	AC ← M[R_1], R_1 ← R_1 + 1

In the above table, NUM denotes a number or operand, ADR represents a memory address, A is an index register, R_1 is the processor register and AC is used for accumulator register. The character # before the operand indicates an immediate mode instruction, @ before memory address indicates indirect address and $ before memory address indicates that the address is relative to the program counter (PC). In addition, register indirect mode is represented by enclosing the register that contains the address in parentheses and the auto increment mode differs from the register indirect mode by placing a '+' sign after the register enclosed in parentheses.

13. Explain data manipulation instructions.

Ans. The data manipulation instructions are used for manipulating data by performing various mathematical operations on them. Depending on the type of operations, the data manipulation instructions are broadly classified into three categories, which are discussed as follows:

- **Arithmetic instructions:** Most computers provide instructions to perform four common arithmetic operations, which include addition, subtraction, multiplication and division. Table 9.6 lists some arithmetic instructions along with their names, mnemonics and functions.

Table 9.6 Arithmetic Instructions

Name	Mnemonic	Function
Addition	ADD	Adds two operands.
Subtraction	SUB	Subtracts one operand from the other.
Multiplication	MUL	Multiplies two operands.
Division	DIV	Divides one operand by the other.
Increment	INC	Increments the operand stored in processor register or memory by one; if a binary number consisting of all 1's and stored in processor register is incremented, we get a binary number with all 0's as the result.
Decrement	DEC	Decrements the operand stored in processor register or memory by one; if a binary number consisting of all 0's and stored in processor register is decremented, we get a binary number with all 1's as the result.
Add with carry	ADDC	Adds two operands and the value of the carry from the previous computation.
Subtract with borrow	SUBB	Subtracts two operands and a borrow if resulted in the previous computation.
Negate	NEG	Creates 2's complement of a number, reversing the sign of an integer if represented in signed 2's complement form.

Computers may provide arithmetic instructions for different types of data such as decimal or binary data, fixed-point or floating-point data and single-precision or double-precision data. For example, a computer may provide three different `ADD` instructions `ADDD`, `ADDF` and `ADDI` for adding two decimal numbers in BCD, two floating-point numbers and two binary integers, respectively. The data type specified by an arithmetic instruction is assumed to be present in the processor registers and is included in the opcode of the instruction during its execution.

- **Logical and bit manipulation instructions:** The logical instructions are used for performing logical operations such as logical AND, OR and XOR, on the individual bits or group of bits stored in the registers. Table 9.7 lists some of the logical and bit manipulation instructions.

Table 9.7 Logical and Bit Manipulation Instructions

Name	Mnemonic	Function
AND	`AND`	Clears a bit or selected bits of the operand to 0 by ANDing the operand with another operand having 0's in the desired bit positions.
OR	`OR`	Sets a bit or selected bits of the operand to 1 by ORing the operand with another operand having 1's in the desired bit positions.
Exclusive OR	`XOR`	Complements a bit or selected bits of the operand by XORing the operand with another operand having 1's in the desired bit positions.
Complement	`COM`	Generates 1's complement of the operand by changing all its 1 bits to 0's and vice versa.
Clear	`CLR`	Replaces each bit of the operand with 0.
Clear Carry	`CLRC`	Clears the carry bit to 0.
Set Carry	`SETC`	Sets the carry bit to 1.
Complement Carry	`COMC`	Complements the carry bit (from 1 to 0 or 0 to 1).
Enable Interrupt	`EI`	Enables the interrupt by setting the flip-flop from 0 to 1.
Disable Interrupt	`DI`	Disables the interrupt by setting the flip-flop from 1 to 0.

- **Shift instructions:** The shift instructions are used for moving the bits of the operand to the left or right direction. Depending on the type of operations specified by the shift instructions, they can be of three types: *logical*, *arithmetic* and *rotate* shift. All these types are discussed here.
  - **Logical shift instructions:** These instructions move the bits to the right or left and a 0 is inserted at the end bit position. In logical shift left (`SHL`) operation, the bits are shifted to the left, the leftmost bit is lost and a 0 is inserted at the rightmost bit position. In logical shift right (`SHR`) operation, the bits are shifted to the right, the rightmost bit is lost and a 0 is inserted at the leftmost bit position.
  - **Arithmetic shift instructions:** These instructions shift a signed binary number to the left or right. In arithmetic shift right (`SHRA`) operation, the sign bit of the number remains as it is. All bits of the binary number including the sign bit are shifted to the right and the rightmost bit is lost. In arithmetic shift left (`SHLA`) operation, the bits are shifted to the left and a 0 is inserted at the end bit position as similar to logical shift left (`SHL`) instruction.
  - **Rotate shift instructions:** These instructions generate a circular shift. The bits shifted out at one end are circulated back to the other end and thus, no information is lost. In rotate left (`ROL`) instruction, all the bits are shifted towards left and the leftmost bit is inserted at the other end.

In rotate right (ROR), all the bits are shifted towards right and the rightmost bit is inserted at the other end. Two more rotate shift instructions include rotate left through carry (ROLC) and rotate right through carry (RORC). The ROLC operation transfers the carry bit in the rightmost bit position, transfers the leftmost bit in the carry bit and the all other bits are shifted towards left. The RORC operation transfers the carry bit in the leftmost bit position, transfers the rightmost bit in the carry bit and the all other bits are shifted towards right.

14. Discuss program control instructions in detail.

Ans. The program control instructions are used for altering the flow of control of program. Generally, the instructions in a program execute sequentially one after the other and the program counter holds the address of the instruction that is to be executed next in sequence. During program execution, each instruction is first fetched from the memory and then executed. Whenever an instruction is fetched, the program counter is automatically incremented to store the address of the next instruction in sequence so that it can be executed next.

However, sometimes a program may contain a loop that causes certain instructions to be executed repeatedly until some specified condition is met. In addition, the program may include certain tests that determine which of the various actions to take place. In such cases, the control may need to be transferred to the instruction that does not necessarily follow the instruction which is currently being executed. For this, a program control type instruction is required that can alter the flow of control of the program by changing the contents of the program counter. Table 9.8 lists some of the program control instructions with their names and mnemonics.

Table 9.8 Program Control Instructions

Name	Mnemonic
Branch	BR
Jump	JMP
Skip	SKP
Call	CALL
Return	RET
Compare	CMP
Test	TST

All these instructions are described as follows:

- **Branch:** It is usually a one-address instruction that is specified as BR ADR in assembly language, where BR stands for branch and ADR is the mnemonic for an address. As a result of execution of this instruction, the program counter is loaded with the value of ADR and thus, the next instruction is fetched from the location ADR. The branch instruction can be *conditional* or *unconditional*. A **conditional branch** instruction involves a condition which when satisfied, the branch address is loaded into the program counter and the next instruction is fetched from that address. In case the condition is not satisfied, the next instruction is fetched from the next location in sequence. On the other hand, in **unconditional branch** instruction, a specified branch address is loaded into the program counter without any conditions.

- **Jump:** It is also a one-address instruction that works similar to branch instruction. It is used to transfer the control of program to some forward or backward location. Like branch instruction, it may also be unconditional or conditional.
- **Skip:** It is a zero-address instruction because it does not require an address field. It can also be conditional or unconditional. In a conditional skip instruction, the next instruction is skipped if the condition is satisfied. To achieve this, the program counter is also incremented during the execute phase along with during the fetch phase. However, if the condition is not satisfied, the control executes the next instruction in sequence.
- **Call and return:** These instructions are used in relation to **subroutine**, which is defined as a self-contained program designed to perform a specific task. During program execution, a subroutine can be called as many times as required in the main program to perform the desired function. When a subroutine is called, a branch is executed to begin executing its set of instructions and after all its instructions have been executed, a branch is made back to the main program. To call a subroutine, the call instruction is used. It consists of an opcode and an address specifying the beginning of the subroutine. The execution of call subroutine instruction causes two operations to be performed: store the return address (the address of next instruction in the program counter) in a temporary location and transfer the control at the beginning of the subroutine.

  The last instruction in every subroutine is the return from subroutine instruction. This instruction when executed specifies the address stored in temporary location to be loaded into the program counter. As a result, the program control is transferred to the address of the instruction that was originally stored in the program counter.
- **Test and compare:** These instructions do not alter the flow of control directly but they set conditions for the conditional branch instructions. The test instruction performs a logical AND operation on two operands and the compare instruction performs subtraction of two operands. The result of any of these operations is not retained; however, certain status bits (discussed in the next question) are updated depending on the result of operation.

15. Explain how the status register works with the status of the accumulator content obtained from ALU.

Ans. Sometimes, the ALU circuit in CPU is supplemented with a status register that stores the status bit conditions (also called **condition-code** bits or **flag** bits). The status register comprises four status bits including carry (C), sign (S), zero (Z) and overflow (V) bits. All these bits are set to 1 or cleared to 0 based on the result of operation performed in ALU (that is, on the content of accumulator).

- **Carry flag (C):** This bit is set to 1 if the operation performed in ALU generates a carry and cleared to 0 if no carry is generated.
- **Sign flag (S):** This bit is set to 1 if the most significant bit in the output obtained from ALU is 1; otherwise, it is cleared to 0.
- **Zero flag (Z):** This bit is set to 1 if the result of the operation contains all 0's; otherwise, it is cleared to 0.
- **Overflow flag (V):** This bit is set to 1 if the operation performed yields an overflow condition; otherwise, it is cleared to 0.

16. What do you mean by program interrupt? Discuss different types of program interrupts.

Ans. Program interrupt refers to the transfer of control from a program that is currently being executed to another service program because of some request generated internally or externally. After the service program has executed, the control returns to the original program that was interrupted. The program interrupts cause a break in the normal execution of a program without depending on any condition. This is referred to as **unconditional transfer of control**.

There are mainly three types of program interrupts, which are discussed as follows:

- **External interrupts:** These are the interrupts that arise from external sources such as an I/O device requesting for the transfer of data, a timing device indicating the time out or some circuit signalling the power failure.
- **Internal interrupts:** These are the interrupts that occur because of incorrect use of data or instructions in the program such as an attempt to divide by 0, stack overflow, use of invalid opcode and register overflow. The internal interrupts (also called **traps**) can occur at either compile time or runtime because of the incorrect syntax or logic used by the programmer.
- **Software interrupts:** These are the interrupts caused by the execution of an instruction. Unlike external and internal interrupts that initiate from signals occurring in CPU hardware, software interrupt is a special call instruction that acts like an interrupt. Thus, the software interrupts can be used by the programmer to initiate an interrupt routine at any desired point in the program.

17. What is the difference between interrupt and subroutine call?

Ans. An interrupt is similar to a subroutine call except the following differences:

- The interrupts (excluding the software interrupts) occur due to external or internal signals, while the call to a subroutine is made from the execution of an instruction.
- It is the hardware that identifies the address of the desired interrupt service program. On the other hand, the address of the called subroutine is determined from the address field of an instruction.
- An interrupt procedure contains all the information that is essential to define the CPU state. In contrast, a subroutine call causes to store only the return address (that is, program counter).

18. List out the differences between external and internal interrupts.

Ans. Some differences between internal and external interrupts are listed in Table 9.9.

Table 9.9 Differences between External and Internal Interrupts

External interrupts	Internal interrupts
They are caused because of some external events.	They are caused because of some exceptional conditions in the program itself.
They are asynchronous with the program.	They are synchronous with the program.
They are independent of the program under execution and depend on external conditions.	They depend on the program under execution. If the same program is re-executed, they occur at the same place every time.
Examples: request from I/O device for the transfer of data.	Examples: division by 0, stack overflow.

19. Describe some major characteristics of CISC and RISC architectures.

Ans. Processors are built with the ability to execute a limited set of basic operations. The collections of these operations are known as the **instruction set** of processor, which determines how the machine language programs can be developed for a specific computer. Earlier, the instruction sets were small in size and easy to understand but with time, the instructions increased in terms of both size and complexity. Based on the instruction sets, there are two types of computer architectures: *CISC* and *RISC*.

CISC Architecture

CISC, which stands for **complex instruction set computer**, includes a large number of instructions, which are put directly into the hardware. These computers also contain a wide variety of data types as well as a number of addressing modes. The main reason behind using the complex instruction set is to simplify the compilation process and thus, increasing the overall performance of the computer. As we know that the job of compiler is to produce a sequence of machine instructions for each statement written in high-level language. This job is simplified if the generated machine instructions can implement the statements directly. The CISC architecture attempts to provide a single machine instruction for each statement and each instruction can directly manipulate the operands residing in the memory.

Characteristics: Some major characteristics of CISC architecture are as follows:

- It includes a large number of instructions typically ranging from 100 to 250.
- It supports multiple addressing modes generally from 5 to 20.
- It provides machine instructions that can directly manipulate the operands in main memory.
- It generally employs microprogrammed control unit.
- It supports the use of variable-length instruction formats.

RISC Architecture

RISC, which stands for **reduced instruction set computer**, includes relatively limited number of instructions. The primary goal of RISC architecture is to keep the instruction set as simple as possible so that the instructions could be executed must faster within the processor; each instruction in RISC architecture can be executed in one clock cycle.

Characteristics: Some major characteristics of RISC architecture are as follows:

- It includes comparatively fewer instructions that consist of mostly register-to-register operations. Simple load and store instructions are used for memory access.
- It supports only few simple addressing modes.
- It generally employs hardwired control unit.
- It supports the use of simple fixed-length instruction format that can be decoded easily.
- It employs comparatively large number of registers in the processor unit because all the computations are performed within the CPU registers.

In respect of the performance equation we can say, the CISC architecture minimizes the number of instructions per program at the cost of number of cycles per instructions. On the other hand, RISC architecture minimizes the cycles per instructions at the cost of number of instructions per program.

20. Compare RISC and CISC machines.

Ans. There is a continuous debate on the comparison of CISC with RISC. Some important differences are listed in Table 9.10.

Table 9.10 Differences between CISC and RISC Machines

CISC	RISC
Uses complex instructions set, where decoding of instructions is a complicated and time-consuming task.	Uses relatively simple instruction sets and the instructions can be decoded easily.
Different instructions take different amount of clock cycles to execute and thus, slow down the overall performance of the machine.	One instruction can be executed in each clock cycle. This is accomplished by means of pipelining in which the fetch, decode and execute cycles of two or more instructions are overlapped.
Incorporates a large number of addressing modes.	Incorporates only a few addressing modes.
Yields smaller and faster programs, thus, improving the performance.	Yields comparatively lengthier programs that take up larger memory.
Needs more hardware logic to implement and support more instructions and addressing modes. As a result, the speed of computation slows down.	The computations are performed at a relatively faster speed.
Uses microprogrammed control unit.	Uses hardwired control unit.
All instructions are present in memory.	All operations are performed within the register.
Minimizes the number of instructions per program at the cost of number of cycles per instruction.	Minimizes the cycles per instructions at the cost of number of instructions per program.
Example: Intel 80486, Celeron computers, Pentium processors, etc.	**Example:** POWER PC, ULTRA SPARC, etc.

21. Consider the seven register organization shown in Figure 9.2 and specify the control word for implementing the following microoperations.

(a) $R_1 \leftarrow R_2 + R_3$

(b) $R_4 \leftarrow R_4 + 1$

(c) $R_5 \leftarrow R_5 \vee R_6$

(d) $R_3 \leftarrow R_1$

(e) $R_1 \leftarrow \sim R_1$

(f) $R_2 \leftarrow \text{SHL } R_3$

(g) $R_1 \leftarrow \text{Input}$

(h) $\text{Output} \leftarrow \text{Input}$

(i) $\text{Output} \leftarrow R_5$

(j) $R_1 \leftarrow 0$

Ans. The following table specifies the control word for the given microoperations.

S. No.	Microoperation	SELA	SELB	SELD	OPR	Control word
a	$R_1 \leftarrow R_2 + R_3$	R_2	R_3	R_1	ADD	010 011 001 00010
b	$R_4 \leftarrow R_4 + 1$	R_4	–	R_4	INCA	100 000 100 00001

Continued…

c	$R_5 \leftarrow R_5 \vee R_6$	R_5	R_6	R_5	OR	101 110 101 01010
d	$R_3 \leftarrow R_1$	R_1	–	R_3	TSFA	001 000 011 00000
e	$R_1 \leftarrow \sim R_1$	R_1	–	R_1	COMA	001 000 001 01110
f	$R_2 \leftarrow$ SHL R_3	R_3	–	R_2	SHLA	011 000 010 11000
g	$R_7 \leftarrow$ Input	Input	–	R_7	TSFA	000 000 111 00000
h	Output ← Input	Input	–	None	TSFA	000 000 000 00000
i	Output ← R_5	R_5	–	None	TSFA	101 000 000 00000
j	$R_1 \leftarrow 0$	R_1	R_1	R_1	XOR	001 001 001 01100

22. Give the infix of the following reverse Polish notations.

(a) ABCDE * / – +

(b) AB + C * D +

(c) AB * CD * + EF *+

Ans. **(a)** ABCDE * / – +

⇨ ABC (D * E) / – +

⇨ AB (C / (D * E)) – +

⇨ A (B – (C / (D * E))) +

⇨ A + (B – (C / (D * E)))

(b) AB + C * D +

⇨ (A + B) C * D +

⇨ ((A + B) * C) D +

⇨ ((A + B) * C) + D

(c) AB * CD * + EF * +

⇨ (A * B) CD * + EF * +

⇨ (A * B) (C * D) + EF * +

⇨ (A * B) + (C * D) EF * +

⇨ ((A * B) + (C * D)) (E * F) +

⇨ ((A * B) + (C * D)) + (E * F)

23. Convert the arithmetic expression A * B + A * (B * D + C * E) into reverse Polish notation.

Ans. The reverse Polish notation for the given arithmetic expression is found as follows:

A * B + A * (B * D + C * E)

= A * B + A * ((B D *) + (C E*))

= A * B + A * (B D * C E * +)

= A * B + A B D * C E * +*

= (A B *) + A B D * C E * + *

= A B * A B D * C E * + * +

24. A computer has 32-bit instructions and 12-bit addresses. If there are 250 two-address instructions, how many one-address instructions can be formulated?

Ans. 32-bit instructions means data lines are of 32 bits.

Given that a single address is of 12 bits. Thus, the total number of addresses the computer may have is 2^{12}, that is, 4 kilobytes.

As there are 250 two-address instructions, the number of one-address instructions that can be formulated is found as follows:

(4K * 32) / (250 * 2)

= (4096 * 32) / (250 * 2)

= 262.144

Thus, total 262 one-address instructions can be formulated.

25. X = (A + B) * (C + D)

Write down the three-address, two-address, one-address and zero-address instructions for the expression.

Ans. Three-address instructions:

Instruction	Operation
ADD R_1, A, B	$R_1 \leftarrow$ M [A] + M [B]
ADD R_2, C, D	$R_2 \leftarrow$ M [C] + M [D]
MUL X, R_1, R_2	M [X] $\leftarrow R_1 * R_2$

Two-address instructions:

Instruction	Operation
MOV R_1, A	$R_1 \leftarrow$ M [A]
ADD R_1, B	$R_1 \leftarrow R_1$ + M [B]
MOV R_2, C	$R_2 \leftarrow$ M [C]
ADD R_2, D	$R_2 \leftarrow R_2$ + M [D]
MUL R_1, R_2	$R_1 \leftarrow R_1 * R_2$
MOV X, R_1	M [X] $\leftarrow R_1$

One-address instructions:

Instruction	Operation	
LOAD A	AC $\leftarrow$ M [A]	
ADD B	AC $\leftarrow$ AC + M [B]	
STORE, T	M [T] $\leftarrow$ AC	M [T] is temporary location.
LOAD C	AC $\leftarrow$ M [C]	
ADD D	AC $\leftarrow$ AC + M [D]	
MUL T	AC $\leftarrow$ AC * M [T]	
STORE X	M [X] $\leftarrow$ AC	

Zero-address instructions: Zero-address instructions are used in stack-organized computers and for such computers the expression must be in reverse Polish notation. Therefore, first we will represent the given arithmetic expression in reverse Polish notation as shown here.

$$X = (A + B) * (C + D)$$
$$= (A\ B\ +) * (C\ D\ +)$$
$$= A\ B + C\ D + *$$

Now, the zero-address instructions for this expression can be written as:

Instruction	Operation
PUSH A	TOS ← A
PUSH B	TOS ← B
ADD	TOS ← A + B
PUSH C	TOS ← C
PUSH D	TOS ← D
ADD	TOS ← C + D
MUL	TOS ← (A + B) * (C + D)
POP X	M [X] ← TOS

26. Write the program to evaluate the arithmetic expression $X = \frac{A * [B + C * (D + E)]}{F * (G + H)}$ using three-address instruction, two-address instruction, one-address instruction and zero-address instruction.

Ans. Three-address instructions:

Instruction	Operation
ADD R_1, D, E	$R_1 \leftarrow M[D] + M[E]$
MUL R_1, R_1, C	$R_1 \leftarrow R_1 * M[C]$
ADD R_1, R_1, B	$R_1 \leftarrow R_1 + M[B]$
MUL R_1, R_1, A	$R_1 \leftarrow R_1 * M[A]$
ADD R_2, G, H	$R_2 \leftarrow M[G] + M[H]$
MUL R_2, R_2, F	$R_2 \leftarrow R_2 * M[F]$
DIV X, R_1, R_2	$M[X] \leftarrow R_1 / R_2$

Two-address instructions:

Instruction	Operation
MOV R_1, D	$R_1 \leftarrow M[D]$
ADD R_1, E	$R_1 \leftarrow R_1 + M[E]$
MUL R_1, C	$R_1 \leftarrow R_1 * M[C]$
ADD R_1, B	$R_1 \leftarrow R_1 + M[B]$
MUL R_1, A	$R_1 \leftarrow R_1 * M[A]$
MOV R_2, G	$R_2 \leftarrow M[G]$
ADD R_2, H	$R_2 \leftarrow R_2 + M[H]$
MUL R_2, F	$R_2 \leftarrow R_2 * M[F]$
DIV R_1, R_2	$R_1 \leftarrow R_1 / R_2$
MOV X, R_1	$M[X] \leftarrow R_1$

One-address instructions:

Instruction	Operation
LOAD D	AC ← M [D]
ADD E	AC ← AC + M [E]
MUL C	AC ← AC * M [C]
ADD B	AC ← AC + B
MUL A	AC ← AC * A
STORE T_1	M [T_1] ← AC
LOAD G	AC ← M [G]
ADD H	AC ← AC + M [H]
MUL F	AC ← AC * M [F]
STORE T_2	M [T_2] ← AC
LOAD T_1	AC ← M [T_1]
DIV T_2	AC ← AC / M [T_2]
STORE X	M [X] ← AC

Zero-address instructions: The reverse Polish notation for the given arithmetic expression is A B C D E+ * + * F G H + * /

Instruction	Operation
PUSH A	TOS ← A
PUSH B	TOS ← B
PUSH C	TOS ← C
PUSH D	TOS ← D
PUSH E	TOS ← E
ADD	TOS ← D + E
MUL	TOS ← C * (D + E)
ADD	TOS ← B + C * (D + E)
MUL	TOS ← A * [B + C * (D + E)]
PUSH F	TOS ← F
PUSH G	TOS ← G
PUSH H	TOS ← H
ADD	TOS ← G + H
MUL	TOS ← F * (G + H)
DIV	$TOS \leftarrow \frac{A*[B+C*(D+E)]}{F*(G+H)}$
POP X	M [X] ← TOS

27. An instruction is stored at location 300 with its address field at location 301. The address field has the value 400. A processor register R_1 contains the number 200. Evaluate the effective address if the addressing mode of the instruction is (a) direct; (b) immediate; (c) relative; (d) register; (e) register indirect; (f) index with R_1 as the index register.

Ans. **(a)** In direct addressing mode, the effective address of the operand is equal to the value stored in the address field of the instruction. Thus, the effective address in this case is 400.

(b) In immediate addressing mode, the second part (address part) of the instruction specifies the operand itself rather than an address. That is, 400 is the operand that is stored at address 301. Thus, the effective address in this case is 301.

(c) In relative addressing mode, the effective address is the sum of address part of instruction and the contents of PC. Since the value of PC after fetching the given instruction (address 301) and during the execute phase is 302, the effective address in this case is 400 + 302 = 702.

(d) In register addressing mode, the processor register R_1 stores the operand itself, that is, 400 is the operand. Thus, there is no effective address in this case.

(e) In register indirect addressing mode, the effective address of the operand is stored in the processor register R_1. Thus, the effective address in this case is 200.

(f) In indexed addressing mode, the effective address is the sum of the address part of the instruction and the contents of index register. As R_1 is used as the index register, thus, the effective address in this case is 400 + 200 = 600.

28. Given the 16-bit value 1001101011001101. What operation must be performed in order to: (a) clear to 0 the first eight bits; (b) set to 1 the last eight bits; (c) complement the middle eight bits?

Ans. (a) The first eight bits of the given 16-bit operand can be cleared to 0 by ANDing it with the operand having 0's in its first eight bit positions, that is, 0000000011111111.

(b) The last eight bits of the given 16-bit operand can be set to 1 by ORing it with the operand having 1's in its last eight bit positions, that is, 0000000011111111.

(c) The middle eight bits of the given 16-bit operand can be complemented (1 to 0 or 0 to 1) by XORing it with the operand having 1's in its middle eight bit positions, that is, 0000111111110000.

29. What is the result of the following operations when executed on an 8-bit processor that uses 2's complement representation for negative integers?

(a) LSH 14, 3

(b) ASH 17, 5

(c) LSH -23, -2

(d) ASH -23, -2

Ans. (a) This instruction indicates logical left shift 14 by three positions. The 8-bit 2's complement representation of 14 is 0000 1110. After shifting left by three positions, we get 0111 0000, which is the integer representation of 112.

(b) This instruction indicates arithmetic left shift 17 by five positions. The 8-bit 2's complement representation of 17 is 0001 0001. As arithmetic left shift operation is similar to logical left shift, after shifting left by five positions, we get 0010 0000, which is the integer representation of 32.

(c) This instruction indicates logical shift operation and –2 denotes shifting to the right by two positions. The 8-bit 2's complement representation of –23 is 1110 1001. After shifting right by two positions, we get 0011 1010, which is the integer representation of 58.

(d) This instruction indicates arithmetic shift operation and –2 denotes shifting to the right by two positions. The 8-bit 2's complement representation of –23 is 1110 1001. Since in arithmetic right shift, the sign bit remains as it is, therefore after shifting right by two positions, we get 1111 1010, which is the integer representation of –6.

30. An 8-bit computer has a register R. Determine the values of status bits C, S, Z and V after each of the following instructions. The initial value of the register R in each case is hexadecimal 72. The numbers below are also in hexadecimal.

(a) Add immediate operand C6 to R.

(b) Add immediate operand 1E to R.

(c) AND immediate operand 8D to R.

(d) Exclusive-OR R with R.

Ans. Given that the value stored in R is hexadecimal 72, that is, 0 1 1 1 0 0 1 0 in binary. Suppose, if we are using 8-bit format, then the values that can be stored in register R can range from –128 to +127.

(a) Add immediate operand C6 to R.

```
         1 1     1 1
72      0 1 1 1 0 0 1 0
C6    + 1 1 0 0 0 1 1 0
        ---------------
        0 0 1 1 1 0 0 0   = 56
```

As there is a carry after addition, C = 1.
As the MSB of the result is 0, it is positive. Therefore, S = 0.
As the result is not 0, Z = 0.
As the result lies in the desired range, there is no overflow. Therefore, *V* = 0.

(b) Add immediate operand 1E to R.

```
        1 1 1 1 1 1
72      0 1 1 1 0 0 1 0
1E    + 0 0 0 1 1 1 1 1
        ---------------
        1 0 0 1 0 0 0 1  =129
```

As there is no carry after addition, C = 0.
As the MSB of the result is 1, it is negative. Therefore, S = 1.
As the result is not 0, Z = 0.
As the result does not lie in the desired range, there is overflow. Therefore, V = 1.

(c) AND immediate operand 8D to R.

On ANDing 72 (01110010) with 8D (10001110), we get 00000010.
For this result, C = 0, S = 0, Z = 0 and V = 0.

(d) Exclusive-OR R with R.

On XORing 72 (01110010) with 72 (10001110), we get 00000000.
For this result, C = 0, S = 0, Z = 1 and V = 0.

MULTIPLE CHOICE QUESTIONS

1. In a stack-organized computer, there is a support for
   (a) PUSH and POP instructions only
   (b) Zero-address instruction only
   (c) Zero-address, PUSH and POP instructions
   (d) None of these

2. The instruction LOAD A is a
   (a) Zero-address (b) One-address
   (c) Two-address (d) Three-address
3. The number of fetch operation(s) required to execute instruction in immediate mode is
   (a) 0 (b) 1
   (c) 2 (d) None of these
4. The LOAD instruction is mostly used to designate a transfer from memory to a processor register known as ___________.
   (a) Instruction register (b) Program counter
   (c) Accumulator (d) Memory address register
5. In reverse Polish notation, the expression A + B * C becomes
   (a) A B C * + (b) A B * C +
   (c) A B C + * (d) A B + C *
6. The ALU takes the data from the temporary storage into ______while performing an operation?
   (a) RAM (b) USB
   (c) Hard disk (d) Register
7. Why addressing modes are used?
   (a) For giving versatility to the programmer
   (b) For reducing the number of bits in an instruction
   (c) For specifying the rules for interpreting and altering the address field of the instruction
   (d) All these
8. In a program using subroutine call instruction, it is necessary to _________.
   (a) Clear the instruction register (b) Initialize the program counter
   (c) Clear the accumulator (d) Reset the microprocessor
9. The status bit is also known as _________.
   (a) Signed bit (b) Flag bit
   (c) Unsigned bit (d) Binary bit
10. Stack overflow is a type of __________.
    (a) Internal interrupt (b) Software interrupt
    (c) External interrupt (d) None of these
11. Which of the following addressing modes is used in instruction PUSH B?
    (a) Immediate (b) Register
    (c) Direct (d) Register indirect
12. Which of the following is not a characteristic of RISC?
    (a) One instruction per cycle (b) Large instruction set
    (c) Simple addressing modes (d) Register-to-register operations

Ans. 1. c 2. b 3. a 4. c 5. a 6. d 7. d 8. a 9. b 10. a
11. c 12. b

10

Input/Output Organization

1. Explain various input–output devices in a computer system.

Ans. A computer system is useful only when it is able to communicate with the external environment. To communicate with the external users, the I/O subsystem (also referred to as I/O) of computer system serves the purpose. It provides an efficient means of inputting data from an outside source to the computer and outputting the results back to the outside users. The I/O devices attached to the computer are also called **peripherals**. The most commonly used input–output devices are keyboard, mouse, visual display unit, printer, plotter and joystick. These input and output devices are explained as follows:

- **Input devices:** These are the electromechanical devices that allow the users to feed data into the computer system for processing. The data entered from the outside world are converted into a form understandable by the computer. Some of the input devices are discussed as follows:
  - **Keyboard**: It is one of the most commonly used input devices, which looks similar to a regular typewriter but with few additional keys. The user can type text or give commands by pressing the set of buttons mounted on the keyboard. Whenever a key is pressed, the input signal is transmitted to the computer and the corresponding character is displayed on the monitor after its processing. The most popular layout for keyboard used is *QWERTY* keyboard. It is named so because the first six keys on the top row of letters are *Q*, *W*, *E*, *R*, *T* and *Y*.
  - **Mouse**: A mouse is a small hand-held pointing device, used for navigating a pointer on the screen. It allows users to move cursor over the screen for selecting or pointing objects on the screen. It works by moving on a smooth surface, stimulating the cursor movement on the monitor. Mouse includes two buttons and a scroll wheel. Whenever one of the buttons is depressed, the system is able to detect the movement of the mouse. It is one of the common and least expensive pointing devices as compared with its counterparts.
  - **Joystick**: This is also a pointing device that moves in all directions and controls the movement of the cursor. The basic design of a joystick consists of a stick that is attached to a plastic base with a flexible rubber sheath. This plastic base houses a circuit board that sits beneath the stick. The electronic circuitry measures the movement of the stick from its central position and sends the information for processing. Joystick also consists of buttons that can be programmed to indicate certain actions once a position on the screen has been selected using stick. Joysticks are mainly used in video games, simulators and controlling industrial robots.

- **Output devices:** These devices are used to take the output (that is, processed data) from a computer system and present to the user either in a printed form or by displaying it on the screen. Since the output from system is in computer understandable form, it first needs to be converted into human readable form by the output devices. The basic functioning of output devices is to take out the information from the computer. The different types of output devices are discussed as follows:
  - **Monitor**: A monitor, also known as **visual display unit** (VDU), is the most basic and commonly used output device for viewing and displaying images. It is similar to a television where the images are represented in the form of **pixels**. Monitors can be developed using either a *cathode ray tube* (*CRT*) or a *liquid crystal display* (*LCD*) technology. A **CRT** is a vacuum tube where the screen pixels are made from phosphor. An electron beam (cathode ray) is emitted by electron gun towards the specified position to strike the phosphor. This causes phosphor to emit light and results in the display of an image. An **LCD** is the most popular video monitor in the market nowadays. It consists of different layers and the rearmost layer is a fluorescent light source. It also comprises various cells aligned in rows across the screen. Each of these cells is fronted by a red, green or blue filter. Light passing through the filtered cells creates the colours on the LCD.
  - **Printer**: To produce hard-copy output, printers are the most used peripheral devices. There are various types of printers available and each of them uses different technologies offering different printing formats. Some of the commonly used printers are *dot matrix printer*, *daisy wheel printer*, *inkjet printer* and *laser printer*. A **dot-matrix printer** is an impact printer, printing one character at a time as a pattern of dots. A **daisy wheel printer** consists of a wheel with the characters placed along its circumference. The wheel rotates to the proper position and an energized magnet presses the letter against the ribbon imprinting the required character. An **inkjet printer** prints a character or an image by spraying small drops of ink through a nozzle on the paper. This printer produces high-quality output than its predecessors. A **laser printer** uses laser source to write information on to a drum coated with a photosensitive material, which when comes in contact with the laser beam, is charged with electricity. A special ink dust is sprinkled on the drum that sticks to the charged area forming the image.
  - **Plotter**: Many engineering design applications require high-quality graphic output on large sheets. To produce outputs for such applications, plotters are used. A plotter is a pen-based output device that is needed to draw high resolution user graphics, blueprint, maps, circuit diagrams and other line-based diagrams. The lines drawn by plotters are continuous and very accurate. The commonly used plotters are *drum plotter* and *flatbed plotter*. In a **drum plotter**, the paper on which the design has to be made is placed over a drum. The drum can move in both clockwise and anticlockwise directions. In case, a horizontal line is to be drawn, the horizontal movement of a pen is combined with the vertical movement of a page via the drum. The curves can also be drawn by creating a sequence of very short straight lines. A **flatbed plotter** consists of a stationary horizontal plotting surface on which paper is fixed. The pen is mounted on a carriage, which can move horizontally, vertically, leftwards or rightwards to draw lines. In flatbed plotters, the paper does not move, the pen-holding mechanism provides all the motion.

2. What is I/O interface? What are the needs for I/O interface?

or

Why the I/O devices cannot be directly connected to the system bus?

Ans. The **I/O interface** refers to a hardware component that facilitates the exchange of information between the external I/O devices and the internal storage devices. Different I/O devices need special communication links to interface with the CPU that could resolve the differences between the CPU and I/O devices. These differences are listed as follows:

- The way computer and memory operate is different from the way I/O devices operate. This is because the I/O devices are electromagnetic and electromechanical devices, whereas CPU and memory are electronic devices. Thus, to resolve this difference, a conversion of signal values is needed.
- A synchronization mechanism is needed to synchronize the data transfer between slow I/O devices and fast CPU.
- Data codes and formats of I/O devices are different from the format of CPU and memory that follow word format.
- Since the mode of operation of each I/O device is different, and hence each one of them is controlled differently so that the operations of one I/O device do not disturb the operations of the other I/O devices connected to the CPU.

To resolve these differences, computer system employs hardware components (called **interface units**) between the peripherals and the processor bus. The role of these interface units is to monitor and synchronize all I/O transfers.

3. Explain the operation of I/O bus of a computer.

Ans. The processor and I/O devices communicate with each other via I/O bus. Figure 10.1 depicts a typical connection between the processor and I/O devices via I/O bus. The I/O bus comprises data, address and control lines. An interface unit is included for each individual I/O and the I/O bus is connected to all I/O device interfaces. The interface unit is responsible for decoding the address and control received from the I/O bus, interpreting them and then providing signals to the I/O controller. In addition, it synchronizes the flow of data and supervises the data transfer between the I/O devices and the processor. Moreover, each I/O device may consist of its own controller, operating that particular electromechanical device.

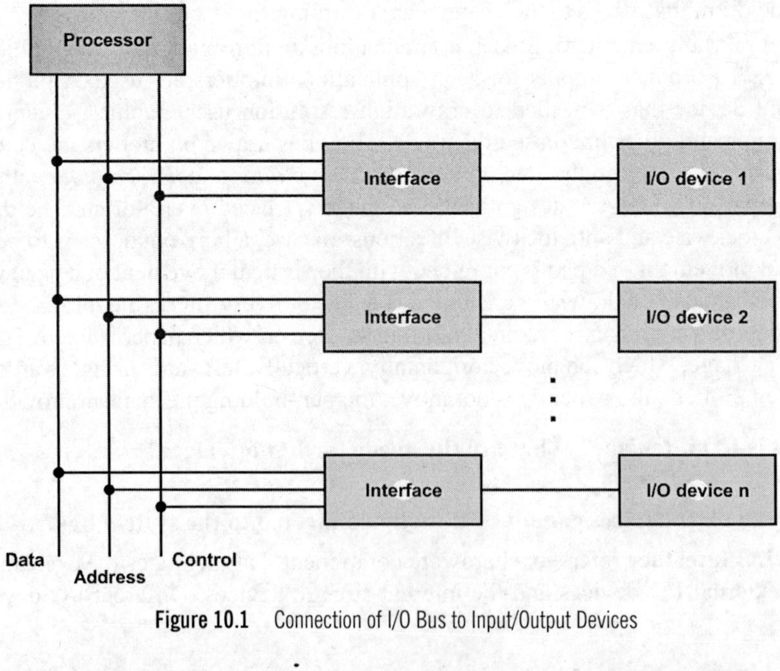

Figure 10.1 Connection of I/O Bus to Input/Output Devices

Whenever a processor wishes to communicate with a specific device, it places the address of that device on the address lines of I/O bus. At the same time, it also gives a function code (referred to as I/O command) in the control lines. The interface units connected to I/O bus decode the address placed in address lines with the help of an address decoder they contain. The interface unit that detects its own address after decoding enables the path between the bus lines and the device it is controlling. While other devices are disabled by their respective interface units. The selected interface interprets the I/O command and proceeds to execute it.

4. List various standards of I/O interfaces.

Ans. The various standards of I/O interfaces are as follows:

- Peripheral component interconnect (PCI)
- Small computer system interface (SCSI)
- Universal serial bus (USB).

5.Write a note on PCI.

or

List various types of commands that can be received by an I/O interface unit.

or

Explain typical desktop/server system using PCI configuration.

Ans. The **peripheral component interconnect (PCI)** is a high-bandwidth bus that can support any processor. When the PCI bus is used in a high-speed I/O subsystem, it delivers better system

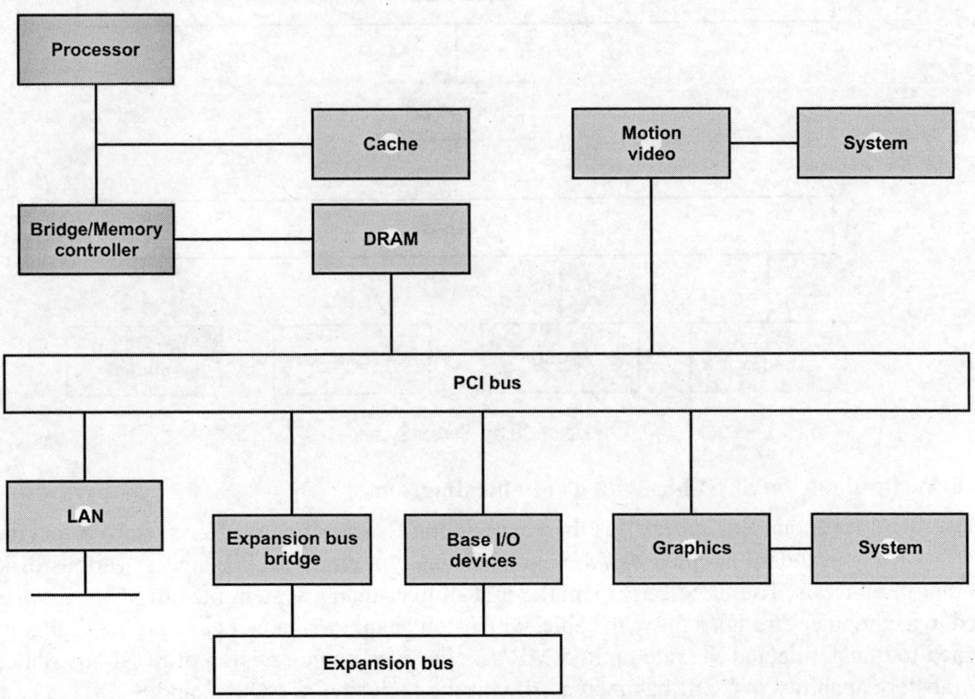

Figure 10.2 Desktop System

performance. The input-output requirements of modern system are economically fulfilled by the PCI as it does not require many chips for implementation. It also supports other buses attached to the PCI bus. Ethernet and Wi-Fi network adapters for both desktop and notebook computers use PCI and it supports many processor configurations including single and multiple processor systems. The PCI cards used in PCs include network and sound card, modems, USB ports, etc. The physical size of the bus, bus timings, electrical characteristics and protocols are specified by the PCI. With the motherboard clock rate, this bus operates either asynchronously operating at any maximum frequency or synchronously. The bus can operate with slower devices with the help of flow control.

Figure 10.2 depicts the use of PCI in a **single-processor system** (also known as **desktop processor system**). In this system, the bridge and DRAM controller connected to the PCI bus provide tight coupling with the processor and thus, enable to achieve high speed of delivering data. Since the speed of the PCI bus may differ from that of I/O capability of processor, bridge acts as a data buffer.

Figure 10.3 depicts the **multiprocessor** or **server system**, in which more than one PCI configuration is connected to processor's system bus by bridges. Cache units, main memory and the PCI bridges are supported by the system bus. The PCI is kept independent of the processor's speed by using bridges, which provide the ability to receive and deliver data rapidly.

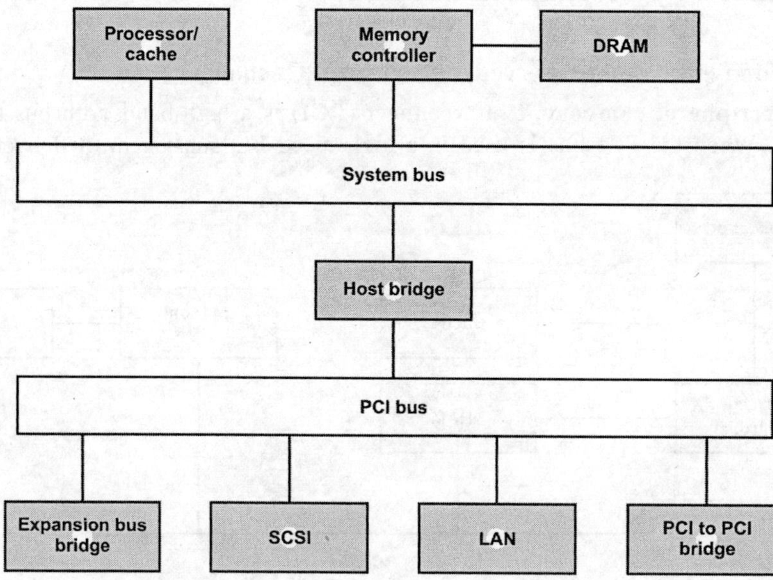

Figure 10.3 Server System

6. Write a note on SCSI bus with a suitable diagram.

Ans. SCSI (pronounced 'scuzzy') is the abbreviation for **small computer system interface**. SCSI bus refers to the standard adopted by ANSI for I/O bus type in 1986. It connects various disk drives and other peripherals. The SCSI bus is smaller and simpler than a system bus. In SCSI, disks are connected to a computer through a 50-wire cable, which can be up to 25 meters in length. Originally, it was designed to transfer data at the rate up to 5 MB/sec, but with some revision of SCSI bus standard, the data transfer capability of SCSI has increased with the inclusion of SCSI-2 and SCSI-3. The original SCSI bus has an 8-bit data line (called **narrow bus**) and it can be used to transfer addresses. A wide

SCSI bus has 16 data lines and can transfer 16 bits at a time. The control functions are performed by 10 additional lines (see Figure 10.4). However, with recent developments, now SCSI bus has wider data buses, more control features and higher data transfer rates.

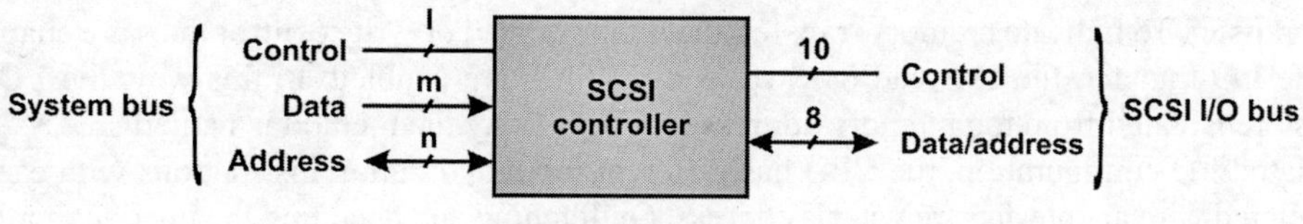

Figure 10.4 SCSI I/O Bus

Maximum capacity of a narrow SCSI bus is eight devices and the capacity of wide bus is 16 devices. An SCSI bus interfaces with the processor-memory bus, through an SCSI controller, which uses DMA to transfer data from a device to main memory or vice versa. The data packets are transferred from the memory to the device through SCSI bus by using DMA.

7. Explain USB.

Ans. **USB** (stands for **universal serial bus**) is an external expansion bus that establishes communication between personal computer and several I/O devices, such as joystick, mouse, keyboard, printers and scanners. USB standard was developed in 1995 with the aim of minimizing the number of ports at the back of PC. USB enables the I/O devices to be added to PC easily and at a low cost. All USB devices come with a USB connector that is plugged into the USB port on the computer. As a USB device is plugged in, it gets configured automatically without requiring restart the PC. For slow devices such as keyboard and mouse, USB offers a maximum speed of 1.5 MB, while for high-speed devices such as webcam, scanners and printers it provides a maximum speed of 12 MB. Originally, it was designed mainly for PCs, but now it has carved its niche for other devices, such as smart phones, video game consoles and PDAs, and as a power cord. Since its evolution, there have been many generations of USBs that are 1.0, 2.0, 3.0 and WUSB (Wireless universal serial bus). Every computer nowadays comes with one or more USB connectors that can attach many I/O devices to the computer easily and quickly. Since every operating system supports USB pretty well, the installation of the USB device drivers is easy and simple enough as compared with other ways of connecting devices to the computer.

8. Explain I/O versus memory bus.

Ans. A processor has to communicate with the memory unit in addition to communicating with the I/O unit. The memory bus consists of data, address and read/write control lines organized in a manner similar to the I/O bus organization. Three ways to use the computer buses for communicating with memory and I/O are as follows:

- Using two separate buses: one for memory and the other for I/O. In this method, an individual set of data, address and control buses are used for memory and I/O. The computers having separate **I/O processor (IOP)** (also called **data channel**), in addition to the central processing unit adopt this kind of procedure. The CPU and IOP communicate with the memory using the memory bus.
- Using a common bus for both memory and I/O, but having separate control lines for each of them. This method is referred to as **isolated I/O**.
- Using a common bus as well as common control lines for memory and I/O. This is referred to as **memory mapped I/O**.

9. Explain isolated versus memory mapped I/O.

Ans. In isolated I/O, a common bus is used for transferring information between I/O or memory and the CPU. However, separate read and write control lines are used to distinguish between the I/O and memory transfer. To indicate memory transfer, the memory read or write control lines are enabled; while to indicate I/O transfer, the I/O read or write control lines are enabled. In this way, the I/O interface addresses are isolated from the memory addresses. That is why the method is named so.

In isolated I/O configuration, the CPU has different input and output instructions with each instruction associated with an interface register's address. On fetching and decoding the opcode of input/output instructions, the CPU puts the address of an interface register on the address lines and activates the I/O read or write control lines. On fetching instructions and operands from the memory, a memory address is placed on the address lines and the memory read or write control lines are enabled. In this way, the external components come to know whether the address is for I/O interface or for a memory word.

The alternative method to isolated I/O is the **memory mapped I/O,** in which the computer uses same address space for both memory and I/O. The interface registers are considered as a part of memory system. However, the addresses assigned to interface registers cannot be assigned to memory addresses, which reduce the range of available memory addresses. The advantage of memory mapped I/O is that there is no specific input or output instructions in this method. The same instructions can be used to manipulate both I/O data residing in the interface registers and the memory words.

10. What do you mean by asynchronous data transfer? List its mechanisms.

Ans. In computers, it is generally required to transfer data between two independent units, such as CPU and I/O interface. If both units share a common clock, the data transfer between them is said to be **synchronous.** However, if each independent unit is supplied with its own clock for internal operation, the data transfer between them is referred to as **asynchronous.** In asynchronous data transfer, control signals need to be transmitted between the communicating units to indicate the time at which data is to be transmitted. This can be achieved by adopting any of the following mechanisms/methods:

- The first method is called **strobe control** in which a strobe pulse is supplied by one of the units, indicating when the transfer has to occur to the other unit.
- In the second method, each data item is transferred along with a control signal indicating the presence of data in the bus. The receiving unit responds with another control signal to acknowledge receipt of data. This method of transferring data is called **handshaking.**

11. What do you mean by strobe control? Explain its data transfer from source and destination initiation.

Ans. In strobe control method, a single control (strobe) line is used to signal the transfer of data. The strobe can be activated by either the source or the destination unit. A bus is used to carry the data between source and destination unit. There are multiple lines in the bus for transferring a byte or word. The strobe line informs about the valid data word available in the bus.

Figure 10.5 shows the block diagram and timing diagram for source-initiated strobe. When the source unit initiates a strobe for data transfer, it places the data on the bus. After a delay when source unit becomes sure that the data has settled to a steady value, it activates the strobe pulse. While data is received by the destination unit, information on the data bus and strobe control signal remains in the active state. For transferring the contents of data bus to one of its internal registers, the destination unit uses the falling edge of the strobe pulse. After the data has been transferred, the source disables the strobe pulse and after a while removes the data from the data bus. Disabling the strobe pulse indicates that the data on the data bus is no more valid. When new valid bit is available, the source again enables the strobe pulse.

In this case, the CPU could be the source and memory unit could be the destination. The CPU indicates a memory-write control signal as the strobe to inform the memory unit that this is a write operation. The CPU then places the word to be written in the memory on the data bus.

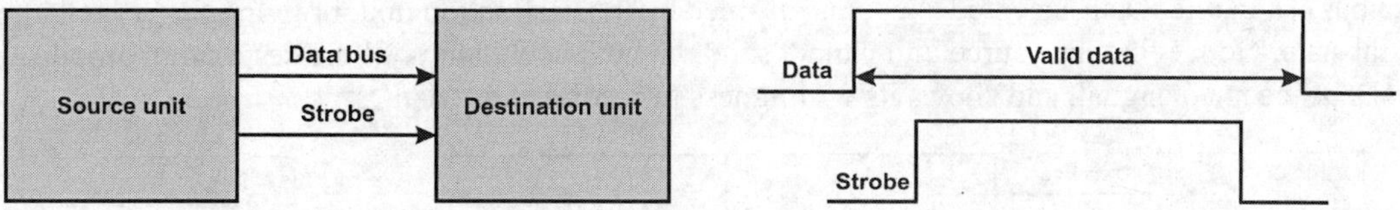

(a) Block diagram (b) Timing diagram

Figure 10.5 Strobe Initiated by Source

Figure 10.6 shows the block diagram and timing diagram for destination-initiated strobe. When the destination unit initiates the data transfer, it activates the strobe pulse to inform the source unit to provide the data. In response, the source unit places the requested data on the data bus. Like source-initiated data transfer, the actual data transfer from data bus to one of the internal registers of destination unit takes place during the falling edge of strobe pulse. The strobe is then disabled by the destination unit and after a pre-determined time interval; the data on the data bus is removed by the source unit.

In this case, the memory unit could be the source and CPU could be the destination. The CPU initiates the memory-read signal as the strobe to inform the memory unit that it is a memory read operation, and requests the memory unit to place a selected word into the data bus.

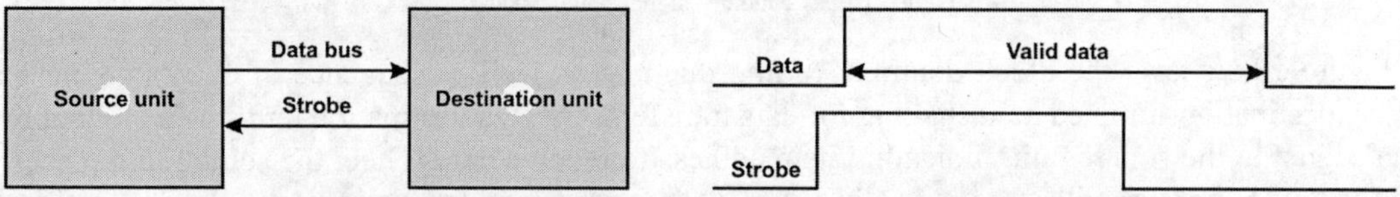

(a) Block diagram (b) Timing diagram

Figure 10.6 Strobe Initiated by Destination

12. What is the disadvantage of strobe control method?

Ans. In the strobe control method, there is no way of knowing whether the data sent by the source unit is accepted by the destination unit or not. There is no acknowledgement as only one control line is there in the same direction from source to destination as the data flows in the bus.

13. What are handshaking signals? Explain the handshake control of data transfer during input and output operations. What are the sequences of events during an input operation using handshake scheme?

Ans. In handshaking mechanism, two control lines are used to transfer data: one for source to destination unit and other in the opposite direction. The first control line is used by the source unit for informing the destination unit about any valid data in the bus. Other control line is used by the destination unit to acknowledge the receipt of data. The handshake control of data transfer during input operation is known as **source-initiated handshaking** and data transfer during output operation is known as **destination-initiated handshaking.**

Figure 10.7 shows the block diagram and timing diagram for source-initiated handshaking. It also depicts the sequence of events that take place during the data transfer. When the source unit initiates the data transfer, it places the data on the data bus and enables the 'Data valid' handshaking signal. The destination unit accepts the data and activates the 'Data accepted' handshaking signal. After receiving 'Data accepted' signals, the 'Data valid' signal is disabled by the source unit invalidating the data on the data bus. Then, the 'Data accepted' signal is disabled by the destination unit, bringing the system into its initial state. Notice that the source unit cannot send the next data item until the destination unit disables its 'Data accepted' signal, and shows its willingness to receive more data.

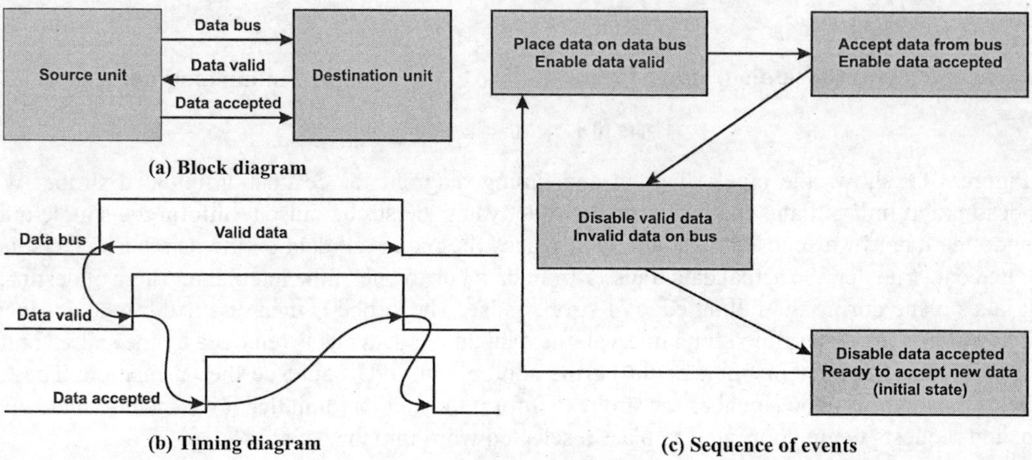

Figure 10.7 Source-initiated Handshaking

Figure 10.8 shows the block diagram, timing diagram as well as sequence of events taking place during destination-initiated handshaking for data transfer. First, the destination unit sends the 'ready for data' signal to the source unit, indicating its readiness to receive data. Then, the source unit places the data on data bus and enables the data valid signal. On receiving the data valid signal, the destination unit accepts the data from data bus and disables the 'ready for data' signal. After this, the source unit disables the valid data signal, informing that the data on data bus is no more valid. Until the source unit receives ready for data signal from the destination unit, it does not place the data on the data bus. From there on the handshaking process is same as that of source initiated.

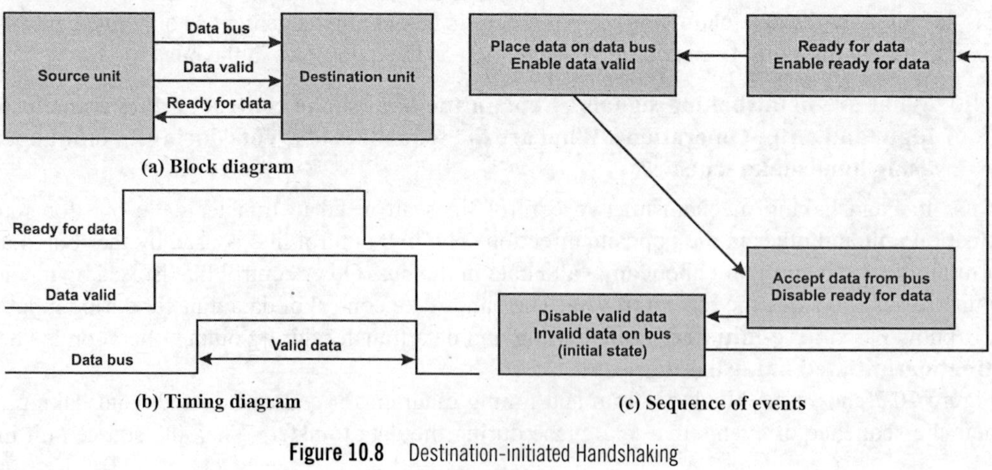

Figure 10.8 Destination-initiated Handshaking

A high degree of flexibility and reliability is provided in the handshaking mechanism as the success of data transfer depends on the active participation of both units. The data transfer will not be complete if any one of the units is faulty. Any error (if occurred) during the data transfer can be detected using the time-out mechanism. This mechanism employs an internal clock that generates an alarm if the time taken for data transfer is more than a pre-determined amount of time. When one of the participating units enables its one of handshaking control signal, the clock starts counting. If the other participant does not respond within a given time, it is assumed that an error has occurred. The time-out signal can be used to interrupt the processor and hence execute a service routine that takes an appropriate error recovery action.

14. Mention different modes of data transfer.

Ans. It is generally required to transfer data between the central computer and the external environment (such as I/O devices). The data to be transferred to an I/O device originates from the memory unit. Similarly, the data coming from some I/O device are ultimately stored in the memory unit. A variety of modes are available for accomplishing the data transfer between the central computer and the I/O devices. Some of these modes require the involvement of CPU, while others directly interact with memory unit to achieve the data transfer. Three possible modes for handling data transfer to and from peripherals include *programmed I/O*, *interrupt-initiated I/O* and *direct memory access* (*DMA*).

15. What is program-controlled I/O or programmed I/O system. Explain with the help of a diagram.

Ans. In program-controlled I/O, the I/O devices do not directly access memory; rather, CPU is involved to accomplish the data transfer. The I/O instructions are written in a computer program that causes the transfer to and from CPU and I/O devices. The CPU needs to execute additional instructions to transfer data to and from CPU and memory, to determine whether the data is available from the device or to count the number of bytes/words to be transferred.

Figure 10.9 shows an example of data transfer between the CPU and I/O device through the interface unit under programm-controlled I/O. The device transfers data one byte at a time. To understand the operation, suppose, the data is to be transferred from the I/O device to memory. When the device is

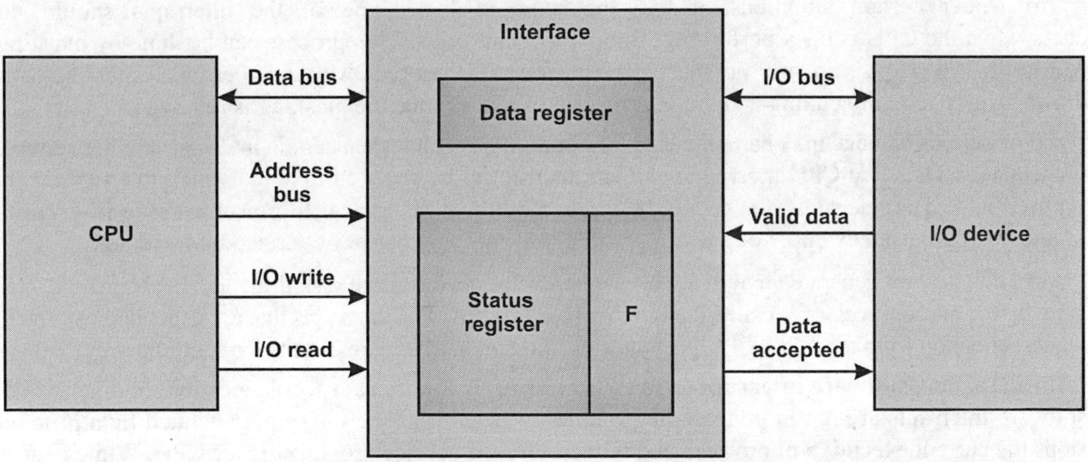

Figure 10.9 Data Transfer from I/O Device to CPU

ready with data, it places data on I/O bus and enables data valid signal. On receiving the data valid signal, the interface loads the data byte into its data register and enables data accepted signal. Along with this, interface sets the Flag bit (F) in its status register to 1. Though, now the I/O device can disable its data valid line, it cannot send next byte until the interface disables data accepted line.

The program-controlled I/O transfer requires CPU to continuously check the `F` bit in the status register of interface. To accomplish this, the CPU reads the status register into one of its internal registers and checks the `F` bit. If `F = 1`, then it indicates a byte to be transferred is available. Thus, the CPU reads the byte from the data register, which is then stored in memory using store instruction. After this, the CPU or interface clears the `F` bit to `0`, and as a result, the interface disables the data accepted line. This indicates the I/O device to transfer next byte of data. On the other hand, if `F = 0`, then the CPU has to wait until some byte is available from the I/O device.

This method is useful only for small low-speed computers where CPU can be dedicated to monitor the device continuously. However, this method proves inefficient because of the difference in the transfer rate of CPU and I/O devices. Once the data transfer is initiated, the CPU stucks in a loop until the data transfer is complete. This results in poor utilization of CPU. This method is very time consuming, as it keeps the CPU busy unnecessarily.

16. Describe the following:

(a) Non-vectored and vectored interrupt

(b) Maskable and non-maskable interrupt

(c) Hardware and software interrupt

Ans. **(a)** When the CPU receives an interrupt signal, it stores the return address from the PC in a memory stack and branches to the service routine that processes the interrupt. There are two ways through which the processor can choose the branch address. One is the **non-vectored interrupt** in which branch address is assigned to a fixed location in memory. The other one is the **vectored interrupt** in which the branch information is given by the source that caused the interrupt. This information is called **interrupt vector**.

(b) Under certain situations, it may be required that some of the interrupts should not occur when the CPU is busy performing some important tasks. This process can be done by masking. **Maskable interrupt** is an interrupt that can be masked off (ignored). Masked interrupts cannot be withdrawn as they remain pending and the interrupt takes place, once the masking is removed.

Some serious damage may harm the data or program or results when certain interrupts are not serviced immediately. Thus, the CPU must know which interrupt to be serviced first and which interrupt can be serviced later. The interrupts that cannot be masked by the CPU are called **non-maskable interrupts**. Memory failure is an example of a non-maskable interrupt that has to be serviced immediately.

(c) The interrupt generated externally by the hardware devices (like disk drive and keyboard) or internally by the microprocessor is called the **hardware interrupt**. The interrupts that are generated externally, request attention from the CPU. CPU generates the internal hardware interrupts for controlling events.

In a program, **software interrupt** (also called a **trap**) is inserted at specific location. In other words, software interrupts are not more than the program instructions. The interrupt generated by a program stops the current execution of program and requests for the service provided by the CPU. While executing a program, when a software-interrupt instruction is encountered, the CPU initiates an interrupt. A perfect example of a software interrupt generated by a program is reading input from the keyboard.

17. What do you mean by interrupt latency?

Ans. Interrupt latency is defined as the delay between receiving an interrupt request and the starting of the corresponding ISR execution. It is caused due to saving of registers.

18. Discuss single-level and multi-level interrupts.

Ans. In general, a number of I/O devices are connected to the computer and each device can generate an interrupt request. Thus, the interrupt system needs to identify the device that caused the interrupt so that the request can be serviced. There are two methods: *single-level* and *multi-level* interrupts, for the selection of the interrupt generated by external device. Both these methods are discussed as follows:

- **Single-level interrupt system:** In this system, there are many interrupting devices that send the interrupt request through a single input pin of the CPU. When CPU gets interrupted by more than one device, it starts polling (checking the logic state of each device) the I/O ports for identifying the requesting device. After the interrupting device has been identified, the CPU services it and then resumes the task it was doing before the interrupt.

  A single-level interrupt system is shown in Figure 10.10. The interrupt requests from all devices are ORed together and connected to the interrupt pin (INT) of the CPU. Thus, every interrupt request gets routed to the processor interrupt input. Once the CPU gets interrupted, it reads the interrupt status of each device and identifies the device that interrupted it.

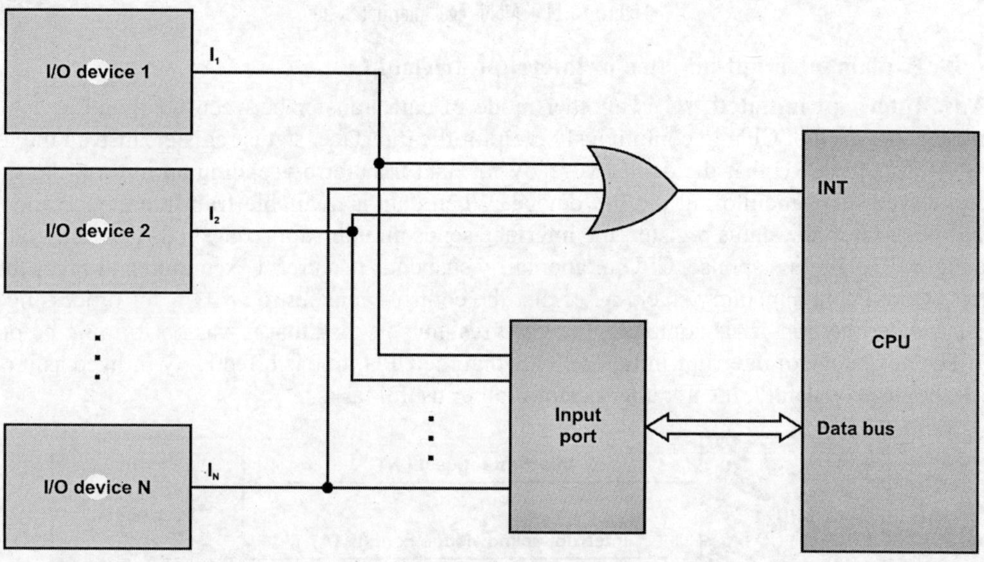

Figure 10.10 Single-level Interrupt System

- **Multi-level interrupt system:** In this system, there are more than one interrupt pins in the CPU and each individual device is connected to its own pin. The advantage of this system is that the CPU can immediately identify the interrupting device upon receiving an interrupt request without having the need to tell I/O ports. This saves the processor time in servicing the interrupt.

  The multi-level interrupt system is shown in Figure 10.11. Each device can send interrupt request to CPU independently by activating the corresponding interrupt pin of CPU. After receiving an interrupt request, the CPU calls a special subroutine to service the interrupt.

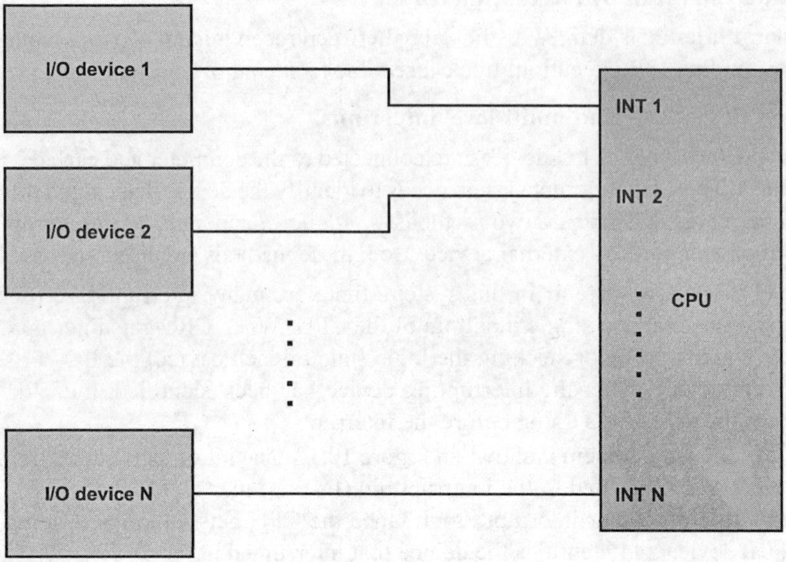

Figure 10.11 Multi-level Interrupt System

19. Explain interrupt-initiated or interrupt-driven I/O.

Ans. Interrupt-initiated I/O is another mode of data transfer between CPU and peripherals. It eliminates the need of CPU to continuously monitor the interface, status register; instead the interface itself informs the CPU that the device is ready for data transfer by sending an interrupt to the CPU. The interface keeps monitoring the I/O device. When data is available from the device and the flag bit has been set in the status register, the interface sends an interrupt request (INT) signal to the CPU (see Figure 10.12). In response, CPU momentarily suspends its current execution and saves the return address from PC in a memory stack. After that the control branches to an `ISR` for processing the I/O transfer. After the transfer is complete, the CPU resumes its task that it was performing before interrupt. The advantage of interrupt-initiated I/O is that the CPU time is effectively utilized as it need not check the flag constantly; it can rather perform other useful tasks.

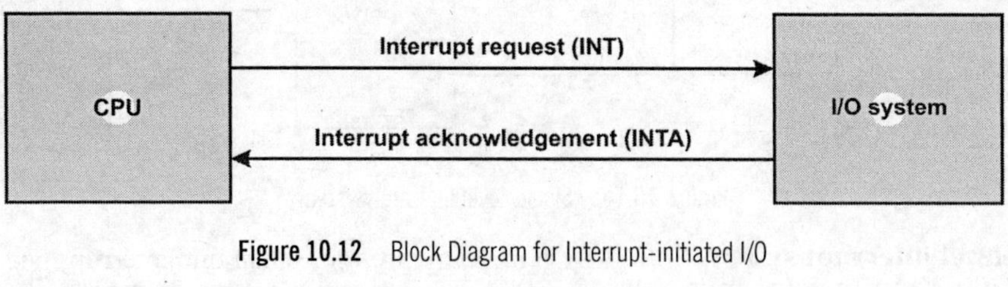

Figure 10.12 Block Diagram for Interrupt-initiated I/O

20. Explain how multiple simultaneous interrupt requests are handled?

or

What happens when more than one interrupt request arrives simultaneously?

Ans. Apart from single interrupt, multiple interrupts can also arise in a CPU. Two approaches used for handling multiple simultaneous interrupt requests are as follows:

- **Disable interrupts:** In this approach, the interrupt line is disabled by the processor when an already existing interrupt is being serviced to ignore the further interrupt requests. The interrupt is disabled immediately when any interrupt arrives during user program execution. The ignored interrupt remains in its pending state and is checked when the processor enables the interrupt. After processing the current interrupt request, the interrupts are enabled and the processor checks the occurrence of any additional interrupt, before resuming the user program. The disadvantage of this approach is that relative priority or time-critical needs are not considered.
- **Define priorities:** In this approach, the interrupts from multiple devices are assigned priorities and the interrupt with higher-priority is serviced before the lower-priority interrupt. To understand, consider a computer system having three I/O devices including a printer with priority 2, a disk with priority 4 and a communication line with priority 5; higher number denotes higher priority. Initially, when a user program is executing, an interrupt from printer arrives. The processor stops the execution of the user program and continues to serve printer interrupt. While this interrupt is being executed, an interrupt from communication line occurs. Since the communication line has higher priority than printer, the processor stops servicing the printer interrupt, pushes it on to the stack and starts processing the communication line interrupt. While communication line interrupt is being serviced, an interrupt from disk occurs. Since the priority of disk interrupt is lower than that of communication line, it is put on hold and the communication interrupt processing task is continued. Once the communication line interrupt has serviced, the processor starts processing the disk interrupt instead of resuming the printer interrupt because disk has been assigned higher priority than printer. After all the interrupts have been serviced, the processor resumes the execution of the user program.

21. What is priority interrupt? Discuss the methods used for establishing priorities of multiple simultaneous interrupts.

Ans. The **priority interrupt** is a system that sets up priorities to multiple interrupt sources for determining which source to service first when two or more interrupt requests arrive at the same time. The system may also determine the conditions that can interrupt the CPU when CPU is already busy in servicing another interrupt. Priorities can be assigned on different basis. For example, the conditions which if delayed can result in serious consequences are given higher priorities. The high-speed devices such as magnetic disk are assigned higher priorities over the slow-speed devices such as keyboard. When more than one device generates interrupt simultaneously, the device with higher priority is serviced first. The priority of simultaneous interrupts can be established either by the hardware or by the software means.

Polling is the procedure to determine the highest priority interrupt source among the multiple simultaneous interrupt sources by software means. In this method, the initial service routine that handles the interrupts is common for all the interrupts. That is, all the interrupts cause CPU to branch to a common address where the initial service routine is located. This service routine examines (polls) all the interrupt sources in the order of their priorities. That is, a higher priority source is tested before the lower-priority source. During examination, the initial service routine tests the interrupt signal of each source and if it is on for some source, the control branches to the service routine for that source. Otherwise, the initial service routine tests the next lower-priority source in sequence and repeats the same process. Thus, the initial service routine identifies the highest-priority device among all the devices that interrupted and branches to one of the several possible service routines. The main disadvantage of polling method is that the time taken in polling several sources in case of multiple interrupts can outgo the time available to service the I/O device.

To speed up the operation, the **hardware priority-interrupt unit** can be used. The role of this unit is to accept the multiple simultaneous interrupt requests, identify the highest priority request among them and then issue an interrupt request to the CPU based on its identification. Each interrupt source comprises its own interrupt vector and thus, can directly access its service routine. This speeds up the operation as polling is not needed. The function of hardware priority-interrupt unit can be established by connecting the interrupt lines serially or in parallel. The former method is referred to as daisy chaining priority, while the latter is referred to as parallel priority method.

22. Explain daisy chaining priority method.

Ans. In daisy chaining priority method, all the devices that request an interrupt are connected serially, with the highest priority device at the first position and the lowest-priority device at the last position. Figure 10.13 depicts a daisy chaining connection between four devices and the CPU.

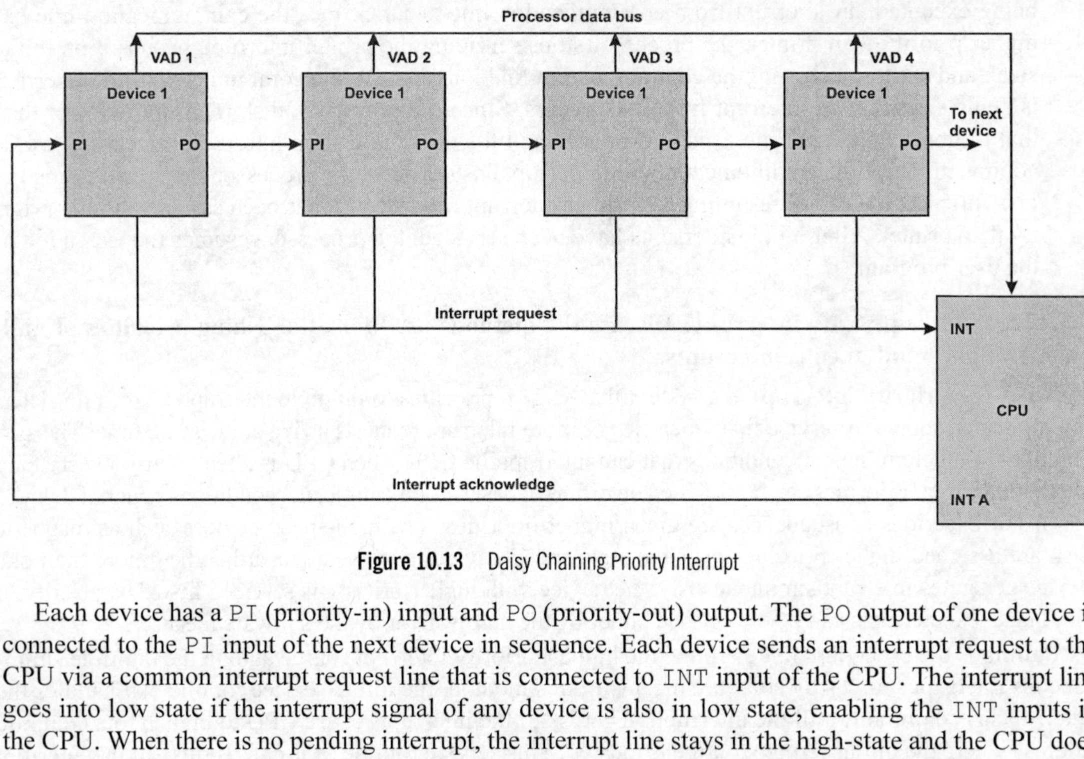

Figure 10.13 Daisy Chaining Priority Interrupt

Each device has a PI (priority-in) input and PO (priority-out) output. The PO output of one device is connected to the PI input of the next device in sequence. Each device sends an interrupt request to the CPU via a common interrupt request line that is connected to INT input of the CPU. The interrupt line goes into low state if the interrupt signal of any device is also in low state, enabling the INT inputs in the CPU. When there is no pending interrupt, the interrupt line stays in the high-state and the CPU does not receive any interrupt. To respond to an interrupt request, the CPU enables the interrupt acknowledge (INTA) line. Initially, it is received by the device 1 at its PI input. If device 1 has not requested for any interrupt, it passes on the acknowledgement signal to the next device through its PO output by setting PO to 1. However, if the device 1 has a pending interrupt, then the acknowledge signal is blocked from going to the next device by clearing its PO output to 0. Then, device 1 puts its own interrupt **vectored address (VAD)** onto the data bus of the CPU for use during interrupt cycle. Thus, if a device having its PI input as 1 is requesting for an interrupt, then it has to place a 0 in its PO output for blocking the acknowledgement signal. Therefore, a device with PI = 1 and PO = 0 has the highest priority among all the interrupt devices and thus, places its VAD on the data bus.

23. Explain parallel priority interrupt method with a diagram.

Ans. Parallel priority interrupt method involves the use of an interrupt register. The individual bits of this register are set by the interrupt signal from each device. The position of bits in register indicates the priority of devices. In addition to the interrupt register, a mask register is also used that controls the status of each interrupt request. When a device with higher priority is being serviced, the mask register disables the lower priority interrupts. In addition, it may allow the higher priority device to interrupt the CPU, while a lower priority interrupt is being serviced.

Figure 10.14 shows the priority interrupt hardware for a system having four interrupt sources. The interrupt register has four bits one corresponding to each interrupt source. The lower the bit position, higher is the priority of associated interrupt source. The bits of this register are set by some external conditions and cleared by program instructions. The number of bits in the mask register is same as that of interrupt register. The bits in the mask register are set or reset with the help of program instructions. Every mask bit and its corresponding interrupt bit are ANDed to produce four inputs (I_0, I_1, I_2 and I_3) for the priority encoder. Thus, an interrupt is recognized only when its corresponding mask bit is set to 1. The priority encoder implements the priority function such that if two or more interrupt requests arrive at the same time, the one with the higher priority gets precedence. It generates three outputs; two of which are the bits of VAD. The two bit VAD generated from the priority encoder is transferred to the CPU.

The third output from the priority encoder is used to set the interrupt status (IST) flip-flop when an unmasked interrupt occurs. The interrupt enable (IEN) flip-flop provides an overall control over the interrupt system and is set or cleared by the program. The interrupt signal for the CPU is obtained by

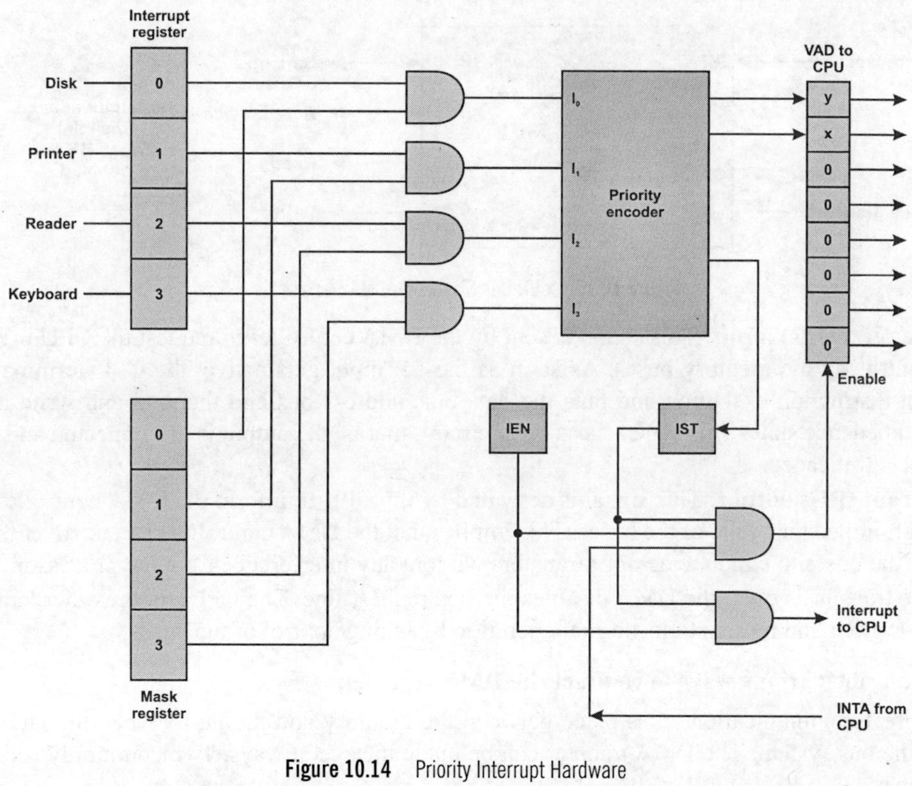

Figure 10.14 Priority Interrupt Hardware

ANDing the outputs of IST and IEN. The INTA signal from CPU when ANDed with IST and IEN enables the bus buffers in the output register and a VAD is put onto the data bus of CPU. Vector address is inserted into the data bus for the CPU to be used during interrupt cycle when one of the device has pending interrupt and it is blocking the acknowledge signal from the next device by placing 0 as the output. The priority encoder's output forms the part of vector address for each interrupt source. Any value can be assigned to the other bits of vector address by appending 6 zeros to the encoder outputs x and y.

24. What is direct memory access?

Ans. The data transfer between fast secondary storage devices (like magnetic disk) and memory is often hampered due to the limited speed of the CPU. The speed of transfer can be improved by removing the CPU from the path and allowing I/O devices to manage the memory buses directly. Such a transfer technique is called direct memory access (**DMA**). During DMA transfer, the CPU does not have any control over the memory buses and remains idle. The control of memory buses is taken over by the **DMA controller**—a part of the I/O device interface—that manages the direct transfer between the memory and I/O device.

25. Describe the CPU bus signals used for DMA transfer.

Ans. During DMA transfer, the CPU remains idle. The CPU can be placed in an idle state in a variety of ways. One common method is to disable the buses. In microprocessors, the buses can be disabled through special control signals. Two control signals are used in the CPU to facilitate the DMA transfer (see Figure 10.15).

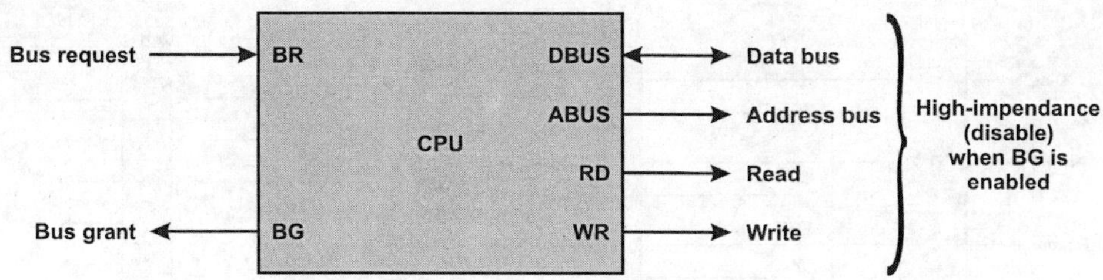

Figure 10.15 CPU Bus Signals for DMA Transfer

- **Bus request (BR) input:** This signal is sent by the DMA controller to request the CPU to release the control on the memory buses. As soon as the BR input gets active, the CPU terminates the current instruction execution and puts the data bus, address bus and the read and write lines in high-impedance state. This state acts as open circuit, that is, the output is disconnected and has no logical significance.
- **Bus grant (BG) output:** This signal is activated by the CPU to inform the DMA controller about the high-impedance state of the buses. This implies that the DMA controller can take over the control of the buses to conduct memory transfers without any interference from the processor.

After the transfer is over, the DMA disables the bus request line. The CPU, on the other hand, disables the bus grant and returns to its normal operation by taking control of the buses.

26. Describe various ways to conduct the DMA transfer.

Ans. Direct communication takes place between the memory and the DMA when the latter takes control of the bus system. The DMA transfer can be made in several ways. Two commonly used ways are as follows:

- In DMA **burst transfer**, a sequence of blocks that consists of a number of memory words is transferred to the memory in a continuous burst.
- An alternative technique to burst transfer is **cycle stealing**, in which DMA controller transfers the words to memory, one word at a time and returns the control of buses to the CPU after each word transfer.

27. Explain the operation of DMA controller along with its block diagram.

Ans. To enable DMA transfer, DMA controller requires control circuits of interface to interact with the CPU and I/O device. It also requires an address register and a set of address lines to directly communicate with memory unit, and a word count register to store the number of words to be transferred.

Figure 10.16 shows the block diagram of DMA controller. The CPU selects the registers in the DMA through the address bus by activating the DS (DMA select) and RS (register select) inputs. The other two inputs read (RD) and write (WR) are bidirectional. The direction in which data is to be transferred is indicated by the status of BG input. If BG = 0, then the CPU can read/write data from/to DMA registers via data bus. On the other hand, if BG = 1, then it indicates that the CPU has released its control of memory buses. Thus, the DMA controller can directly read/write data from/to memory by placing the desired memory address onto the memory bus and activating the RD or WR input, respectively. The DMA request and DMA acknowledge lines are used by the DMA to communicate with the external I/O, following the handshaking mechanism.

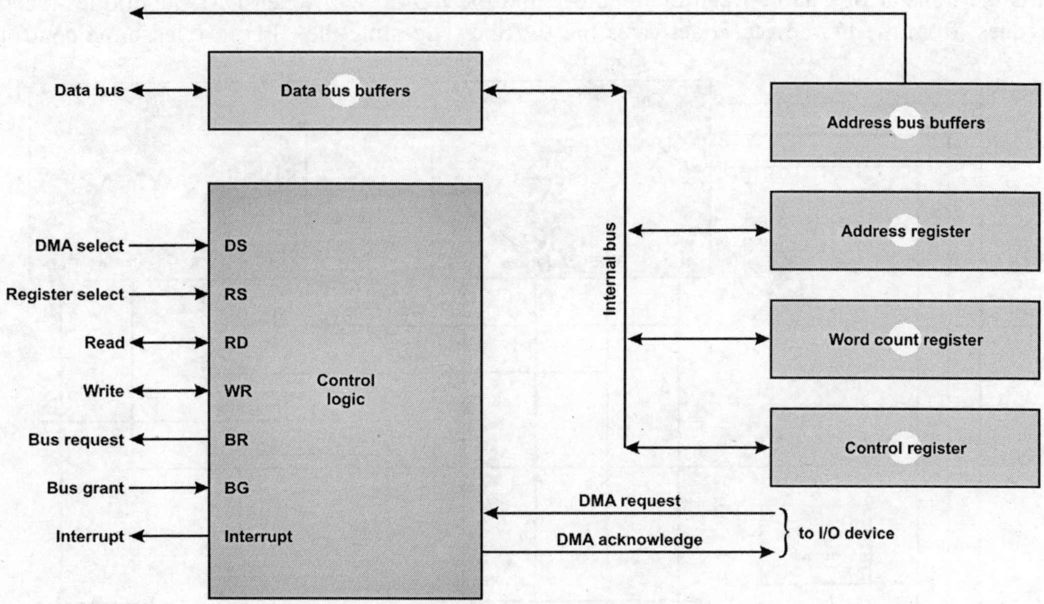

Figure 10.16 Block Diagram of DMA Controller

Registers in DMA controller: There are three registers in DMA controller, namely, *address register*, *word count register* and a *control register*. The desired location (address) in memory where the data is to be read from or written to is specified in the **address register**. The address bus buffers help in passing the address bits into the address bus. After the transfer of each word into memory, the address register is incremented. A count of number of words to be transferred is kept in the **word count register**. When each word is transferred, the word count register is decremented by one and tested for zero. The mode of transfer is specified by the **control register**. The CPU takes all the registers in the DMA controller as I/O interface registers and can read from or write into DMA registers through the data bus under program control.

DMA initialization: Before starting the DMA transfer, DMA needs to be initialized by the CPU. The initialization process is a program that consists of I/O instructions, which specify the address for choosing specific registers in DMA. After the DMA has been initialized, the data transfer between peripheral and memory unit continues to proceed until the complete memory block is transferred. To initialize DMA, the CPU sends the following information via data bus.

- The starting address of the memory block where the data is to be read from or written to.
- The total number of words in the memory block, that is, the word count.
- A control for specifying the mode of transfer, such as read or write.
- A control for starting the DMA transfer.

28. Explain DMA transfer along with its diagram.

Ans. The CPU and DMA communicate with each other through the address and data buses as depicted in Figure 10.17. The DMA has its own address that activates the DS and RS lines. After that the CPU initializes the DMA using the data bus. On receiving the start control command, the DMA starts the transfer of data between the memory and the I/O device. When DMA controller receives a request from the I/O device, it activates the BR line requesting the CPU to release the control of

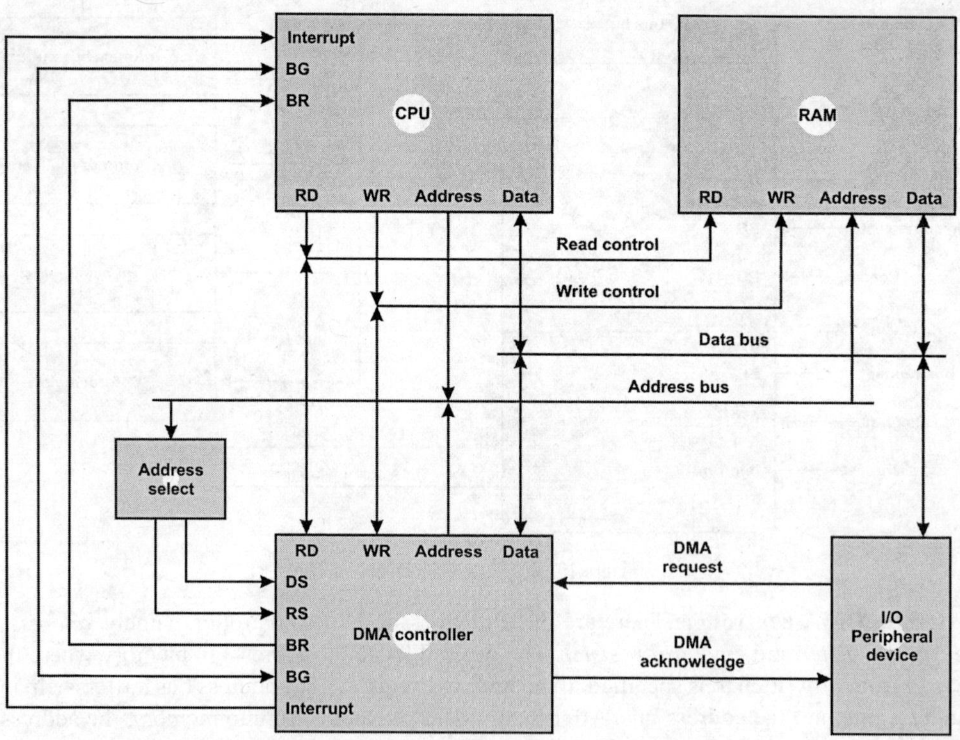

Figure 10.17 DMA Transfer in Computer System

memory buses. In response, the CPU activates the bus grant (BG) line, informing the DMA about the disabling of buses. DMA comes to know about the disabling of buses when the CPU responds with its BG line. The DMA then places the current address in its address register onto the address bus, activates the RD (for read operation), WR (for write operation) and sends a DMA acknowledge signal to the I/O device. As RD and WR signals are bidirectional, the value of BG determines the direction of transfer. If BG = 0, then the direction of RD and WR will be from CPU to memory, while if BG = 1, then the direction of transfer will be from DMA controller to memory. Through data bus, the I/O device can communicate with memory for transferring data directly between the two units while the CPU is temporarily disabled.

After receiving the DMA acknowledge signal, the I/O device can directly interact with the memory unit, while the CPU remains blocked for that moment. The I/O device receives a word from (in case of read operation) or supplies a word onto (in case of write operation) the data bus.

The address register of DMA is incremented and the word count register is decremented after every word transfer. DMA checks the request line coming from the I/O device, if the word count does not reach zero. If the I/O device is of high speed, then the line is made active immediately after the previous transfer gets completed and the second transfer process can be started that will continue until the whole block gets transferred. In contrast to a low-speed device, the DMA request line may arrive late. In such a case, the DMA disables the line allowing the CPU to execute its program. The DMA requests again to the CPU for the buses.

When the word count register reaches zero, the DMA removes its bus request and stops transferring any data. It informs the CPU about the termination by sending an interrupt signal. In response to this signal, the CPU reads the content of the word count register. The zero value in the word count register makes the CPU realize that all the words are transferred successfully. To check how many numbers of words had already been transferred, the CPU can read the word count register at any time.

29. Explain I/O processor.

or

Discuss I/O processor and its organization.

Ans. An **input–output processor (IOP)** is defined as an external processor that has direct memory access capability and is employed to directly communicate with the I/O devices. The IOP is designed for handling details of I/O processing independent of the CPU and the CPU is relived from the tasks involving I/O transfers. The IOP can be considered similar to CPU; however, it is dedicated only to I/O. Though IOP has DMA capability, it does not require the CPU to entirely set up the DMA controller, rather it fetches and executes its own instructions to read data from or write data to memory.

A computer can have more than one IOP in addition to the CPU. Figure 10.18 shows the block diagram of a computer having one IOP. Several I/O devices of the computer are connected to IOP through the I/O bus and the IOP is connected to memory unit through memory bus. Here, the role of the CPU is to process the data required while solving the computational task and of the IOP is to provide data path for transfer between memory transfer unit and I/O devices. Once the CPU initializes the process, the IOP continues to operate without any involvement of CPU.

The IOP and the devices attached to it communicate in a manner similar to that of a program control method of transfer. Based on the level of sophistication included in the system, the way of communication between CPU and IOP is determined. In most of the computer systems, CPU acts as the master

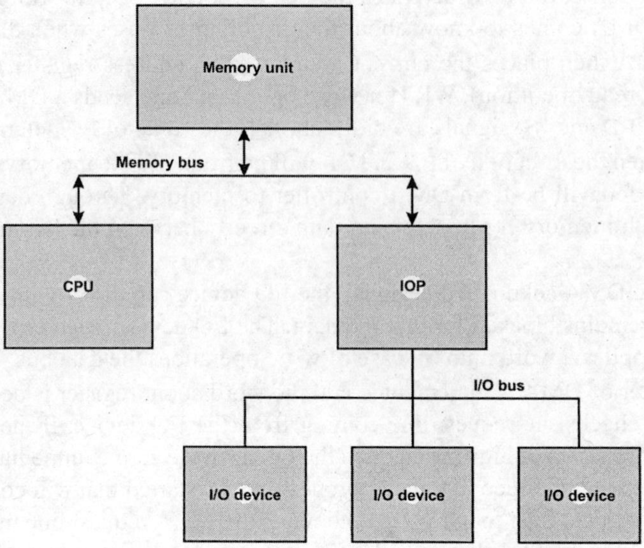

Figure 10.18 Block Diagram of Computer with IOP

processor and IOP acts as the slave processor. The task of initiating all operations is assigned to the CPU, while IOP executes I/O instructions. The operations to start an I/O transfer and to test I/O status conditions for making decisions on various activities of I/O are provided by CPU instructions. When IOP needs CPU, it sends an interrupt signal to the CPU. The IOP requests CPU by sending interrupt signal and responds to CPU requests by specifying a status word in a specific memory location. This status word is later examined by a CPU program. When an I/O transfer is desired, CPU informs the IOP where to find the I/O program in memory and afterwards IOP continues with the transfer process. The transfer details are also provided to the IOP by the CPU.

30. Explain CPU–IOP communication.

Ans. Depending on the computer configuration, there can be different forms of communication between CPU and IOP. However, in most computer configurations, the memory unit acts as a message centre where one processor can store information for the other processor. Figure 10.19 shows a flowchart illustrating the steps involved in a simplified form of CPU–IOP communication.

Initially, the CPU sends an instruction to IOP for checking the IOP path. The IOP responds by putting the status word in a specific memory location. This status word is checked by the CPU. The status word bits imply the condition of IOP and I/O device such as device busy and device ready, based on which the CPU decides the next step. If the status bit conditions are `OK`, then an instruction is sent to IOP by CPU for starting the I/O transfer. This instruction indicates IOP the address in memory where the I/O program is located.

Once the data transfer has been initiated, the CPU continues with the program which was interrupted earlier, whereas the IOP is busy in executing its I/O operations. The interrupt request signal is sent to the CPU by IOP after the completion of the specified task. The CPU responds to this interrupt by sending an instruction to read status from IOP. The IOP then places the contents of the status report into a particular memory location. The status word in the status report is checked by the CPU to determine whether the transfer has been completed successfully.

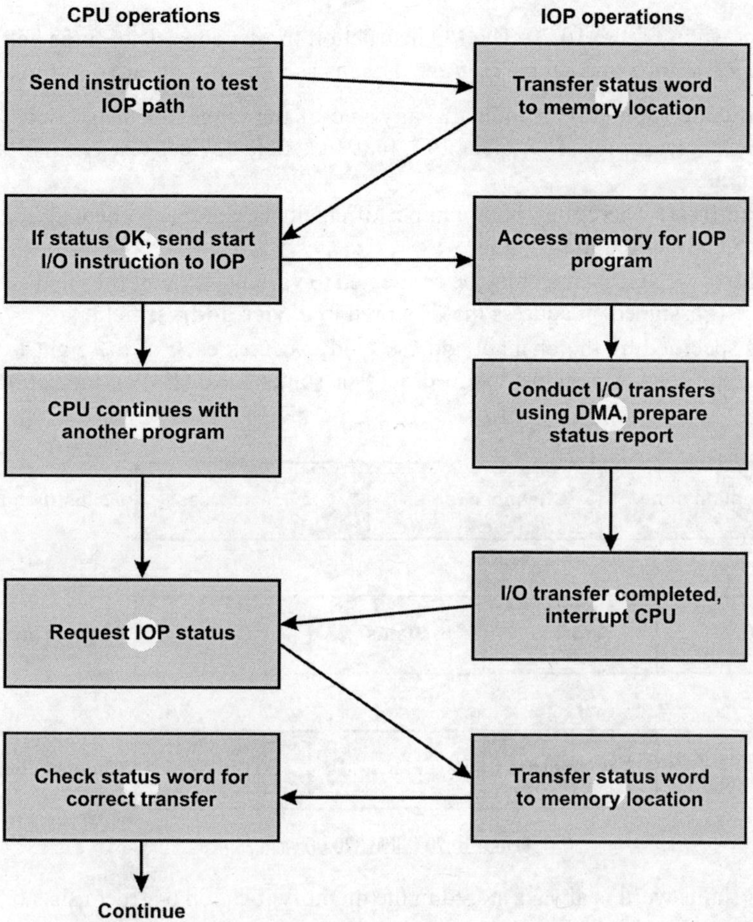

Figure 10.19 CPU–IOP Communication

31. Explain the IBM 370 I/O channel.

Ans. The name **channel** is given to the I/O processor used in IBM 370 computers. Through dedicated control lines, the direct communication between the CPU and the channels can be done. The CPU can indirectly communicate through reserved storage area in memory. A number of channels are included in a typical system configuration where each channel is attached to one or more I/O devices. The channels are of three types: *multiplexer, selector* and *block-multiplexer*. These channels are described as follows:

- **Multiplexer:** This channel is connected to many slow- and medium-speed devices. It can operate with a number of devices at the same time, however, transfers only one byte at a time.
- **Selector:** This channel can control one high-speed device and can handle only one I/O operation at a time.
- **Block-multiplexer:** This channel combines the features of both the multiplexer and the selector channels. It is connected to various high-speed devices and can transfer entire block of data at a time.

There can be direct communication between CPU and channels via dedicated control lines or indirect communication via reserved storage areas in memory. The word formats associated with the channel operation are shown in Figure 10.20. The I/O instruction format consists of three fields, namely, *operation code*, *channel address* and *device address*. The instruction formats are described as follows:

- **Operation code (opcode):** It indicates any one of the eight I/O instructions, that is, start I/O, start I/O fast release, test I/O, clear I/O, halt I/O, halt device, test channel and store channel identification.
- **Channel address:** There may be a number of channels, and each channel is assigned a specific address, which is stored in this field.
- **Device address:** Each channel may be connected to various devices, thus to distinguish the device, each device is assigned an address that is stored in **device address** field.

The channel specified by the channel address field executes each of the eight I/O instructions and sets one of the four condition status bits in processor status word (PSW), indicating the result of I/O operation.

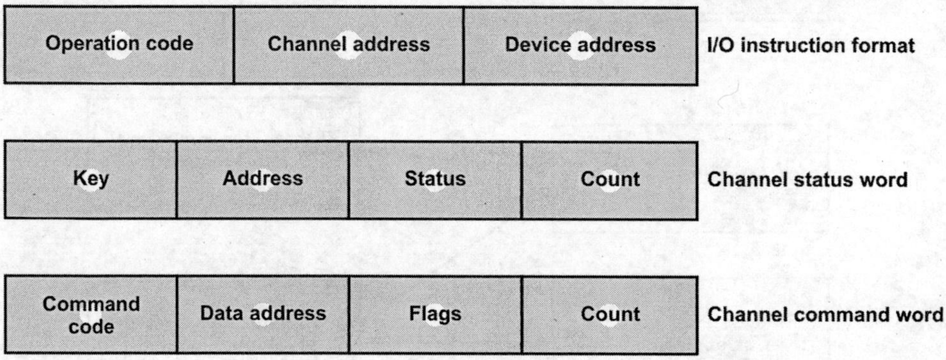

Figure 10.20 IBM 370 I/O Word Formats

The channel status word is always stored in the memory location 64. It consists of four fields, which are as follows:

- **Key:** The field in this format is used to prevent the unauthorized access by a user to the information of other user or of operating system.
- **Address:** This field specifies the address of the last command word used by the channel.
- **Status:** This field indicates the status of device and channel, and any errors that occurred during transfer of data.
- **Count:** This field is used to give the remaining count after the transfer process is over. The count field shows zero if the transfer has successfully completed.

After receiving any of the start I/O or start I/O fast release instruction, the channel refers to memory location 72 for the address of the first channel command word (CCW). The CCW consists of four fields, which are discussed as follows:

- **Command code:** This field contains an operation code, which corresponds to one of the six types of I/O operations including write, read, read backwards, control, sense and transfer in channel.
- **Data address:** This field contains the first address of a memory buffer.
- **Count:** This field specifies the number of bytes that are involved in transfer.
- **Flags:** In each CCW, there are six flag bits that give additional information for the channel.

32. A DMA controller transfers 16-bit words to memory using cycle stealing. The words are assembled from a device that transmits characters at the rate of 2400 characters per second. The CPU is fetching and executing instructions at an average rate of 1 million instructions per second. By how much will the CPU be slowed down because of DMA transfer?

Ans. CPU refers to memory on an average once every μsec ($1/10^6$).
Character arrives every 1/2400 = 416.6 μ sec
Since DMA controller can transfer a 16-bit word during each memory cycle, two (of 8 bits each) from peripheral can be sent simultaneously.
The time taken to send two characters = 2 × 416.6
= 833.3 μ sec.
The CPU is slowed down by no more than 1/833.3 × 100 = 0.12%.

MULTIPLE CHOICE QUESTIONS

1. Which printer is used for printing one character at a time?
   (a) Dot matrix (b) Daisy wheel
   (c) Laser (d) Inkjet
2. ___________ provides the way for transferring binary information between internal storage and I/O device.
   (a) I/O bus (b) I/O interface
   (c) Output interface (d) Input interface
3. In ________, the processor treats I/O devices as locations in memory and uses the same instructions to access them.
   (a) Synchronous communication (b) Memory-mapped I/O
   (c) Asynchronous communication (d) Polling
4. When the processor reads from input or writes to output on every clock cycle, this is called___________.
   (a) Interrupt-driven I/O (b) Synchronous communication
   (c)Memory-mapped I/O (d) Asynchronous communication
5. Which asynchronous data transfer functions as both a transmitter and a receiver?
   (a) Strobe control (b) Asynchronous serial transfer
   (c) Handshaking (d) Asynchronous communication interface
6. In the FIFO buffer, data can be inserted if the _________ signal is enabled.
   (a) Output ready (b) Insert
   (c) Input ready (d) Input
7. ___________ operations are the result of I/O instructions written in the computer program.
   (a) DMA (b) Interrupt-initiated I/O
   (c) Interrupt (d) Programmed I/O
8. An interrupt for which hardware automatically transfers the program to a specific memory location is known as
   (a) Software interrupt (b) Hardware interrupt
   (c) Maskable interrupt (d) Vector interrupt

9. What advantages does interrupt-driven I/O have over polling?
   (a) Interrupt-driven I/O is synchronous while polling is asynchronous.
   (b) Interrupt-driven I/O does not require any additional hardware.
   (c) Interrupt-driven I/O allows the computer to process other tasks while waiting for I/O.
   (d) Interrupt-driven I/O can be memory mapped while polling cannot.
10. When two or more requests arrive simultaneously, a _________ will establish priority over various sources to determine which condition to be serviced first.
    (a) Priority interrupt (b) Priority
    (c) Interrupt (d) Parallel priority interrupt
11. Which procedure is used to determine the higher priority interrupt source among multiple simultaneous interrupt sources?
    (a) Memory-mapped I/O (b) Synchronous communication
    (c) Asynchronous communication (d) Polling
12. Who controls the data transfer in DMA?
    (a) Microprocessor (b) RAM
    (c) I/O devices (d) Memory
13. Which protocol in serial communication is based on the binary code of a character set?
    (a) Character-oriented protocol (b) Bit-oriented protocol
    (c) Byte-oriented protocol (d) Word-oriented protocol

Ans. 1. a 2. b 3. b 4. b 5. d 6. c 7. d 8. b 9. c 10. a

11. d 12. c 13. a

11

Memory Organization

1. What does memory mean?

Ans. Memory refers to an electronic holding place where data can be stored and retrieved later whenever required. It is an integral part of any computer system. Memory is divided into two broad categories: *main memory* and *auxiliary memory*. The memory unit that communicates directly with the CPU is called as the **main memory** (also called as **primary memory**). It holds the instructions and data currently being processed by the CPU, the result of intermediate calculations and the recently processed data.

Usually, the capacity of main memory is limited and not enough to accommodate all the programs in a typical computer. Moreover, not all the stored programs are needed by the CPU at the same time. Thus, it is preferable to store the information not currently being used by the CPU in low-cost storage devices, referred to as **auxiliary memory** or **secondary memory**. A variety of auxiliary storage devices are available such as magnetic tapes, magnetic disks etc. These devices are used to store data, files, application and system programs. The auxiliary memory also serves as a backup storage.

2. Define the term memory location and address.

Ans. Memory can be viewed as a storage unit. It is divided into several physical parts referred to as **memory locations**, where each location is capable of holding certain piece of information. Each location is identified with the help of an address (in binary form), referred to as **memory address** of that location.

3. Differentiate between the word addressable and byte addressable computers.

Ans. The computers may be *byte addressable* or *word addressable*. In a **byte-addressable computer**, each memory address refers to a single byte of storage. If the data to be stored are larger than a single byte, they are stored in multiple consecutive memory addresses. In contrast, in **word-addressable computers**, each memory address identifies a portion of storage larger than a byte. This implies that each memory location in word-addressable computers can hold larger amount of data as compared with byte-addressable computers.

4. Discuss different memory operations.

or

How read and write operations are performed in memory?

Ans. Retrieving a word from a specified memory location is termed as **memory read operation**. This operation can be performed using the following three steps:

1. The memory location from where the word is to be read is loaded into the memory address register (MAR).
2. The CPU issues the read signal to indicate that the word, whose address is specified in MAR, is to be read into the memory data register (MDR).
3. The required word is loaded by the memory into MDR after a little delay. Now, the word is ready to be used by the CPU.

Storing a word in a specified memory location is referred to as **memory write operation**. This operation can be performed using the following three steps:

1. The CPU loads the given word into MDR.
2. The CPU loads the address of the locations where the word is to be stored into MAR.
3. A write signal is issued by the CPU to indicate that the word stored in MDR is to be stored in the memory location specified in MAR.

5. Write a short note on hierarchy of memory?

or

Justify the use of hierarchical memory system.

or

Explain different components of memory hierarchy.

Ans. A computer system generally employs a variety of storage devices such as auxiliary memory, main memory and cache memory. All these memory components can be organized into a hierarchy on the basis of storage capacity, access speed and the cost per bit of storage [see Figure 11.1(a)]. The lowest level of hierarchy, the low-cost, slow but largest storage capacity, is auxiliary memory, which includes magnetic tape, magnetic disk, optical disk, etc. The magnetic tape and optical disk are used to store the removable files, while the magnetic disk is used as backup storage.

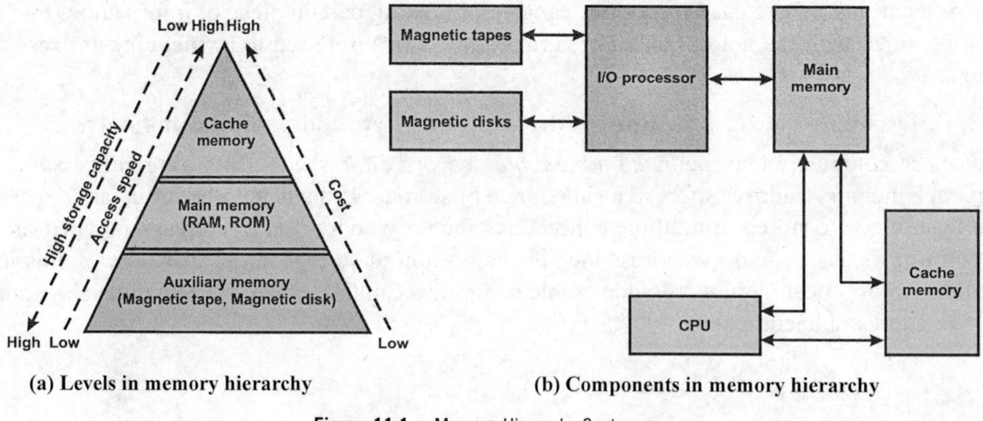

(a) Levels in memory hierarchy (b) Components in memory hierarchy

Figure 11.1 Memory Hierarchy System

The next level of hierarchy, the relatively expensive, faster and less storage capacity, is main memory which includes random access memory (RAM) and read only memory (ROM). The reason behind placing the main memory at the central location is that it can communicate with the CPU directly and with the auxiliary memory via an I/O processor [see Figure 11.1(b)]. When the programs currently required by the CPU are not available in the main memory, they are transferred from auxiliary memory to main memory. The reason behind the CPU not directly accessing the auxiliary memory is that if the CPU has to access the auxiliary memory constantly to retrieve every piece of required data, it would operate very slowly. However, when the data are kept in main memory, the CPU can access it more quickly. When some programs are not currently required in the main memory, they are transferred to auxiliary memory to make room for currently used programs.

The highest level of hierarchy, the small, most expensive and very high-speed, is cache memory which can be directly accessed by the CPU. The cache memory makes the currently required data and instructions available to the CPU at a rapid rate, resulting in increased processing speed. The cache memory is used in computer systems to cover the speed mismatch between the processor and main memory. Usually, the access time of main memory is much higher than the processor speed. As a result, the processing speed of CPU gets limited by the speed of main memory. To compensate this speed mismatch, the cache memory whose access speed is nearly equal to the CPU clock cycle time is employed between the CPU and main memory. The cache memory stores parts of the program that are currently being executed and the data that are frequently being accessed by the CPU so that the CPU could avail them immediately when needed, without having the need to access the main memory. This increases the performance rate of the computer as well.

6. Explain the characteristics of different memory devices.

Ans. There are various types of storage media available in the market. Each of them provides different functionality based on various characteristics, such as volatility, accessibility, capacity, etc. Thus, while choosing a specific memory device, these characteristics must be considered. The different characteristics of the memory devices are discussed as follows:

- **Volatility:** This characteristic determines whether the data stored in the device are lost or remain intact when the power supply is turned off. In the former case, the memory is said to be volatile while in the latter-case, the memory is non-volatile. For example, the volatile memory device is suitable where very fast accessing speed is needed. On the other hand, non-volatile memory is suitable where information needs to be stored for a longer time period.
- **Mutability:** This characteristic determines whether the memory device can be overwritten once or multiple times. The storage devices that allow to be overwritten multiple times are called **mutable storage devices**. For example, RAM, CD-RW and flash memory are mutable. On the other hand, the storage devices that can be written only once after manufacture are called **immutable storage devices**. The immutable devices support multiple read and write once operations. CD-R is an example of immutable storage device.
- **Accessibility:** Accessibility of memory devices can be measured in terms of access time, access rate and access mode. They are discussed as follows:
  - **Access time:** The time period from the beginning of a read instruction signal and preparation of the availability of the desired word in memory buffer register (MBR) is known as memory access time.
  - **Access rate:** The number of words that can be accessed from memory during a specific time interval is known as **access rate** of the memory. It is measured in words per seconds. Access rate is the inverse of access time.

- **Access mode:** It defines the way the information can be accessed from the memory (serially or directly). The most commonly used access methods are sequential access, direct access and random access. In sequential access mode, the memory locations can be accessed only in a predetermined order. However, in direct and random access, memory locations can be accessed in any order. The only difference between direct and random access method is that in the latter the access time is independent of the location, that is, the time to access any two locations in memory is always same.

- **Capacity:** The storage capacity of a memory device can be defined as the total amount of data that can be held by the storage device. It is expressed using two terms: word size and number of words. The word size is expressed in bits or bytes. The commonly used word sizes are 8, 16 and 32 bits. For example, if memory capacity is 4K x 8, then it means that 4K (that is, 4096) words can be stored in memory and size of each word is 8 bits.
- **Performance:** The performance of a storage device can be measured in terms of latency and throughput. **Latency** is the total time taken to access a specific location in the storage device. Usually, for the primary storage devices, this time is measured in nanoseconds. In case of secondary storage, latency is measured in milliseconds and in case of tertiary storage, it is measured in seconds. **Throughput** is defined as the amount of data that can be read from or written to the memory device per unit of time. Usually, it is measured in terms of megabytes (MB) per second.

7. Discuss the types of main memory.

Ans. The main memory is the central storage system of the computer that stores data and programs currently being executed. It communicates directly with the CPU, making the data access rate high. It is constructed using the semiconductor integrated circuit's technology. It can be classified into two categories: *RAM* and *ROM.*

- **RAM:** RAM is like the computer's scratch pad. It allows the computer to store data for immediate manipulation and to keep track of what is currently being processed. It is the place in a computer where the operating system, application programs, and data in current use are kept so that they can be accessed quickly by the CPU. For a memory to be random access means that the time to access any location in memory is same. RAM is much faster to read from and write to than the other kinds of storage in the computer such as hard disk. Integrated circuit RAM chips are available in two operating modes: *static* and *dynamic*.
  - **Static RAM (SRAM):** The word 'static' indicates that the memory retains its contents as long as power is being supplied. However, as the power gets down, the data are lost. This makes SRAM a volatile memory. SRAM is made up from a number of internal flip-flops, which hold the binary information. It is very fast and has access time in the range of 10–30 ns. Due to its high speed, it is often used for caches and high-speed registers. In addition, it is easier to use, and has shorter read and write cycles as compared with DRAM. However, it is much more expensive than DRAM.
  - **Dynamic RAM (DRAM):** It is named so because it is very unstable. The data continue to move in and out of the memory as long as power is available. DRAM is made up of capacitors that are provided within the chip by MOS transistors. These capacitors hold the binary information in the form of electric charge applied to them. The stored electric charge on capacitors continues to decay with passage of time. Therefore, DRAM must be periodically refreshed to restore the charge, thereby maintaining the data. This refreshing is done by placing the memory on a refresh circuit that rewrites the data every few milliseconds for restoring the charge.

DRAM is used for most system memory because it is smaller, cheaper and has relatively high capacity. However, it is slower than SRAM because refreshing needs to done in a frequent interval of time.

- **ROM:** Though major portion of main memory is constructed using integrated RAM chips, a portion is constructed with integrated ROM chips. Unlike RAM, ROM is non-volatile which means that the information in ROM is not lost even when the power is turned off. Moreover, it is read only memory, that is, the data and instructions stored in ROM can only be read and used but cannot be altered. Therefore, ROM is used for storing programs that are to reside permanently in computer and not subject to change once the production of computer is over.

The most common application of ROM is to store the **bootstrap loader**—the initial program needed to start the computer operating after the power is turned on. Whenever power is turned on and computer is started, there is nothing in RAM, and the hardware of computer enables the execution of bootstrap loader stored in ROM by storing the first address of this program in program counter (PC) register. The bootstrap loader then loads the operating system from hard disk to main memory and the control is handed over to the operating system to make it ready for general use. There are different types of ROM, some of which are as follows:

- **Programmable ROM (PROM):** It is a type of ROM which can be programmed. Blank PROM chips can be bought economically and coded by the users with the help of a special device known as **PROM-programmer**. However, once a PROM has been programmed, its contents can never be changed. Therefore, PROM is referred as **one-time programmable (OTP)** device. PROMs offer flexible and economical storage for fixed programs and data.
- **Erasable Programmable ROM (EPROM):** An EPROM is programmed in exactly the same manner as a PROM. However, unlike PROM, an EPROM can be erased and reprogrammed repeatedly. It can be erased by simply exposing the device to a strong source of ultraviolet light for a certain amount of time. Note that an EPROM eraser is not selective; it will erase the entire EPROM. Although EPROM is more expensive than PROM, its ability to be reprogrammed makes it more useful.
- **Electrically Erasable Programmable ROM (EEPROM):** This type of ROM can be erased by an electrical charge and then written to by using slightly higher-than-normal voltage. EEPROM can be erased one byte at a time, rather than erasing the entire chip with ultraviolet light. Hence, the process of reprogramming is flexible, but slow.

8. Explain the RAM and ROM chips with the help of their block diagram.

or

How read and write operations are performed in RAM and ROM chips? Explain with the help of a block diagram.

Ans. The RAM and ROM chips are discussed as follows:

A **RAM chip** employs one or more control inputs to communicate with the CPU. These inputs select the chip whenever required by the processor. Figure 11.2 shows the block diagram of a RAM chip having two chips select (CS) control inputs: CS1 and $\overline{\text{CS2}}$. The capacity of RAM is 128 words with each word containing three more inputs: read (RD), write (WR), and a 7-bit address (AD7) bus input. It is connected to an 8-bit bidirectional data bus. The bidirectional data bus enables the data transfer between CPU and memory. During read memory operation, the data are transferred from memory to CPU, while in opposite direction during memory write operation.

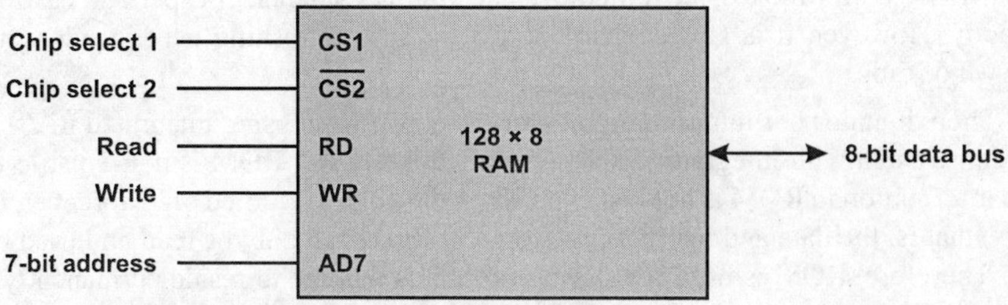

Figure 11.2 RAM Chip

To construct a bidirectional data bus, a three-state buffer can be used which can have three possible outputs: logic-1, logic-0 and high impedance state. The logic 1 and logic 0 denote simple digital signals while the high impedance state acts as an open-circuit which implies that the output does not carry a signal and has no logical significance.

The operation of RAM chip is specified in the function table shown in the Figure 11.3. Observe that RAM chip is in operation only when CS1 and $\overline{CS2}$ are active, that is, (CS1 = 1 and $\overline{CS2}$= 0). When either of the control inputs is disabled or both control inputs are disabled or the control inputs are enabled but read write inputs are disabled, the memory is inhibited and the data bus is in high-impedance state. After enabling the control inputs, the memory is inhibited and read and write operations can be performed by enabling the read and write inputs, respectively. When the RD input signal is enabled, the contents of the input memory location whose address is specified by the address input lines are placed on the data bus. When WR input signal is enabled, the contents on the data bus are stored into the memory location specified by address on address bus input. Thus, RD and WR signals are used to control the bus buffers associated with data bus in addition to performing the memory operations.

CS1	$\overline{CS2}$	RD	WR	Memory function	State of data bus
0	0	×	×	Inhibit	High-impedance
0	1	×	×	Inhibit	High-impedance
1	0	0	0	Inhibit	High-impedance
1	0	0	1	Write	Input data to RAM
1	0	1	×	Read	Output data from RAM
1	1	×	×	Inhibit	High-impedance

Figure 11.3 Function Table for RAM

ROM chip

The **ROM chip** works in the same manner as that of RAM chip. However, unlike the RAM chip, only the read operation can be performed on ROM chip. Thus, a one-way data bus is needed instead of a bidirectional data bus. Figure 11.4 shows the block diagram of ROM chip. Notice that the internal binary cells of a ROM take less space in memory. Therefore, more number of ROM bytes can be stored in a same size chip as compared with RAM bytes. In other words, the capacity of a ROM chip is greater than that of RAM chip of same size. That is why the capacity of ROM chip shown in Figure 11.4 is 512 bytes, while that of RAM chip shown in Figure 11.3 is 128 bytes, though both chips are of same size.

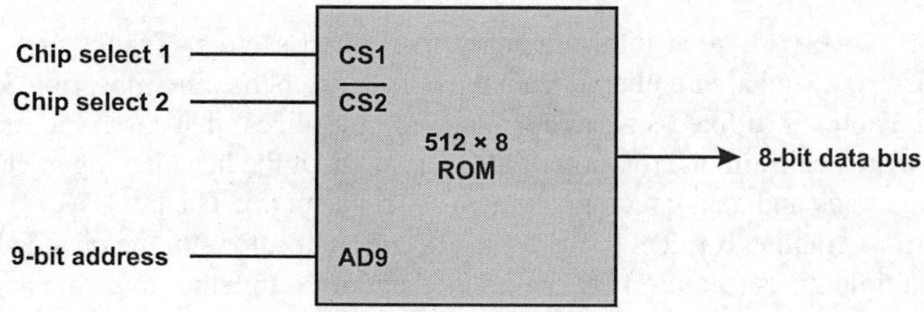

Figure 11.4 ROM Chip

ROM chip has two chip select (CS1 and $\overline{CS2}$) control inputs and a 9-bit address (AD9) input. The chip is in operation when CS1 = 1 and $\overline{CS2}$ = 0. After enabling the control inputs, the read operation can be performed. The address input specifies address of any one of the 512 bytes whose contents are then placed on the data bus for the CPU.

9. What is the difference between memory access time and memory cycle time? How are they affected due to destructive and non-destructive readout?

Ans. **Memory access time** is defined as the time period between an address is sent to memory and the word is read/written from/to that address. Usually, it is expressed in nanoseconds. **Memory cycle time** is defined as the sum of access time and the additional time required before the next access can start. It is concerned with only RAM.

Destructive and non-destructive readout, both are the methods of reading data. In **destructive readout,** the data are erased from the source after the read operation is completed. To restore the original data, it has to be rewritten on that location that is, memory needs to be refreshed. On the other hand, in **non-destructive readout,** the data are not erased from the source after the completion of read operation. In case of destructive readout, the next read or write in memory cannot be processed until the refresh operation has been carried out. This increases the memory access time as well as memory cycle time. In non-destructive readout, restoring and refreshing operations are performed automatically. Data can be read from the same location without rewriting. Thus, access rate as well as memory access time is less in comparison to destructive readout memory.

10. What is auxiliary memory? Discuss any one of the auxiliary memory devices.

Ans. The memory unit used for permanent storage of data is called **auxiliary memory.** As the main memory of computer system is volatile in nature, data are lost in case of power failure or when power is turned off. Thus, there should be such a media that can store large size data files and other backup information permanently and economically. This is provided by auxiliary memory. Auxiliary memory is less expensive and has a low access speed. Some of the most commonly used auxiliary memory devices are magnetic disks, magnetic tapes, magnetic drums, magnetic bubble memory and optical disks. Here, we are discussing the magnetic disk.

Magnetic Disk

Magnetic disks are the widely used and popular medium for direct access secondary storage. They offer high storage capacity and reliability and have capability to access the stored data directly. A magnetic disk consists of a plastic/metal circular plate/platter, which is coated with magnetic oxide layer. Data are represented as magnetized spots on a disk. A magnetized spot represents 1 and the absence of a magnetized spot represents 0.

The surface of a disk is divided into imaginary tracks and sectors. **Tracks** are concentric circles where the data are stored, and are numbered from the outermost to the innermost ring, starting with zero. **Sectors** refer to the number of fixed-size areas (imaginary pie slices) that can be accessed by one of the disk drive's read/write heads, in one rotation of the disk, without the head having to change its position. An intersection of a track and a disk sector is known as **track sector.** The track sectors are grouped into a collection known as **cluster**. It refers to the basic allocation unit for storage on a disk.

Frequently, multiple disks (platters) are maintained and used together to create a large disk storage system. Typically, two or more platters are stacked on top of each other with a common **spindle**, which rotates them. There is a gap between the platters, making room for magnetic read/write head. There is a read/write head for each side of each platter and all the heads are attached to a single assembly called a **disk arm assembly**, which can move them towards the central spindle or towards the edge (see Figure 11.5). All the read/write heads are on the equal diameter track on different platters at one time. The tracks of equal diameter on different platters form a **cylinder**. A close look at the internal structure of magnetic disk is shown in Figure 11.5.

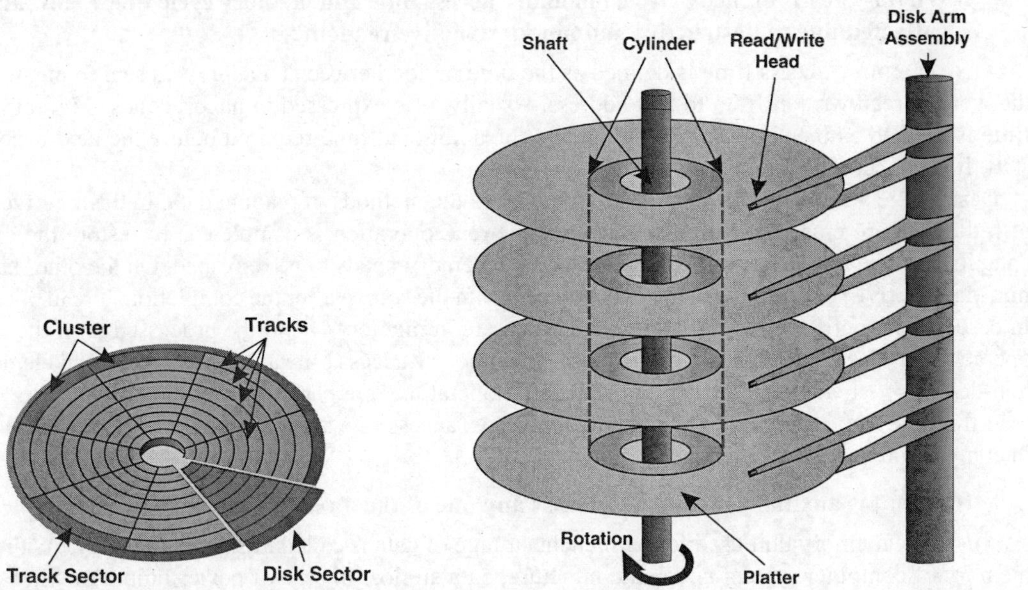

Figure 11.5 Magnetic Disk

The storage capacity of a disk can be calculated as:

Storage capacity $= s \times p \times q \times n$ bytes

Where,

s = total number of surfaces

p = number of tracks in each surface

q = number of sectors in each track

n = number of bytes in each sector

The process of accessing data from a magnetic disk comprises the following three steps:

1. **Seek:** As soon as the disk unit receives the read/write command, the read/write heads are positioned on the specific track on the disk platter. The time taken in doing so is known as **seek time.** It is the average time required to move the heads to the desired track on the disk.
2. **Rotate**: Once the heads are positioned on the desired track, the head of the specific platter is activated. As the disk is rotated constantly, the head has to wait for the required sector or cluster (desired data) to come under it. This waiting time is known as **rotational delay time** or **latency** of the disk.
3. **Data Transfer**: Once the read/write head is positioned over the desired sector, the data can be transferred to or from the disk to main memory. The rate at which the data are read from or written to the disk is known as **data transfer rate**. It is measured in kilobits per second (kbps). The data transfer rate depends upon the rotational speed of the disk.

The combined time (seek time, latency and data transfer time) is known as the **access time** of the magnetic disk.

11. Write a short note on magnetic tape.

Ans. Magnetic tape appears similar to the tape used in music cassettes. It is a plastic tape with magnetic coating on it. The data are stored in the form of tiny segments of magnetized and demagnetized portions on the surface of the material. Magnetized portion of the surface refers to the bit value '1' whereas the demagnetized portion refers to the bit value '0'. The amount of data or the number of binary digits that can be stored on a linear inch of tape is the **recording density** of the tape.

The magnetic tape is divided into vertical columns (**frames**) and horizontal rows (**channels** or **tracks**). The data are stored in a string of frames with one character per frame and each frame spans multiple (usually 7 or 9 tracks). Thus, a single bit is stored in each track, that is, one byte per frame. The last track (7th or 9th) stores the parity bit. A read/write head is mounted on each track to record and read data as a sequence of characters.

On a magnetic tape, data are recorded in form of blocks where each block consists of a grouping of data (known as **records**) that is written or read in a continual manner. Between these blocks, the computer automatically reserves some blank space called **inter-block gap (IBG)**. One block may contain one or more records that are again separated by blank space (usually 0.5 inch) known as **inter-record gap (IRG)**. In case of reading data from a moving tape, whenever an IRG is reached, the moving tape is stopped. It remains in immobile motion until the record is processed.

The data on the tape cannot be addressed and can only be retrieved sequentially in the order in which they were written. Thus, if the record to be accessed lies at the end of the tape, earlier records must have to be read before reaching to the desired one. Thus, the access time of magnetic tape is very high in comparison to magnetic disk.

12. Write a short note on optical disks.

Ans. Apart from magnetic tapes and magnetic disks, another storage medium, which is more popular, is the optical disk. An **optical disk** is a flat, circular, plastic disk coated with material on which bits may be stored in the form of highly reflective areas and significantly less reflective areas, from which the stored data may be read when illuminated with a narrow-beam source, such as a laser diode. These disks are capable of storing enormously high amount of data in a limited amount of space. The optical disk storage system consists of a rotating disk coated with a thin layer of metal (aluminium, gold or silver) that acts as a reflective surface and a laser beam, which is used as a read/write head for recording data onto the disk. Some of the common examples of optical disks include compact disk (CD), digital versatile disk (DVD) and Blu-ray disk.

13. Write notes on the following:

(a) CD-ROM

(b) WORM

Ans. (a) CD-ROM

A CD is an optical disk that was originally intended only for storing music (in the form of digital audio). It can record more than 60 minutes of uninterrupted playing time. A **compact disk-read only memory (CD-ROM)** is capable of being used as a data storage device along with storing of digital audio. CD-ROM reading devices are frequently included as a component in personal computers. A CD-ROM disk is a shiny, silver colour metal disk of 12 cm in diameter. It is the most popular and the least expensive type of optical disk and as the name implies, it comes pre-recorded with the data, which cannot be altered. A typical optical disk is made up of three layers: a **polycarbonate base** through which light can pass, a **layer of aluminium**, and a protective **layer of acrylic** on top of that.

A CD-ROM has one track that spirals from the centre to the outside edge. This track is divided into sectors of equal length and density. Files are stored on these particular contiguous sectors. CD-ROM drives are characterized by the **spin rate**. The spin rate is the rotation speed of the disk and it influences the information retrieval speed (access time). Currently quad, hex and octal-speed CD-ROM drives are available where quad means 4 ×, hex means 6 × and octal means 8 ×. Thus, octal-speed drive will be the fastest and, as a result, the most expensive.

(b) WORM

As the name suggests, write once-read many (WORM) disks can be used to read as well as to write (usually only once) data onto their surfaces. Data can be written, but cannot be erased on an optical disk. The reason is the technology used for recording. The most common type of a WORM disk is the compact disk-recordable (CD-R). It is a thin (1.2 mm) disk made up of polycarbonate with a 120 mm diameter that is mainly used to store music or data. A CD-R disk is similar to a standard CD, but has subtle differences to enable the storage and removal of data. The disk is coated on the side with the spiral groove with a very thin layer of a special dye and subsequently with a thin, reflecting layer of silver, a silver alloy or gold. Finally, a protective coating of a photo-polymerizable lacquer is applied on top of the metal reflector and cured with UV-irradiation.

14. Explain the different memory access methods?

Ans. There are three methods of accessing data from the memory devices:

- **Sequential access:** Sequential access means that the data can be accessed from the memory device in the order it was stored. Whenever an access request arrives, the device is searched from the beginning until the desired data are found. The most common sequential access storage device is magnetic tape where data are stored and processed sequentially. To understand, suppose a tape contains information regarding employees of an organization. Now, to look for the information of employee number 100, the computer will have to start with employee number 1 and then go past 2, 3, and so on, until it finally comes to 100. The sequential access method is quite simple than the other methods but searching for data is slow.
- **Direct access:** Direct access means that the data stored on the memory device can be accessed in any order. The location, where the desired data are stored can be accessed directly and data can

be retrieved immediately. The most common direct access storage devices are magnetic disk and optical disk. In these devices, the data are stored as a numbered sequence of blocks, which can be accessed in any order. For example, one can access first block 12, then access block 78 and then block 2. The direct access method is ideal for applications such as airline reservation systems or computer-based directory assistance operations. In these cases, there is no fixed pattern of the requests for data.

- **Random access:** Random access is similar to direct access, that is, data from any memory location can be accessed directly. However, in random access, the time taken to access data from the storage unit is independent of the location of data in storage unit. This implies that each separate location is as easy to access as any other location and takes same amount of time. On the other hand, in direct access, the time taken to access two different locations may differ. The most common example of random access memory device is RAM.

15. What is associative memory? Explain its hardware organization.

Ans. The memory unit that can be accessed on the basis of data contents instead of memory addresses or location is called **associative memory** or **content addressable memory (CAM)**. The associative memory can be accessed in parallel as well as simultaneously on the basis of data content. During write operation no address is specified; rather the memory unit itself finds some empty unused locations to store the word. During the read operation, the contents of the word or a part of the word are specified. The memory unit searches through the memory and marks the words that match the specified content for reading. As search is made based on the contents rather than addresses, the search time reduces significantly.

Associative memory is better suited to situations where a number of search operations are to be performed in parallel. In addition, the entire word or some particular field of the word can be used for the search operation. However, associative memory is much more expensive than RAM. This is because each cell in associative memory must have storage capability and logic circuits to compare the cell contents with an external argument. Therefore, associative memory is primarily used for search-critical applications.

Hardware organization: Figure 11.6 shows the block diagram of associative memory which consists of a memory array and logic for n words where each word consists of `m` bits. There is an argument register `A`, key register `K`, each of `m` bits one per each bit of word. A match register `M` of `n` bits, one per each word is also used.

While searching the data from associative memory, the search content is specified in the argument register. Then each word is compared in parallel with the argument register's content. If a word matches then the bit corresponding to the matching word is set. Thus, eventually the words having the corresponding bits 1's in the match register are the matching words. Now, a sequential access can be made to the memory to read the word for which we have corresponding 1-bit in the match register.

In case the search operation is to be performed based on some particular field or key in the argument register, the key register provides the mask for choosing the desired field. If the key register contains all 1's, all bits of the argument register are compared with each memory word; otherwise, only those bits of the argument register are matched with the memory words which are having 1's in their corresponding bit positions in the key register. To understand, consider the following scenario:

```
A = 010 110010
K = 111000000
```

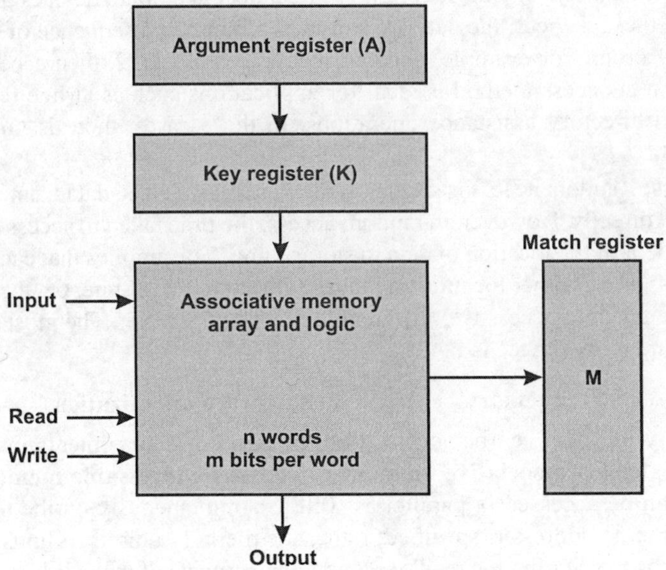

Figure 11.6 Block Diagram of Associative Memory

Now, only the unmasked argument field (that is, first three bits of A starting from MSB) will be compared with each memory word. For example, if W_1 = 010001100 and W_2 = 101110010, then only W_1 matches, but W_2 does not.

16. What is cache memory? Also, explain its operation.

Ans. Cache is a very high-speed small memory that aims to speed up the memory access operation. It is placed between the CPU and the main memory (see Figure 11.7). The cache memory is organized to store the frequently accessed data and instructions so that the average memory access time can be reduced, thereby reducing the total execution time of the program. The cache memory tends to reduce the access time of main memory by a factor of 5–10.

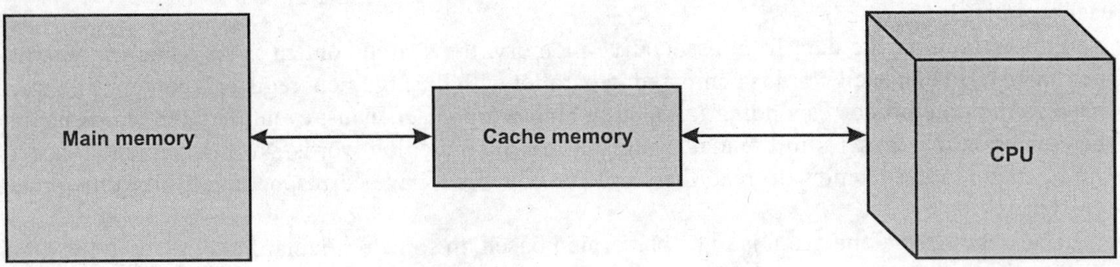

Figure 11.7 Cache Memory

Operation of Cache

The cache organization concerns with the transfer of information between CPU and main memory. Whenever processor needs to access any memory word, first of all, this word is searched in cache memory. If the required word is present in the cache, it is read from there. However, if the word is not found in cache then main memory is accessed to read the word. The recently accessed block of words that has been accessed from main memory is then transferred to the cache memory so that next time if this word is required, it can be accessed from cache, thus, reducing the memory access time. The block size can vary from one word to 16 words adjacent to the required word. If cache is already full, then it is overwritten, else the contents are appended.

17. Describe the advantages and disadvantages of using cache memory?

Ans. Cache memory is used for faster accessing of data or to minimize the average access time. It is used to compensate for mismatch in the speed of main memory and CPU. Cache memory has several advantages. Some of the advantages are as follows:

- CPU has direct access to cache memory. Thus, the data that resides in cache can be accessed without any delay and at less processing cost.
- Cache increases the performance and the processing speed of CPU.
- In case of shared-memory multiprocessor architecture, where all the processors share a common memory of the server, but have their own private caches, the reliability is increased. This is because in case of server down, all the processors can directly access the frequently accessed data from their own caches.
- The use of cache results in increased CPU utilization due to faster accessing of data.

Although, cache memory has several advantages, there are some disadvantages also. Some of them are as follows:

- As cache is small in size, the cost per bit of storing data is high. Thus, the use of cache memory increases the hardware cost.
- Cache suffers from the problem of coherency, that is, inconsistent data in case of multiprocessor system. In this system, each of the processors has its own private cache along with shared resources. If the same value of data exist in multiple caches, the changes made in one cache required to update the other copies of cache also. However, absence of identical changes creates the problem of inconsistent data.
- The cache memory suffers from the problem of synchronization in client-server system, when multiple accesses can be made on the database. This problem occurs when there is no proper integration between the cache and the RDBMS used. The single access on the database does not create a problem. However, another access by a different application can cause problem.

18. Define the following terms:

(a) Cache hit
(b) Cache miss
(c) Cache hit time
(d) Cache miss time penalty
(e) Hit ratio
(f) Miss ratio

Ans.

(a) Cache hit: Whenever a read operation is to be performed, the cache memory is examined at first. If the required data are found in cache, a cache hit is said to have occurred. In case of a cache hit, the processor immediately fetches the word from the cache and performs the operation.

(b) Cache miss: If the data are not found in cache, it is termed as cache miss.

(c) Cache hit time: The time taken to access the data from cache in case of cache hit is known as cache hit time.

(d) Cache miss time penalty: In case of cache miss, the required data are to be fetched from the main memory, transferred to cache and then accessed. The time required to fetch the required block from the main memory is called **cache miss time penalty.**

(e) Hit ratio: It is defined as the number of cache hits divided by the total number of CPU references (including both cache hits and cache misses), as given here:

$$\text{Hit ratio} = \frac{\text{Number of hits}}{\text{Hits} + \text{Misses}}$$

The hit ratio always lies in the close interval of 0 and 1. A sufficiently high value of hit ratio indicates that the processor accesses cache memory most of the time instead of main memory. Thus, the access time becomes approximately equal to the access time of the cache memory.

(f) Miss ratio: Miss Ratio is defined as the ratio of number of cache misses divided by the total number of CPU references.

$$\text{Miss ratio} = \frac{\text{Number of misses}}{\text{Hits} + \text{Misses}}$$

Alternatively, it can be defined as the subtraction of hit ratio from 1, as given here:

Miss ratio = 1 – hit ratio

19. Derive an equation to compute the average access time if the cache memory is employed between the CPU and main memory.

Ans. When the cache memory is employed between the CPU and main memory, the CPU first examines the cache for the required word. In case of cache hit, the CPU accesses only the cache and the main memory is not accessed. On the other hand, in case of cache miss, the CPU has to access the main memory as well as cache. Let t_C and t_M denote the time taken to access cache and main memory, respectively, and h denotes the hit ratio. Then, the average access time (say, t_A) can be computed using the following equation:

$$t_A = ht_C + (1-h)\ (t_C + t_M)$$

where, $(1 - h)$ denotes the miss ratio.

20. How cache size is used to improve the performance of CPU?

Ans. A high number of cache misses decreases the performance of CPU. Thus, to increase the CPU performance, the number of cache misses must be reduced. This can be accomplished by increasing the size of cache memory. A larger cache can hold more information; therefore, it is more likely that the CPU finds the required data in the cache itself. As a result, the number of cache hits increases and the average access time is reduced. Thus, a large cache can help in improving the performance of CPU.

Unfortunately, in some cases, large cache sizes can lower the performance also. With the large cache size, the number of locations in cache also increases and the CPU has to search through all these locations for the required piece of information. Thus, the larger size slows down the cache speed. Therefore, the cache size should be optimum so that the performance of the CPU can be maintained.

21. Discuss the different types of mapping process while considering the organization of cache memory.

or

What does the mapping function mean? Discuss different techniques of mapping process?

Ans. The process of transforming the data from the main memory to cache memory is referred as the **mapping process.** There are three types of mapping procedures, namely, *associative mapping, direct mapping* and *set-associative mapping,* which are discussed as follows:

- **Associative mapping:** The most flexible and the fastest cache organization employ an associative memory as cache. The associative memory holds the address as well as data of the memory word (see Figure 11.8).

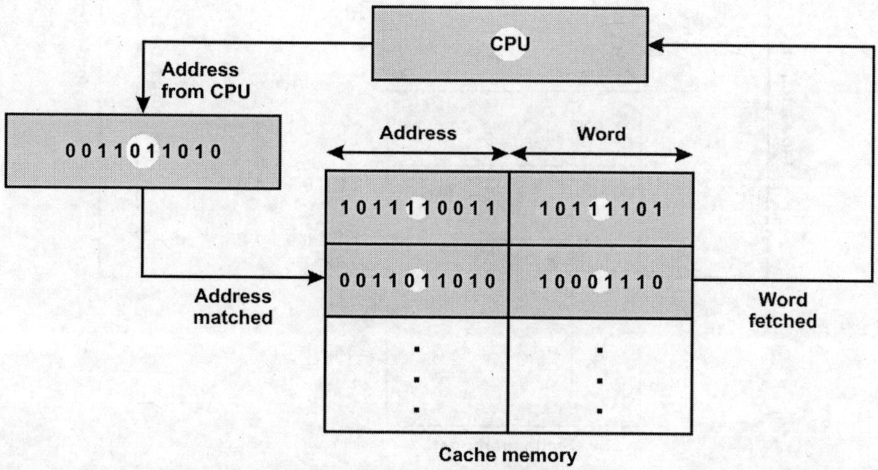

Figure 11.8 Associative Mapping

When the CPU needs to access some word, the address of that word is specified in the argument register. This address is then compared with the address stored in the associative memory to find a match. If a match is found, the data corresponding to the matched address are read and given to the CPU. On the other hand, if a match is not found, the word is accessed from the main memory. Along with this, the address–data pair of the word thus read is transferred to the associative cache memory. If the cache is already full, then some existing address–data pair must be removed so that the new required pair can be accommodated. The decision as to which pair should be removed is taken with the help of a replacement algorithm, chosen by the designer.

Associative mapping results in faster access to data. However, it is expensive and requires an additional logic circuit in each cell to implement the searching by content rather than the address.

- **Direct mapping:** This method of cache organization tends to reduce the cost by using a random access memory for the cache. The address of each memory word is divided into two fields, namely, *index* and *tag.* The number of address bits (starting from LSB) required for accessing the cache memory form the index field and the rest address bits form the tag field. For example, if the capacity of main memory is 2^n, that is, each address in main memory is n-bits long, and the capacity of cache is 2^m, then the least significant m bits of an n-bit address in main memory denote the index field, while remaining (n−m) bits denote the tag field. Each memory word in cache memory contains the data and its corresponding tag bits and is stored in cache memory at the address specified by the index bits of that word (see Figure 11.9).

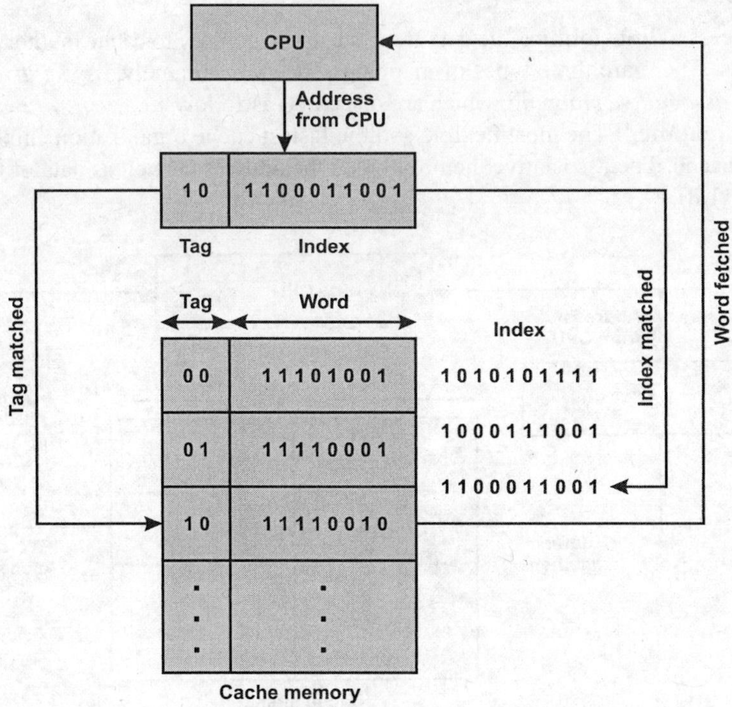

Figure 11.9 Direct Mapping

When CPU needs to access some word, the index bits of the address specified by the CPU are used to access a location in cache memory. Now, the tag bits stored at that location is matched with tag field of the address to be found. If a match occurs, the desired word is read from cache. However, if two tags do not match, the desired word is read from main memory. Then, it is stored in the cache memory, replacing the existing tag field with new tag field.

Till now, we have considered the block size of one word. In case a block contains more than one word, the index is divided into two parts: *block* and *word*. For example, if each cache block in a cache of size 512-words can hold eight words, then there will be total 64 (2^6) blocks (as 512/8 = 64). Now, if index is of n bits, then 6 bits out of n bits are needed to address a block and (n–6) bits are needed to address the word within that block. All words within a single block contain the same tag value. An entire block is transferred from main memory to cache memory in case of cache miss. Though, it increases the access time, a considerable improvement in the hit ratio is achieved.

The disadvantage of direct mapping is that two memory words with same index value but different tag value cannot be present in the cache memory at the same time. Moreover, the hit ratio may reduce significantly if such words need to be accessed repeatedly.

- **Set associative mapping:** This cache organization overcomes the limitations of direct mapping organization by allowing two or more memory words with same index but different tags to reside together under the same index address in the cache memory. The data of the words are stored along with its associated tag-data items in one words of cache constitute a set. Figure 11.10 shows the block diagram of a set associative cache organization with set size two. Two data words and their associated tags can be stored at each index address. This increases the number of bits required in each word of cache.

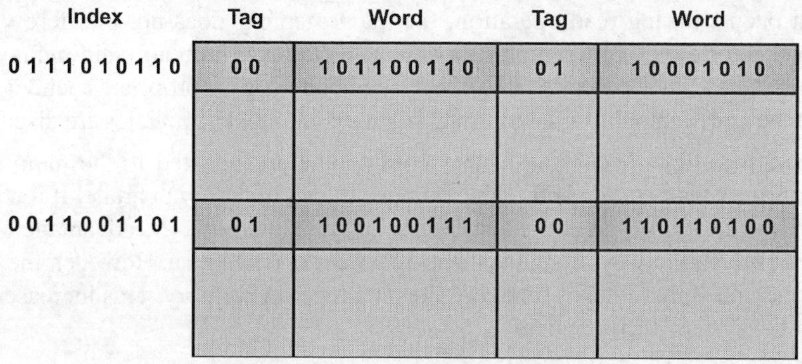

Figure 11.10 Set Associative Mapping

When CPU specifies the address to access a memory word, the index value of that address is used to access the cache memory. Then, the tag value of the given address is matched against the both tag values stored in the cache. If a match occurs, the data word is accessed for the desired word. Then the recently accessed data tag pair is inserted in the cache at the corresponding index address. In case the cache is already full, one of the data–tag pairs needs to be replaced with the new one, using some page replacement algorithm.

The advantage of set associative mapping cache is that the hit ratio increases with increase in size of set as more data words having same index but different tags can be accommodated in a word of cache. However, it also increases the number of bits required in each word of cache. In addition, the more complex comparison logic is needed to match with the tags within a set.

22. Discuss various page replacement algorithms of cache memory.

Ans. While searching any word in cache, if a miss occurs then that word has to be accessed from the main memory and then placed in the cache. If cache is full then its old contents need to be replaced with the new one. The decision of replacing the memory block is determined by the replacement algorithm. There are various types of page replacement algorithms. Some of the commonly used replacement algorithms are discussed as follows:

- **Least recently used (LRU):** This replacement algorithm is based on the assumption that a word (tag–data pair) in cache that has been recently accessed is likely to be accessed again in the near future. Therefore, it replaces the word from cache that has not been used for the longest period of time.
- **First-in, first-out (FIFO):** This is the simplest replacement algorithm. As the name suggests, the first word loaded into the cache memory is the first word to be replaced. That is, the words are replaced in the order in which they were loaded into the cache memory. This algorithm is easier to implement as compared to other replacement algorithms. However, it is rarely used as it is not very efficient.
- **Least frequently used (LFU):** This algorithm replaces the word from the cache memory that has accessed the least number of times.

- **Random replacement:** In this algorithm, no specific criterion is used for choosing a word from cache for replacement. The word to be replaced is chosen at random from the cache.

23. What are the cache write policies? Briefly explain each of them?

Ans. In cache system, same data may exist at two different locations: in cache and main memory. When cache hit occurs during read operation, the main memory does not interfere with the transfer process. However during write operation, data should be updated in both main memory and cache to avoid any inconsistency. To accomplish this, the system can adopt appropriate cache write policy (also referred to as cache updating policy). Two commonly used cache write policies are discussed as follows:

- **Write-through policy:** According to this policy, data are updated in the main memory during every memory write operation and cache memory is also updated in parallel if it contains the word at the specified location. This is the simplest and easiest method. The advantage of this method is that the main memory always contains the most recent updated data. However, the disadvantage of using this method is that it takes time to write data in main memory. This increases the bus traffic, hampering the system performance.
- **Write-back policy:** According to this policy, only the cache, not the main memory is updated during the write operation. The updated location in cache then marked with a flag to indicate that whenever the word at this location is to be removed from cache, it must be first copied to main memory. The reason behind adopting the write-back policy is that as long as word remains in cache, all the memory requests for that word will be fulfilled from cache itself without needing to access main memory. Thus, it does not matter whether or not the main memory obtains the updated value. It is essential to update the main memory only when the word is to be removed from cache.

24. Write a short note on virtual memory? Explain with the help of an example.

Ans. Virtual memory is a technique that allows executing a program that is partially in main memory. The main benefit of this technique is that the programs to be executed can be larger than the available physical memory. Only those parts of program or data are loaded into main memory which is currently needed for the execution of the program. The rest part is kept on the auxiliary memory devices and is loaded into the memory only when needed. Virtual memory gives the illusion to the programmers that the system has much larger memory than actually available memory. This eases the task of programming as the programmers no longer need to worry about the constraints of physical memory limitation.

In a virtual memory system, each addresses generated by a user program is referred as **virtual address** and the set of all virtual addresses generated by a user program is known as its **address space**. Each address in main memory is referred to as **location** or **physical address**. Whenever a program is brought into main memory for execution, it occupies certain number of memory locations. The set of all physical addresses used by the program is known as its **physical address space** or **memory space**. In virtual memory systems, the address space can be larger than the memory space.

To demonstrate the concept of virtual memory, suppose that the capacity of the main memory of a computer is 32K words and the auxiliary memory can store 1024K words. This implies that the auxiliary memory can store information equal to capacity of 32 main memories. If we denote address space by N and memory space by M, we can write that N = 1024K and M = 32K.

For our example, 15 bits are required to specify each physical address as $32K = 2^{15}$ and each virtual address is of 20 bits as $1024K = 2^{20}$. That is, CPU refers instructions and data with 20-bit address; however, the information at this address is to be taken from the main memory having 15-bit addresses.

Therefore, it is required to map a 20-bit virtual address to a 15-bit physical address. For this, a memory mapping table is used which can be stored in main memory or separately. Figure 11.11 demonstrates the mapping of a virtual address using memory mapping table.

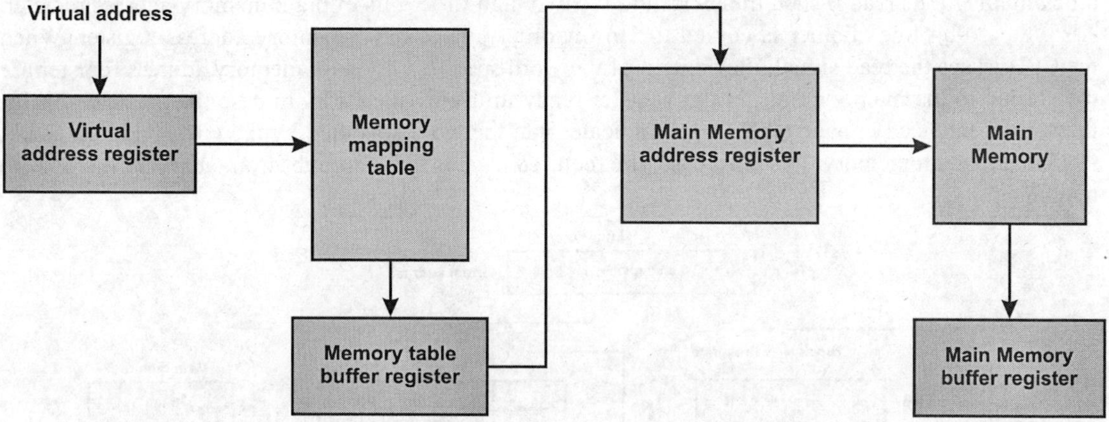

Figure 11.11 Memory Table for Mapping a Virtual Address

25. Briefly explain the paged-virtual memory system.

Ans. In a paged-virtual memory system, both the address space and memory space are split into groups. The address space is divided into fixed-size groups called **pages** and the memory space is divided into fixed-size groups called **blocks** (sometimes called **page frames**) which are of same size as that of pages. In addition, the user programs are also considered to be partitioned into pages. During a program execution, the required portions of the program are loaded from auxiliary memory to main memory in units of pages. To understand the concept of paging, consider we have a computer with address space of 8K and memory space of 4K. If a page or block size is assumed to be 1K, then we will have eight pages in address space and four blocks in memory space.

Each address generated by the CPU is divided into two parts: a page number address [high-order bits] and a line address within that page [low-order bits]. If the address space is 2^m and we choose a page size of 2^n (bytes or words), then the low-order n bits will specify the line address (d) and the high-order m−n bits will specify the page number address (p). For example, in our case, the address space is 2^{13} (as $8K = 2^{13}$) and page size is 2^{10} (as $1K = 2^{10}$). Therefore, 10 low-order bits of the virtual address will specify the line address and three high-order bits will specify the address of page number. As the line address is same in both address and memory space, only the mapping from a page number to block number is needed.

To map from a page number to block number, a **paged-memory map** (also referred to as **page table**) is maintained for each user program. The page table keeps track of which block is allocated to which page. It consists of as many numbers of words as there are pages in the address space (for example, in our case eight words). The page table stores the block number allocated to each page and the page number is used as index to the table. The page table also consists of presence bit field associated with each page. The presence bit for a page is set to 1 if the page is available in main memory; otherwise, it is set to 0.

To illustrate how address mapping is performed, consider the memory system shown in Figure 11.12. The page table indicates that the pages 2, 3, 5 and 7 are available in blocks 1, 3, 0 and 2, respectively.

Now, suppose the given 13-bit virtual address is 0110011011101. This virtual address gives p = 011 (three high-order bits) and d = 0011011101 (10 low-order bits). The content of page table at address 011 which is 11 is read into the memory table buffer register. As the corresponding presence bit is 1, the block number thus read is then transferred to the two high-order bits of main memory address register. Also, the 10-bit line number is copied to 10 low-order bits of main memory address register. When the CPU issues the read signal, the content of the word specified by main memory address register are transferred to the main memory buffer register ready to use by the CPU. In case the presence bit for the word referenced in page table is 0, it indicates that the word specified by the virtual address is not available in main memory. In such a case, the required page is to be brought from auxiliary memory to main memory.

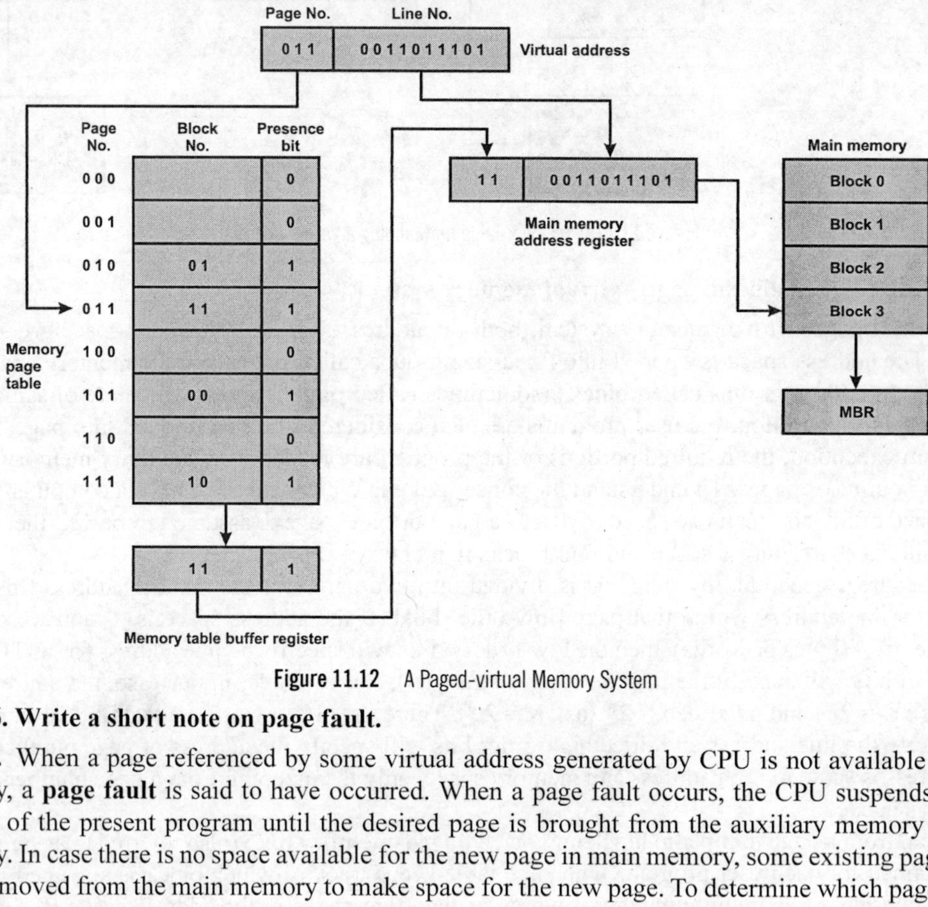

Figure 11.12 A Paged-virtual Memory System

26. Write a short note on page fault.

Ans. When a page referenced by some virtual address generated by CPU is not available in main memory, a **page fault** is said to have occurred. When a page fault occurs, the CPU suspends the execution of the present program until the desired page is brought from the auxiliary memory to main memory. In case there is no space available for the new page in main memory, some existing page needs to be removed from the main memory to make space for the new page. To determine which page should be removed, some page replacement algorithm is used. Two most commonly used page replacement algorithms include FIFO and LRU.

27. How many memory chips are needed to construct 2M × 16 memory system using (512K × 8) static memory chips?

Ans. Given, size of static memory chip = 512K × 8.

The required memory size is 2M × 16, that is, 2 × 1024K × 16. Thus,

$$\text{Number of required static memory chips} = \frac{2\times1024\times16}{512\times8} = 8\,\text{chips}$$

Hence, eight static RAM chips of size 512K × 8 are required to construct a memory system of size (2M × 16).

28. How many 256 × 4 RAM chips are needed to provide a memory capacity of 2048 bytes?

Ans. Given, size of RAM chip = 256 × 4

Required memory capacity = 2048 bytes = 2048 × 8 bits.

Thus,

$$\text{Number of required ROM chips} = \frac{2048\times8}{256\times4}$$

$$\text{Number of required ROM chips} = \frac{2048\times8}{256\times8} = 16\,\text{chips}$$

Hence, 16 RAM chips of size 256 × 4 are required to provide a memory capacity of 2048 bytes.

29. A computer employs RAM chips of 256 × 8 and ROM chips of 1024 × 8. The computer system needs 2K bytes of RAM, 4K bytes of ROM, and four interface units, each with four registers. A memory mapped I/O configuration is used. The two highest-order bits of the address bus are assigned 00 for RAM, 01 for ROM and 10 for interface registers.
(a) How many RAM and ROM chips are needed?
(b) Give the address range in hexadecimal for RAM, ROM and interface.

Ans. Given,
Size of RAM chip = 256 × 8 = $2^8 \times 8$
Size of ROM chip = 1024 × 8 = $2^{10} \times 8$.
The RAM size required by the system = 2K = 2 × 1024 = 2^{11} bytes.
The ROM size required by the system = 4K = 2^{12}.

(a) $$\text{Number of required RAM chips} = \frac{2^{11}\times8}{2^8\times8} = 2^3 = 8\,\text{chips}$$

$$\text{Number of required ROM chips} = \frac{2^{12}\times8}{2^{10}\times8} = 2^2 = 4\,\text{chips.}$$

Thus, the computer system needs eight RAM chips and four ROM chips.

(b) There are four interface units and each interface unit has four registers. Thus, there are total 16 (that is, 2^4) registers for interface. The address range for RAM, ROM and interface in hexadecimal notation is as follows:

		Hexadecimal Address
	RAM	0000 – 07FF
Similarly,	ROM	4000 – 4FFF
	Interface	8000 – 800F

30. A certain magnetic disk has the following specification:
Number of recording surfaces = 10
Number of tracks/surface = 256
Number of sectors/track = 32
Number of bytes/sector = 128
Disk rotation speed = 2400 rpm
Calculate (a) disk capacity, (b) transfer rate and (c) latency time.

Ans. Given number of surfaces, s = 10.

Number of tracks/surface, p = 256.

Number of sectors/track, q = 32.

Number of bytes/sector, n = 128.

(a) Disk capacity $= s \times p \times q \times n$
$= 10 \times 256 \times 32 \times 128$
$= 10 \times 2^8 \times 2^5 \times 2^7$
$= 10 \times 2^{20}$
= 10 MB.

(b) Capacity of one track $= q \times n$
$= 32 \times 128$
$= 2^{12}$ bytes.

As the disk rotation speed is 2400 rpm, one rotation is completed in 64/2400 = 1/40 seconds. This implies that 2^{12} bytes of data can be transferred in 1/40 seconds. Thus, the amount of data that can be transferred in 1 second can be calculated as:

Data transfer in 1 second $= 2^{12} \times 40$ bytes
$= 40 \times 4 \times 2^{10}$ bytes
= 160 KB.

Thus, the transfer rate = 160 KB/sec.

(c) Latency time = (time in one rotation)/2
= (1/40)/2
= 1/80 sec.

31. A hierarchical cache memory subsystem has following specification:
i Cache access time of 50 ns.
ii Main storage access time is 500 ns.
iii 80% of memory requests are for read operation.
iv Hit ratio is 0.9 for read access and write through scheme is employed.

Now on the basis of this information, calculate:
(a) What is the average access time of the system considering only memory read cycles?
(b) What is the average access time of the system for both read and write request?
(c) What is the hit ratio taking into consideration for write cycle?

Ans. Given that cache access time, $t_C = 50$ ns.
Memory access time, $t_M = 500$ ns.
Probability of read operations, $P_R = 0.8$.
Thus, the probability of write operations, $P_W = 1 - 0.8 = 0.2$.
Hit ratio for read operations, $h_R = 0.9$.

(a) If only read operations are considered, the average access time (t_R) can be calculated as:

$t_R = h_R \times t_C + (1 - h_R)(t_C + t_M)$
$= 0.9 \times 50(1 - 0.9)(50 + 500)$
$= 45 + 55$
$= 100$ ns.

(b) As write-through policy is used, the data are written to main memory during every write operation. The average access time (t_A) when both read and write operations are considered can be given as:

$t_A = P_R \times t_R + P_W \times t_M$
$= 0.8 \times 100 + 0.2 \times 500$
$= 80 + 100$
$= 180$ ns.

(c) Hit ratio (h) when write cycle is also considered can be computed as:

$h = P_R \times h_R + P_W \times h_W$

Where h_W is the hit ratio for write cycles. Thus,

$h = 0.8 \times 0.9 + 0.2 \times 0$
$= 0.72.$

32. Comment on direct mapping function of 2048 word cache memory onto 65536 word main memory.

Ans. In a 65536 word main memory, each memory address will be of 16 bits (as $65536 = 2^{16}$). In a 2048 word cache, an 11-bit (as $2048 = 2^{11}$) address is required to access each word in cache. Thus, the least 11 significant bits of each memory address serve as index and remaining 5 bits will serve as tag.

33. A block set associative cache consists of a total of 64 blocks divided into four block sets. The main memory contains 4096 blocks, each consisting of 128 words.
(i) How many bits are there in a main memory address?
(ii) How many bits are there in each of the TAG, SET and WORD fields?

Ans. Given,

(i) Main memory size = 4096×128 words
$= 2^{12} \times 2^7$
$= 2^{19}$.

Hence, main memory address consists of 19 bits.

(ii) Given, main memory size, $M = 4096$ blocks
$= 2^{12}$ blocks.

Thus, the number of bits required to address each block in main memory, $m = 12$

Cache memory size, $N = 64$ blocks
$= 2^6$ blocks.

Thus, the number of bits required to address each block in cache, $n = 6$

Number of cache sets = $64/4 = 16$
$= 2^4$.

Set size, $S = 4$ blocks
$= 2^2$ blocks.

Thus, the number of bits required to address each set in cache, s = 2.

Now, the number of bits in tag, set and word field can be calculated as:

Tag = m − n + s = 12 − 6 + 2 = 8 bits
Set = n−s = 6 − 2 = 4 bits
Word = 128 = 2^7 = 7 bits.

MULTIPLE CHOICE QUESTIONS

1. Which of the following is used to store the initial program needed to start the computer operating?
   (a) Auxiliary memory (b) RAM
   (c) SRAM (d) ROM
2. Associative memory uses _______ search procedure for accessing the data.
   (a) Parallel (b) Sequential
   (c) Direct access (d) None of these
3. In dynamic RAM the last electric change on the capacitors are\is restored by performing ______ operation?
   (a) Cycling (b) Dynamic
   (c) Refresh (d) None of these
4. The cache memory is placed between the ________ and _________.
   (a) RAM, ROM (b) CPU, main memory
   (c) Buffer, main memory (d) ROM, auxiliary memory
5. A large fraction of memory request is found in fast cache memory because of _________.
   (a) High hit ratio (b) Locality of reference property
   (c) Less number of miss (d) None of these
6. How many memory chips of 128 × 8 RAM chips are needed to provide a memory capacity of 2048 bytes?
   (a) 64 (b) 24
   (c) 16 (d) 128
7. If memory access takes 20 ns with cache and 110 ns without it, and the cache access time is 10 ns, then the hit ratio is:
   (a) 90% (b) 88%
   (c) 93% (d) 87%
8. The method of updating the main memory as soon as a word is removed from the cache is called _________.
   (a) write-through (b) protected write
   (c) cache-write (d) write-back
9. In direct mapping technique, if main memory is of 64K words and cache memory is of 1K words than there will be __________.
   (a) 9 index bits and 6 tag bits (b) 6 index bits and 9 tag bits
   (c) 10 tag bits and 6 index bits (d) 10 index bits and 6 tag bits

10. How many different addresses are required by the memory that contains 16K words?

(a) 16,380 (b) 16,382
(c) 16,384 (d) 16,386

11. A part of the computer system that supervises the flow of information between auxiliary memory and main memory is called _________.

(a) Memory management system (b) Paging
(c) Segmentation (d) None of these

Ans. 1. d 2. a 3. c 4. b 5. b 6. c 7. a 8. d

9. d 10. c 11. a

12

Pipelining

1. What is parallel processing? How parallelism can be achieved?

Ans. Parallel processing is a class of techniques that provide simultaneous data processing. It helps in increasing the execution speed of the computer system. In a conventional computer, each instruction is executed sequentially. However, in parallel processing system, simultaneous processing of data can be performed. For example, a system with multiple ALU units can execute more than one instruction simultaneously, resulting in improved performance. Even in a conventional system with a single processor, concurrent processing can be performed to improve the performance. For example, when ALU is executing an instruction, subsequent instruction can be read from the memory.

The main benefit of parallel processing is that it helps in enhancing the computation speed and throughput of the system. For supporting parallel processing, more hardware is needed in system. This requirement increases the cost of the system. However, with the advancement of the technology, the cost of hardware decreases and using parallel processing techniques becomes economically feasible.

One way to achieve parallelism is to have more than one functional unit in the system and distributing the tasks to them. Multiple functional units may or may not perform same task but these must be able to operate in parallel with each other. For example, the unit responsible for arithmetic calculations may be divided into functional units operating in parallel as shown in Figure 12.1.

In Figure 12.1, the operation that a functional unit can carry out is specified in the block representing the functional unit. For example, arithmetic operations on integers are carried out by the functional units *Adder-subtractor* and *Integer Multiply*. Further, all the units are capable of executing in parallel. Hence, while an arithmetic operation like addition is being performed on two numbers, shift operation can be performed on another number. Generally, a complex control unit is required with a multifunctional unit to coordinate all the activities among various units.

Following are the applications of the parallel processing computers.

- Numerical weather forecasting
- Computational aerodynamics
- Finite element analysis
- Remote sensing application
- Genetic engineering
- Weapon research defense

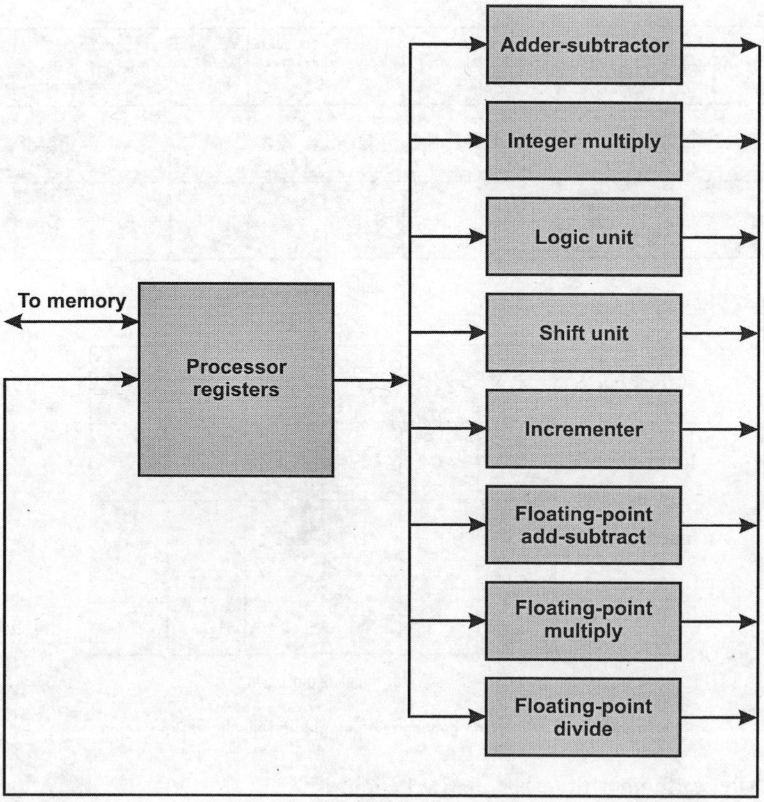

Figure 12.1 Processor with Multiple Functional Units

2. What is pipelining? Explain how processing is done in the pipelining.

Ans. Pipelining is a technique in which instructions are divided into sub-instructions with each sub-instruction being executed in a different segment. In other words, each segment does partial processing on the instruction and the outcome of a segment is transferred to the next segment in the pipeline. Segments can operate concurrently with other segments of the pipeline.

In a traditional method, instructions were executed sequentially, that is, one after the other. Hence, the performance of system is low. On the other hand, pipelining improves the performance as more than one instruction is being executed in different stages at the same time. The comparison between the sequential execution and pipelined execution of instructions is shown in Figure 12.2. In this figure, the pipeline is assumed to have four segments, namely, *fetch* (*F*), *decode* (*D*), *execute* (*E*) and *write* (*W*).

It can be observed that the pipelined processing of instructions takes only six clock cycles as compared to the twelve clock cycles required in the sequential processing of the same instructions.

Structure of pipeline

A pipelined organization comprises m segments each of which consists of one or more input registers and a combinational circuit. The input registers are used to store data and prevents interference among various segments while the combinational circuit executes the sub-instruction in a particular segment. The outcome of combinational circuit of a given segment is supplied to the input register of its subsequent segment. The execution of instruction is completed only when it gets executed in every segment

Clock cycle	1	2	3	4	5	6	7	8	9	10	11	12
	Instruction 1				Instruction 2				Instruction 3			
	F	D	E	W	F	D	E	W	F	D	E	W

(a) Sequential processing

Clock cycle	1	2	3	4	5	6
Instruction 1	F	D	E	W		
Instruction 2		F	D	E	W	
Instruction 3			F	D	E	W

(b) Pipeline processing

Figure 12.2 Comparison between Sequential and Pipelined Processing

of the pipeline. After sufficient time has elapsed (time in which a segment completes its activity), a clock is applied to all the registers. In other words, all the registers receive new input after every clock cycle. In this way, every segment does its processing in one clock cycle.

To understand the pipeline organization, consider executing the following operation.

$$X_i \times Y_i + Z_i \quad \text{for } i=1, 2, \ldots, n$$

The given operation is a combination of two operations, multiply and addition, on a sequence of numbers. For pipelined processing, each of the two operations is implemented in a different segment as shown in Figure 12.3. This pipelined organization uses five registers R1 through R5 and two combinational circuits *Multiplier* and *Adder*.

All the five registers are loaded with new data after every clock cycle. In the clock cycle 1, registers R1 and R2 are loaded with the values of X_1 and Y_1. In the clock cycle 2, the Multiplier produces the product of these two inputs and supplies the result to register R3. In the same clock cycle, X_2 and Y_2 are supplied to registers R1 and

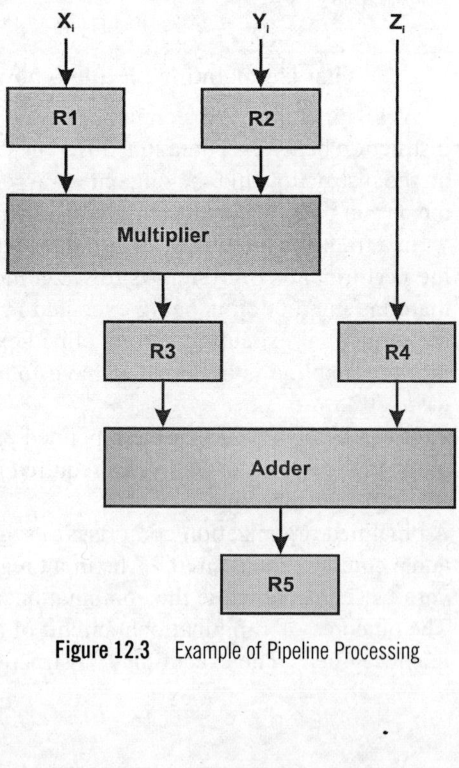

Figure 12.3 Example of Pipeline Processing

R2 and Z_1 is supplied to register R4. In the clock cycle 3, all the segments operate simultaneously. The Adder adds the values it gets from registers R3 and R4 and produces the first result. In addition, X_3 and Y_3 are supplied to R1 and R2, the product of X_2 and Y_2 is supplied to R3 and Z_2 is supplied to R4. Following the third clock cycle, a result is produced with every clock cycle. This process goes on until new input data flows in the system. It is to be noted that clock must continue until the last output is produced by the pipeline. The operations performed in every clock cycle are shown in Figure 12.4.

Clock cycle	Segment 1		Segment 2		Segment 3
	R1	R2	R3	R4	R5
1	X_1	Y_1	–	–	–
2	X_2	Y_2	$X_1 \times Y_1$	Z_1	–
3	X_3	Y_3	$X_2 \times Y_2$	Z_2	$X_1 \times Y_1 + Z_1$
4	X_4	Y_4	$X_3 \times Y_3$	Z_3	$X_2 \times Y_2 + Z_2$
5	X_5	Y_5	$X_4 \times Y_4$	Z_4	$X_3 \times Y_3 + Z_3$
6	X_6	Y_6	$X_5 \times Y_5$	Z_5	$X_4 \times Y_4 + Z_4$
7	X_7	Y_7	$X_6 \times Y_6$	Z_6	$X_5 \times Y_5 + Z_5$
8	–	–	$X_7 \times Y_7$	Z_7	$X_6 \times Y_6 + Z_6$
9	–	–	–	–	$X_7 \times Y_7 + Z_7$

Figure 12.4 Operations Performed in Every Clock Cycle

3. What are the advantages of pipelining?

Ans. The pipelining technique has got many advantages which help in improving the performance of a system. The advantages are as follows.

- It requires less time for executing the instructions as compared to sequential processing.
- In a pipelined machine, multiple instructions can be executed simultaneously.
- Pipelining helps in efficient use of CPU resources.
- By using pipelining, throughput and speed increases without using any special hardware technique.

4. Why does pipeline improve performance?

Ans. In an un-pipelined processor, each instruction is executed completely before the execution of next instruction can begin. The cycle period should be chosen long enough so that an instruction can execute completely in one clock cycle. Long cycle period decreases the rate at which instructions can be executed.

In case of the pipelined processor, the instructions are decomposed into number of stages and as an instruction completes its first stage, the execution of next instruction can begin. The clock period can be chosen much shorter than the clock period of un-pipelined processor as the instruction has to complete only one stage in one clock cycle. Due to this, the execution rate of instruction increases, which improves the performance.

5. What are speedup, throughput and efficiency of a pipelined architecture?

or

How the performance is measured in a pipeline processing?

or

Find an equation for the speedup, efficiency and throughput of a k-stage pipeline.

Ans. The processing of the tasks in pipeline is represented with the help of **Gantt chart** (also known as **space-time chart**). Gantt chart shows how instructions proceed through the segments of a pipeline with every clock cycle. The vertical axis of the chart represents the sub-instructions in the segments of pipeline and the horizontal axis represents the time. A sample Gantt chart of a 4-segment pipeline executing four instructions is shown in Figure 12.5. The figure depicts that segment 1 handles instruction I_1 in first clock cycle. In the second clock cycle, instruction I_1 proceeds to the segment 2 and instruction I_2 enters segment 1. This process continues and the instruction I_1 passes through all the segments of the pipeline and completes its execution in four clock cycles. Here onwards, one instruction completes its execution with every clock cycle. For example, I_2 completes its execution in fifth clock cycle, I_3 in sixth clock cycle and so on.

Clock cycle	Fetch	Decode	Execute	Write
1	I_1			
2	I_2	I_1		
3	I_3	I_2	I_1	
4	I_4	I_3	I_2	I_1
5		I_4	I_3	I_2
6			I_4	I_3
7				I_4

Figure 12.5 A Sample Gantt Chart

The pipelined execution of instructions improves performance that can be evaluated using the three measures: speedup S(k), efficiency E(k) and throughput U(k), where k represents the number of segments in the pipeline. If the duration of clock cycle is t and the number of instructions is n, the three measures can be calculated as follows.

Speedup: It can be defined as the ratio of time required to complete n instructions using sequential processing over the time required to complete n instructions using pipeline processing. Total time required to complete n instructions is n × k × t clock cycles using sequential and k+n−1 clock cycles using pipeline processing. Hence,

$$S(k) = \frac{n \times k \times t}{(n + k - 1) \times t} = \frac{n \times k}{(n + k - 1)}$$

$$\lim_{n \to \infty} S(k) = k \quad \text{(k fold increase in the speed)}$$

Efficiency: It can be defined as the ratio of actual speedup to the maximum speedup.

$$E(k) = \frac{\text{Actual Speedup}}{n} = \frac{n}{(n + k - 1)}$$

$$\lim_{n\to\infty} E(k) = 1$$

Throughput: It represents the number of instructions executed per unit time.

$$U(k) = \frac{n}{(n + k - 1) \times t}$$

$$\lim_{n\to\infty} U(k) = 1 \text{ assuming } t = 1$$

6. Explain how the arithmetic pipeline works.

Ans. The pipelining that is used for performing arithmetic operations is known as **arithmetic pipeline**. The complex and slow operations like multiplication and floating point arithmetic are broken into various sub-operations, which are executed in different segments of the pipeline. It helps in increasing the performance. Let us take an example of floating-point adder/subtractor having two normalized floating point binary numbers.

$X = m_A \times 2^a$
$Y = m_B \times 2^b$

Here, m_A and m_B are the two fractions that represent the mantissas and a and b are the two exponents. For executing floating-point addition/subtraction, the following sub-operations need to be performed.

- Exponent comparison.
- Equalize or align the mantissas and choose larger exponent.
- Add/subtract mantissas.
- Normalize the result.

All these four sub-operations are segmented into four different stages. In the first stage, exponent comparison is performed by subtracting them to determine the difference. In the second stage, the larger exponent is chosen as the exponent of the result. Difference in the first stage determines how many times the mantissa related with the smaller exponent is shifted to the right to align it with another mantissa. The two mantissas are added or subtracted in the third stage. In the last stage, the result is normalized. In case, overflow occurs, the mantissa of the output is shifted right and the exponent is incremented by one. But in case of underflow, the number of leading zero's in the mantissa determines the left shift for mantissa and the number to be subtracted from the exponent. The flowchart for floating point addition and subtraction discussions about the pipeline stages is shown in Figure 12.6. R (register) stores the outcome of sub-operations. Consider the two normalized floating numbers X and Y on which addition is to be performed.

$X = 0.10110 \times 2^3$
$Y = 0.11010 \times 2^4$

The addition operation is divided into the sub-operations performed in the following stages:

Stage1: Exponent comparison

$|a - b| = |3 - 4| = 1$

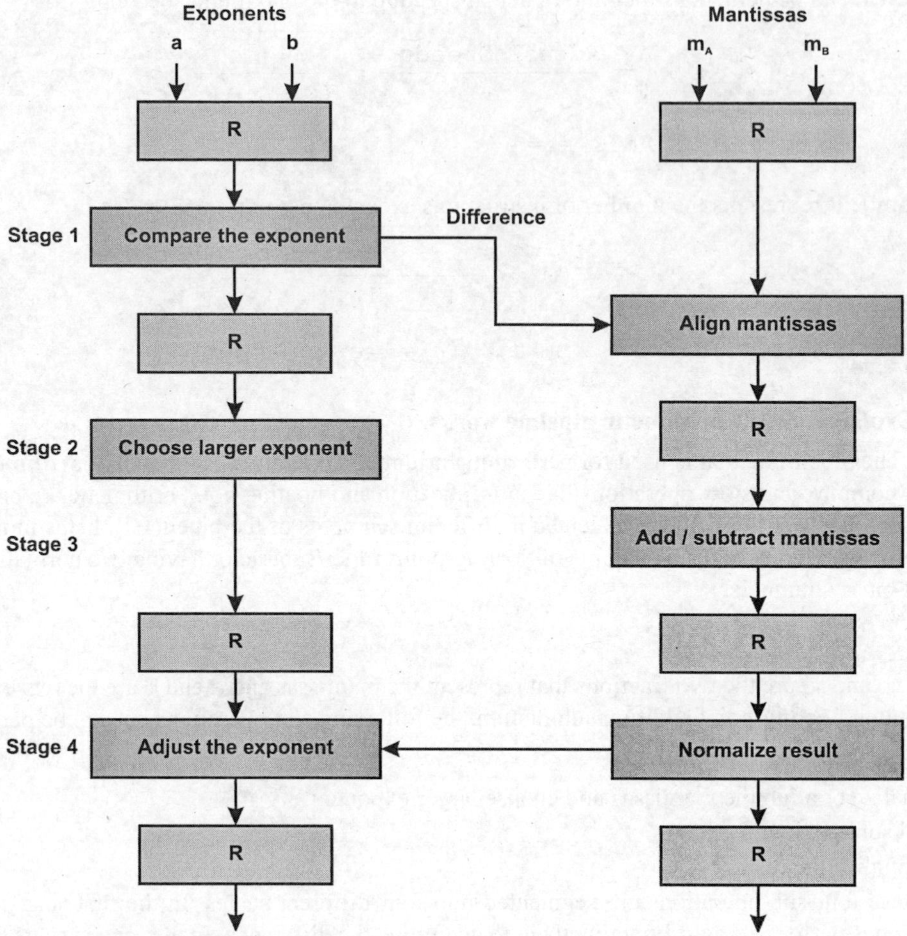

Figure 12.6 Pipeline for floating-point addition and subtraction

Stage2: Align the mantissas and choose the larger exponent

Larger exponent is b that is 4

So the mantissa m_A will be shifted. After shifting, the two numbers are:

$X=0.01011 \times 2^4$

$Y=0.11010 \times 2^4$

Stage3: Add the mantissas

Addition of mantissa is $m_R=0.01011+0.11010=1.00101$

$m_R=1.10101 \times 2^4$

Stage4: Normalize the result

$m_R=0.110101 \times 2^5$

In Figure 12.6, the comparator, shifter, incrementer, decrementer and adder/subtractor are implemented with the combinational circuit. Now suppose, the time delays of the four segments are

t_1=40ns, t_2=60ns, t_3=90ns and t_4=50ns and the inter-stage delay d=10ns, the time period of clock cycle can be computed as:

$$t = \max(t_i)_1^k + d$$
$$= 90ns + 10ns$$
$$= 100ns$$

The amount of time needed while executing floating point addition/subtraction using the non-pipeline floating point adder/subtractor is:

$$T_1 = t_1+t_2+t_3+t_4+d$$
$$= 40+60+90+50+10$$
$$= 250ns$$

Hence, for this particular pipeline the speedup is:

$$\frac{250}{100} = 2.5$$

7. Explain how the instruction pipeline works.

Ans. In addition to the data stream, the pipelined processing can occur in the instruction stream. In the instructions pipeline, the consecutive instructions are read from the memory while the previous instructions are being executed in other segments. An instruction pipeline operates on a stream of instru ctions by overlapping the fetch, decode and execute stages of different instructions. This method is also known by **instruction look ahead**. Overlapping of different stages helps in reducing the overall processing time. Virtually, all the high-level computers are now using instruction execution pipelines.

An instruction pipeline consists of five stages (see Figure 12.7), which are as follows:

1. **Instruction Fetch (IF):** The instructions are fetched by the control unit from the memory.
2. **Instruction Decode (ID):** The control unit decodes the instruction to determine the type of operation to be executed.
3. **Operand Fetch (OF):** When the opertion needs operand, the control unit detemines the address of each operand and fetches them from memory.
4. **Execute (EX):** The operation is executed on the operands.
5. **Write back (WB) or Store:** The output is stored in the specified location.

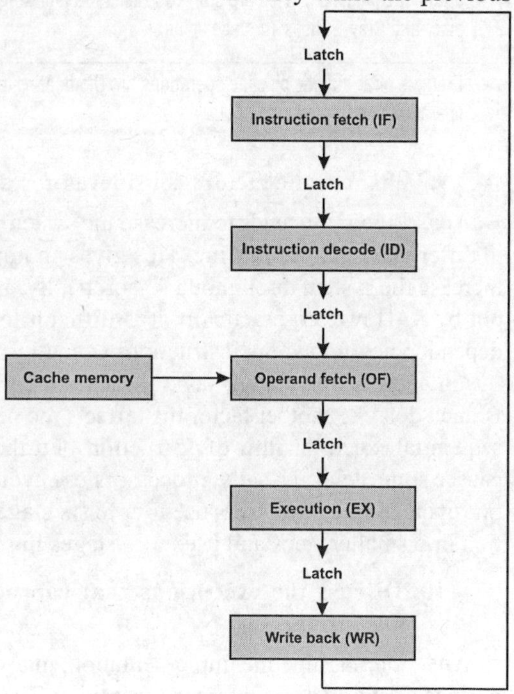

Figure 12.7 Stages in Instruction Pipeline

8. Explain the difference between instruction pipeline and arithmetic pipeline.

or

How the instruction pipeline differs from the arithmetic pipeline?

Ans. The differences between the arithmetic and instruction pipelines are listed in Table 12.1.

Table 12.1 Differences between Arithmetic and Instruction Pipelines

Arithmetic pipeline	Instruction pipeline
In an arithmetic pipeline, the operations are decomposed into sub-operation for execution in different stages.	An instruction pipeline operates on a stream of instructions by overlapping the fetch, decode and execute stages of different instructions.
Arithmetic pipeline cannot execute different operations at the same time. To do so, a vectored arithmetic unit is to be included in the CPU.	Different operations can be executed simultaneously.
Arithmetic pipeline is synchronous. The word synchronous means each stage is operated in a fixed number of clock cycles. Therefore, no buffering is required between the phases.	In instruction pipeline, buffering is required.
Some examples of high-speed and modern computers where arithmetic pipeline is used are star-100 (uses the four stages pipe) and Cray-1 (uses 14 stages pipe).	Almost all modern computers support the use of instruction pipelines.
Example of arithmetic pipeline operations are the floating-point operations performed in the ALU	Example of instruction pipeline operations can be seen in the RISC pipeline.

9. What are the factors considered for deciding the number of pipeline stages in a system?

Ans. Pipelining tends to increase the system throughput by allowing multiple instructions to execute in different stages at one time. This gives an impression that a large number of stages should be used to increase the system throughput. Theoretically, a pipeline with n stages may increase the system throughput by n. However, practically it is difficult to achieve the theoretical maximum speedup because of dependencies among the instructions executing simultaneously. The dependence of one instruction, say I_2, on another instruction, say I_1, causes the pipeline to stall until instruction I_1 executes completely. Branch delay is another factor that affects the performance of system as branch instruction may alter the sequential execution flow of instructions. Further, ALU also takes time in performing operations, which causes some delay. Usually, processors use cycle time such that one ALU operation can be completed in one cycle. Some processors use four to six stages in pipeline while others decompose instruction execution into smaller steps and use more stages in pipeline, decreasing the clock cycle time.

10. Discuss the exceptions that can occur during the pipeline operation along with the resolution.

Ans. During pipeline implementation, many exceptions tend to occur. These exceptions can be categorized as external and internal exceptions. The exceptions that immediately take place after the instruction has entered into the pipeline are known as **external exceptions**. On the other hand, the exceptions that occur in the middle of execution of an instruction are called **internal exceptions**.

During exception handling, when nobody knows what internal activity is taking place in the pipeline unit is called **imprecise exceptions**. Here, no effort is made to solve any issues during or after the exceptions. On the other hand, **precise exceptions** are those which clearly define the rules what is to be done with the instructions in pipeline during, before and after the exception is handled. As an example, consider the divide by zero exception that may occur in the ALU stage of an instruction. In this case, the instructions ahead of the faulty instruction in the pipeline are permitted to finish their execution. Handling the faulty instruction is difficult especially in machines where multiple pipelines are used. One way suggests storing the contents of the registers at the time of occurrence of exception for future reference and aborting the faulty instruction. The instructions preceding the faulty instruction in the pipeline can be restarted after handling the faulty instruction.

11. What are the pipeline hazards? How do they affect the speedup?

or

Why hazards occur in a pipeline?

Ans. A pipeline stalls when a particular instruction requires extra time to perform its operation in one stage making other stages to become idle. A pipeline functions effectively as long as one instruction completes its execution in a stage in every clock cycle. However in practice, a program may involve dependency among various instructions in a pipeline, which may affect the smooth functioning of the pipeline, thus, resulting in **pipeline hazards** (also known as **pipeline bubble**).

To understand how a pipeline may stall, consider a situation where a cache miss occurs while performing an instruction fetch operation. Suppose there are five instructions I_1, I_2, ..., I_5 and instruction I_2 incurs a cache miss. Thus to fetch the instruction I_2, extra time unit are required, due to which the fetching of the instruction I_3 and subsequent instructions is delayed (see Figure 12.8). The occurrence of such situation is known as pipeline hazards. This leads to wastage of time units and the time required for executing the five instructions increases as well. Thus, it hampers the overall performance in the pipeline.

The pipeline hazards are classified into three types: *data*, *instruction* and *structural hazards*.

Clock cycle	Fetch	Decode	Execute	Write
1	I_1			
2	I_2	I_1		
3			I_1	
4				I_1
5				
6				
7	I_3	I_2		
8	I_4	I_3	I_2	
9		I_4	I_3	I_2
10			I_4	I_3
11				I_4

Figure 12.8 Effect of Cache Miss on the Pipeline

- **Data hazard:** It refers to a situation in which either the source or the destination operand of the next instruction in the pipeline is not available in the expected clock cycle. This causes the instruction to wait and the pipeline to stall. There are three types of data hazards, which are explained using the pipelined execution of the following instructions.

I_1: $R_1 \leftarrow R_2 + R_3$
I_2: $R_4 \leftarrow R_4 - R_1$
I_3: $R_4 \leftarrow R_4 - R_5$
I_4: $R_5 \leftarrow R_6 + R_7$

- **RAW (read after write):** It is a hazard in which an instruction, say I_b, uses the data as its source which is being written by another instruction, say I_a, in the pipeline where I_a appears before I_b in program. For example, the instruction I_2 needs the data that are to be written by instruction I_1. In the pipelined execution, the instruction I_1 calculates R_1 in the execute (EX) phase during clock cycle 4 and updates the operand corresponding to it in the store phase during clock cycle 5 (see Figure 12.9). However, the instruction I_2 reads the operand in fetch operand (FO) phase during clock cycle 4. If the instruction I_2 is allowed to execute without stalling the pipeline, it reads the wrong value in R_1 and causes the value of R_4 to be incorrect.

Clock cycle	IF	ID	FO	EX	Store
1	I_1				
2	I_2	I_1			
3		I_2	I_1		
4			I_2	I_1	
5				I_2	I_1
6					I_2

Figure 12.9 RAW Hazard

One solution to this problem is **hardware interlocks**. This technique uses the interlock circuit to identify such dependencies among the instructions and delays the dependent instructions for enough clock cycles. With this technique, the instruction I_2 will be delayed for two clock cycles. Clearly, this solution degrades the performance.

An alternate solution is **data forwarding**, also called **operand forwarding**. This technique uses the forwarding hardware to detect whether the previous ALU operation has updated the register corresponding to the operand being used as a source in the current instruction. If this is the case, the control logic discards the value of the operand read from memory and uses the ALU value as the input for performing the operation. In our example, the instruction I_1 updates the value of R_1 in clock cycle 4. The forwarding hardware detects that the instruction I_2 needs the value of the operand corresponding to R_1 as a source in clock cycle 5. Hence, rather than using the value of this operand read in clock cycle 4, it uses the ALU value as input in clock cycle 5.

- **WAW (write after write):** It is a hazard in which an instruction, say I_b, writes some operand, say X, before it is written by a previous instruction, say I_a, leaving the value written by I_a as the final value of X. This hazard can occur in the pipeline that allows an instruction to proceed while a previous instruction is stalled. In our example instructions, both I_2 and I_3 write the same data. If instruction I_2 is stalled for some reason and pipeline allows I_3 to update R_4, the WAW hazard will occur. One solution to this hazard is to stall all the instructions in the pipeline following the stalled instruction until it does not start proceeding.

- **WAR (write after read):** It is a hazard in which an instruction, say I_b, writes some operand, say X, before it is read by a previous instruction, say I_a. This hazard can also occur in the pipeline that allows an instruction to proceed when a previous instruction is stalled. In our example, instruction I_4 updates R_5, which is read by I_3. If instruction I_3 is stalled for some reason and pipeline allows I_4 to update R_5, the WAR hazard will occur. One solution to this hazard is to stall all the instructions in the pipeline following the stalled instruction until it does not start proceeding.

- **Instruction hazard:** It is a hazard in which the decision of executing the next instruction in the pipeline depends on the execution of the current instruction. The instruction on which such a decision can be based is branch instruction. A branch instruction can be unconditional or conditional. Unconditional branch always breaks the sequential execution flow of pipeline. On the other hand, conditional branch may or may not break the sequential execution flow of pipeline. In this case, the next instruction to be executed depends on the result of the branch condition. The methods to deal with unconditional and conditional branch instructions are discussed in Q13.
- **Structural hazard:** It is a hazard in which the system does not have the resource to support simultaneous operations of two or more instructions executing in different stages of pipeline. When this hazard occurs, pipeline allows one instruction to execute its operation and stalls the others. For example, suppose a pipelined processor uses single memory pipeline for both data and instructions. When an instruction is accessing data from memory in a stage of pipeline, an instruction reference cannot be allowed at the same time as this causes resource conflict. One simple technique to resolve this hazard is to stall the pipeline for one clock cycle so that the required resource is ready for service.

12. What role the cache memory can perform in pipeline implementation?

or

Describe the role of cache memory in pipelined system.

or

How can memory access be made faster in a pipelined operation? Which hazards can be reduced by faster memory access?

Ans. In pipelining, each stage should complete its operation in one clock cycle. The clock period should be chosen such that the stage with the longest task can be completed in it. If any stage finishes up its task earlier, it remains inactive for the rest of the clock period. If all the stages of a pipeline have tasks that can be completed in about the same time period, pipelining results in improved performance.

Figure 12.10 demonstrates the pipelined execution of four instructions. The figure indicates that the fetch stage is assigned with the clock cycle equal to the clock cycle of the other stages. However, if every fetch stage needs memory access, the fetch stage becomes much slower than a basic operation inside the processor like addition. Hence, the fetch stage cannot be completed in the clock cycle in which the other stages can be completed. If the clock cycle is chosen long enough that the fetch stage involving memory access can be completed in it, the other stages remain idle in the clock cycle after completing their task. Hence, pipelining will be of little use.

One solution to this memory access problem is the use of cache memory. Cache memory exists on the same chip as the processor. Hence, access time to cache memory is almost equal to the time required

Clock cycle	1	2	3	4	5	6	7
Instruction I_1	F_1	D_1	E_1	W_1			
Instruction I_2		F_2	D_2	E_2	W_2		
Instruction I_3			F_3	D_3	E_3	W_3	
Instruction I_4				F_4	D_4	E_4	W_4

Figure 12.10 Instruction Execution Divided into Four Steps

for basic operations inside the processor. This makes it possible to complete the fetch stage in almost the same clock cycle in which the other stages can be completed and thus, pipeline can have all the stages of equal clock cycle.

13. What can be the resolution when an instruction pipeline stalls?

Ans. An instruction pipeline may stall because of instruction dependency and data dependency among the instructions in a program. Following methods are used to reduce pipeline stall due to instruction dependency.

- **Unconditional branching:** This type of branching always changes the sequential order of execution of instructions. Reducing the impact of unconditional branching on pipeline requires identifying the branch instruction before fetching the wrong instructions.
  - **Reordering of instructions:** Some smart compiler changes the sequence of instructions in a way that reduces the impact of unconditional branching while ensuring the correctness of the final result produced by the execution of the reordered instructions. Consider some instructions appearing in the program in the order I_1, I_2, I_3, I_4, I_5, I_6, I_7 and I_8, which are to be executed with a four-stage pipeline. Assume that I_4 is an unconditional branch instruction whose target instruction is I_8. If these instructions are executed in the same order as they appear, the instructions I_5, I_6 and I_7 will be fetched for execution before I_4 is executed. The execution of the instruction I_4 changes the target instruction from I_5 to I_8, which results in discarding of I_5, I_6 and I_7 instructions and fetching of I_8 instruction. Alternatively, if the instructions are reordered by the compiler as I_4, I_1, I_2, I_3, I_5, I_6, I_7 and I_8 for execution, fetching of wrong instruction will not take place (see Figure 12.11). Note that the order of only those instructions which have no dependency can be changed. Otherwise, the execution of the reordered instructions produces an incorrect result.
  - **Use of dedicated hardware along with instruction reordering:** In this method, the fetch unit is associated with a special hardware. It is assumed that the hardware unit identifies the unconditional branch instruction and its target instruction as early as possible so that fetching of incorrect instructions can be avoided. It is also assumed that the special hardware does the assigned task in no additional time. This assumption is unrealistic as no task can be completed without taking any time units. Typically, the hardware unit takes some additional time units for

Clock cycle	IF	ID	FO	EX
1	I_4			
2	I_1	I_4		
3	I_2	I_1	I_4	
4	I_3	I_2	I_1	I_4
5	I_8	I_3	I_2	I_1
6		I_8	I_3	I_2
7			I_8	I_3
8				I_8

Figure 12.11 Reordering of Instructions by Smart Compiler

completing its task. If some other instructions can be executed simultaneously with the task of hardware unit, the negative impact of the additional time units on system performance can be minimized. The instructions to be executed in the mean time can be provided by reordering of instructions by the compiler, if possible.

- **Conditional branching:** The techniques discussed above for dealing with the unconditional branching may not work while dealing with conditional branching. This is because in conditional branching, the target instruction will not be known until the branch condition is computed. There are various methods that can be used to deal with the conditional branch instructions.

  One method to deal with the problem of executing next instruction following a branch instruction is to stall the pipeline until branch condition is evaluated. This method yields performance loss as the execution of the next instruction is delayed until the branch condition is evaluated (see Figure 12.12). In the figure, I_2 is assumed to be a branch instruction. When this branch instruction is decoded in clock cycle 3, the instruction I_3 is halted and no more instructions are fetched in the pipeline until the branch instruction is executed in clock cycle 5. After this, the next instruction is fetched. In the figure, it is assumed that branch changes the execution flow, hence, instruction I_3 is discarded and I_4 is fetched for execution.

  Another method to deal with this problem is **branch prediction**. In this method, some additional logic is used to make a prediction of branch condition and accordingly the subsequent instructions are fetched and pipelined without any delay. If the prediction is correct, pipeline progresses with the full speed. However, if the prediction is incorrect, pipeline is stalled. Now, pipeline has to be cleaned and the next target instruction has to be fetched.

  One more method to deal with the problem is **delayed branch**. In this method, instructions are rearranged such that the instructions independent of the outcome of the branch instruction can be executed in the delay slots after the branch instruction. This rearrangement of instructions is the responsibility of the compiler. When the outcome of branch is available, the next target instruction is fetched during execution of the independent instructions. In such a way, pipeline keeps progressing without or minimal interruption.

The method that can be used to reduce pipeline stall due to data dependency is **operand forwarding**. Operand forwarding can be performed in both hardware and software. Operand

Clock cycle	IF	ID	FO	EX	Store
1	I_1				
2	I_2	I_1			
3	I_3	I_2	I_1		
4	Delay slot	Delay slot	I_2	I_1	
5	Delay slot	Delay slot	Delay slot	I_2	I_1
6	I_4	Delay slot	Delay slot	Delay slot	I_2
7		I_4	Delay slot	Delay slot	Delay slot
8			I_4	Delay slot	Delay slot
9				I_4	Delay slot
10					I_4

Figure 12.12 Delay caused by Branch Instruction

forwarding with hardware is discussed in Q11. Alternatively, operand forwarding can be performed in software by the compiler. In this case, the compiler should provide the outcome of the instruction as operand for the subsequent instructions as quickly as possible. To support this feature, the compiler should perform data dependency analysis to identify which operand can be made available for subsequent instructions. Basically, analysis requires recognition of the following three forms.

- **Store-fetch:** In this form, the result produced by an instruction is needed as a source in the next instruction. For example, consider the following two instructions in order.

  I_1: $M[R_1] \leftarrow R_2$

  I_2: $R_3 \leftarrow M[R_1]$

  In this case, the value of operand corresponding to register R_1 is needed as source by instruction I_2. This value is already available in register R_2. Hence, a smart compiler can replace the instruction I_2 with following instruction.

  $R_3 \leftarrow R_2$

- **Fetch-fetch:** In this form, the data fetched by an instruction is also needed as an operand by the next instruction. For example, consider the following two instructions in order.

  I_1: $R_1 \leftarrow M[R_2]$

  I_2: $R_3 \leftarrow M[R_2]$

  In this case, instruction I_1 fetches the value of operand corresponding to register R_2 and stores it in register R_1. This value is also needed by instruction I_2. A smart compiler can replace the instruction I_2 as shown below to immediately move the required value in register R_3.

  $R_3 \leftarrow R_1$

- **Store-store:** In this form, the data written by an instruction are also written by the next instruction. For example, consider the following two instructions in order.

  I_1: $M[R_1] \leftarrow R_2$

  I_2: $M[R_1] \leftarrow R_3$

In this case, the value of an operand corresponding to register R_1 by instruction I_1 is overwritten with the value of register R_3 by instruction I_2. If there is no instruction between instruction I_1 and I_2 that fetches the value of this operand, the smart compiler can replace the two instructions with the following instruction.

$M[R_1] \leftarrow R_3$

14. A branch instruction causes the pipeline to stall for three clock cycles. Give the mechanism to improve branch penalty by one clock cycle.

Ans. Consider some instructions appearing in the program in the order I_1,I_2,I_3 and I_4, which are to be executed with a four-stage pipeline. Assume that I_2 is a branch instruction whose target instruction is I_4. When these instructions are executed in the same order, pipeline has to be stalled for three clock cycles while I_2 is in pipeline (see Figure 12.13). This is because the next instruction to be executed after instruction I_2 is not known until the execution of instruction I_2. Figure 12.13 shows the instruction pipeline when branch has not changed the target instruction.

Clock cycle	IF	ID	FO	EX
1	I_1			
2	I_2	I_1		
3	Delay slot	I_2	I_1	
4	Delay slot	Delay slot	I_2	I_1
5	Delay slot	Delay slot	Delay slot	I_2
6	I_3	Delay slot	Delay slot	Delay slot
7	I_4	I_3	Delay slot	Delay slot
8		I_4	I_3	Delay slot
9			I_4	I_3
10				I_4

Figure 12.13 Penalty of Three Clock Cycles because of Branch Instruction

Now, if the instructions are reordered by the compiler as I_2, I_1, I_3 and I_4 for execution, assuming that the instructions I_1 and I_2 have no data or instruction dependency, branch penalty can be decreased to two clock cycles, achieving improvement of one clock cycle (see Figure 12.14).

15. Compute the speedup, efficiency and throughput measures for a four-stage pipeline having delays of 15, 25, 45 and 30 ns of the different stages while processing 100 jobs. Assume a latch delay of 5 ns.

Ans. We have to compute the performance measure for a four-stage pipeline, hence k is 4. Further, the delays of each stage of pipeline are t_1=15 ns, t_2=25 ns, t_3=45 ns and t_4=30 ns and the latch delay is 5 ns. The cycle time, represented by t, for this pipeline should be the sum of latch delay and the maximum of t_1, t_2, t_3 and t_4, that is, 45+5=50 ns. The total number of tasks to be completed by the pipeline, represented by n, is 100.

The speedup can be computed as:

Clock cycle	IF	ID	FO	EX
1	I_2			
2	I_1	I_2		
3	Delay slot	I_1	I_2	
4	Delay slot	Delay slot	I_1	I_2
5	I_3	Delay slot	Delay slot	I_1
6	I_4	I_3	Delay slot	Delay slot
7		I_4	I_3	Delay slot
8			I_4	I_3
9				I_4

Figure 12.14 Improvement of One Clock Cycle by Reordering of Instructions

$$S = \frac{n \times k}{n + k - 1}$$

$$= \frac{100 \times 4}{100 + 4 - 1} = 3.88$$

The efficiency can be computed as:

$$E = \frac{n}{n + k - 1}$$

$$\frac{100}{103} = 0.97$$

The throughput can be computed as:

$$U = \frac{n}{(n + k - 1) \times t}$$

$$= \frac{100}{103 \times 50} = 0.019$$

MULTIPLE CHOICE QUESTIONS

1. Which part of the following employs parallel processing?
   (a) Pipeline processing (b) Vector processing
   (c) Array processor (d) All of these
2. The performance of a pipeline in processing the tasks can be calculated with the help of _______.
   (a) Gantt Chart (b) Unit time
   (c) Arithmetic operation (d) None of these
3. The pipeline which involves complex and slow arithmetic operations is known as ________.
   (a) Instruction pipeline (b) Arithmetic pipeline
   (c) RISC pipeline (d) None of these

4. The hazard in which the execution of one instruction depends upon the previous instruction is known as ________.

   (a) Instruction hazard (b) Data hazard
   (c) Structural hazard (d) None of these

5. The pipeline hazard can be of ________ types.

   (a) One (b) Two
   (c) Three (d) Four

6. RAW (Read after write) is a type of ________ hazard.

   (a) Instruction hazard (b) Data hazard
   (c) Structural hazard (d) None of these

7. The performance of pipelined processor suffers when:

   (a) The pipelined stages have different delays
   (b) Consecutive instructions depend on each other
   (c) The pipeline stages share hardware resource
   (d) All of these

8. The two types of exception handling mechanisms are ________.

   (a) Precise and imprecise (b) Zero and non-zero
   (c) Instruction and data (d) None of these

9. The branch direction is predicted based upon the information at ________ stage.

   (a) Execute stage (b) Fetch stage
   (c) Decode stage (d) None of these

10. Data forwarding is also known as ________.

    (a) Pipeline bubble (b) Register by passing
    (c) File passing (d) None of these

Ans. 1. d 2. a 3. b 4. a 5. c 6. b 7. a 8. a 9. c 10. b

13

Vector Processing and Array Processors

1. Explain the term vector processing. List down some of the application areas where vector processing is important.

Ans. Vector is a set of scalar data items usually stored at contiguous memory locations. It is generally used to represent the data in science and engineering applications that require very long computations. This computation when performed by a traditional sequential computer may take several days or weeks because such a computer is capable of processing single or pair of data items at once. Such processing is known as **scalar processing**. Generally, scalar processing is slow and less efficient. Hence, processors with vector processing capabilities are required for applications involving long computations. Such processors are called **vector processors**. Applying operation including arithmetic or logical operation directly on vectors is **vector processing**. Notice that the vector processors allow specifying operations with special instructions known as **vector instructions**, which have several properties including the following:

- Single vector instruction is equivalent to multiple instructions of traditional sequential computer. In other words, one vector instruction can specify the amount of work that is specified by multiple instructions of conventional computer, such as a loop instruction.
- Vector instruction allows pipelining the operations as computation of one operation is independent of outcome of the previous operation.
- Typical vector instruction includes the base address of source operands, base address of destination operand, the operation to be performed and the vector length.

The computers having capabilities of vector processing are needed in special applications. Some of the application areas where vector processing is important are listed below:

- Image processing
- Medical diagnosis
- Artificial intelligence and expert systems
- Long-range weather forecasting
- Petroleum explorations

- Mapping the human genome
- Aerodynamics and space flight simulations

2. How operations can be performed on vectors?

Ans. A vector is a set of scalar data items usually stored at contiguous memory locations, that is, arranged in the form of a one-dimensional array. Most applications need to perform arithmetic operations on such large array of numbers. However, since a conventional sequential computer can process only one operand at a time, performing an arithmetic operation on a vector requires splitting into single computations with subscripted variables. An element V_i of vector V is represented as V(I), where I specifies the memory address or the register containing the number.

To understand how vector operations are performed, assume that P and Q are two vectors of length 50 stored in the form of arrays. The elements of vector Q are subtracted from vector P, producing the third vector R. The machine language implementation for this subtraction operation is as follows:

```
            Initialize I = 1
BACK        READ P(I)
            READ Q(I)
            STORE R(I) = P(I) - Q(I)
            INCREMENT I = I + 1
            If I ≤50 go to BACK
            Continue
```

This code section makes to fetch a pair of operands from arrays P and Q, perform the subtraction operation and store the result in array R. The loop control variable I (that was initialized with 1) is then incremented by one and the entire process is repeated until I becomes greater than 50.

The vector processing facilitates removing the loop overhead associated with the time taken for fetching and executing the instructions in the loop. A single vector instruction is sufficient to specify the above task, which is written as follows:

```
R(1:50) = P(1:50) - Q(1:50)
```

This vector instruction is a composite structure of several components such as base addresses of the operands, vectors length and the operation to be performed.

3. Discuss the matrix multiplication operation using a vector processor.

Ans. Matrix multiplication is one of the most common used operations in computers performed through vector processors. An $m \times n$ matrix, where m denotes the number of rows and n denotes the number of columns, is organized as an $m \times n$ vector. The multiplication operation of two $n \times n$ matrices requires n^2 inner products with each inner product requiring n multiply and add operations. Hence, a total of n^3 multiply-add operations are required for computing the product of two matrices.

Consider P and Q are the 3×3 source matrices and R is the product matrix. The product matrix R can be calculated using the following formula:

$$R_{ij} = \sum_{k=1}^{3} P_{ik} \times Q_{kj}$$

For example, the element in the first row and third column of matrix X can be calculated as:

$$R_{13} = P_{11}Q_{13} + P_{12}Q_{23} + P_{13}Q_{33}$$

In the above instruction, three multiplication and three addition operations are used, assuming that R_{13} is initialized with 0. Hence, the total number of operations required is 27, that is, 3^3.

Before starting the multiplication operation, the output vector R is initialized with 0. The matrices that are to be multiplied (that is, P and Q) can be stored in either memory or processor register. To compute the inner product of two matrices on a pipeline vector processor, two floating-point pipelines including multiplier and adder are used. Figure 13.1 depicts the multiplier and adder pipelines having five segments each for calculating the inner product of matrices P and Q.

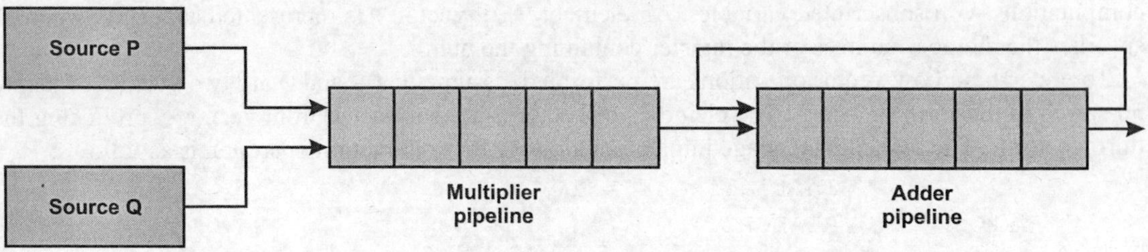

Figure 13.1 Calculation of Inner Product using Pipeline

Initially, each segment register in the multiplier and adder pipeline is initialized to 0. Hence, for the first ten cycles, the adder pipeline produces 0 as the output. To start with, the pairs of elements from P and Q are brought in the multiplier pipeline and the multiplication operation is performed on one pair per each clock cycle. After five cycles when the multiplier pipeline is full, the products computed in the multiplier pipeline start getting added to the output of the adder pipeline. For the next five cycles, a 0 is added to each product coming to the adder pipeline. At the end of tenth cycle, the adder pipeline contains first five products (P_1Q_1, P_2Q_2, P_3Q_3, P_4Q_4 and P_5Q_5), while the multiplier pipeline contains next five products (P_6Q_6, P_7Q_7, P_8Q_8, P_9Q_9 and $P_{10}Q_{10}$). Hence, during the eleventh cycle, the first elements in both pipelines (that is, P_1Q_1 and P_6Q_6) are added in the adder pipeline. Then during the next clock cycle, the addition of P_2Q_2 and P_7Q_7 is performed. This process continues until all the terms have been added. This pattern splits the summation into five sections as shown here.

$$
\begin{aligned}
R = P_1Q_1 &+ P_6Q_6 + P_{11}Q_{11} + P_{16}Q_{16} + P_{21}Q_{21} + \ldots \\
&+ P_2Q_2 + P_7Q_7 + P_{12}Q_{12} + P_{17}Q_{17} + P_{22}Q_{22} + \ldots \\
&+ P_3Q_3 + P_8Q_8 + P_{13}Q_{13} + P_{18}Q_{18} + P_{23}Q_{23} + \ldots \\
&+ P_4Q_4 + P_9Q_9 + P_{14}Q_{14} + P_{19}Q_{19} + P_{24}Q_{24} + \ldots \\
&+ P_5Q_5 + P_{10}Q_{10} + P_{15}Q_{15} + P_{20}Q_{20} + P_{25}Q_{25} + \ldots
\end{aligned}
$$

Finally, when the multiplier pipeline is empty, zeros are inserted in each segment of that pipeline. However, the adder pipeline still contains five partial sums, one in each segment. These partial sums are then added together to produce the final sum.

4. Write a short note on the following:
(a) Memory Interleaving
(b) Supercomputers

Ans. (a) Memory interleaving: Generally, the simultaneous memory access is required by the pipelines and vector processors from two or more different sources. One of the efficient means of facilitating simultaneous access is to divide the memory into several modules where each module is attached to a common memory address and data bus. A memory module is essentially a memory array having its own address register (AR) and data register (DR). The different memory modules are distinguished on the basis of certain least significant bits of the address on address bus.

Figure 13.2 depicts the memory organization of n modules, with all modules connected to the same address and data bus. The AR receives the address bits from the common address bus and DR is used to communicate or exchange the data with the bidirectional data bus. A memory module can initiate a memory access when other modules are performing read/write word from/to memory. In addition, each module can serve a request independent of the state of the other modules.

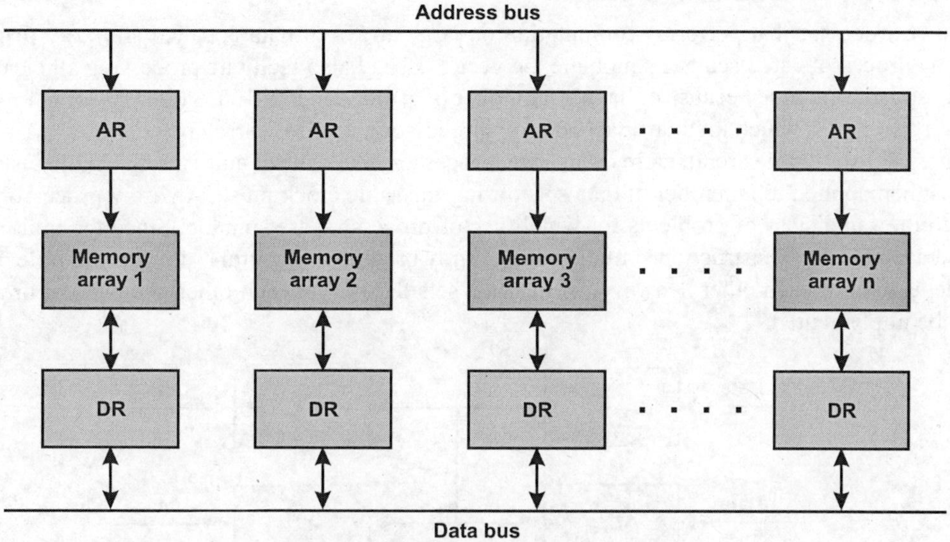

Figure 13.2 Memory Organization of n Memory Modules

The modular memory system supports the use of a technique, named **interleaving.** In this technique, each memory module is assigned a different set of addresses. If the number of modules (n) in the memory system is in the power of 2, that is, if $n = 2^k$, then the least k significant bits of the address are used to identify the desired module and rest bits are used to identify the location within that module.

(b) Supercomputers: A supercomputer is a commercial computer that comprises vector instructions and performs arithmetic operations using floating-point pipelines. These are very powerful and high-performance machines used for computation in most scientific problems. The components of a supercomputer are packed tightly with each other so that the electronic signals have to cover a shorter distance, thus speeding up the operation. Since the closeness of components may result in burning up of components, supercomputers employ special techniques to remove the heat from the circuits.

The supercomputers use the same instruction set as that of conventional computers, such as data transfer instructions, data manipulation instructions and program control instructions plus the instructions that process the vectors and combination of scalars and vectors. They provide faster computational speed, fast and large memory systems and extensive use of parallel processing. A supercomputer consists of multiple functional units each of which has its own separate pipeline configuration.

Though like other computers the supercomputers can also be used for general-purpose applications, their use is limited to certain scientific applications, such as weather forecasting and space research. They are specially designed for the numerical calculations that involve vectors and matrices of floating-point numbers. The reason behind the limited use and limited market of supercomputers is that they are quite expensive.

Supercomputers are the special-purpose machines, which are specially designed to maximize the numbers of **flops (floating-point operations per second)**. Any computer below one gigaflop/sec is not considered a supercomputer. The basic cycle time for a typical supercomputer lies in the range of 4 – 20 ns. CRAY-3, Cyber 205 and PARAM are some well-known supercomputers.

5. Describe the term array processor.

Ans. A processor that performs computation on large arrays of data is called an **array processor**. The array processors are used to manipulate the vectors. They also facilitate processing all elements of an array at the same time because of having a number of arithmetic logic units (ALU). Array processors can be of two types, which include attached array processor and SIMD array processor.

Figure 13.3 shows the architecture of an array processor. The control unit issues a single instruction, which is then applied to a number of data sets during the same clock pulse. An array processor is well suited to the same class of problems for which vector processors are suitable. Since the multiple data sets operate on a single instruction simultaneously, array processor is useful as long as multiple data sets are independent of each other. However, if the data sets depend on each other, the parallel processing cannot be implemented.

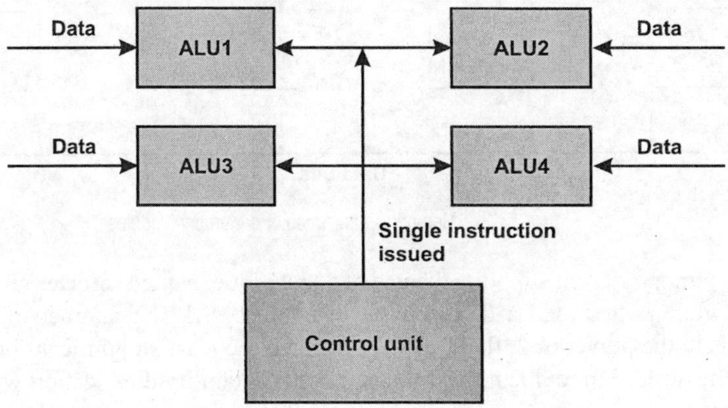

Figure 13.3 Architecture of an Array Processor

6. Which of the array processors serves as a peripheral for a conventional host computer and how?

or

Describe in brief the attached array processors.

Ans. An attached array processor serves as a peripheral for the conventional host computer. It provides vector processing capability to the computer, thus enhancing its performance. It supports parallel processing by employing multiple functional units. This helps to achieve high performance. The array processor includes an arithmetic unit that has one or more pipelined floating-point adders and multipliers. The users can program the array processor to make it deal with a number of complex arithmetic problems.

The attached array processor is interconnected with the host computer in the way as shown in Figure 13.4. Here, the host computer is a general-purpose commercial computer and the attached array processor is a backend machine under the control of the host computer. The attached array processor is connected to the host computer via an input–output interface. It communicates with the main memory through the local memory which is connected to the main memory via a high-speed bus. For conventional data processing, the host computer without the attached array processor is sufficient, while for the complex arithmetic calculations, the host computer works in conjunction with the attached array processor.

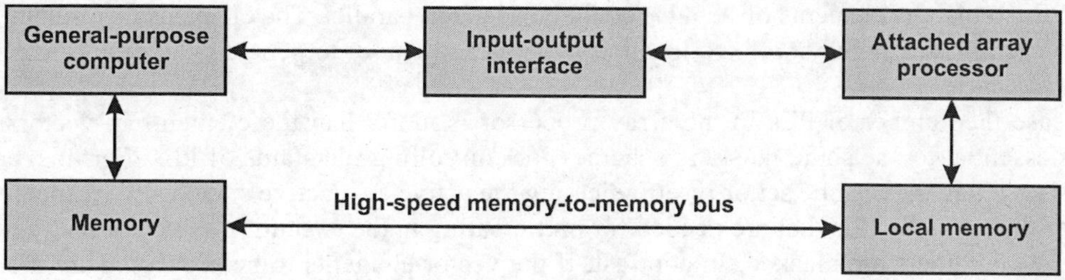

Figure 13.4 Attached Array Processor with Host Computer

7. Explain the SIMD array processor along with its architectural diagram.

Ans. An **SIMD array processor** is a computer which contains multiple processing elements (PEs) that operate in parallel to perform the same operation. All the PEs are under the control of a single control unit, which results in single instruction stream, multiple data stream (SIMD) organization. Figure 13.5 shows the general block diagram of an SIMD array processor organization. It includes `n` PEs with each PE attached to its own local memory `M`. Each PE contains an ALU, a floating-point arithmetic unit and other working registers. The master control unit is responsible for controlling the operations of all PEs and the main memory stores the programs to be executed.

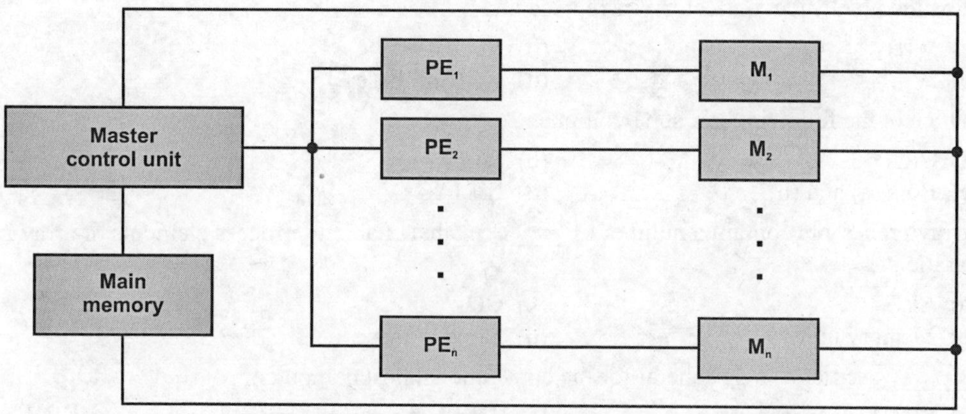

Figure 13.5 SIMD Array Processor Organization

During the execution of a program, the master control unit decodes an instruction and determines how it will be executed. If the decoded instruction is of scalar or program control type, it is executed inside the master control unit itself. However, if it is a vector instruction, it is provided to all PEs simultaneously so that the instruction operation can be executed in parallel. Before starting parallel execution, the required vector operands are stored in local memory of PEs. Thus, each PE can fetch the required operand directly from its local memory instead of accessing the main memory.

To understand how vector instructions are executed in SIMD array processor, assume that P, Q and R are the three vectors and the vector operation R = P + Q is to be performed. To start with, the master control unit transfers the ith elements of vectors P and Q (which are P_i and Q_i) to the local memory M_i, where i = 1, 2,..., n. Then, it provides the floating-point add instruction $R_i = P_i + Q_i$ to all PEs so that the elements of P and Q could be added in parallel. The elements of resultant vector R from each PE are stored at a fixed location in its local memory to generate the desired vector sum in one add cycle.

In case the number of PEs in the array processor is more than the elements in vectors, it becomes essential to use some masking schemes for controlling the status of PEs. For this, each PE comprises a flag that can be set or reset indicating the active or inactive state of PE, respectively. It ensures that only the PEs that are needed for participating in the execution of vector instruction are active, while others are masked. In contrast, if the vector elements to be processed are more than the number of PEs,elements need to be divided into groups and the number of elements in each group is equal to the number of PEs in the array processor. ILLIAC IV is one of the best examples of the SIMD array processor which was developed by the Burroughs Corporation. at the University of Illinois.

MULTIPLE CHOICE QUESTIONS

1. For which of the following applications, vector processing is required?
   (a) Image processing (b) Weather forecasting
   (c) Medical diagnosis (d) All of these
2. How the ith element of vector V is represented?
   (a) V (I) (b) Vi
   (c) iV (d) None of these
3. Which of the following is a supercomputer?
   (a) CRAY-3 (b) PARAM
   (c) Both (a) and (b) (d) ILLIAC IV
4. Array processors contain a number of ________ that enable to process elements of array in parallel.
   (a) ALUs (b) CUs
   (c) Memory units (d) None of these
5. ________ serves as a peripheral for the conventional host computer.
   (a) SIMD array processor (b) Attached array processor
   (c) Supercomputer (d) Vector processor
6. ILLIAC IV is one of the best examples of the ________.
   (a) Vector processor (b) Attached array processor
   (c) SIMD array processor (d) None of these
7. The data register is used to communicate or exchange the data with the ________.
   (a) Address bus (b) Data bus
   (c) Memory bus (d) None of these

8. In SIMD array processor, each PE contains the ALU, floating-point arithmetic unit and other __________ registers.

   (a) Working (b) Data

   (c) Instruction (d) None of these

Ans. 1. d 2. a 3. c 4. a 5. b 6. c 7. b 8. a

14

Multiprocessor

1. What is multiprocessor? Name two different sets of architectural models for a multiprocessor.

Ans. A **multiprocessor** is an MIMD computer system containing two or more processors where all the processors share common sets of memory modules, I/O channels and peripheral devices. Each processor may have its own local memory and private I/O devices along with shared memory and I/O devices. The entire system is controlled by a single integrated operating system that allows the communication between processors and their programs. Two main characteristics of a multiprocessor system are as follows:

- It is a single computer that contains multiple processors.
- All processors communicate and cooperate with each other at different levels for solving a problem.

Based on the memory organization, there are two different sets of architectural models for a multiprocessor which are:

- Loosely coupled multiprocessors.
- Tightly coupled multiprocessors.

2. Describe the desirable features in a processor for multiprocessing.

Ans. A number of desirable features are needed in a processor for being effective in a multiprocessor environment. Some of these features are discussed below:

- **Process recoverability:** The processes and the processor should be considered two different entities in multiprocessor environment. In the case of a processor failure, the interrupted process should be retrieved and executed by another processor. If a processor does not support this feature, the reliability of multiprocessor is reduced. Most of the processors maintain the state of currently executing process in the internal registers that cannot be accessed from outside the processor and in the case of failure, these are not written in the memory. Hence for process recoverability, it is desirable to separate the general-purpose registers from the processor. This has become possible with current technology without any significant loss of speed.

- **Efficient context switching:** The processor should support more than one addressing domain (context) and thus, an efficient context switching for the effective utilization of resources. The context switch time is the total time taken to switch from one process to another process, which includes saving the current state of one process and restoring the state of new process. A special instruction and a number of register sets are used to accomplish the context switching efficiently. The multiprocessor architecture should support such instruction and the register sets.
- **Large virtual and physical address space:** The processor should support large physical address space to allow programs to access large amount of data if required. It should also support a large virtual address space. The virtual memory space should be segmented to achieve modular sharing. It should also provide the mechanisms for memory protection and checking software reliability.
- **Effective synchronization primitives:** The processors should provide implementation of some mechanisms that can be used to establish mutual exclusion among concurrently executing cooperating processes. The mechanisms for achieving mutual exclusion need certain operations to be treated and executed as indivisible operations. Semaphore is one of the generally used mechanisms to achieve mutual exclusion.
- **Interprocessor communication mechanism:** The processors that are used to build multiprocessor must have support for interprocessor communication. The mechanism for interprocessor communication must be implemented in the hardware. Such a mechanism becomes especially useful when processors frequently exchange requests for services.

3. Explain the difference between multicomputer and multiprocessor systems.

Ans. The multiprocessor systems have certain similarities with multiple computer (simply called multicomputer) systems as both support concurrent operations in the system. However, there exist some important differences between them, which are listed in Table 14.1.

Table 14.1 Differences between Multicomputer and Multiprocessor Systems

Multicomputer	Multiprocessor
A multicomputer system consists of several autonomous computers that may or may not communicate with each other over the network.	Multiprocessor system is a single integrated system that contains multiple processors.
In a multiple computer system, each system has a separate memory configuration.	In a multiprocessor system, all processors share the same memory space. They do not have separate memory configuration.
The processors can communicate by sending messages because they do not have shared memory.	The processor can communicate by sending message as well as sharing common memory space.
Every system has its own separate operating system.	All processors are controlled by a single operating system.
Multicomputer has fast processing power because every processor has separate memory.	Multiprocessor has less processing power because all processors share the same memory space.
The structure of multicomputer is complex because more than one computer is used to build the multicomputer system.	The structure of multiprocessor system is less complex.
A multicomputer system needs more space because it includes number of separate computers to perform all the tasks.	Multiprocessor are more space effective because single motherboard is used for all the processors.
Multicomputer is more efficient as in case of unexpected shut down of a computer, one can continue working on another computer.	Multiprocessor is less efficient because in case of unexpected shut down of the system, one has to wait until the system reboots or gets repaired.

Continued...

Table 14.1 (Continued)

Each processor can perform a different task. Hence, several tasks can be performed simultaneously with a multicomputer system.	Several processors are involved in processing a single task.
Multicomputer system is classified as no remote memory access (NORMA).	Multiprocessor system is classified as a MIMD computer.
An example of multicomputer system is IBM attached support processor system.	An example of multiprocessor system is Deneclor's HEP system.

4. Briefly explain the loosely coupled multiprocessor system. Explain how the intra and inter-processor communication takes place in non-hierarchal loosely coupled system.

Ans. In a **loosely coupled multiprocessor system**, each processor has a separate set of I/O devices and a large local memory (LM) to access data and instructions. A processor with its local memory and I/O interface is often termed as **computer module**. The processes that execute on different computer modules can communicate with each other through message transfer system (MTS). The MTS supports communication between different modules by exchanging messages. As the degree of coupling between the computer modules is loose, a loosely coupled system (LCS) is also referred to as **distributed system.** Figure 14.1 shows *N* loosely coupled computer modules in a non-hierarchical LCS. Each computer module comprises a processor, a local memory, local I/O devices and a channel and arbiter switch (CAS).

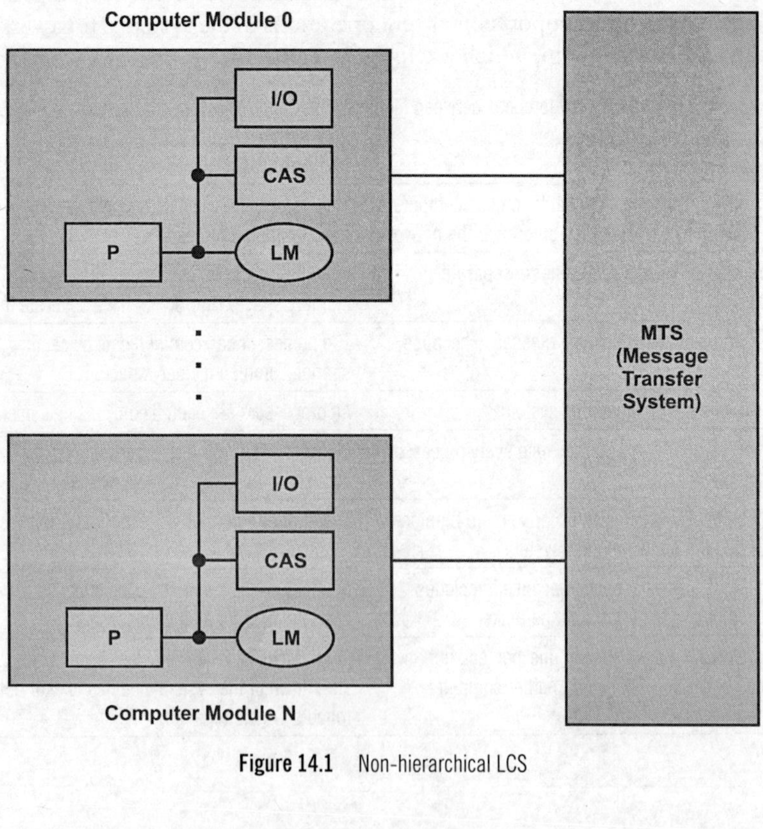

Figure 14.1 Non-hierarchical LCS

A LCS is more efficient when minimum interaction is required among two or more computer modules. If two or more different computer modules send request for accessing the physical segment of MTS simultaneously, then collisions occur. In such cases, CAS decides which of the requesting computer modules can access the segment. The decision to choose a request from multiple requests is made based on the given service discipline, and other requests are delayed until the current request has been completely serviced. The channel within the CAS can have a high-speed communication memory that is used for buffering block transfers of messages. This communication memory is accessible by all the processors.

MTS is one of major factors in determining the performance of a non-hierarchical LCS. It can be implemented as a single time-shared bus or a shared memory system. The performance of LCS that is configured using a single time-shared bus is limited by several factors such as message arrival rate on the bus, the message length and the bus capacity. In addition, as the number of computer modules increases, the contentions for the bus also increase. On the other hand, for a LCS configured using shared memory system, the performance is limited by the memory conflicts arisen due to processor–memory interconnection network.

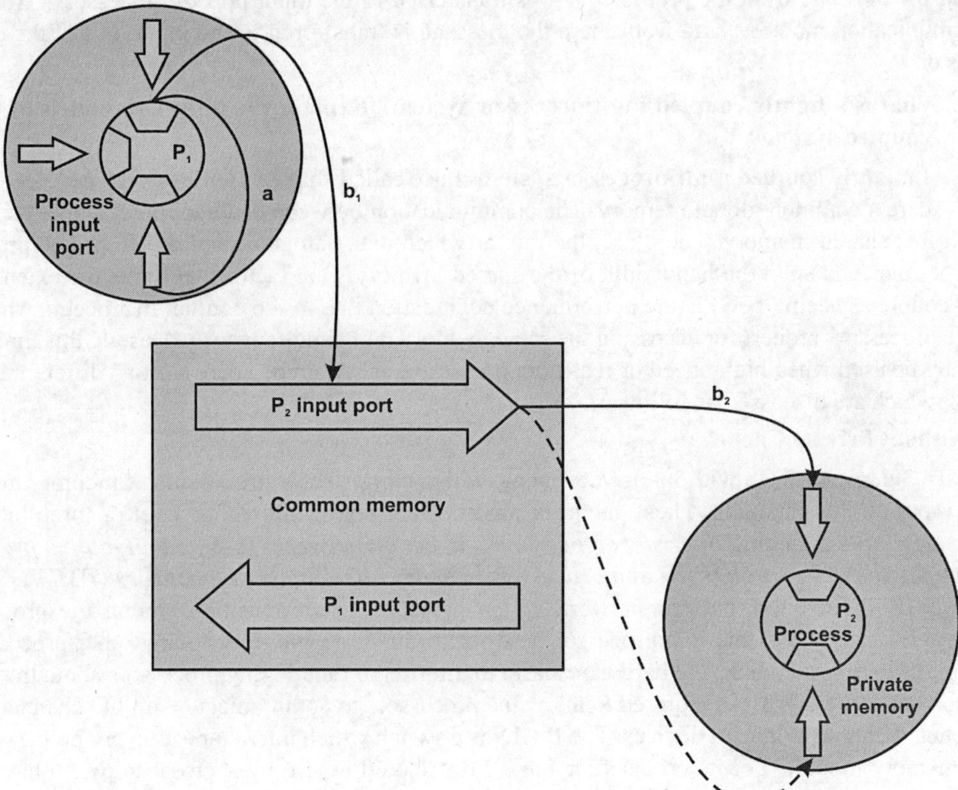

Figure 14.2 Communication between Processes in a Multiprocessor Environment

The communication memory can be centralized and connected to the time-shared bus or can be a part of the shared memory system. It can also be distributed. In either case (centralized or distributed) it is assumed to be consisting of various logical ports that can be accessed by the processors. A process (task) executing on a processor can communicate with other processes executing on the same processor or some different processor. Each process is associated with an input port that is stored in the local memory of the processor executing that process. In addition, each processor is associated with a communication port residing in communication memory as its input port. During communication, the messages issued by the source process are directed to the input port of the destination process. When the processes executing on the same processor communicate, the communication takes place through local memory only. On the other hand, the communication between processes executing on different processors takes place through a communication port.

Figure 14.2 shows the communication between processes. A process executing on the processor P_1 communicates with another process on P_1 by directly placing a message in the input port of that process (indicated by the arrow 'a' in the figure). On the other hand, the communication between a process on P_1 and a process on P_2 takes place in two steps (indicated by the arrows 'b1' and 'b2' in the figure). Initially, the message from the process on P_1 is transferred to the input port of processor P_2 (residing in communication memory) and from there the message is transferred to the input port of the desired process on P_2.

5. What is a tightly coupled multiprocessor system? Explain the different models of tightly coupled systems.

Ans. In **tightly coupled multiprocessor systems** (also called **shared memory systems**), all the processors share a common global memory. The communication between different processors takes place through this shared memory. Therefore, the rate at which data can communicate from one processor to another depends upon the bandwidth of the shared memory. One factor that limits the extension of tightly coupled system (TCS) is the performance degradation due to the conflict that occurs when two or more processors request for accessing the same memory unit simultaneously. Despite this limitation, TCS may be used when high-speed or real-time processing is required. There are two different models of TCS, which are discussed as follows:

TCS without Private Cache

Figure 14.3 depicts a TCS without private cache, which comprises P processors, M memory modules and C input/output channels. These memory modules are connected using a set of three interconnection networks including *interrupt signal interconnection network* (*ISIN*), *input–output processor interconnection network* (*IOPIN*) and *processor–memory interconnection network* (*PMIN*).

The **ISIN** is an interprocessor network which provides synchronization among the processors. Processors basically use this interprocessor network to direct an interrupt to any other processor. In addition, ISIN is used to buzz the hardware alarm to inform the functioning processors about the failure of a processor. The **IOPIN** is required to allow the processors to communicate with I/O channel which is attached with the peripheral devices. The **PMIN** is a switch which interconnects every processor with every memory module. For its proper function, PMIN should be a P by M crossbar switch having PM sets of crosspoints with each set of crosspoints interconnecting one processor with one memory module. Alternatively, the crossbar switch can be distributed across the memory modules. With this configuration of PMIN, a multiported memory is designed.

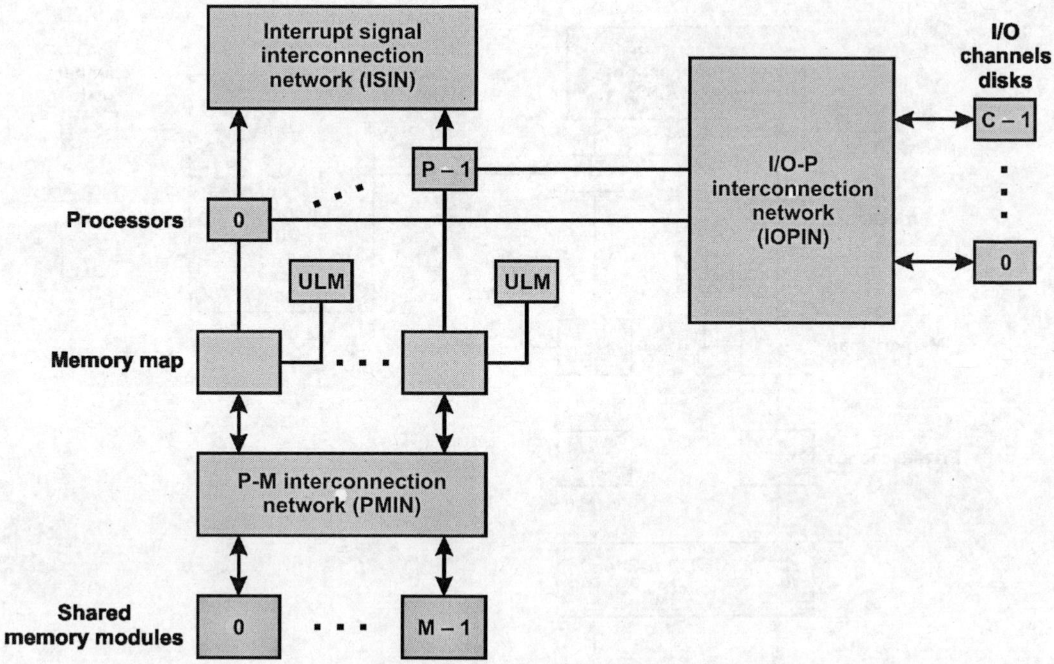

Figure 14.3 TCS without Private Cache

In TCS without private cache, one memory module can serve the request of one processor at a given time. When two or more processors attempt to access the same memory module at the same time, memory conflict occurs. Resolving memory conflicts is the responsibility of the PMIN switch as each memory reference goes through it. To reduce the number of memory conflicts, systems usually have as much memory modules as the processors. Alternatively, a local memory, known as **unmapped local memory (ULM)**, is associated with each processor. This storage area is used to store the Kernel code and the operating system tables, which are used by the processes executing on the processor. For example, on a multiprogrammed processor with ULM, task switch is handled by saving the current state of the executing task in the ULM and switching to the new task. This method reduces the traffic on PMIN switch and thus, reducing the memory conflicts.

In addition to the above problem, this organization suffers with another problem. As each memory access request is handled by PMIN switch, processor–memory switch causes delay. This delay increases the instruction cycle time, resulting in decreased system throughput.

TCS with Private Cache

The architecture of TCS with private cache is shown in Figure 14.4. This architecture is similar to the architecture of TCS without private cache except that every processor has a private cache associated with it.

Associating private cache with processors helps in reducing the instruction time delay as most of the memory references made by a processor are handled by the cache itself instead of going to the PMIN switch. Clearly, this reduces the traffic at PMIN switch and thus, reducing the contention at crosspoints. However, this organization suffers with cache coherence problem. Cache coherence problem and its resolution are discussed in Q12.

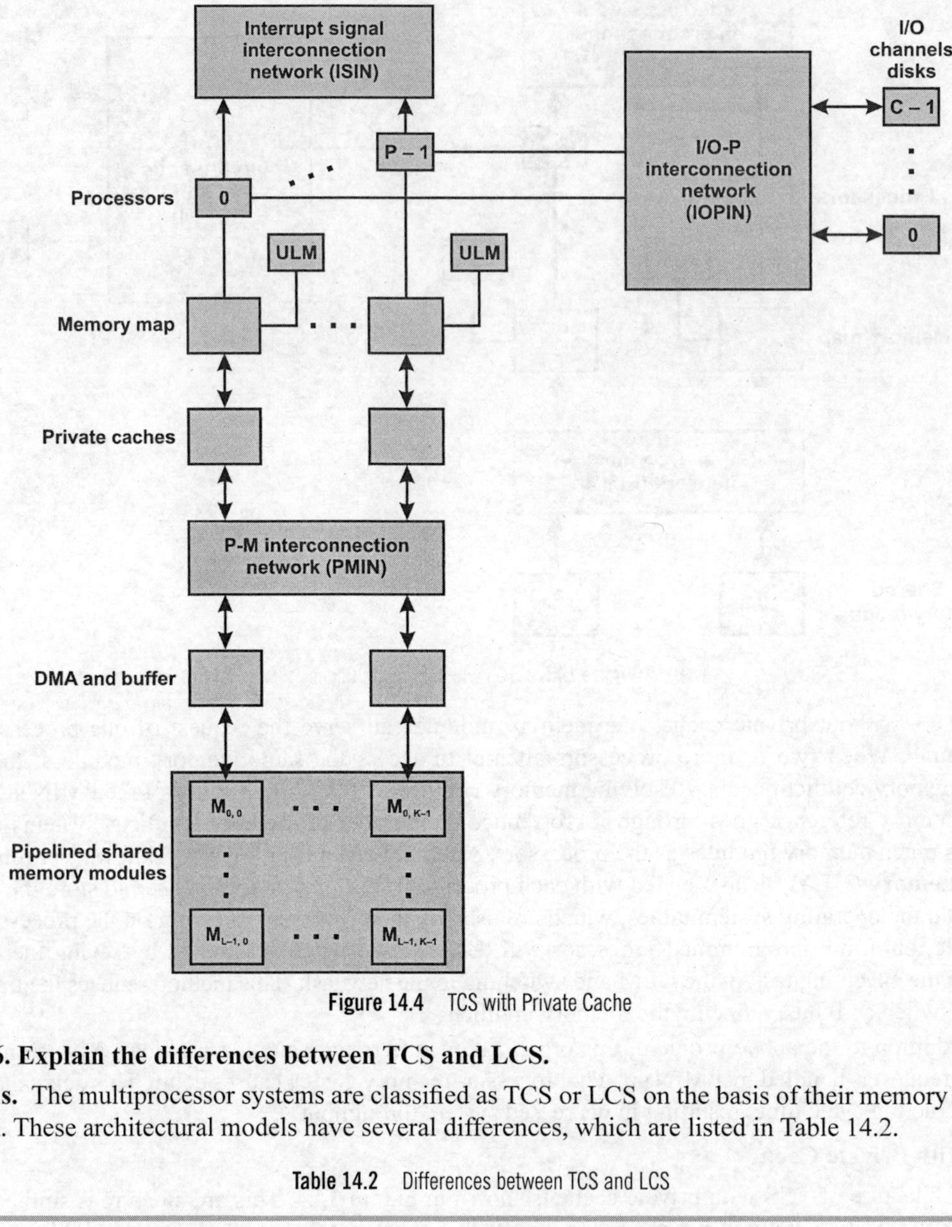

Figure 14.4 TCS with Private Cache

6. Explain the differences between TCS and LCS.

Ans. The multiprocessor systems are classified as TCS or LCS on the basis of their memory organization. These architectural models have several differences, which are listed in Table 14.2.

Table 14.2 Differences between TCS and LCS

TCS	LCS
Processors share a single global memory.	Processors do not share memory.
Different processors communicate through shared memory.	Processors communicate with each other by sending messages in the form of packets through MTS.
TCSs are efficient even when interaction among tasks is high as interaction does not significantly affect the performance.	LCSs become inefficient when there is much interaction between tasks.

Continued…

Table 14.2 (Continued)

TCS	LCS
It requires high initial investment and depreciates rapidly.	LCS is an interconnection of nodes, which are usually inexpensive. Further, nodes can be replaced individually and hence, no high investment is needed at once.
The data rate at which processors can communicate is high.	The data rate is low when messages are sent from one machine to another.
In TCS, all processors are highly dependent on each other.	In LCS, all processors are less dependent on each other. They perform their task individually.

7. What is an interconnection network? List the different schemes available for establishing an interconnection network.

Ans. A multiprocessor system is composed of various components such as CPUs, input/output processors (IOP) attached to I/O devices and a memory unit divided into a number of modules. All these components communicate with each other through an interconnection network. The structure of interconnection network depends on the number of paths available among the processing elements (PE) in a LCS or between the processors and shared memory in a TCS. An interconnection network can be set up based on any of the following forms:

- Time-shared common bus
- Multiport memory
- Crossbar switch
- Multistage switching network
- Hypercube system

8. Differentiate between time-shared common bus and multiport memory. Also draw the figure for both systems.

Ans. Although both time-shared common bus and multiport memory use the concept of bus to provide the interconnection, they have several differences. Some of the differences between them are listed in Table 14.3.

Table 14.3 Differences between Time-shared Bus and Multiport Memory Interconnection Network

Time-shared common bus	Multiport memory
The memory unit and the processors (including CPUs and IOPs) are connected through a common bus (see Figure 14.5).	The memory modules and CPUs are connected through separate buses (see Figure 14.6). Each processor has a bus comprising data, address and control lines and each memory module has a number of ports, one per each processor bus.
The communication can occur between a processor and the memory unit or between two processors at a time.	When one processor is communicating with a memory module, another processor can communicate with any other module at the same time.
A processor has to determine the availability status of the bus before starting a transfer operation. If bus is busy, processor has to wait.	Each memory modules has an internal control logic that decides which port will have access to the memory, when multiple CPUs want to access the same memory module.

Continued...

Table 14.3 Differences between Time-shared Bus and Multiport Memory Interconnection Network (Continued)

Transfer conflicts can occur in the system as bus is shared by all the processors. These conflicts are resolved by the bus controller, which establishes priorities among the requesting processors.	Memory access conflicts can occur when two or more processors attempt to communicate with the same memory module at the same time. These conflicts are resolved by assigning fixed priorities to each memory port.
The transfer rate is limited because this system has only a single path for exchanging the data.	System facilitates high transfer rate because of having multiple paths between processors and memory modules.
It needs less wires and simple control logic for implementation. Thus, it is less expensive.	It needs expensive memory control logic with a large number of cables and connectors that make it quite expensive.

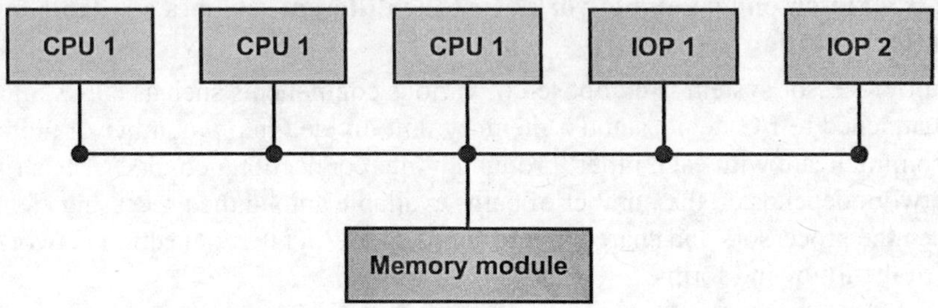

Figure 14.5 Time-shared Common Bus

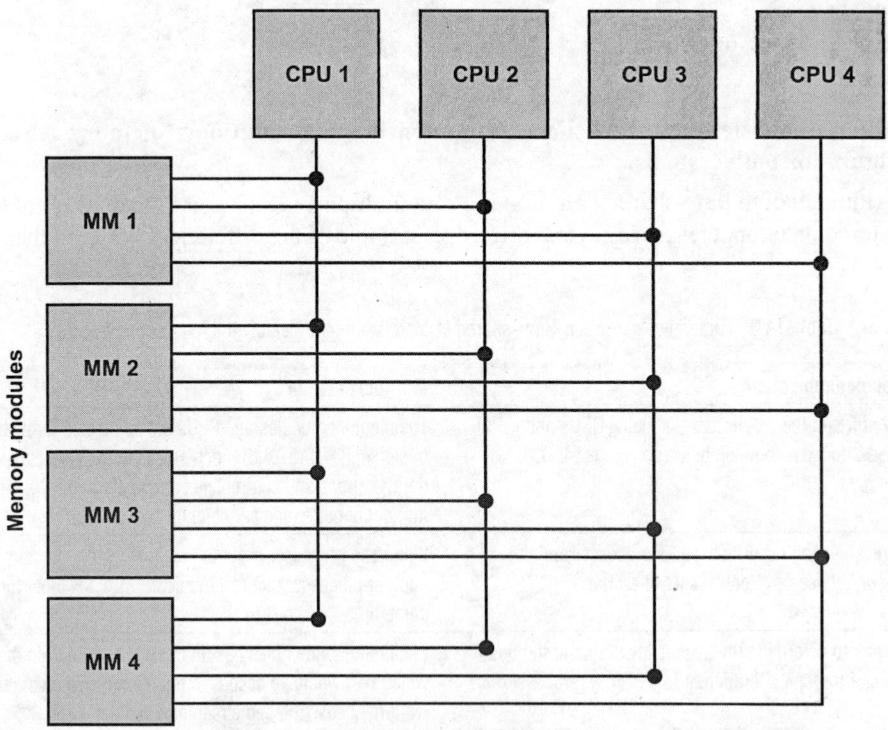

Figure 14.6 Multiport Memory

9. How crossbar switch interconnection network can be created?

Ans. A crossbar switch uses an $N \times N$ matrix organization to connect N processors with N memory modules. Figure 14.7 shows the crossbar switch organization for four CPUs and four memory modules. Each processor is connected to a memory module through a separate bus. At the intersection of each processor bus and paths of a memory module, a crosspoint is placed. A **crosspoint** is an electric switch (indicated by the small square in figure) that has the control logic to establish the data transfer path between a processor and a memory module. The control logic first checks the address placed on the bus to determine whether the address refers to its specific module. If yes, it allows the data transfer. In case multiple processors request to access the same memory module, the control logic resolves the conflicts on the basis of predetermined priorities.

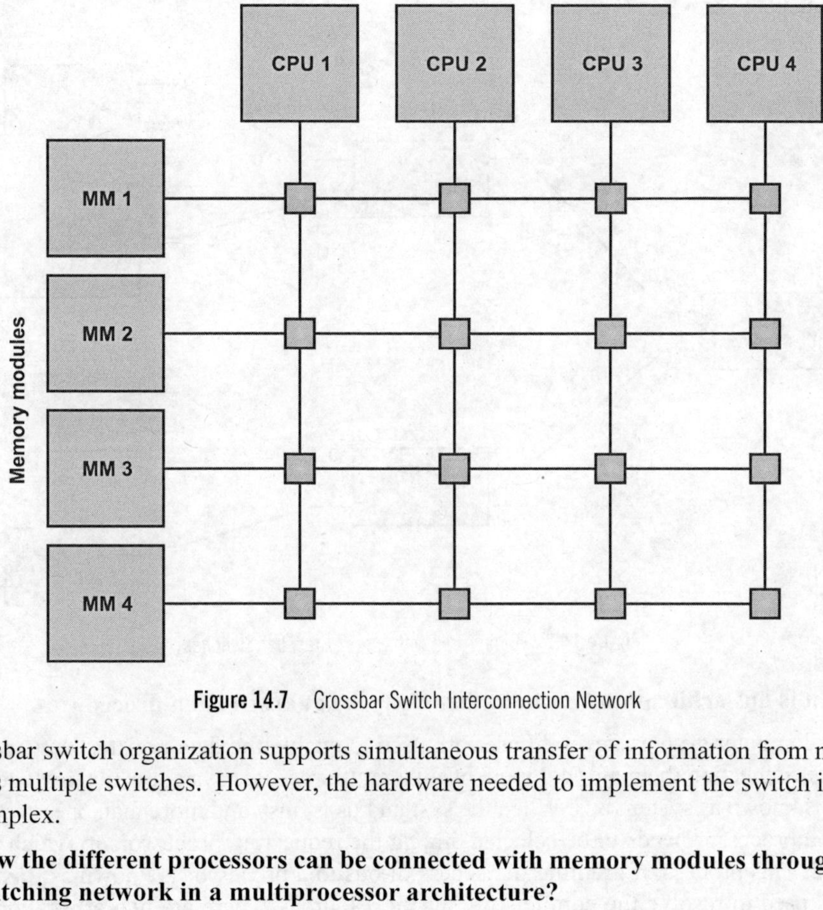

Figure 14.7 Crossbar Switch Interconnection Network

The crossbar switch organization supports simultaneous transfer of information from memory modules as it has multiple switches. However, the hardware needed to implement the switch is very expensive and complex.

10. How the different processors can be connected with memory modules through multistage switching network in a multiprocessor architecture?

Ans. A **multistage switching network**, as the name implies, consists of several stages with each stage containing 2×2 crossbar switches. A 2×2 crossbar switch has two inputs and two outputs (0 and 1). Each input can be connected to any of the two outputs. The control signals associated with a switch determine to which output an input is to be connected. In addition, the switch can also resolve conflicts that arise when both inputs want to connect to the same output. In such a case, the switch allows one input to connect and the other is blocked.

Using the 2 × 2 crossbar switches, a multistage network controlling communication between a number of sources and destinations can be designed. Figure 14.8 depicts a binary tree connecting two processors (P_1 and P_2) with eight memory modules (designated by binary 000 through 111) by means of switches. When a processor wishes to communicate with a memory module the path for data transfer needs to be determined as there are multiple paths. The data transfer path between a processor and a specific memory module is determined by the binary bits of the destination memory module. To understand how, suppose the processor P_1 wishes to communicate with the memory module whose binary is 101. Now, the first bit in the destination number (which is 1) indicates that the processor P_1 should be connected to switch output 1 in the first stage, to switch output 0 in the second stage and to the switch output 1 in the third stage. Thus, the data transfer between the processor P_1 and third memory module 101 follows the path shown in Figure 14.8.

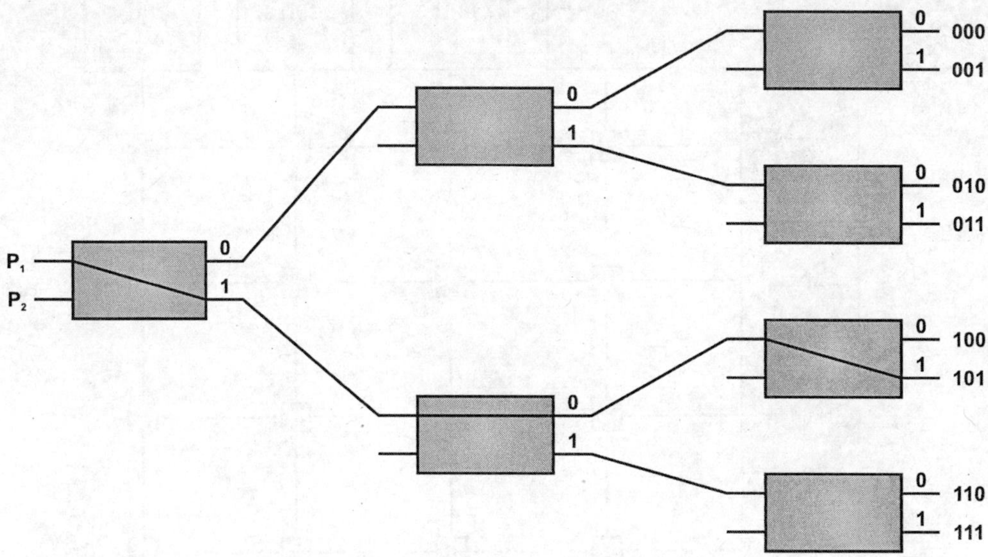

Figure 14.8 Binary Tree with 2 × 2 Crossbar Switches

11. What is bus arbitration? Explain the two types of arbitration procedures.

Ans. In a computer system, several buses are used to enable the data transfer between the components. The bus connecting the major components of a multiprocessor system which include CPUs, IOPs and memory is known as system bus. When the system bus is busy and more than one processor request the bus, then a processor needs to be selected among the requesting processors to which the access of bus is granted. This process of granting the access of bus to a processor is known as **bus arbitration**. Arbitration is used to resolve the conflicts for shared resources. There are two arbitration procedures, namely, *serial* and *parallel* arbitration to resolve the interprocessor conflicts. Both these procedures take the established priorities of the processors into account to resolve the conflicts. The serial and parallel arbitration procedures are discussed as follows:

- **Serial arbitration:** This arbitration procedure is also named as **daisy chain arbitration**. In this method, the processors requesting the control of bus are serially connected. The priority is assigned to every processor according to its connection to the priority control line. The processor closely connected to the priority control line is assigned the higher priority as compared to the one that is connected farther from the priority control line. When multiple processors request for the control of common bus at the same time, the priority is used to resolve the conflict. The processor with the highest priority is given the permission to use the system bus first.

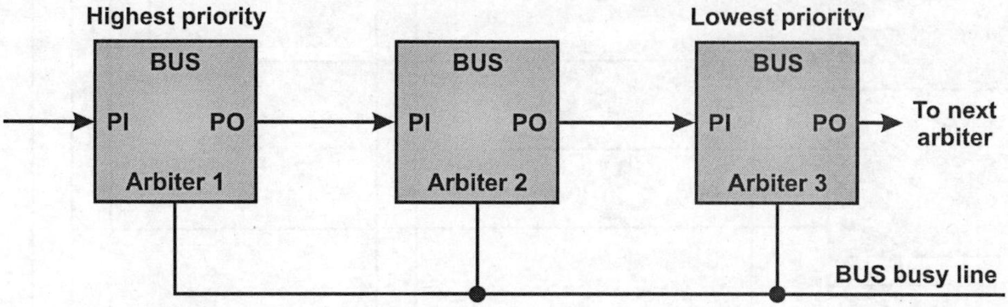

Figure 14.9 Daisy Chain Arbitration

Figure 14.9 shows the serial connection of three arbiters. Each processor has its own bus arbiter logic along with two lines: *priority-in* (*PI*) and *priority-output* (*PO*). The `PO` of each arbiter is connected to the `PI` of the next lower arbiter. The `PI` of the processor with highest priority is kept at logic 1. The `PO` of any arbiter will be 1 if its `PI` is 1 and the associated processor has not requested for the use of bus. However, if `PI` of any arbiter is 1 and the associated processor has also requested for the use of the bus, the arbiter logic sets its `PO` to 0. The other low priority arbiters get 0 as `PI` inputs and produce 0 as `PO` outputs. Thus, the processor having `PI` = 1 and `PO` = 0 is granted the use of bus.

A problem may arise when the control of the bus is allocated to some processor and in the meanwhile some higher priority processor requests for it. At that time, the lower priority processor must complete its bus operation, before releasing the control of the bus. To transfer the control in an orderly manner, the bus busy line is used, which is common to all the arbiters. When a processor is granted the access of bus (that is, `PI` = 1 and `PO` = 0), it examines the bus busy line. If this line is found to be inactive, that is. the bus is not being used by any processor, the control of bus is granted to the corresponding processor by activating the bus busy line of the arbiter. However, if the bus busy line is active, it means some processor is already using the system bus and thus, the processor has to wait until the bus busy line becomes inactive.

- **Parallel arbitration:** In this arbitration procedure, an external priority encoder and a decoder are used for assigning priorities to the processors. Each bus arbiter consists of bus acknowledge input line and a bus request output line (see Figure 14.10). Whenever a processor requires the control of bus, its arbiter enables the bus request output line and it is granted the use of bus when its acknowledge input line gets enabled. The bus request output lines from each arbiter form the input for the priority encoder, which generates as output a 2-bit code representing the highest priority processor among the requesting processors. This output code becomes the input to a 2×4 decoder, which enables the appropriate acknowledge input line to grant the access of the bus to the highest-priority processor. After the system bus is allocated to a particular processor, the required bus transfer is performed.

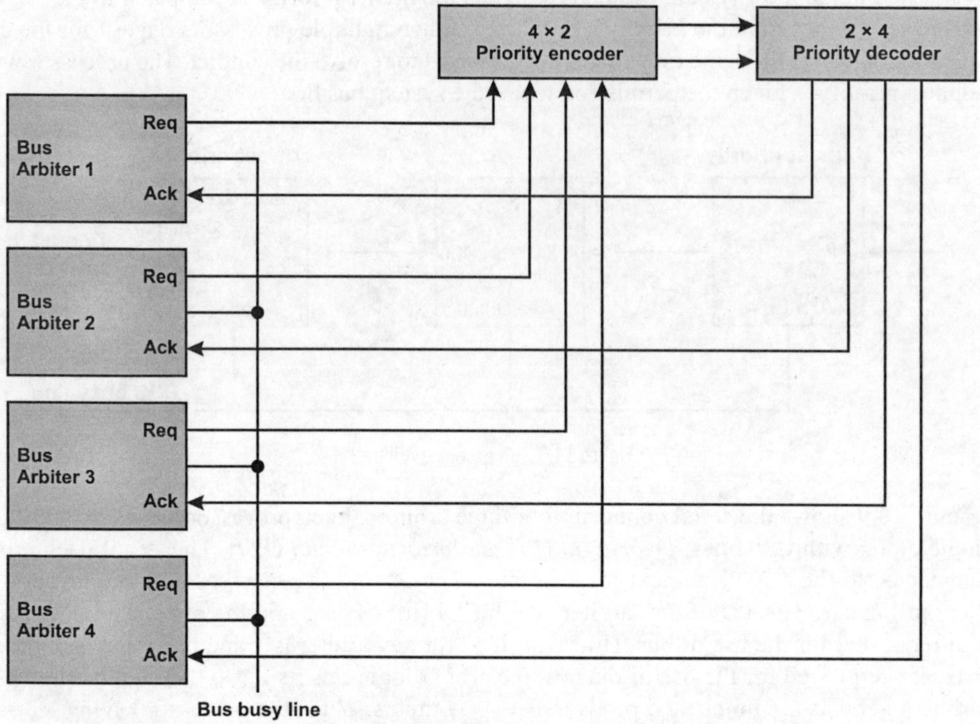

Figure 14.10 Parallel Arbitration

12. What do you mean by cache coherence? Discuss the different problems of cache coherence and propose solution.

Ans. The cache memory is used for reducing the average access time in uniprocessors. There are basically two memory operations, read and write. During memory read operation, as long as the processors find the desired word in cache, the main memory is not engaged in the transfer. However, during the memory write operations, there are two procedures, namely, *write-through* and *write-back* that are used to update the memory. In **write-through** policy, both cache and main memory are updated during every write operation, whereas in **write-back** policy, only cache is updated and the updated location is marked so that later it can be copied to the main memory. In a multiprocessor system where all the processors share a common memory and each processor has its own private cache also, it is possible that same data are available in multiple caches as well as main memory. In case one copy of such data is changed, other copies must be updated to ensure the correct memory operations; otherwise, data inconsistency may arise. This is known as **cache coherence problem.**

The problem of cache coherence arises in multiprocessors with private caches because in such systems the writable data need to be shared. The read-only data can be securely copied without facing any cache coherence problem. To understand, consider four processors P_1, P_2, P_3 and P_4 with each processor having a private cache (see Figure 14.11). During the operation, an element (say, Z with value 63) from main memory is loaded into these processors. Thus, the element Z = 63 is also copied into private caches of these processors.

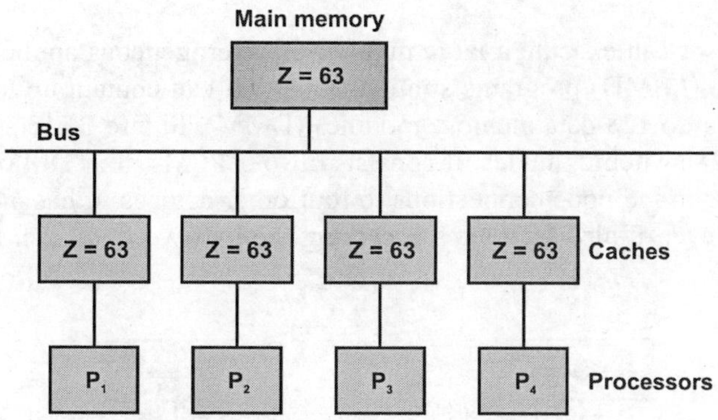

Figure 14.11 Cache Configuration after a Load on Z

Now, if one of the processors (say, P_1) changes the value of Z to 130, other copies of Z become inconsistent. Moreover, the main memory will also be inconsistent, depending on the cache write policy in use.

- If the write-through policy is in use, the modified value of Z (which is 130) is stored into P_1 and the main memory is also updated to the current value of Z. Thus, there remains consistency between the main memory and the originating cache; however, the other three caches come in the state of conflict because they still hold the old value of Z [see Figure 14.12 (a)].
- If the write-back policy is in use, only the originating cache has Z = 130, while the main memory and other three caches are still inconsistent [see Figure 14.12 (b)].

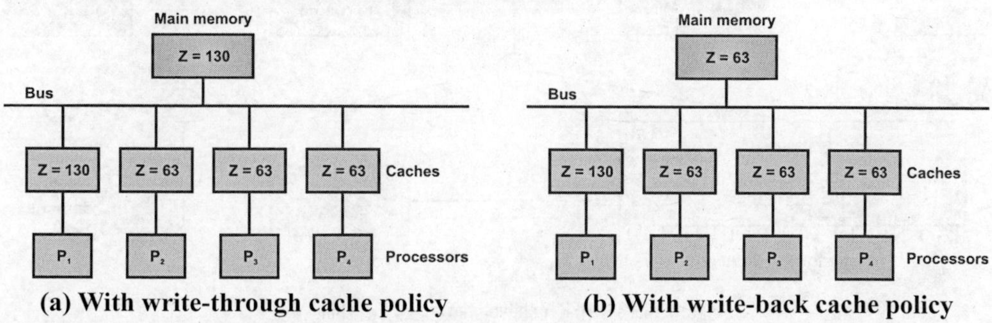

Figure 14.12 Cache Configuration after Updating Z by processor P_1

One solution to the cache coherence problem is not to permit the use of private cache for each processor and allow the shared cache memory attached with main memory. The shared cache is accessed for each memory access. Though this scheme avoids the cache coherence problem, it increases the average memory access time thus, suppressing the real benefit of the cache memory.

13. What is HEP system? Draw the figure to show the configuration of HEP system with 28 switching nodes.

Ans. Heterogeneous element multiprocessor (HEP) is a large-scale scientific multiprocessor system. It is the first commercially available MIMD multiprocessor system. As the name suggests, this scientific multiprocessor can execute a large number of heterogeneous applications such as sequential (SISD) or parallel (MIMD) programs simultaneously. It can contain up to 16 process execution modules (PEM) and up to 128 data memory modules (DMM). Figure 14.13 shows the configuration of HEP system with 28 switching nodes. It consists of four PEMs, four DMMs, a mass-storage subsystem, an I/O processor and node connections to four other devices. It has 64 bits wide instructions and data words. However, it also facilitates accessing the half-word, quarter-word and bytes within the PEM.

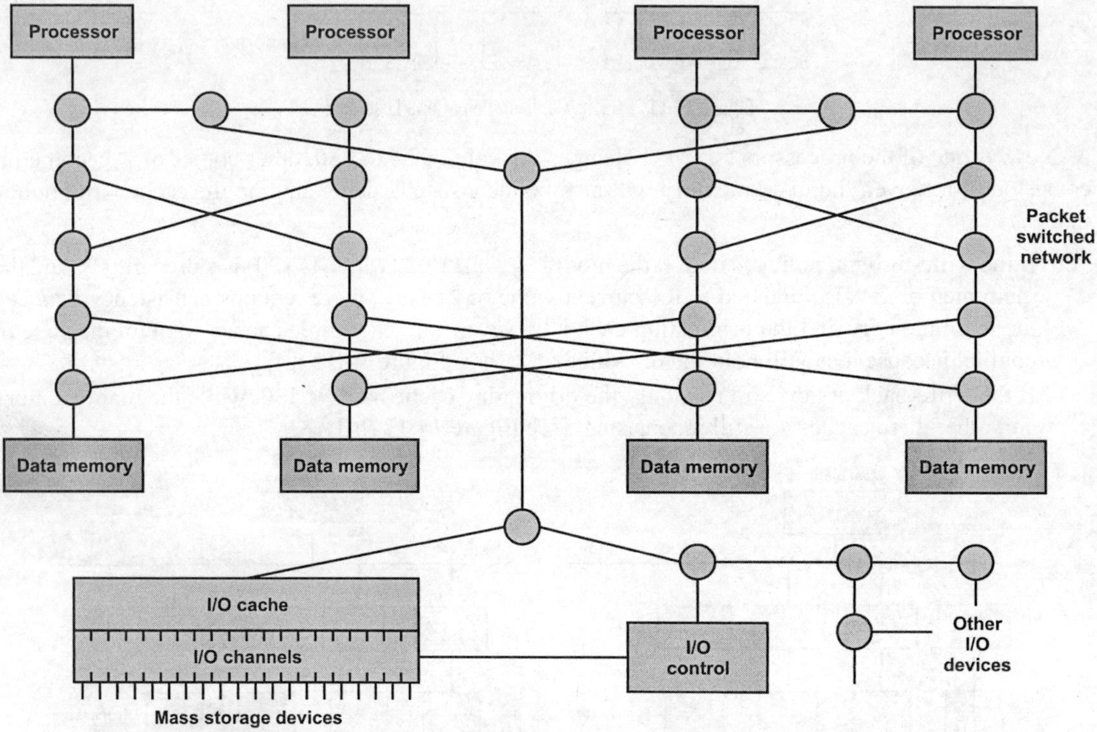

Figure 14.13 HEP Architecture with 28 Switching Nodes

14. Name some mainframe multiprocessor systems.

Ans. A mainframe multiprocessor system achieves concurrency and high system performance through parallelism rather than by decomposing the user SISD algorithm into MIMD processes. It executes non-interacting and independent processes concurrently. The degree of coupling in commercial multiprocessors is usually low, though degree of coupling varies from system to system. Some of the mainframe multiprocessor systems are:

- IBM 370/168 MP, 3033 and 3081.
- UNIVAC 1100/80 and UNIVAC 1100/90 series.
- The Tandem Non-stop system.

MULTIPLE CHOICE QUESTIONS

1. How many different sets of architectural models of multiprocessors are there?
   (a) One (b) Two
   (c) Three (d) Four
2. The processor provides context switching and gives support to more than one _________.
   (a) Addressing domain (b) Network domain
   (c) User domain (d) None of these
3. In a multicomputer, every processor has a separate operating system.
   (a) True (b) False
   (c) Cannot define (d) None of these
4. How many models are there in a tightly coupled multiprocessor?
   (a) One (b) Two
   (c) Three (d) Four
5. The crossbar switch uses the ________ format to connect the processors and memory.
   (a) Table (b) Multiple
   (c) Matrix (d) None of these
6. HEP stands for
   (a) Heterogeneous element processor (b) Heterogeneous element process
   (c) Heterogeneous equal processor (d) None of these
7. There are two types of bus arbitration
   (a) Single and multiple (b) Serial and parallel
   (c) Serial and multiple (d) None of these
8. Which of the following are the examples of a multicomputer?
   (a) IBM attached support processor system (b) Deneclor's HEP system
   (c) IBM 370/168 MP, 3033 (d) Tandem Non-stop system
9. Which of the following are not mainframe multiprocessor systems?
   (a) IBM 370/168 MP (b) Univac 1100/80
   (c) Tandem Non-stop system (d) HEP system
10. The multistage network can be constructed by using ___________.
    (a) 4×4 switch (b) 8×8 switch
    (c) 2×2 switch (d) None of these

Ans. 1. b 2. a 3. a 4. b 5. c 6. a 7. b 8. a 9. d 10. c

15

Introduction to 8085 Microprocessor and Assembly Language

1. What is microprocessor? Draw the block diagram of microprocessor.

Ans. A **microprocessor** (shortened as **μp**) is a programmable logic device integrated on a silicon chip that performs all the logical, computational and data processing tasks of the computer as similar to a CPU. As it acts like the CPU, it is also referred to as the brain of the computer. It comprises a limited number of on-chip locations referred to as registers that can store information. There is an arithmetic logic unit (ALU) and a control unit (CU) inside the chip. ALU is responsible for performing all the arithmetic and logical operations on the data stored in registers. CU is responsible for generating control signals to direct the operations of external devices as well as for internal on-chip circuitry. The microprocessor programming is done using the assembly language.

A number of microprocessors have evolved over the years, which can be differentiated on the basis of the following characteristics:

- **Instruction set:** It refers to a group of instructions that can be executed by the microprocessor.
- **Bandwidth:** It refers to the number of bits that can be processed in a single instruction. A microprocessor having the higher bandwidth is more powerful.
- **Clock speed:** It refers to the number of instruction that can be executed in one second by the microprocessor. Usually, the clock speed is measured in megahertz (MHz). Higher the clock speed, faster will be the processing.

Figure 15.1 depicts the block diagram of a microprocessor that includes ALU, accumulator (`AC`), general purpose registers, stack pointer (`SP`), program counter (`PC`), clock and timing circuit and interrupt circuit.

2. Differentiate between 8-bit and 16-bit microprocessors.

Ans. The microprocessors operate on binary digits (bits), that is, 0 and 1. The bits are represented in machines in the form of electric voltages. The low voltage level, usually 1 V, represents the bit 0 and the

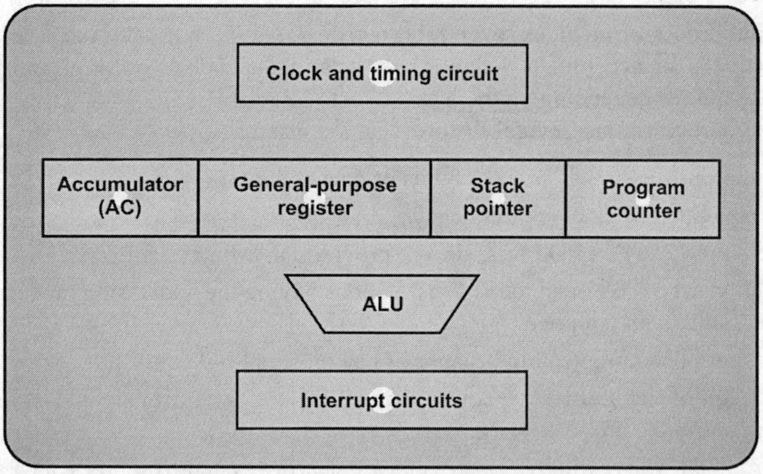

Figure 15.1 Block Diagram of a Microprocessor

other high voltage level represents the bit 1. Each microprocessor is capable of processing a group of bits (referred to as **word**) and different microprocessors are organized based on their word length. For example, a processor that can recognize and process an 8-bit word is called 8-bit microprocessor. Similarly, a microprocessor having word length 16 is referred to as 16-bit microprocessor. Apart from word length, the 8-bit and 16-bit microprocessors have several others differences that are listed in Table 15.1.

Table 15.1 Differences Between 8-bit and 16-bit Microprocessors

8-bit Microprocessor	16-bit Microprocessor
An 8-bit microprocessor has less memory addressing capacity	A 16-bit microprocessor can address comparatively more number of memory locations
The execution speed of 8-bit microprocessor is comparatively less	A 16-bit microprocessor can execute at a relatively faster speed
The instruction set of 8-bit microprocessor is less powerful as it has less number of instructions	The instruction set of 16-bit microprocessor is more powerful as it has more number of instructions
Some examples of 8-bit microprocessors are Z80, MC 6800, Hitachi HD 64180 and 8085 microprocessors	Some examples of 16-bit microprocessors are Intel 8086/8088 microprocessors

3. Write a short note on 8085 microprocessor. Also explain the features of 8085 microprocessor.

Ans. The 8085 microprocessor, also sometimes referred to as **8085A**, is an 8-bit general-purpose microprocessor, introduced by the Intel in 1976. It is an enhanced version of its predecessor, that is, the Intel 8080A. Its instruction set is compatible with that of 8080, meaning that it has several new instructions along with the 8080 instruction set. The digit 5 in the name of 8085 microprocessor has come from the fact that it needs a power supply of +5V to complete its operation. The 8085 comprises an 8-bit data bus and a 16-bit address bus. This implies that it can process 8 bits at a time and can address up to 2^{16} (that is, 64K) memory locations. The 8-bit data bus is multiplexed with the lower part of 16-bit address bus to reduce the number of pins up to 40.

The 8085 microprocessor includes seven 8-bit registers, that is, A, B, C, D, E, H and L. The six registers except A (that is, an accumulator) can be used as an independent byte registers or as three 16-bit registers BC, DE and HL depending on the instruction to be processed.

The 8085 microprocessor has several features that are listed below:

- The 8085 microprocessor can process 8 bits of data at the same time.
- It can operate with 3 MHz clock frequency.
- It can access upto 256 (2^8) I/O ports, since it provides an 8-bit I/O address.
- The instruction set of 8085 includes 74 instructions having the addressing modes: immediate, register, direct, indirect and implied.
- It facilitates serial communication because of having serial I/O control.
- It does not require an external bus controller as it generates control signals including IO/$\overline{M}$, $\overline{RD}$ and $\overline{WR}$ to control the bus cycles.
- In an environment where muliple processors are sharing system resources such as I/O and memory, the external hardware that can be another microprocessor or equivalent master can determine which of the machine cycle is being executed by the microprocessor with the help of status signals (IO/$\overline{M}$ S_0 and S_1).
- It allows exchanging large amount of data between I/O devices and memory at high speed by sharing the system bus with direct memory access controller.

4. Describe the architecture of 8085 microprocessor.

Ans. The architecture of 8085 microprocessor is shown in Figure 15.2. It consists of various architectural elements, which are functionally organized into the following blocks:

- **Register set:** The 8085 microprocessor incorporates various registers to perform several computing tasks. These registers except temporary register are accessible by the programmer to perform the operations. The register set of 8085 microprocessor is discussed in detail in Q6.
- **Arithmetic logic unit (ALU):** It is responsible for performing the arithmetic and logic operations bitwise on 8-bit variables. These operations include addition, subtraction, AND, OR, NOT, XOR, rotate and clear. The branching decision is also considered by the ALU.
- **Address buffer:** It is an 8-bit unidirectional buffer used to hold the eight high-order bits (A_8–A_{15}) of the address bus. In case of certain conditions such as reset, hold and halt conditions or when the address lines are not in use, the address buffer can tri-state the high-order address bus.
- **Address/data buffer:** It is an 8-bit bi-directional buffer used to hold information from multiplexed address/data bus (AD_7–AD_0), that is, eight low-order bits of the address bus (A_0–A_7) and 8 bits of data bus (D_0–D_7). In case of certain conditions such as reset, hold and halt conditions or when the address/data lines are not in use, the address/data buffer can tri-state the multiplexed address/data bus.
- **Increment/decrement address latch:** It is a 16-bit register that is responsible for incrementing or decrementing the contents of the program counter or stack pointer as a part of the instruction that is being executed.
- **Instruction decoder:** It decodes the operation code (opcode) of the instruction stored in instruction register. Then, it generates the timing and control signals according to the instruction for controlling the registers, data buffers, ALU and external peripherals.

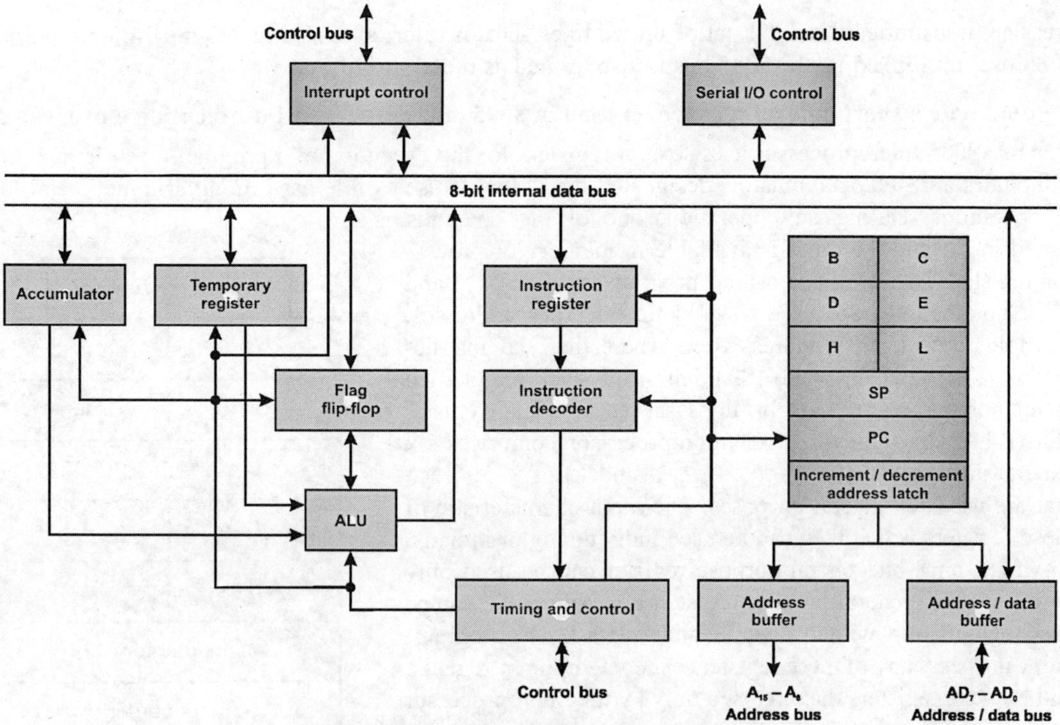

Figure 15.2 Architecture of 8085 Microprocessor

- **Interrupt control:** Usually, the instructions are executed in sequence, that is, one after the other. However, sometimes the execution of one of the special routines (group of instructions) is necessary under certain conditions within a program. This condition is referred to as **interrupt**. After executing the routine corresponding to the interrupt, the control must be transferred back to the program executing prior the interrupt. The block contains interrupts such as RST 5.5, RST 6.5, RST 7.5, TRAP and INTR along with one interrupt acknowledgement signal $\overline{\text{INTA}}$.
- **Serial I/O control:** It is responsible for bit-by-bit transmission of data. This block provides two signals for serial communication: SID and SOD. The SID signal is used to receive data serially and the SOD signal is used to send data serially.
- **Timing and control circuitry:** The control circuitry generates control signals required to perform all the operations such as signals to fetch, decode and execute the instructions and to interface the peripheral devices to the processor. All the operations as well as the control circuitry are synchronized with the help of clock signals.

5. What is address multiplexing in context of 8085 microprocessor?

Ans. In 8085 microprocessor, the data bus is 8-bit wide, that is, 8 bits of data can be transferred in parallel. The address bus of 8085 is 16-bit wide, which means that it can directly address up to 2^{16} (64K bytes) memory. The eight most significant bits (A_8–A_{15}) of a 16-bit memory address are transferred through the eight dedicated address lines and the eight least significant bits (A_0–A_7) of the memory address are transmitted through eight data lines. Thus, the data and a part of the memory address are transmitted through a set of shared lines. This is referred to as **address multiplexing**. Since 8085 uses multiplexing, the 8085 bus is also termed as **multiplexed bus**.

6. Write a short note on register set used in 8085 microprocessor for executing a program.

Ans. 8085 microprocessor uses several registers for the execution of a program (see Figure 15.3). It includes an 8-bit accumulator (designated by `A`) that is used while performing arithmetic and logic operations. During any operation, one of the operands is stored in `AC` and the other is available in memory or processor register. Two 16-bit registers, program counter (`PC`) and stack pointer (`SP`) are used to hold the memory addresses. `PC` holds the memory address from where the next instruction is to be fetched, while `SP` points to a stack maintained in memory. A set of five flip-flops serves as a flag register of five bits. In addition, 8085 microprocessor comprises six general-purpose registers (`B`, `C`, `D`, `E`, `H` and `L`) of 8 bits each that are used for several purposes. The main characteristic of these registers is that they can be used individually or in pairs. However, an 8-bit general-purpose register can be used only with a specific general-purpose register. For example, `B` can be used together only with `C`, `D` with `E` and `H` with `L`. The programmer can access any of these registers except temporary register, and `W` and `Z` registers that are used only by the microprocessor for performing internal operations.

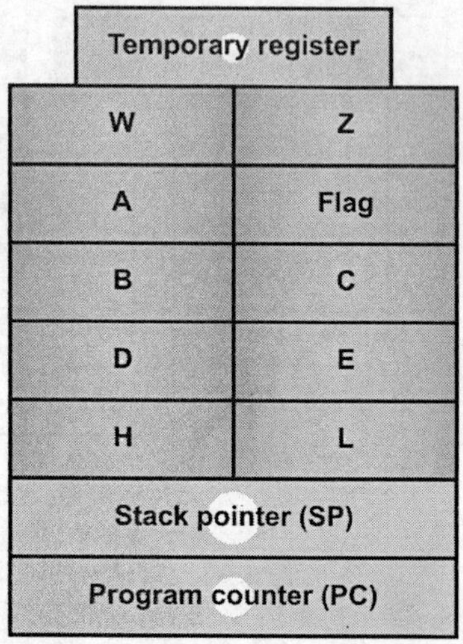

Figure 15.3 Register Set in 8085 Microprocessor

7. Explain the classification of 8085 microprocessor instructions.

Ans. The functions that a microprocessor can perform are determined by its instruction set, which is a group of instructions available inside the microcomputer. In 8085 microprocessor, the instructions vary on the basis of number of bytes contained in them. The 8085 microprocessor uses one, two or three byte instructions for performing different operations. A 1-byte instruction tells only about the operation to be performed. In contrast, 2-byte and 3-byte instructions indicate the operand or the address of the operand along with the operation code (see Figure 15.4). In 2-byte and 3-byte instructions, all the bytes are stored consecutively in memory.

The different instructions available in 8085 microprocessor are categorized into five functional groups, which are as follows:

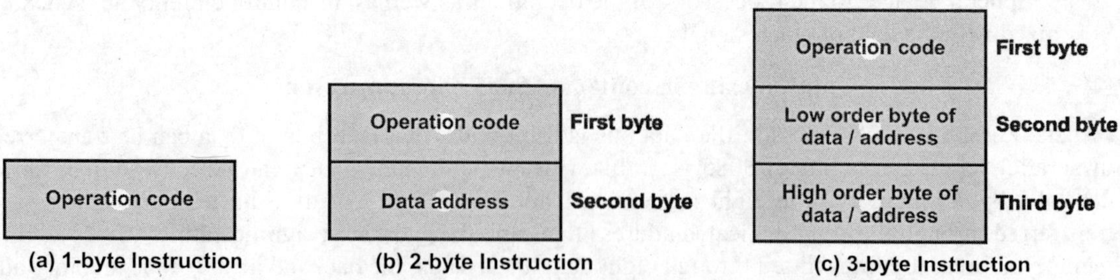

Figure 15.4 Instruction Format in 8085 Microprocessor

- **Data transfer instructions:** The instructions in this group are used for copying contents from source to destination without changing the contents of source. The source can be a register, a memory location, a specific byte from memory or an I/O device. Similarly, the destination can be a register, memory location or the accumulator. This group includes load, store, move and exchange instructions. For example, consider the following instruction:

  ```
  MVI B, 40H
  ```

  This instruction loads the hexadecimal value 40H into the register `B`.
- **Arithmetic instructions:** The instructions in this group are used to perform arithmetic operations such as add, subtract, increment and decrement the data stored in registers or memory. For example, consider the following instruction:

  ```
  ADD R
  ```

  This instruction adds the contents of the register `R` with the contents of `A` and stores the result back in `A`. That is,

  $A \leftarrow A + R$
- **Logic and bit manipulation instructions:** The instructions in this group are used to perform logic operations on the data stored in registers or memory. The 8085 microprocessor provides several logical operations such as AND, OR, XOR, compare, rotate and complement. For example, consider the following instruction:

  ```
  ANA R
  ```

  This instruction performs the logical `AND` operation on the contents of register `R` and `A`, and stores the result back in `A`. That is,

  $A \leftarrow A \wedge R$
- **Branch instructions:** The instructions in this group are used for changing the sequence of the program execution either conditionally or unconditionally. The branch instructions include conditional or unconditional jumps, call to subroutine, return from subroutine and restart operations. For example, consider the following instruction:

  ```
  JMP addr
  ```

  This instruction transfers the control to the address specified by `addr`.
- **Stack, I/O and machine control instructions:** The instructions in this group are used for maintaining the stack, reading from input ports, writing to output ports, setting and reading interrupt masks and setting and clearing flags. For example, consider the following instruction:

  ```
  HLT
  ```

  This instruction causes the processor to stop the processing and wait.

8. Discuss various addressing modes available in 8085 microprocessor.

Ans. A method used to specify the operand address in an instruction is known as **addressing mode**. 8085 microprocessor supports five different addressing modes, which are as follows:

- **Immediate addressing mode:** In this addressing mode, the actual operand of 8 or 16 bits is specified in the instruction itself. The immediate addressing mode is indicated by the letter `I`. Thus, the instructions having letter `I` come under this category. For example, consider the following instruction:

  ```
  MVI A, 60H
  ```

  This instruction transfers the 8-bit immediate data (that is, 60H) into `A`.
- **Register addressing mode:** In this addressing mode, the source operand or destination operand or both are stored in registers which are specified in the instruction. For example, consider the fol-

lowing instruction:

```
ADD B
```

This instruction adds the contents of register B with that of A and stores the sum in A.

- **Direct addressing mode:** In this addressing mode, the 16-bit address of the operand is specified in the instruction itself. This 16-bit address is specified in the second and third bytes of the instruction. For example, consider the following instruction:

```
LDA 3000H
```

This instruction to loads the 8-bit contents stored in the memory location 3000H into A.

- **Indirect addressing mode:** In this addressing mode, the memory address of the operand is specified in the instruction by means of a register pair. For example, consider the following instruction:

```
LDAX B
```

This instruction loads A with the contents of memory location pointed by the BC register pair. Though the register C is not explicitly specified in the instruction, it will be used with B to store the 16-bit address of a memory location, which further stores the address of the operand.

- **Implied addressing mode:** In this addressing mode, the operand is implicitly specified in the definition of instruction. For example, consider the following instruction:

```
CMA
```

This instruction complements the contents of A as A is the implicit operand in this instruction.

9. What is the relationship between instruction cycle, machine cycle and T-states?

Ans. The microprocessor executes the instructions of a program in a sequential manner, unless not specified. It continues fetching, decoding and executing the instructions one after the other until it finds a halt (HLT) instruction. The **instruction cycle** (consisting of fetch, decode and execute phases) for each instruction may involve transferring of data between processor and I/O or memory. Each data transfer operation between processor and I/O or memory requires a specific time period known as **machine cycle**. Further, each machine cycle includes certain number of clock periods, referred to as **T-states**. Generally, each instruction cycle involves one to five machine cycles and each machine cycle involves three to six T-states (see Figure 15.5).

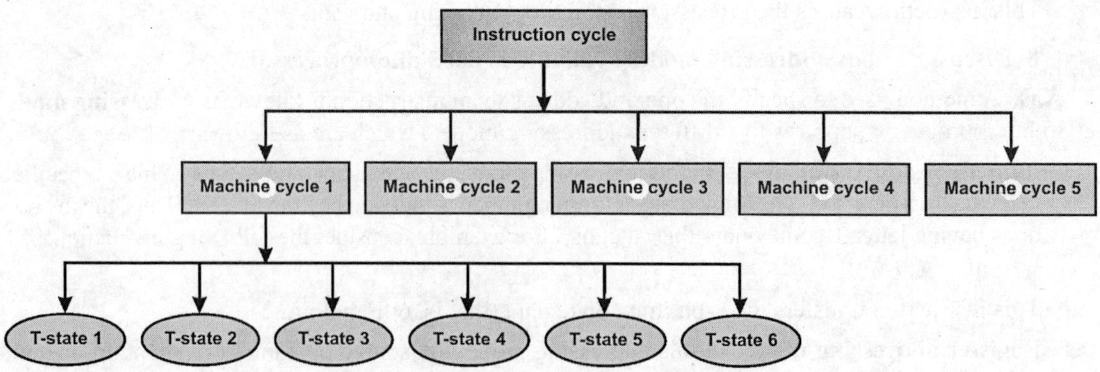

Figure 15.5 Relationship Between Instruction Cycle, Machine Cycle and T-states

10. Draw and explain the pin diagram of 8085 microprocessor.

Ans. The 8085 microprocessor comprises 40 pins, which are functionally organized into seven groups. Figure 15.6(a) shows the configuration of all 40 pins of the 8085 microprocessor and Figure 15.6(b) shows their functional organization. The description of each functional group of pins is as follows:

- **Power supply and frequency signals:** This group comprises five pins: V_{cc}, V_{ss}, X_1, X_2 and `CLK OUT`. The 8085 microprocessor needs +5V power supply, which is connected at pin V_{cc}. The ground power supply is connected at pin V_{ss}. The other two pins X_1 and X_2 are used to connect the tuned circuits such as LC, RC or crystal. The frequency of a crystal tuned circuit must be 6 MHz in order to operate the system at 3 MHz. This is because the oscillator frequency of the system is always divided by 2 by the internal clock generator. The `CLK OUT` is used as a system clock for all other devices. The frequency of the `CLK OUT` is half of the oscillator frequency.
- **Data bus and address bus:** In 8085 microprocessor, eight data bus lines (D_0–D_7) are multiplexed with the eight low-order bits (A_0–A_7) of 16-bit address bus. As a machine cycle consists of at least three T-states, during the first T-state the eight low-order bits of the memory or I/O address are placed into the multiplexed address/data bus and during the remaining T-states the multiplexed lines are used as bi-directional data bus. On the other hand, the high-order 8 bits of the memory or I/O address are placed into the eight high-order address bus lines (A_8–A_{15}).
- **Control and status signals:** The 8085 microprocessor includes several control and status signal such as $\overline{RD}$, $\overline{WR}$, `ALE`, `READY` and IO/$\overline{M}$, which are described as follows:
  - **$\overline{RD}$ and $\overline{WR}$:** These signals indicate the direction of data transfer between processor and I/O or memory. When $\overline{RD} = 0$, the data are to be read from the specified memory locations or I/O port through the data bus. When $\overline{WR} = 0$, the data are to be written to specified memory location or I/O port through the data bus.
  - **Address latch enable (ALE):** The eight low-order bits (A_0–A_7) of address are available on the multiplexed address/data bus during the first T-state only. During other T-states, the multiplexed bus is used only for data. However, the eight low-order bits of address are needed during the remaining T-states of the machine cycle also. Therefore, it becomes necessary to latch the eight low-order bits during the first T-state of machine cycle to make them available throughout all the T-states of machine cycle. The latching is done through an external latch and `ALE` signal from 8085 microprocessor.
  - $\overline{IO}/\overline{M}$, S0 and S1: The IO/$\overline{M}$ signal specifies either the memory or I/O operation. The signals S0 and S1 indicate which of the machine cycles is being executed.
  - **READY:** This signal indicates whether a peripheral is ready for data transfer. If this signal is active, then data transfer from processor to peripheral can start; otherwise, the processor has to wait.
- **Interrupt signals:** The 8085 microprocessor has five pins including INTR, RST 5.5, RST 6.5, RST 7.5 and TRAP at which it can receive interrupt requests. In addition, the 8085 microprocessor includes an $\overline{\text{INTA}}$ signal that indicates the acknowledgement to the interrupt request received at `INTR`.
- **Serial I/O signals:** The 8085 microprocessor has two serial I/O signals, which are serial input data (`SID`) and serial output data (`SOD`). These signals are used for performing bit-by-bit operations in serial. The signal `SID` is an input signal that accepts data from external devices in serial order, that is, bit-by-bit. While the signal `SOD` is used to transmit the data bit-by-bit to the external device.

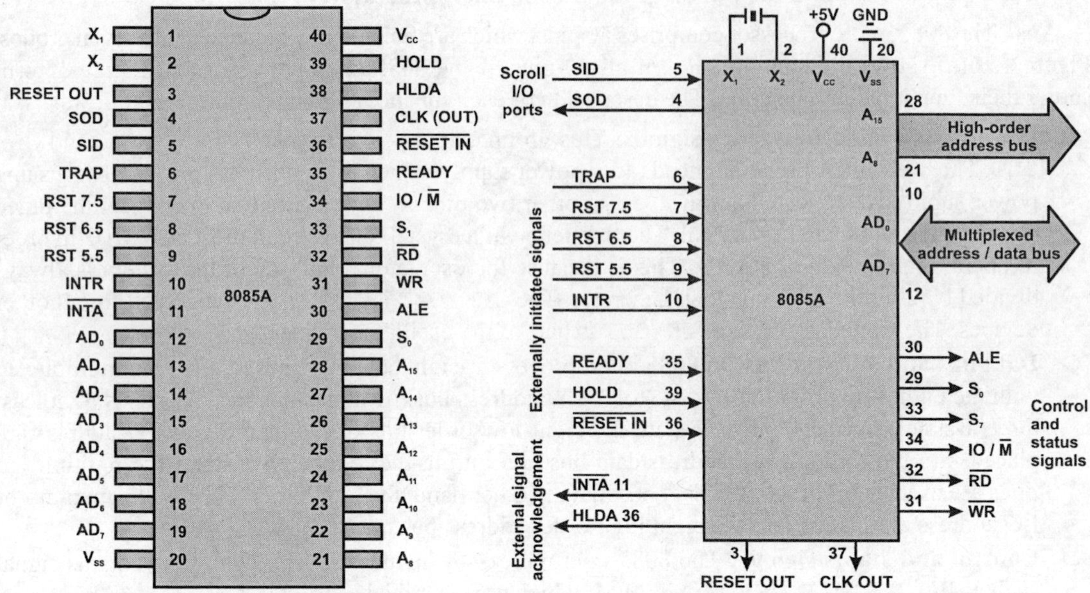

(a) Pin Configuration (b) Functional Organization

Figure 15.6 8085 Microprocessor Pin Configuration and Functional Organization

- **DMA signal:** There are two DMA signals in 8085 microprocessor including `HOLD` and `HLDA`. The `HOLD` signal indicates that the use of address, data and control bus is being requested by another master. The `HLDA` signal is used to acknowledge the `HOLD` request.
- **RESET signals:** The 8085 microprocessor has two reset signals, that is, `RESET IN` and `RESET OUT` signals. The `RESET IN` signal when set to low is used to set `PC` to zero (that is, 0000H), and reset the `IE` and `HLDA` flip-flops. It can also tri-state all the three buses (data, address and control). On the other hand, the `RESET OUT` signal is used to reset the processor. It can also be used to reset other devices connected to the system. This signal is synchronized with the processor clock.

11. Describe the hardware interrupts of 8085 microprocessor.

Ans. The 8085 microprocessor includes five hardware interrupts that can be initiated by external devices by placing an appropriate signal on the corresponding interrupt pin. The interrupts are enabled/disabled by setting/clearing the `IE` flip-flop, which is internal to the processor. Various hardware interrupts of 8085 microprocessor are described as follows:

- **INTR:** This is a maskable interrupt and thus, can be disabled in case the microprocessor is busy in performing some higher priority task. It can be disabled by using disable instruction (`DI`) and `SIM` (set interrupt mask) instruction pair or by resetting the system/processor. The microprocessor checks the `INTR` line during the execution of each instruction. If the input to the `INTR` signal goes high and the `IE` flip-flop is enabled, then the processor finishes the execution of the current instruction and then, disables the interrupt. With this, the acknowledgement is sent to the interrupt source at `INTA` pin. Now, the processor cannot receive further interrupt requests until the `IE` flip-flop is set. `INTR` is a non-vectored interrupt and has the lowest priority. It is a level-sensitive interrupt that means once it goes high, it needs to be kept high until detected by the processor.

- **RST 5.5 and RST 6.5:** These interrupts are maskable and can be disabled by using the `DI` and `SIM` instruction pair or by resetting the system/processor. These interrupts are level triggered, which means that once they go high, they remain high until detected by the processor. If the microprocessor cannot respond immediately to `RST 5.5` and `RST 6.5` interrupt requests, an external hardware must be used to store them. The priority of `RST 6.5` and `RST 5.5` is third and fourth, respectively.
- **RST 7.5:** This is a maskable interrupt and can be disabled using `DI` instruction or by resetting the system/processor. It is a positive edge-sensitive interrupt and thus, it can be triggered even with a short pulse. Once this interrupt signal goes high, there is no need to maintain it at high state until detected by the processor. This is because it is stored internally in a `D` flip-flop until either the microprocessor responds or it is cleared. It has the second highest priority among all the interrupts.
- **TRAP:** This is a non-maskable interrupt and thus, cannot be disabled. It is a vectored interrupt and has the highest priority among all the interrupts. It is level- and edge-sensitive triggered, which implies that the level of input line should go high and stay high until acknowledged by the microprocessor. The `TRAP` interrupt can be cleared by supplying an external signal to reset the microprocessor or by giving a high `TRAP` acknowledge through an internal signal.

12. Define the term microcomputer. Also show its block diagram.

Ans. A **microcomputer system** is constructed by integrating components such as read only memory (ROM), read/write memory (RAM) and peripheral devices with the microprocessor (see Figure 15.7). Along with these components, some special-purpose devices such as interrupt controller, programmable timers, programmable I/O devices and DMA controllers can also be included in the microcomputer to improve the capacity, performance and flexibility of the system.

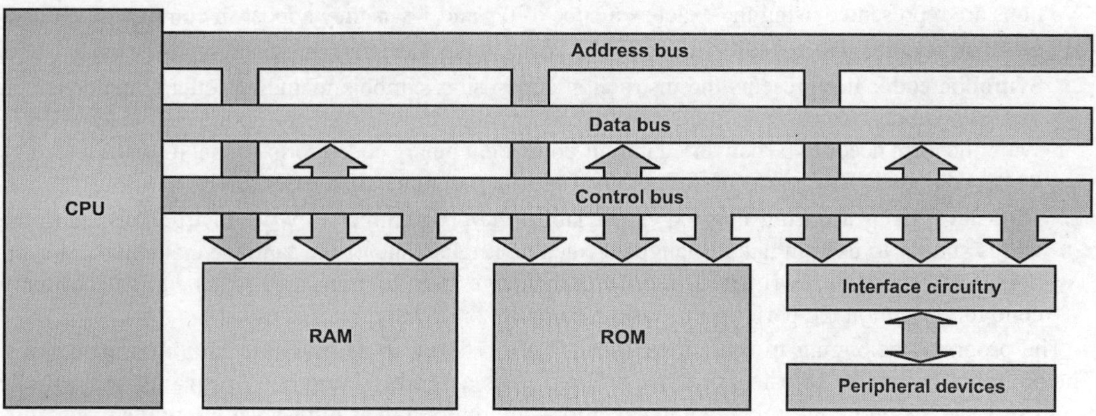

Figure 15.7 Block Diagram of Microcomputer System

13. How do we develop a program?

Ans. A program consists of a series of instructions that the computer processes to perform the required operation. It includes some fixed data required to execute the instructions and the process of defining those instructions and data. Thus, in order to design a program, a programmer must determine three basic fundamentals:

- The instructions to be performed.
- The order in which those instructions are to be performed.
- The data required to perform those instructions.

To perform a task using a program, a programmer has to consider various inputs of the program along with the process, which is required to convert the input into the desired output. Suppose we want to calculate the sum of two numbers A and B and store the sum in C. Here, A and B are the inputs, addition is the process and C is the output of the program (see Figure 15.8).

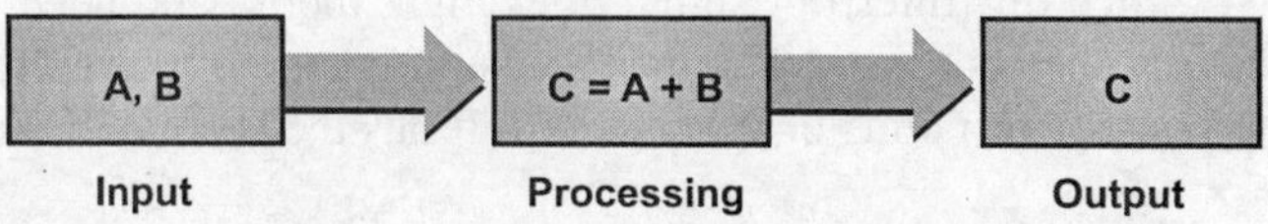

Figure 15.8 Program Performing a Task

14. Describe the categories a computer program may belong to.

Ans. A computer needs to be instructed using programs (a set of instructions) to perform all its tasks. To write computer programs, a programming language is required as computers do not understand natural languages like English. A **programming language** consists of a set of characters, symbols and usage rules that allow the user to communicate with the computer. A variety of programming languages are available, however, the computer understands only the programs written in binary form. Thus, a program written in any other programming language needs to be converted into an equivalent binary form so that it can be executed by the computer.

The computer programs may belong to one of the following categories:

- **Binary code:** It refers to the programs written in binary format. The data (operands) and instructions are represented using the exact sequence of 0's and 1's as they appear in computer memory.
- **Octal or hexadecimal code:** It is the equivalent octal or hexadecimal representation of the binary code.
- **Symbolic code:** It represents the instruction code using symbols including letters, numerals and special symbols. However as the computer understands only the binary code, each instruction in symbolic form needs to be converted into its equivalent binary coded form so that it can be executed by the computer. This task is performed by a special program called **assembler**.
- **High-level programming language:** It enables the programmer to write instructions using the words similar to used in natural language such as English and/or the familiar mathematical symbols. Each instruction written in high-level language must be translated to its equivalent binary code for execution. To perform this task, a compiler or an interpreter is used.

The programs belonging to categories 1 and 2 are referred to as **machine language programs**. The programs belonging to category 3 are referred to as **assembly language programs** or **symbolic programs** and the programs belonging to category 4 are referred to as **high-level language programs**.

15. What do you understand by machine language?

Ans. The first ever language used in the computers and machines was binary, also known as **machine language**. In this language, all instructions and data should be written using 0's and 1's. Machine language is also known as computer's 'native' language as this system of codes is directly understood by the computer. Each instruction in machine language consists of two parts. The first part is an **opcode**, telling the computer what function needs to be performed and the second part is the **operand**, telling the computer where to find the data on which the desired operation is to be performed.

16. Write a short note on assembly language. Describe different fields used in an assembly language instruction.

Ans. The complexities of machine language led to the search of another language. The assembly language has been developed in the early 1950s. It allows the programmer to interact directly with the hardware. This language assigns a mnemonic code to each machine language instruction to make it easier to remember or write. It allows better human-readable method of writing programs as compared with writing in binary bit patterns. However, the set of rules for assembly language varies from computer to computer as the instruction set of microprocessor is different for each computer.

Assembly language provides symbolic instructions, usually three letters long, corresponding to each machine instruction. The letters are usually abbreviated indicating what the instruction does. For example, `ADD` is used to specify an addition operation. The set of rules for assembly language defines how the symbols should be used and combined to construct a **line of code**—a fundamental part of a program written in assembly language. Each line of an assembly language program consists of three fields: *label*, *instruction* and *comment*. The general format of an assembly language instruction is

```
[Label] <Instruction> [Comment]
```

Here, `[]` indicates that the enclosed specification is optional and thus, may or may not appear in the instruction. The description of the fields included in assembly language instruction is as follows:

- **Label:** This is an optional field that (if present) specifies a symbolic address. A **symbolic address** is made up of one, two or three alphanumeric characters, where the first character is essentially an alphabet, while the other two can be alphabets or numerals. The symbolic address specified in the label field must be separated from the instruction field by a comma (`,`).
- **Instruction:** This field specifies the instruction that can be one of the following three types:
  - **Memory-reference instruction (MRI):** An MRI comprises two or three symbols separated by spaces. The first symbol consisting of three letters specifies the operation code, second specifies a symbolic address and the third specifies the direct or indirect address. There are total seven MRIs whose symbols and description have been discussed in *Chapter 7*.
  - **Register-reference or input/output instruction (non-MRI):** A non-MRI does not include an address field. It comprises a three-letter symbol representing the input-output or register-reference instruction. There are total 18 non-MRIs including 12 register-reference and six input/output instructions. The symbols and description for these instructions have been discussed in *Chapter 7*.
  - **Pseudoinstruction:** A pseudoinstruction is different from the above two instructions as it is not a machine instruction. It refers to an instruction that provides information to the assembler regarding some phase during the translation. Some pseudoinstructions that an assembler can recognize are listed in Table 15.2.

Table 15.2 Pseudoinstructions

Symbol	Information to the assembler
`ORG N`	Informs to store the instruction or operand specified in the line following the pseudoinstruction in the memory location specified by `N`
`END`	Indicates the termination of the symbolic program
`DEC N`	Specifies how to convert the signed decimal number `N` into binary
`HEX N`	Specifies how to convert the hexadecimal number `N` into binary

- **Comment:** This field specifies a comment or may be empty. The comments are not a part of the actual program, but are used only for reference purposes, that is, for specifying what actually the instruction will do. A comment if included in a line of code is preceded by a semicolon (`;`) so that the assembler could recognize the beginning of the comment field.

17. List the rules for defining labels in assembly language programs.

Ans. A label is the first and an optional part in a line of assembly language code. It is included to provide identification to a line of code or the memory location that needs to be referenced by the other parts of the program. There are certain rules that must be followed while defining the labels in an assembly language program. These rules are listed as follows:

- It must start from the first column in the program with the first character always being a letter.
- It is neither a machine instruction nor an instruction to the assembler. Rather, it is a user-defined identifier.
- Though it can be referenced by other lines of code in the program, it can never be reused. In other words, the same label name cannot be used by two or more lines of code in the same program.

18. Write a short note on assembler.

Ans. The assembly language is nothing more than a symbolic representation of machine code, which allows symbolic designation of memory locations. However, no matter how close assembly language is to machine code, the computer still cannot understand it. Therefore, the assembly language program must be translated into machine code before being executed. This job is performed by a program called **assembler**. The assembly language program is also known as the **source code**, while the final machine language program is designated as **object code**. The assembler takes the source code and produces the object code.

19. How is the symbolic program represented in memory?

Ans. An assembly language program (also called **symbolic program**) must be placed in memory for execution. The user types the characters of the symbolic program on the terminal and a system program named **loader** inputs these characters in the memory. As the program comprises symbols, an alphanumeric character code such as ASCII is to be used for representing those symbols in memory. All the characters of a line of code are stored in consecutive memory locations and each memory location holds two characters because of having capacity of 16 bits. The label field of the line of code is followed by a comma, the operation and address symbols are separated by spaces and the end of line is denoted with `CR` (carriage return) code.

Memory word	Symbol	Hexadecimal code
1	B E	42 45
2	G I	47 49
3	N ,	4E 2C
4	S T	53 54
5	A	41 20
6	V A	56 41
7	R	52 20
8	I CR	49 CR

Figure 15.9 Memory Representation of BEGIN, STA VAR I

To understand the memory representation, consider the following line of code:

```
BEGIN, STA  VAR I
```

This line of code is stored in eight adjacent locations in memory as shown in Figure 15.9.

20. Describe the major tasks performed by the assembler during translation of a symbolic program.

OR

Explain the working of a two-pass assembler.

Ans. The assembler takes a symbolic program in ASCII as input and produces an equivalent binary program as output. To perform the translation, the assembler scans the given symbolic program in two passes. The tasks performed by the assembler in each pass are described as follows:

- **First pass:** During the first pass, no translation is performed; rather each instruction or operand of the program is assigned a memory location. Since the lines of code (whether containing machine instruction or operands) in a symbolic program are placed in consecutive memory locations, the sequential memory locations are assigned up to the end of the program. Moreover, no memory locations are assigned to `ORG` and `END` pseudoinstructions as they do not represent any instruction or operand. The assembler generates an address symbol table that correlates the labels used in the program with their respective locations.

To start with, the assembler uses a memory word named **location counter** (**LC**), which holds the memory location assigned to the instruction or the operand currently being processed. The tasks performed by the assembler during the first pass are described in the algorithm given below:

```
1. Start the first pass
2. Set LC to 0
3. Scan the next line of code
4. If the line includes a label then
      Store the label along with the content of LC in the address symbol
      table
   Else
      Test the instruction field
      If instruction field has ORG pseudoinstruction then
       Set LC to the value following ORG
       Go to step 3
      Else
       If instruction field has END pseudoinstruction then
             Go to step 7
       End if
     End if
   End if
5. Set LC = LC + 1
6. Go to step 3
7. End of first pass
```

- **Second pass:** During the second pass, the assembler adopts a table lookup procedure for translating machine instructions to their binary equivalent. Four tables including pseudoinstruction, MRI, non-MRI and address symbol are used by the assembler for this purpose. The pseudoinstruction table stores the four symbols of the pseudoinstructions (discussed in Q16) along with the address of their respective subroutine processing that pseudoinstruction. The MRI table stores seven symbols of the memory-reference instructions and their 3-bit equivalent opcode. The non-MRI table stores 18 symbols of the register-reference and input-output instructions and their 16-bit equivalent binary code. The address symbol table is obtained from the first pass.

To start the translation process, the assembler initially sets `LC` to 0. Here, it is important to note that during this pass, the assembler ignores the label in the line of code and directly jumps to the instruction field for examining the first symbol occurred. The tasks performed by the assembler during the second pass are described in the algorithm given below:

```
1.  Start the second pass
2.  Set LC to 0
3.  Scan the next line of code
4.  Jump to instruction field and take the first symbol
5.  Search the symbol in the pseudoinstruction table
6.  If the symbol found in pseudoinstruction table then
       If symbol matches with ORG pseudoinstruction then
       Set LC to the value following ORG
       Go to step 3
       Else
       If symbol matches with END pseudoinstruction then
             Go to step 10
       Else
       Convert the DEC or HEX operand into binary
       Replace the symbolic instruction with binary code
       End if
    End if
    Else
       Search the symbol in the MRI table
       If the symbol matches with an MRI then
       Extract the respective opcode from the MRI table and set
    bits 2 to 4 of the instruction
       Take the second symbol (a symbolic address) of MRI
       Search the address symbol table to get the binary
    equivalent of the symbolic address and set bits 5 to 16
    of the instruction
       If the third symbol (I) is present in MRI then
             Set I = 1
       Else
             Set I = 0
       End If
       Combine all parts of the binary instruction
    Else
       Search the symbol in the non-MRI table
       If the symbol is a valid non-MRI then
             Extract its 16-bit binary code from the non-MRI
       table
       Else
             Print 'Error in given line of code'
```

```
            Go to step 8
        End if
    End if
  End if
7. Store the binary instruction code in the location specified by LC
8. Set LC = LC + 1
9. Go to step 3
10. End of second pass
```

21. Discuss the steps involved in executing an assembly language program.

Ans. A program written in assembly language is always saved with the extension `.asm`. Suppose the given source program is `first.asm`. The execution of this program involves three sequential steps, which are *assembly*, *link* and *execute*. These steps are described as follows:

1. **Assembly:** In this step, the source program (`first.asm`) is given to the assembler, which translates it to the object code, creating `first.obj` file.
2. **Link:** In this step, the object file (`first.obj`) is given to the linker that converts it into executable machine code, creating `first.exe` file. Before producing the executable file, the linker combines the separately assembled modules (if any) of the program into one executable program.
3. **Execute:** In this step, the executable file (`first.exe`) is loaded into memory by the loader for execution.

22. What is assembler directive?

Ans. Assembler directives are the statements that allow a programmer to control the way the program should be assembled and linked. These are the directions for the assembler (or the linker), indicating something that it needs to know for carrying out the assembly process. The assembler directives are processed by the assembler during the assembly phase and not by the processor at runtime. Thus, no machine executable code is generated corresponding to these statements. Some of the common assembler directives are described as follows:

- **SEGMENT:** An assembly language program is divided into three main segments: code, data and stack. Each segment is defined using SEGMENT directive. The keyword `SEGMENT` indicates the beginning of a segment and the keyword `ENDS` indicates the end of the segment. Each segment is identified with the help of a label. The labels of the `SEGMENT` directive and its corresponding `ENDS` directives must match.
- **HEX:** This directive permits to use the hexadecimal values in the assembly language program. It instructs the assembler that the values beginning with the dollar (`$`) sign in the program should be treated as numeric constants in hexadecimal notation.
- **EQU:** This directive provides the same functionality as the `#define` directive used in C language. It is used to define the strings or constants in the program that can be used during assembly. The format of EQU directive is:

  ```
  <Label> EQU <value>
  ```

  For example, consider the following statement:

  ```
  SUM EQU 50
  ```

  Now during the assembly phase, whenever the assembler finds `SUM` label in the source program, it replaces the label with 50.

- **PROC:** This directive is used to define a procedure in the program. A procedure refers to a block of code within the code segment of the program. The beginning of a procedure is indicated using the `PROC` directive and its end is indicated using the `ENDP` directive. The identifying labels of the `PROC` and its corresponding `ENDP` must match.
- **END:** This directive is used to indicate the end of the program. It is the last statement of an assembly language program that informs the assembler that the program has finished.

23. While executing a program, when the 8085 microprocessor completes the fetching of machine code located at memory address 2057H, what will be the contents of program counter?

Ans. As we know that the program counter contains the address of the next instruction to be executed, the contents of program counter will be 2058H.

24. Write a code segment to
a. Clear the accumulator
b. Add 47H (use ADI instruction)
c. Subtract 92H
d. Add 64H
e. Display the results after subtracting 92H and after adding 64H

Ans. The program to perform the given operation is as follows:

```
SUB A              ; Clear accumulator
ADI 47H            ; ADD 47H to the accumulator
SUI 92H            ; A=B5H
OUT PORT1          ; Display B5H
ADI 64H
OUT PORT1          ; Display 19H
HLT
```

25. Write instructions to load the hexadecimal number 65H in register C and 92 H in the accumulator. Display the number 65H at PORT0 and 92H at PORT1.

Ans.

```
MVI   C, 65H
MVI   A, 92H
OUT   PORT1             ; DISPLAY 92H
MOV   A, C              ; Copy C into A
OUT PORT0               ; Display 65H
HLT
```

26. Write instructions to
a. Load 00H in the accumulator
b. Decrement the accumulator
c. Display the answer
Specify the answer you would expect at the output port.

Ans.

```
MVI          A, 00H         ; (A = 0 0 0 0 0 0 0 0
DCR          A              ;      -0 0 0 0 0 0 0 1
OUT PORT1                   ;     -----------------
HLT                         ;      1 1 1 1 1 1 1 1 = FFH
```

27. Write a program loop using a pointer and a counter to clear the contents of hex locations 500 to 5FF with 0.

Ans. The program loop to clear the contents from location 500 to 5FF is as follows:

```
      LXI H, X500H          ; Pointer to source address in memory
      MVI D, X100H
      SUB A                 ; Clear accumulator
      MVI D, X100H          ; Set up register D as a counter
LOOP: STAX H                ; Clear memory
      INX H                 ; Point to the next memory location
      DCR D                 ; Update counter
      JNZ LOOP              ; Repeat until D=0
      HLT
```

28. Write instructions to clear the CY flag, to load number FFH in register C and to add 01 to (C). If the CY flag is set, display 01 at an output port; otherwise, display the contents of register C.

Ans. The program with given requirement is as follows:

```
         SUB A              ; Clear the CY flag
         MVI C, FFH         ; Load number FFH in register C
         MOV A, C
         ADI 01H            ; Add 01 to register C
         MOV C, A
         JNC DISPLAY ;        Display the result
         MVI A, 01H
DISPLAY: OUT PORT 1         ; Output = 01H because INR does
         HLT                ; not set CY flag
```

29. Write a program in assembly language to find and display the greatest number between two numbers. If both are equal, display 01H at the output port.

Ans.

```
         MVI B 30H
         MVI C 40H
         MOV A, B
         CMP C
         JZ EQUAL
         JC GRT
         OUT PORT1
         HLT
EQUAL:   MVI A 01H
         OUT PORT1
         HLT
GRT:     MOV A, C
         OUT PORT1
         HLT
```

MULTIPLE CHOICE QUESTIONS

1. Which of the following is not a characteristic of the microprocessor?
   (a) Instruction set (b) Bandwidth
   (c) Clock speed (d) Timing signal
2. Which of the following is not an 8085 interrupt?
   (a) RST 4.5 (b) RST 5.5
   (c) RST 7.5 (d) TRAP
3. The length of the address bus in 8085 microprocessor is ________.
   (a) 8 bits (b) 16 bits
   (c) Any of these (d) None of these
4. Which of the components of 8085 microprocessor is used to transfer the multiplexed address to low order bus?
   (a) Address buffer (b) Address latch
   (c) Address/data buffer (d) Instruction decoder
5. The programmer cannot access ________ register in 8085 microprocessor.
   (a) Temporary registers, accumulator (b) W, Z and temporary registers
   (c) Both (a) and (b) (d) None of these
6. The instruction `CMA` falls under the category of ________ addressing mode in 8085 microprocessor?
   (a) Register (b) Immediate
   (c) Direct (d) Implied
7. The instruction `HLT` falls under the functional group of ________ in 8085 microprocessor.
   (a) Data transfer instructions (b) Branch instructions
   (c) Arithmetic (d) Stack, I/O and machine control instructions
8. Which pin is connected to the 8085 microprocessor for power supply?
   (a) V_{cc} (b) V_{ss}
   (c) Either (a) or (b) (d) Both of these
9. The instruction code using symbols including letters, numerals and special symbols is known as ________.
   (a) Memory-reference instruction (b) Symbolic code
   (c) Pseudoinstruction (d) None of these
10. Which of the segments is not used in an assembly program?
    (a) Code (b) Stack
    (c) Data (d) Control
11. In a microprocessor system, if TRAP, HOLD and RESET pin got activated at the same time, while the processor was executing some instructions, then it will first respond to:
    (a) TRAP (b) HOLD
    (c) RESET (d) None of these

Ans. 1. d 2. a 3. b 4. c 5. b 6. d 7. d 8. a 9. b 10. d 11. a

Index

A

B

N

O

P

Q

R

S

X

Z